Some problems are so difficult they can't be solved in a million years unless someone thinks about them for five minutes.

H. L. Mencken

MANAGING DP HARDWARE

Prentice-Hall Series in Data Processing Management
Leonard Krauss, Editor

Capacity Planning, Cost Justification, Availability, and Energy Management

JAMES W. CORTADA

Prentice-Hall, Inc., Englewood Cliffs, New Jersey 07632

Library of Congress Cataloging in Publication Data

Cortada, James W.   (date)
    Managing DP hardware.

    (Prentice-Hall series in data processing
management)
    Bibliography; p.
    Includes index.
    1. Electronic data processing—Management. I. Title.
II. Title: Managing D.P. hardware. III. Title: Managing
data processing hardware. IV. Series.
QA76.9M3C67   658.4'038   82-405
ISBN 0-13-550392-2   AACR2

Editorial/production supervision
    by *Gretchen K. Chenenko*
Manufacturing buyer: *Gordon Osbourne*
Cover design by *Edsal Enterprises*

Managing DP Hardware: Capacity Planning, Cost Justification,
    Availability, and Energy Management

Printed in the United States of America

10 9 8 7 6 5 4 3 2 1

ISBN 0-13-550392-2

Prentice-Hall International, Inc., *London*
Prentice-Hall of Australia Pty. Limited, *Sydney*
Prentice-Hall Canada Inc., *Toronto*
Prentice-Hall of India Private Limited, *New Delhi*
Prentice-Hall of Japan, Inc., *Tokyo*
Prentice-Hall of Southeast Asia Pte. Ltd., *Singapore*
Whitehall Books Limited, *Wellington, New Zealand*

TO NINA

Contents

Preface

In the past decade alone, companies have spent hundreds of billions of dollars on data processing. Easily a third of that expense went toward DP equipment. In the decade to come additional billions will be spent. The purpose of this book is to provide data processing management, nontechnical users of DP, and executives specific time-proven suggestions for managing the use and cost of such equipment. The proliferation of various devices, possible configurations, and vendors make it necessary to take a more rationale approach toward decision making regarding such common issues as time sharing, computers, minis, micros, terminals, software to drive them, who to buy from, and financial strategies. Better management of data processing hardware encourages the selection of those devices which best serve the interests of an organization in a cost-effective manner. Proper control over installation of new, more, or different devices ensures that services continue to users without interruption. This is an important issue if one keeps in mind that today over half of the work force in the industrialized world is directly dependent on computers to carry on their jobs. This book will show how to take advantage of current and newly available technologies, maximize their use, and control their expense through specific recommendations.

This book is written for both technical management in DP and for the larger population of managers who must make data processing decisions with little or no background. The discussion is nontechnical, with DP decisions and recommendations translated into business terms comparable to considerations that are weighed in other sectors of an organization.

Chapter 1 is devoted to giving the reader a perspective on how hardware is used today, what forms it takes, and the financial impact it has. It shows how to take advantage of changing technologies and thus improves a company's productivity. Chapter 2 deals with capacity planning—a topic hardly understood by most managers, with the consequence that companies spend billions of dollars unwisely. Capacity planning—knowing how much work your hardware does today against what you need tomorrow—describes budgetary and financial strategies, contributes to the costing of applications, and assists in the management of hardware changes. Because capacity planning is one of the most basic activities any manager should perform who is considering new hardware acquisitions today, it describes computers, minis, micros, peripherals, terminals of various types, distributive processing, and word processing, to mention only a few. There are proven methods and tools available today to make capacity studies easy and extremely cost beneficial. This chapter illustrates why and how to perform such planning and gives specific examples of the methods employed.

Once an organization understands its hardware capability and its capacity requirements for the near future, justifying various rental, lease, purchase, and vendor options becomes possible. It is then necessary and feasible to identify what makes sense for an organization instead of being confused by a flood of concepts and thoughts involving such issues as centralization, distributive processing, data bases, minis, micros, intelligent terminals, and so on. In short, simple, rationale, business decisions can be the outcome of a properly analyzed set of financial and technical options. Because so many people today depend on computers to do their work properly, managing the actual installation of equipment and training people to use such devices is even more vital to the health of any organization than mere financial analysis. Therefore, Chapter 3 has been devoted to this subject to ensure that severe crises and cost overruns can be avoided. Hand in glove with such activity is concern that equipment be properly loaded with work. Given the rapidly changing technology impressed upon us today, Chapter 4 has been devoted to the whole question of how to maximize productivity from these devices. Such issues as keeping a machine running and making sure that it does the maximum amount of work possible are fundamental to the question of DP productivity today.

There is hardly a department in any company today that does not use some sort of DP device or service. Most companies also support data processing departments with data centers crammed full of equipment, using up vast quantities of electricity, air conditioning, heating, and space. With the cost of energy rising by over 50% each year overall, electricity by at least 15% annually for commercial users, and technical personnel by an equal amount, it has become imperative that management control the use of energy by DP. Chapter 6 deals with the issue of energy consumption, making specific recommendations on how to control costs while providing expanded data processing services. We also provide suggestions on how a company can use data processing to save an organization thousands of dollars in each of its buildings every month, employing proven methods.

Chapter 7 concerns the problem of communications. User managers and general executives constantly complain that they do not understand what DP is all about. They are asked to endure situations they find increasingly unacceptable and complex, to spend vast sums of money, and to live in a state of confusion that is unnecessary. They have rebelled and in the past several years have increased pressure on data processing management to communicate their problems and needs in nontechnical language—to justify and present their proposals in business terms familiar to all. This chapter takes time-honored methods for communicating thoughts in business and applies them specifically to DP as it is today. As with previous chapters, the concern has been to illustrate the virtues of clarity of thought, brevity of expression, and application of business concerns to better management of DP.

Chapter 8 deals with disaster planning. This is a topic that is only now beginning to draw serious attention on the part of organizations heavily dependent on data processing. It focuses on how to restore hardware and software services to an organization following a major disaster through preventive actions employing a methodology that improves the chances of a rapid recovery.

To enhance the usefulness of this book, a glossary of data processing terms is provided, with particular emphasis on words that have only recently crept into the vocabulary and on words used extensively in this book. A short bibliography by chapter is included to provide references for additional reading. Each chapter is introduced by a one paragraph road map of its contents, and the body of the text is subheaded for additional ease of use. An index provides yet another avenue to get at information quickly. All the chapters are enhanced with examples and case studies drawn from current situations, existing and new technologies, and live and evolving trends.

Checklists and other aids, such as sample reports and logs, are included to reinforce key management principles.

ACKNOWLEDGMENTS

A number of people have contributed their time and talents in helping me make this a useful book. Bernard Goodwin of Prentice-Hall enthusiastically supported the project, and the production staff, especially Gretchen Chenenko, quickly moved the book through production. Mike Elia, Technical Services Manager at Worthington Pump, did pioneering work on disaster planning while the architect of the process as described in this book is Ed Allen, Senior Systems Engineer at IBM. Suraj Bhatia, also of IBM, critiqued most of the chapters and taught me a great deal about capacity planning and availability management. It would have been very difficult to have written the chapter on capacity planning as well without the expert advice of Robert Guttman, MIS Director at Fedders Corporation. Eric Smith, DP manager at Alltrans Corporation, shared his staff's experiences on tuning with me. James Kelly, MIS Director at Worthington Pump Corporation, sharpened my awareness of how communications with non-DP management can be made more effective. In preparing this book, I relied on the advice and comments of data processing, financial, and general management, specialists in the industry, and my colleagues. Although I received much encouragement from my friends within IBM, this book is the product of my own work and should not be considered in any way as an official statement of my employer. I alone am responsible for any weaknesses or failures this book may have and for which I hope the reader will forgive me.

JAMES W. CORTADA

Progress, therefore, is not an accident, but a necessity.

Herbert Spencer

Chapter 1 reviews where data processing hardware is used in most organizations, what types of devices they are, and how they are changing. The costs and functions are described together with the potential benefits of taking advantage of them for any company. Tracking what is installed and suggestions on how to maximize this kind of information to control costs are discussed. Finally, proven methods of taking full advantage of new technology are reviewed.

CHAPTER ONE

DP Hardware and Its Role
in the Organization

Today data processing (DP) hardware is rapidly changing in function, form, design, and cost, and is of increasing importance within all organizations. Changes are coming faster than they ever have before and industry pundits suggest that the rate of evolution will actually increase as we pass through the 1980s. The form of data processing equipment, and the speed with which it changes, become increasingly important as the percent of the work force dependent on the use of computerized applications expands. In most organizations today in the industrialized world, over 50% of all workers rely on computers to one degree or another to help them carry out their functions. Computerized reports on which decisions are made, terminals that tell a worker how to build a product, and terminals that secretaries use for typing (now more fashionably called "word processing") are all obvious forms of dependence on DP hardware. An understanding of its form and changes in DP hardware, where it is best and typically used, some cost trends, and tracking its use thus become managerial functions of considerable significance.

MAJOR COMPONENTS OF DP HARDWARE

Data processing equipment consists of several types of devices. The first is the central processing unit (we know it as the computer), which actually takes data and uses them to run programs with information to generate data or reports that someone wants. There are printers to which computers send information for reproduction on paper, and data storage devices on which information is stored in such devices as tape, disk, or diskette. A vast array of telecommunications equipment supports terminals throughout an organization. Other equipment includes card reading and punching units, and data entry devices such as typewriter terminals and the more widely used cathode ray devices (known as CRTs), which look like television sets equipped with typewriters.

Computer Systems

Computers range in size from hand-held calculators that we buy for almost nothing today to those that control national airline reservation systems with on-line terminal networks involving hundreds of CRTs and printers. There are several general types of computers, however, which management typically must deal with in any organization. First, there is the central computer, also known as the *mainframe,* which would be found in a company's data center. This device, usually a large computer, might serve the majority of an organization and probably do all its data processing. Typical examples of mainframes are the IBM 4300 series or its widely used predecessors, the 370 family of computers. They tend to come in various sizes of memory and speed so that a company can operate the one it needs and upgrade to larger units when required, with almost full compatibility. Several chapters of this book discuss in more detail how this is done wisely and cost effectively. Mainframes are general-purpose computers that do both commercial work and more specialized engineering or scientific computing. They support a wide range of peripheral devices, a variety of operating systems, and a substantial number of programming languages, often capable of operating several jobs concurrently.

Another type of computer, the *mini,* is typically not only much smaller than a mainframe but might only support one application or one department within a company. As a general rule, minis might be found in small companies that do several million dollars worth of business annually, as a one-application machine (e.g., laboratory testing or physical distribution in a warehouse to mention two), or to support a small unit of an organization, such as one plant, an engineering design department, or a sales group. Often these are acquired together with a special application package designed to run on this device. Given the massive increases in computing power today, some of the more common minis have more power than large mainframes of the 1960s. Remember—power is relative—because one of the characteristics of evolving DP technology has been the overall increase in computing power, memory, storage, speed, and so on, with every new generation of equipment.

A third class of even smaller devices than the minis are the *micros,* which are typically integrated into some other piece of equipment. They are often used, for instance, in automated processing and manufacturing equipment. Thus one might find micros as part of a papermaking machine or an automatic conveyor belt in a distribution center; more recently, they have turned up in automobile engines to improve fuel economy and in microwave ovens. Micros are a relatively new entry into the computer arena, having been on the scene for less than 10 years. A by-product of space exploration technology, these small units are capable of carrying logic from programs fairly inexpensively and thus are used widely today in all kinds of industrial and consumer machinery. They are almost a throwaway technology and verge on being considered simply as sophisticated parts. Electric calculators have micros, as do memory typewriters. Most electric scales in supermarkets and many time and attendance devices also utilize micros. Typically, these are programmed for a specific set of functions and, unlike most minis and all mainframes, usually cannot be reprogrammed to perform other activities. The only exception to the rule is the hand calculator, particularly the programmable models, which are simply sophisticated micros. (See Figure 1-1.)

Most common within organizations are mainframes. Invariably they are the preserve of a data processing department, although increasingly they are turning up as one-application machines in manufacturing plants, distribution centers, and offices. But the larger units are usually housed in data centers run by a staff of specialists who are also responsible for a sizable collection of peripheral devices, such as printers, disk and tape units, and possibly as data-entry devices. Minis tend to be found in those parts of an organization where non-DP users rely on their services, such as plants and departments. For the most part they are designed to be operated by non-DP personnel and are often stand-alone devices that are not dependent on the main data center. In fact, in some companies there are so many minis that a data processing manager might find that most are not compatible with the data center's equipment or with each other, thereby complicating any effort to keep track of them or to have minis serving as backup to other minis when they break down. They are attractive in many cases because they are generally easy to install and maintain, often with prewritten software.

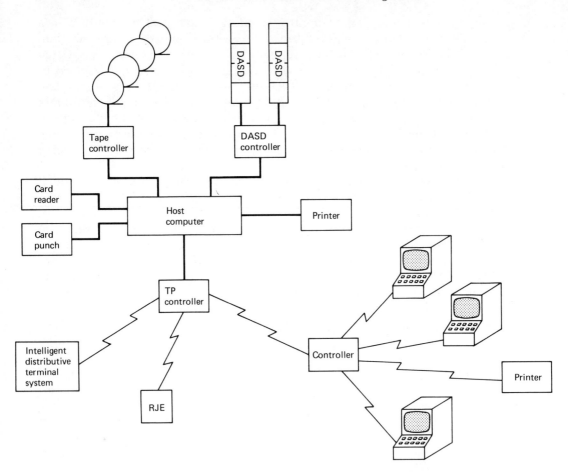

Figure 1-1. Example of a central-site computer configuration.

Micros are hidden from view simply because they are part of other equipment and rarely come into an organization independently of some other device. Thus they are operated indirectly by personnel operating other hardware, such as industrial plant or otherwise technical devices. Training for the operation of technical equipment of a non-DP nature often includes instructions on operating that portion of the unit which is in fact a micro (such as the controls). (See Figure 1-2.)

Printers

Mainframes and minis are usually equipped with one or more high-speed printers running from about 300 lines per minute (lpm) to over 20,000 lpm (the latter typically laser technology). Micros might have a smaller printer to produce reports on the performance of equipment. Typically, such printers

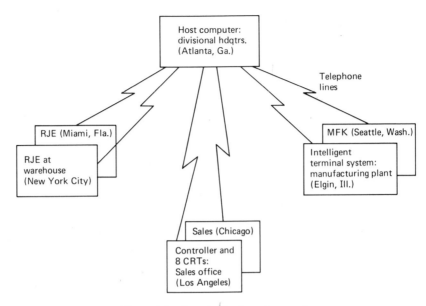

Figure 1-2. Sample distributed network.

are measured in terms of characters per second (cps) printed rather than lines per minute, and they are always much slower, intended for much lighter printing requirements. Typical line speeds for printers on minis may range from 300 lpm to 1000 to 2000 lpm. There is a major gap in print speed, ranging from 2000 lpm for impact mechanical devices to over 13,000 lpm for laser-technology printers. Laser printers are often used in large companies that might have several mainframes in one data processing department, producing millions of pages of reports per month.

Data Storage

Data storage devices exist for micros up through mainframes and come in a variety of sizes and forms. *Direct-access storage devices* (DASD) are typically used for information that must be retrieved often and quickly by going directly to specific files (often for programs that are run frequently and for users of CRTs). These devices are continually being added to computer systems as the demand for storage increases. DASD may store as few as several million characters of information (each character is called a *byte*) or may support billions of bytes of data in mass storage units. A second form of data storage are *diskettes,* which look much like 45-rpm records. Data are usually keyed from a terminal onto these diskettes and are either transmitted via telephone lines to a host computer or are mailed if not used locally on terminals. Each diskette can typically hold the same amount of information that a box of computer cards can hold, about 144,000 characters as a minimum. They cost about five times as much as a box of cards but, unlike cards, are reusable and thus the cost is easily justified. Furthermore, they take up less space than cards and when dropped, the information they contain is not scattered out of order all over the floor.

Another type of data storage widely used is *tape*. Data are stored on tape in sequential order much as on an open-reel tape recorder, and the amount is limited only by the size of the tape. The density at which information can be stored varies widely, but the most compact units today can hold about 6200 bytes per inch. A typical reel of 2400 feet can therefore hold a great deal of information. The speed at which tape can be written to or read from ranges from a slow several hundred bytes per second to hundreds of thousands per second and approaching a million. Measured in terms of the cost of storing a byte of data, tape is cheaper than disk. However, because it has the disadvantage of reading and writing data sequentially, it is generally used only for large sequentially operated jobs (e.g., running a company payroll) or more often as a backup file for disk. An organization might make a copy of all its disk files on tape and store the latter in another building as a backup in case something happened to the disk copies.

Control Units

Less visible, but very important, are control units that manage the functions of various devices. In a data center these might include such units as a tele-processing controller, which is, in effect, a mini. It has the responsibility of coordinating the communications from the host computer out to all the various types of intelligent (those with memory) or dumb terminals, keeping track of problems on telephone lines and related equipment, perhaps editing out control data so that only your information travels down the line, thus speeding up transmission of data at lower costs. These typically have software (programs) in them and often also microcode (programs permanently installed in the equipment by the manufacturer). Other control units include smaller ones that manage clusters of terminals near the computer in the same building or at remote locations. They could also control communications among a variety of computers, minis, and micros. Today, organizations often distribute their data processing, which means that micros might talk to minis. This in turn could mean that minis might communicate with main-frames, some of which require telecommunication control units to manage the network of hierarchical computing power.

Another commonly used type of control unit is for DASD. As the number of disk drives increases, the need to control what data come into and out of the computer first, second, third, and so on, at what speed, and to which DASD device, increases. Today such control is vested in control units, many of which are driven by microcode, although programmable units are increasingly becoming the norm. Tape drives are also managed by control units. In years past, control units were usually large, boxy, expensive units. Recently, there has been a trend toward reduction in size or the integration of their functions within the computer or into the peripheral device itself. The other trend has been to offload from the mainframe the responsibility for managing the flow of data and the operation of large numbers of peripherals through the installation of programs and microcode within control units. Often this is done by the manufacturer, thus freeing data processing personnel to concentrate on programming.

Specialized Devices

Another group of devices used in data processing are the less frequently seen diskette readers, diskette-to-tape readers, keypunch machines with which to prepare the all-too-familiar 80-column computer card, and machines to sort and read cards—most of which are being retired as this technology of the 1950s and 1960s is replaced by disk-oriented systems. Other units include a variety of data-reading devices, such as electronic scanners, optical card readers (OCRs, which most people have seen to grade computerized tests in schools), and monitors in hospitals, which keep track of pulse and breathing or even analyze blood. In fact, most computerized or mechanized hospital equipment have micros designed to perform one function, such as to analyze blood or to prepare a variety of x-rays or scans of patients.

Terminals

Terminals represent a major portion of data processing equipment, often the most visible in a company. There are basically three general types. The first, and most popular, are CRTs, which allow individuals to examine files currently residing on disk and to update them directly. They are used for every type of application imaginable, from order entry to shop floor data control to data entry and financial modeling. In short, they are used whenever there is a need for direct and immediate interaction between people and data. Often, near one or more such devices there might be a small printer that can reproduce data and reports viewed on a screen. CRTs can be in one color (called monochrome) or may have as many as seven different colors, highlighting certain types of data or illustrating charts and graphs. They include diagnostic microcode (logic) to determine if there is anything wrong with the unit or with the telecommunications hookup to the computer. Some even include some memory, used to store data prior to being transmitted to a control unit or a computer. They can come equipped with teleprocessing components that allow them to communicate over telephone lines to other locations, or can be attached with others to a local control unit that handles communications to a mini or mainframe elsewhere.

Another type of terminal is a hard-copy device, which in effect is a typewriter with reams of paper but no television screen. It, too, can communicate directly to a host far away or share a local control unit that performs the same function. It often has an additional feature—the ability to write data directly to a diskette or some sort of DASD for local storage physically within the same unit—which is often useful for data collection at a time when it is not convenient to send information directly to a computer. Such data can then be transmitted at another more convenient time. The most primitive form of hard-copy terminal is the teletype. Like these older units, being mechanical units, hard-copy terminals run more slowly than CRT devices.

Terminals are as varied as applications and vendors. In the past several years, application-oriented terminals have appeared increasingly. Examples abound in every industry. Laser scanning devices at grocery checkout counters, by which cans and packages are passed over a beam instead of being mechanically charged out on a cash register by a clerk, are common and fast. Wands to read magnetic stripes (similar to the dark bands appearing on the backs of credit cards) in manufacturing plants represent another. Automated teller window devices in banks and credit-card style identification card readers at doors and entrances are terminals. Together with the more traditional CRTs, the word-processing terminal, which is a combination of CRT, typewriter, magnetic card data storage, micro with text-processing code, and possibly telecommunication capability, is the most rapidly expanding terminal in use today. Engineers designing on-line via a screen now have their own special devices, with large CRTs, capable of handling vast quantities of data and quickly presenting such information in graphic form. Micros attached to industrial equipment often have specially designed CRTs to display data on the activities of a machine.

Another set of widely used equipment which is increasingly evident throughout organizations are copiers with telecommunications capability. The old xerographic devices that made a copy of a letter from one sheet of paper to another are being changed to devices that have the ability to store the information in machine-readable form for later reproduction. Also common is the ability for such copiers to communicate data across telephone lines to other copiers or to computers for (as an example) consolidation with other reports into new reports. Such devices can operate concurrently with others or by themselves and with multiple functions. For instance, you could be copying a letter while the copier is communicating a massive report to another device across the country. Or two copiers could talk to a host sending the same type of data for consolidation into one report. Both devices could be controlled locally or by someone at a host computer thousands of miles away. The future promises even more functions for copiers as they are refined to provide the ability to store information in machine-readable form at costs less than those to store the same data on paper.

In the preceding paragraphs we have suggested that there is a variety of equipment available today for those using data processing and that all of these units are constantly undergoing refinement. In fact, in any organization it would probably be impossible to catalog where all of these units are located, particularly as some of them are integrated under the covers of other types of equipment. Yet there are some general statements that can be made about areas in which organizations have found it cost effective to use data processing hardware. Although the comments below might not all be true for a specific organization, they can serve as a general guide.

Typically, mainframes and their large amounts of peripheral equipment are located somewhere in the data processing department. If the company has other data centers scattered about the country, again the hardware is usually physically located within a data processing department. Distributed remote job entry (RJE) stations (terminals used to transmit or receive reports and data) can be anywhere in an organization, usually not within a DP department. Distributed intelligent terminals, which may include computers, DASD, tape, and printers, may be located in a mini-DP department or within an office environment. Micros are typically the most difficult to find because they are embedded within other equipment in hospitals, manufacturing devices, trucks, conveyor belts, or processing units. Terminals can be found anywhere from the office of the chairman of the board to a deserted storage room. Typically, they are in office and plant locations. In short, wherever a telephone might exist within your organization, so could a terminal, particularly the popular CRT variety. Most often, they are located in departments that process work with large amounts of information and are administrative in nature. These include order servicing departments; in accounting, finance, personnel, administration, and distribution; at foreman's stations; by entrances to buildings; and in laboratories. Hardened industrial varieties, which are resistant to dirty environments and heat, are used increasingly on plant floors. (See Figure 1-3.)

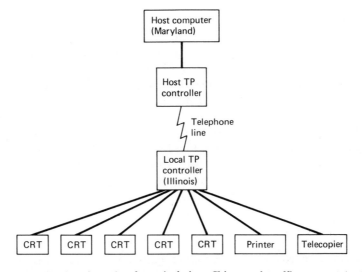

Figure 1-3. Sample node of terminals in a Chicago sales office communicating with host computer in Bethesda, Maryland.

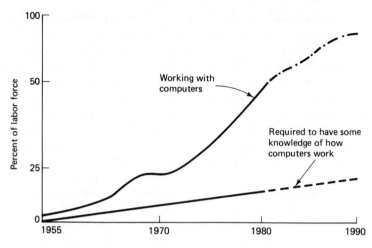

Figure 1-4.   Growth of dependence on computers.

All industry pundits forecast that the number of devices of all types that will be used in the next 10 years will increase sharply, and that they will appear in every nook and cranny of an organization. The reasons for this view can be summarized quickly. First, the DP industry is growing at over 25% each year in the industrialized world—faster than almost any other sector of an economy. It increasingly sells its products and services to that sector of the world economy also involved in services and industrialization, representing more than 85% of the economy of the Western world. Second, the percentage of the work force dependent on computerized technology has been increasing each year. In the 1970s alone, that dependence went from about 25% to over 50%, and by the end of the 1980s is expected to top 75%. Moreover, as the need to understand the technical details of DP in order to use it decreases, the impulse to use the technology will increase. In 1955 almost everyone using DP had to be technically versed in its fine points. By 1970 that figure had dropped by half and by 1980 to less than 20% of those using DP. Increasingly, use of DP equipment has become like driving an automobile or using an oven—neither of which requires that you understand the underlying technology. For instance, the requirements that the user understand how to fix equipment or program in complex languages are disappearing. More will be said later about the massive price/performance revolution that continues to take place, making data processing a very cost-effective tool and providing another reason for our increased dependence on computers. (See Figure 1-4.)

Hardware Trends

Because hardware is changing constantly—and more so today than ever before—some additional general comments should be made about its characteristics as reflected by trends in equipment evolution. First, devices are being increasingly more integrated so that each does more than ever before, many performing functions that might earlier have been performed by two or more devices. For example, more terminals are being built with integrated control units under their covers. Computers are absorbing functions often performed in the past by separate units (to control CRTs, DASDs, printers, and tapes). The result is that the cost of peripheral control units is declining, and in some configurations, actually disappearing. By-products of such a trend include the decline in air conditioning needed to support control units, a drop in the amount of costly electricity (in some cases by over 60%) used, smaller data processing rooms because many new devices can be in office environments or in factories, and smaller technical staffs to operate and maintain such devices.

Second, as the use of chip technology continues to replace older, more mechanical units, equipment will have fewer moving parts to break down and fewer components. This will mean that costs will continue to push downward, making the use of additional devices more affordable. Furthermore, with fewer moving parts, the opportunities to improve uptime (availability) with fewer and faster repairs becomes possible.

Third, more vendors are integrating within their products programs (software) to replace mechanical devices as well as programs once written by users, thus making equipment more reliable, much less expensive, and easier to operate. The trend toward the use of firmware (the marriage of software and hardware), usually in the form of microcode (often residing on diskettes or in chips), has also encouraged vendors to add increasing amounts of self-diagnosis in their equipment. These aid service personnel and users in keeping devices operational for longer periods of time between breakdowns, while reducing the cost of maintenance. Such diagnostic and correcting tools identify a variety of problems and can even correct some of them. Computers, for example, can notify an operator when a part requires replacement, so that when a telephone call is placed to the maintenance engineers, they know exactly what parts to bring with them without having to come to the data center first, determine the problem, go back for the parts, and then do the repair work. Other diagnostic capabilities can alert maintenance personnel when certain portions of a device are beginning to fail so that preventive care can be taken on a planned basis.

EVOLUTION OF HARDWARE TECHNOLOGY

Because one of the chief characteristics of data processing has always been continuous and dramatic change, it becomes imperative to understand it better before planning what devices to have in an organization and for how long. Otherwise, the cost in lost productivity, economic and financial opportunities, or inconvenience may be great. It is a fact of life that although these changes have often resulted in less expensive hardware and more productive systems of great benefit, change has also made it far more complex for management to control, let alone to take advantage of new equipment or better price performance. And with the cost of hardware still absorbing about a third of most DP budgets, this concern for managing cost and technological changes to an organization's advantage continues, especially when one remembers that the amount of hardware forecasted to be used in the years to come will actually go up rather than down. The risks of faulty product strategies by vendors on the one hand, and implementation plans out of step with new advances on the other, can continue to cause serious problems if not handled properly. In short, by understanding the thrust of certain key changes, some of which have already been mentioned, management can make more intelligent decisions about hardware acquisitions, how best to finance them, and where to use hardware. The measurement of hardware evolution involves changes in technology, applications, and cost. In the following discussion, primary attention will be paid to technology and applications.

Computers

During the 1970s, a number of vendors introduced large, multipurpose mainframe computers that build on the dramatic technological changes of the 1960s, which saw a wide range of compatible computers with highly increased levels of reliability introduced into the marketplace. Some of the typically new products of the 1970s included IBM's 370s, Itel's V series, and CDC's 6000/7000. Performance speeds advanced more than fourfold over the largest systems of the 1960s. The new operating systems (system control programs) that were introduced and widely used provided more function, yet increased the complexity of data processing. For example, the demand for more programmers and operators increased sharply. The population of programmers in the United States alone went from about 165,000 in 1970 to some 275,000 by about 1980.

Plug-compatible vendors, such as Amdahl Corporation and Itel, introduced additional computer products with increases in speed and size. Thus a number of new vendors and products came into existence as the decade progressed. The result was that by the end of the 1970s, someone buying a computer had dozens of choices that could be made for every possible size of device, and for some units, such as terminals, the options ran into the hundreds. Equipment became dramatically more reliable, had increasing amounts of microcode diagnostics, and were running with better operating systems. Maintenance of this technology became more technical but less labor intensive with each new introduction of diagnostic capabilities and inherent self-correcting features.

The 1970s was the decade in which minicomputers came into their own, as dozens of vendors marketed cost-effective systems. The standardization of technology increased as the 32-bit chip came to dominate, leading to more standard forms of byte constructions (length of words as measured in bits per byte), in operating systems (especially in large computers), and later in application package design architectures. Larger minis came into the marketplace in a variety of forms, often competing against smaller mainframes. New applications generated specialized minis, as for example by the end of the 1970s for word processing and graphic design. In the important example of word processing, typewriter-like devices were part of many mini systems that could stand by themselves in offices with little or no connection to a data processing department. Dozens of major vendors introduced mini systems in the late 1970s: IBM, Wang, and DEC, to mention just three.

Peripheral Devices

Peripherals also experienced substantial changes, characterized by increases in speed, capacity, and miniaturization. More diagnostic capabilities, together with increased ease of use, often paralleled developments with computers. Intelligent DASD systems became common and far less costly in the 1970s. In DASD alone, access speeds increased to 20 milliseconds or more and capacities jumped to over 1000 megabytes per drive. Transfer rates kept up with faster channel speeds on computers, thus allowing data to move directly from DASDs to central processing units at speeds as high as 40 megabits per second. Mass storage systems allow billions of on-line data to be available at cost-effective rates. The IBM mass storage unit, for instance, allows trillions of bits of data to be stored. Tape drives doubled, then tripled their speeds and multiplied the density at which data could be stored on tape.

Printers became smaller, less noisy, and faster. Impact printers ranged in speed from a slow 40 characters per second to over 2000 lines per minute. Many became desktop models at half the price of the larger slower varieties of the 1960s. The 1970s was the decade in which laser printers and ink jet technology also came into their own, signaling a new level of sophistication and quality in the industry. Programmable units made it possible to reduce the cost of preprinted forms by using stock paper and allowed for changes in report printing without slowing or stopping printers to change paper in order to generate new items. And with the introduction of various telecommunication disciplines (such as IBM's SNA), remote printing became extremely easy and common for remote locations.

Application Trends

On-line applications made the 1970s a decade in which large numbers of managers became convinced that terminals and their related applications increased productivity. Terminal populations increased annually at rates of 10%, 20%, 30%, and more. The CRT became as common in business as the

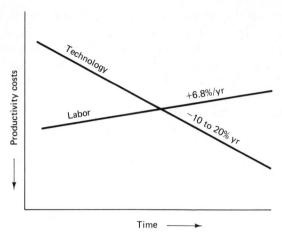

Figure 1-5. Productivity gains made by technology versus cost of labor (measured in U.S. dollars; data from 1970s).

telephone and the typewriter. The productivity gains achieved by using on-line systems to replace manual, paper-bound functions were so great that terminals increased their percentage of a department's hardware budgets by a percentage point a year in many organizations. Managers began to talk about productivity gains of more than 25% over manual systems. Keypunch data entry, when converted to key-to-disk devices, also resulted in productivity gains closer to 40% or more. The successes as measured in reduced operational costs, increased control over business functions, and improved working conditions clearly ensure that during the 1980s more on-line applications will come about in areas previously ignored by data processing. (See Figure 1-5.)

What developments can be expected in the 1980s? Industry watchers are all in agreement on at least one point: the DP industry will continue to experience a dramatic period of growth and change equal to that witnessed during the 1970s. A number of factors account for this situation. As the DP industry matures, with a more clearly identifiable role to play in the world economy and more narrowly within organizations, acceptability of this technology will continue to grow. There is also the turnpiking effect of convenience. As organizations continue to find more useful ways to use data processing while expanding the use of existing applications, their dependence on data processing as a tool with which to run a business increases. The pattern in an obvious and well-known one in which the demand for expanded use of useful applications grows almost exponentially. Something as simple as the number of terminals in an organization can be charted typically with a straight line going up from left to right. Moreover, as management continues to increase its experience with data processing, people will find more applications to cost-justify and install, in turn contributing to the expansion of data processing's role in an organization. There is even an element of peer pressure and competition involved. Companies that saw others use data processing to automate distribution centers successfully, for example, will do so themselves if for no other reason than simply to remain competitive in service. Those who today still have manual manufacturing or customer order servicing systems are expected to take advantage of DP, which for many thousands of organizations has proven to be cost effective. New companies continually start with computerized applications while older organizations are branching out into new application areas that include energy conservation, service to customers, or specialized applications (as in the health industry), often using data processing in ways that have become traditional within their industry only within the past 10 years.

There are also new applications which are just now coming into their own, either because of changing economics in a particular industry or national economy (such as the recent sharp increase in the cost of energy) or because of evolution in the function and cost of data processing. The most obvious and fashionable one at the moment is computing in the office. In the past, American companies, for example, made capital investments of about $5000 per worker in plants for machinery but perhaps 10 to 20% of that amount per office worker. Yet the number of office workers has increased faster in the 1970s than plant personnel and the salaries of white-collar staffs have traditionally been high. In the 1980s, this trend toward more office personnel will continue as the industrialized economy increasingly concentrates its growth in the service sector and less in manufacturing or in agriculture. Thus the need to increase the productivity of office workers has generated a sharp demand for data processing applications in that area. (See Figure 1-6.)

In the United States alone, forecasts for office systems are dramatic but not necessarily ambitious. The U.S. Bureau of Labor Statistics shows that clerical employees will number about 20 million by the mid-1980s. Industry watchers have suggested that by 1990 a similar number of terminals would

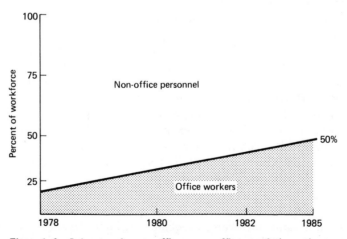

Figure 1-6. Labor trends: non-office versus office population estimates.

Filling out forms
Standard letters (e.g. dunning notices)
Supply acquisitions (purchases)
Budgets
Travel reservations and expenses
Appointments and calendar management
Appraisals
Planning, reviews, controls
Records and file management
Internal-use-only document control
Time cards
Funding proposals
Training
Electronic mail and message systems
Other

Figure 1-7. Office functions suitable for computerization.

be used in office systems. The reasons for this projected growth in the demand for office applications are not hard to find. The rapidly escalating cost of people, the sheer number of them involved, coupled with current inefficient distribution of information (manifested in such symptoms as a sharp rise in paperwork and government requirements for reports) dictate that many of these functions be computerized. Companies have watched their management successfully increase the productivity of plant personnel, for example, through the use of data processing technology all through the 1970s and early 1980s, while that of office personnel has remained static. While managers have noted that productivity gains have come anywhere but in the office at a time when office work is actually increasing, some have turned to automation for help, and this has meant data processing.

Properly designed office systems involve the use of computers, printers, CRT terminals, on-line typewriters, text processing, and photocopying with telecommunications to transmit documents, reports, proposals, and so on, as part of an electronic mail system within a company. Any survey of what it costs to move information about within a company (most information transmission is within an organization, not to the outside) clearly suggests a large number of applications perfect for computerization and specialized hardware. Figure 1-7 suggests some of the potential application areas. Figure 1-8 shows what internal communications within one company actually cost in salaries, manual systems, and so on, which, when multiplied across thousands of desks and people represented a sizable expense.

Paper file systems and slow research methods are also expensive, and can be done faster and less expensively with office systems, saving, in addition, on space, file cabinets, clerks—all with the potential for more accurate information. Currently installed systems suggest that the potential savings in time for professional staff people using office applications range from 10 to 20%, that of clerical help from 25 to 40%, while that of secretaries range from 30 to 40%. Savings in salaries alone more than offset the cost of programming and hardware, especially in large organizations with thousands of office personnel.

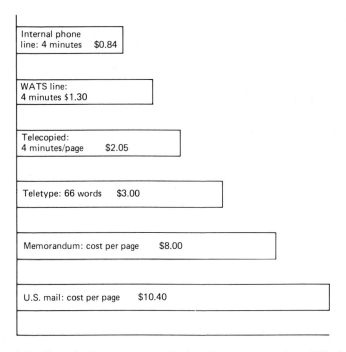

Internal phone
line: 4 minutes $0.84

WATS line:
4 minutes $1.30

Telecopied:
4 minutes/page $2.05

Teletype: 66 words $3.00

Memorandum: cost per page $8.00

U.S. mail: cost per page $10.40

Figure 1-8. Costs for internal communications in a company where 80% of all correspondence was internal.

A second area of productivity gains that will increasingly generate additional demands for hardware is engineering. Today, we know that an engineer can design 40 to 85% faster using a computer than manually on paper. The simple act of drawing new patterns is speeded up, and the geometric calculations can be done faster and more accurately by the computer. For example, various iterations of a design can be made quickly, and mockups can be prepared with confidence that the math that designates curves and angles was done correctly by the designer. Increased accuracy alone can save a great deal of money in expensive tooling. Draftsmen can increase their productivity at least as much as engineers by allowing designs stored in computers to be drawn by computer-driven plotters faster than anyone could draw them and just as neatly. Considering the rapidly escalating costs of engineers and draftsmen, productivity gains of more than 40% in throughput, coupled with more than a 50% reduction in cost, are normal expectations today. Thus one can expect a series of technological developments in hardware and software in this area alone throughout the 1980s.

A third major new application area virtually guaranteed to drive up the need for more and different types of data processing hardware is the home. Energy management systems, which are becoming increasingly common in business (and about which more is said in Chapter 6), are beginning to appear in private homes on a smaller scale. As in business structures, they help control the use of hot water (such as by turning the hot water heater off at night and on again before people wake up in the morning) and electricity, balance the temperature inside with that on the outside, and manage the use of heating oil and natural gas to ensure increased efficiency. Micro technology is embedded in many microwave ovens to monitor cooking; video machines record television programs when people are out; and the record industry has introduced visual phonograph records that provide sight with sound. Already common are television games and games played with hand calculators. Educational specialists are talking increasingly of learning in the home using CRTs attached to computers in an education center, thus following the path many companies and governments have taken in training their own personnel. Games alone annually generate millions of dollars in sales, and video machines and CRT-based learning systems promise to generate even more revenues for vendors in the next 5 to 10 years.

Other applications driving the need for hardware could be mentioned, but suffice it to say that traditional uses for such technology and new ones constantly suggest that data processing will continue to find itself in demand in all its forms and in most organizations. So what technologies can management expect to be using in the next few years? For one thing, our perspective is changing, with an obvious impact on how we approach technology and, by implication, how we select it. Our fascination with speed and size is beginning to diminish; concern now turns more to quality. In the 1970s machines became faster and cheaper. One has only to recall the impact of the hand calculator and its price evolution. Earlier devices costing $700 have been superseded by better models priced below $50. Computers are continuing to increase in function while decreasing in cost. Throughout the 1980s this trend is expected to continue at the same rate as at the start of the decade. Similar statements could be made about peripherals and terminals. Technological barriers will thus not be as great an issue in the years to come as they were in the past. The quantity of devices used will instead become a characteristic of the future. Micros will become more common than small machines, minis more common than engines or mechanical devices. In the home cable television will be managed by computer, and at the office minis equal in power to larger computers of the 1970s, yet at the cost of copiers, will provide local processing and control functions. (See Figure 1-9.)

First shipped new technology	Cost/million instructions
1955	$40.00
1961	2.00
1965	0.40
1971	0.11
1977	0.08
1979	0.04
1981	0.02

Figure 1-9. Cost of processing using IBM computers. (Source: IBM Corporation.)

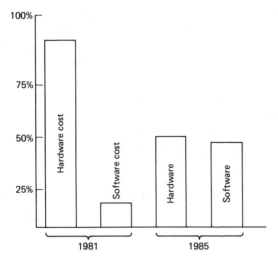

Figure 1-10. Relative cost trends of hardware and software.

To improve reliability, more software will become integrated into hardware, and companies will probably be charged greater amounts for code than they were before. It is believed by some industry pundits that the expense of software in computers will account for nearly 90% of the cost of a system by the early 1990s, whereas in 1981 it represented about 50% on large computers. Similar amounts are being spent in distributive processing computers as well. For minis, the current percent of cost for a system taken by software is between 5 and 10%, but these numbers are expected to grow rapidly to nearly 50% by the early 1990s. Thus the trend toward increased software costs relative to hardware is clear and unmistakable. Recent computer product announcements in the late 1970s and early 1980s by all the major manufacturers of such equipment have made this fact a reality and all have stated that this is the direction they will go throughout the next few years. (See Figure 1-10.)

Benefits of New Technologies

The benefits to companies of these trends are varied but several are universal and very real. They can be summarized as follows:

- Technical staffs can concentrate more on applications and less on hardware or systems software problems, thereby increasing amounts of cost-justified applications being generated by less technically oriented personnel.

- Technical improvements will continue to increase the percent of time that equipment is operational while reducing the number of hours required to make repairs. Increased availability of systems will reduce the amount of idle time on the part of computer users who in the past could not perform their jobs without using data processing. Productivity gains from this benefit alone can be measured easily in the number of people that would not have to be hired while the amount of work that existing staffs could do could go up.

- Miniaturization of parts and reduction in costs permit greater redundancy within devices to make it possible for systems to operate through alternative means when specific components fail, thereby ensuring increased uptime (availability).

- Additional storage capacity for an organization's data in large banks of DASD or mass storage units will make increasing amounts of information more easily available for management to use in running businesses. It is not unreasonable to assume that by the end of the 1980s trillions of bytes of information could be stored and managed at reasonable costs in large and medium-size companies.

Price Performance

Throughout the preceding discussion, price performance improvements have been mentioned. A closer examination of this issue suggests that the cost of hardware has been going down, thereby stimulating the acquisition of even more devices by replacing manual systems that have become more expensive. In 1955, the cost of performing 1 million instructions in a computer was roughly $40. By 1971, this cost had dropped to 11 cents and at the start of the 1980s to 0.02 cents. This trend in the United States during the 1970s alone resulted in a growth in hardware acquisitions of over 30% annually. Between 1980 and 1990, this same market will buy hardware at the rate of $100 billion per year in the Western world as opposed to the rate of about $20 billion per year experienced in the early 1970s. Computers alone have dropped dramatically as illustrated above, but so have other devices. CRTs that might have rented for $135 per month in 1970 by the early 1980s were renting for less than $80 and proved to be better devices than their predecessors.

Disk storage provides another and important example of increased price performance. In 1970, for one dollar a DP department could store 3800 bytes of data on DASD. By the end of the decade, one dollar allowed an organization to store 16,269 bytes of information. This did not represent a fourfold increase in price performance since, with inflation, the value of the dollar declined, making the increased bytes per dollar closer to eight times the rate for 1970. Another important storage medium—computer memory— experienced price performance improvements as well. The purchase price of 1 megabyte of memory in 1970 was about $600,000, but by the end of the decade the same amount of memory cost $15,000. Technological improvements in memory alone contributed substantially, therefore, to the drop in

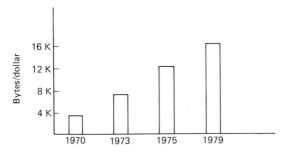

Figure 1-11. Amount of DASD available per dollar based on purchase prices.

rental and purchase prices of all computers continually throughout the past 15 years. (See Figure 1-11.)

Measuring the cost of systems within a DP department provides another avenue closer to our individual organizations for appreciating what is happening to the expense of hardware. In 1977, for example, a company's cost for a computer system (central processor, peripherals, software, maintenance) without taking into account the cost of operators, would have looked something like this: about 60% for computer hardware, roughly 20% for peripherals, and the rest for software and maintenance. Five years later the same quantity of computing power would have broken down as follows: computer 45%, peripherals less than 20%, software would have gone from about 8 to 9% up to approximately 14 to 15% (not including new and additional application programs that might have been added over the years), and maintenance would have inched up a point or two.

In the 1970s, the percentage of a DP department's budget going toward hardware was roughly a third. By the early 1980s (using the trends outlined in the paragraph above), the portion going toward equipment had dropped to just slightly more than 25% of a total budget. Yet because of increased demands for data processing, the DP budget as a whole continued to grow not only in actual dollars but as a percentage of a company's overall expenses. More terminals, DASD, computers, minis, and micros were installed. This fact alone accounted for the bulk of the forecasted growth expected in shipments of equipment throughout the 1980s, as suggested by industry watchers and computer vendors. In short, the cheaper it got, the more it was used and that is still true.

Another way in which management can look at the expenditures it makes on data processing, and thus plan for it, is by measuring the overall cost of DP within an organization. In the 1970s, approximately 0.8 to 1.5% of all dollars coming into a company or agency was spent on data processing. Certain industries spent more (such as banks and manufacturing concerns), others less (distribution and forest products). Yet by the early days of the 1980s, the overall percentage had increased to roughly 2%, with industry forecasters suggesting that this figure would grow to as high as 5% by the late 1980s. And this figure would seem conservative when one con-

siders that some companies in the 1970s spent as much as 10% on data
processing. Hardware dollars obviously jumped by leaps and bounds throughout this period. Even in 1980, for instance, which was a year of economic
uncertainty, expenditures in the United States alone had gone up over 9%,
to a national total of approximately $17 billion, and record levels were spent
in Western Europe. The annual reports of major hardware vendors for 1980
also provided specific evidence that the sheer number of units shipped to
their customers had jumped over the previous year by 10%, 30%, and in
some cases by even more.

Because a large portion of the anticipated increase in expenditures, therefore, will involve hardware (with increased portions going toward software),
the question arises as to which portion of an organization's hardware costs
will increase the most. This question should be asked within each company
so that an acquisition strategy can be put in place. Some general comments
applicable to everyone might help identify potential trends in any individual
company. Clearly, the number of computers (and their size) will increase,
easily doubling. DASD installations will grow at rates equal to that of the
1970s, while capacities will probably double quickly and increase manyfold.
But nothing will become more visible or as common as the terminal, as
familiar even as our telephones had become by the 1960s. In 1970 in the
United States alone, vendors shipped about 100,000 terminals. By the end of
1979, this annual rate had grown to over 750,000 and was expected to exceed 1 million long before 1985. Typically, demand for terminals was many
times that. As Figure 1-12 suggests, however, the demand for terminals will
actually increase more sharply than in the past and equally important, the
DP industry will not be able to satisfy it. Therefore, at the local level, management will have to do a better job of understanding how many terminals

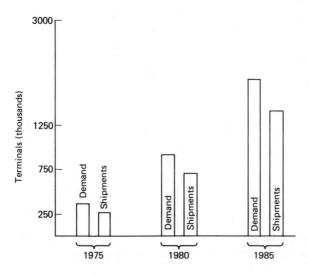

Figure 1-12. Demand for CRTs versus
actual shipments in the United States.

it needs and ordering them far in advance. It also means that older terminals will remain in an organization far longer than many have expected. For most companies, therefore, purchasing their installed base of terminals would usually make more sense than leasing them for many years. New terminals would be used side by side with older ones, most of which would be compatible with the newer devices.

There are thus a number of implications for management, with increasing amounts of hardware becoming more visible throughout an organization, not just limited to DP departments. Briefly:

- More computers and their smaller peripherals will be physically located where they are used in plants, warehouses, laboratories, and offices without the requirement of specialized electrical outlets, power sources, or additional air conditioning.

- As new buildings are constructed and older ones remodeled, more attention will be paid to installing energy management systems to hold down the cost of operation, and additional cabling for terminals will go in much as telephone lines do today.

- Greater emphasis will be placed on providing hardware availability (improving uptime and reliability), and more units will be installed in offices and conference rooms where none existed before. Terminal-based information systems will continue to overcome manual operations in rapid fashion.

- Increasingly, local building codes and DP industry standards will call attention to how and where data processing hardware is used in buildings, calling for management to make decisions regarding who is responsible for maintenance (the DP department or users) and how the inventory of equipment will be controlled.

- Greater portions of non-DP departmental budgets will have line items documenting the cost of hardware and other DP services and software, suggesting that increasing numbers of managers will, in various functional areas, want to make decisions regarding the acquisition of hardware and determine how to expense its costs on the company's books.

- As the need for standards grows, there will be increasing emphasis on how hardware is to be acquired, paid for, and disposed of company-wide. Normal accounting practices regarding capitalization will have an influence on establishing these standards so as to take into account company-wide acquisition discounts, capital strategies, tax laws, and the vagaries of the DP hardware market.

- As the amount of money being spent on DP hardware increases, so is the attention paid by DP management on providing upper management with financial strategies that best control and manage this cost.

Such strategies will have to take into account tax laws, the cost of capital, changes in the secondhand-computer marketplace, and the introduction of new technologies and products by a company's major vendors. Implied in the requirement to develop financial plans is the requirement that DP departments establish standards for compatibility of systems and software across the entire organization, particularly when applications cut across several departments (such as word processing, electronic mail systems, and order servicing). Compatibility of hardware would allow for the movement of equipment from one division or department to another, thereby preventing the wasting of a company's assets (particularly if the device in question were already purchased).

The overall benefit to management of a more coordinated look at all hardware expenditures within an organization are becoming increasingly obvious. Quantity discounts, compatibility of systems, backup, and timing of new acquisitions all take advantage of new and more cost-effective hardware. But with more departments making acquisitions in the years to come, the complexity of decision making coupled with an obvious need to coordinate acquisitions make the management of hardware costs more difficult. DP departments lacking in financial knowledge, let alone financial strategies or in not reporting directly to top management, may find their monopoly on hardware acquisitions quickly and sharply broken. With simple and more application oriented software packages becoming available, often with easier-to-install hardware being sold directly to end users, DP departments could find their role within an organization eroding at the same time that the use of data processing was actually increasing. In fact, one could argue that given the amount of data processing non-DP departments have already become involved with, the age of the data processing department may come to an end in this century. Regardless of what happens to data processing departments, managements in general are devoting more attention than ever before to the better use of equipment in the most cost-effective manner possible. As the percent of a company's budget devoted to data processing increases, therefore, so will the need to manage data processing better, regardless of who does it.

HOW MANAGEMENT CAN TAKE ADVANTAGE
OF ECONOMIC TRENDS

In the previous pages several fundamental trends were described that have serious implications for the cost of hardware. First, individual pieces of equipment are becoming less expensive to lease and purchase. Maintenance costs are dropping dramatically. For example, a computer purchased in the 1970s may have cost $3000 a month for maintenance, whereas the same power in new technology may now cost only $500. Second, the speed with which new products were announced in the 1970s increased sharply over the 1960s, from an average of every seven years to less than four. This has meant that purchased equipment had to be amortized faster and in some cases, companies elected to lease for fear of being stuck with overpriced older technologies. Third, the percentage of total cost for data processing going toward hardware decreased while that for software increased. Fourth, the amount of technical expertise required to install and operate equipment declined, making it possible for non-DP departments to acquire equipment independent of the data processing department. These trends clearly suggest that management will want to pay more attention to financial and cost strategies in the future. Although Chapter 3 discusses this issue in more detail, some general points can be made based on the experience of the 1970s to guide management in avoiding some obvious and unnecessary costs.

1. Establish a Life for an Application   Too often applications are developed or packages purchased without any consideration of the number of years the particular function should be around. Consequently, hardware that is acquired for it may not be amortized either to take into account how long it will be used for this application or the need to replace it because of new products or changing requirements not addressed properly in the beginning. If, after a proper and detailed study of word-processing requirements, for example, a company designs a system that it feels will be around for approximately seven years, the cost justification for such a system should take into account spreading the cost of developing the application over the life of the project, thereby following good accounting practices and appropriate tax laws. Equipment for such an application can then be selected on the basis of its suitability to support the particular application. And because technology changes frequently enough, management would be in a position to insist that whatever vendor's equipment is chosen should have the capacity to perform future functions anticipated to come on stream within the life of the seven-year project. That means making sure that a vendor's product is current and has a direction that provides a reasonable feeling that its follow-on will be compatible with the application in question. Thus if a company put in a word-processing system that had just been introduced by a vendor, the chances of that product being current for three or four years makes it appear that the equipment would stay in the company that long and therefore, in this case, would be a candidate for purchase with amortization over three to four years, possibly five to satisfy tax laws. However, if the equipment in question has been available in the marketplace for three years, it should be considered as a candidate for lease for two years in anticipation of a follow-on product announcement by the vendor. These comments are sample strategies; individual companies would have to analyze their situations in light of their own needs. But the point is that the first step in managing the introduction and eventual disposal of equipment in cost-effective terms is to understand what it will be used for and for how long.

2.   Insist That Compatibility of Systems across the Company Be Maintained Whenever Reasonably Possible   Since operating systems and programs will inevitably require some technical expertise from a data processing department, new acquisitions should have the capability of being supported by a company's professional data processing group. Using an IBM example, bringing in a computer that uses the DOS/VSE operating system for a particular application when the DP department has no knowledge of this software may make little sense if it is a user manager's intention of having the DP department support the software. Although mixed systems may have justification, lack of expertise or training does not. Compatibility can extend to the hardware itself. For instance, using the word-processing case illustrated above, by insisting that all the terminals used in this application be usable in all word-processing stations throughout the organization ensures that boxes can be switched about. Using a common technology on CRTs would also ensure that if a particular application was no longer needed, these terminals could then be taken from the defunct application and be used in another with minimal fuss. Cross-application terminal compatibility also suggests that if one application needed a terminal immediately, possibly a device could be taken away from some other use; in short, buy yourself some flexibility and simplicity.

There are other logical benefits that come with compatibility of hardware, as with software. One department's computer or DASD could serve as backup for another's while knowledge of a particular device in one sector of the company can be shared with others without having to undergo the cost of learning about new technologies, not to mention the time wasted. Compatibility can also be an insurance policy against faulty forecasts on demand. For example, if for word processing a computer was purchased and is planned for amortization over five years, with management saying in the third year that it needs a bigger device to support the application, what can be done? There are two options that quickly come to mind. First, management could eat the cost of two years' remaining amortization (by rolling this expenditure into that of the new computer's) or second, management could find another home for the smaller unit within the organization for some new cost-justified application (or upgrade). The second option simply requires the transfer of the remaining book value to be amortized to the expense of the new application, in the process probably reducing the cost of hardware for it. Although this second option is the smarter move to make, it would not be possible if the equipment were not compatible with other existing hardware.

Since the issue of compatibility is so important and the problem so common, another example of a frequent situation can help illustrate the need to deal with the issue. Many companies have multiple data centers, each with budgets running into the millions of dollars. Say that shop 1 has an IBM 4331 computer and that shop 2 has a small Honeywell. Assume that the first shop is rapidly expanding and soon finds that its purchased 4331 is no longer adequate for its needs and wants to replace it with the next larger unit, a 4341. Management might say that the 4331 still had two years' worth of amortization left or about $35,000, and so suggests that it be transferred to the second shop, which has also been growing and could use the additional capacity.

The 4331 could not displace the Honeywell system since they are technically incompatible. Conversion of the programs running in the second shop would probably cost hundreds of thousands of dollars—far in excess of the $35,000 book value of the 4331. Therefore, in this common instance, the company would either keep the 4331 somehow, or sell it possibly for less than $35,000 and thus take a loss, and finally will probably have to up-grade the computer in the second location anyway. Money was wasted in both shops, not to mention the loss of opportunity in using each other's applications and expertise. Such a scenario is so common that it is probably safe to say that in one form or another, every company with more than one data center has experienced it at one time or another. And invariably the fix is either unsatisfactory or some manager ends up making a "bite the bullet" decision of some sort that could have been avoided in the first place.

3.   Establish a Formal Procedure for Full Financial Analysis of Hardware Acquisitions above a Certain Value   Less frequently today within DP departments but still common among non-DP shops, equipment will be acquired without any reasonably detailed financial analysis that takes into account such options as purchase versus lease, alternative financing scenarios, or consideration of company-wide expense and capital plans and strategies. Set a threshold amount that if exceeded requires a formal financial analysis of alternatives. Sample thresholds might be any device that leases for more than $5000 per year or which has a purchase price in excess of a similar amount. The monetary value set should not be any lower; otherwise, every-one will be sitting around doing financial analyses instead of their regular jobs. On the other hand, it should not be so high that only rarely is any financial work ever done. In all probability threshold values above $5000 would be most reasonable. Analysis of alternatives should not be limited just to computers (as is still the case in too many organizations). By making the requirement a monetary value comparable with those set for other industrial equipment within an organization, DP technologies can change together with prices and values without affecting the requirement. Thus if computers become a minor expense with software taking the major share, the requirement for analysis will then force examination of alternative soft-ware costs. This approach would also eliminate some rules that have become silly over the years. For example, in many companies all computer decisions are made by the chairman of the board. Thus in a multibillion-dollar company, it would be conceivable that a decision to acquire a $20,000 mini would have to go to the top; what a waste of a valuable executive's time on such a relatively small decision!

With changing patterns of acquisitions, financial analysis gets done, then, where it is relevant to do so. For example, if, over the past five years, 75% of all hardware acquisitions involved terminals and peripherals with average monthly lease prices of between $100 and $1500 and purchase prices of $3000 to $45,000, a reasonable expenditure level requiring analysis might be $500 on lease and $10,000 on purchase. This company might also require that if the total number of devices of a particular kind have a monetary value equal to or greater than the threshold amount, financial analysis should be performed. In our example, management also checks periodically to see if the right devices are being studied, because in one year the volume acquisitions might be terminals and in the next, DASD. Thus the rule could be that the guidelines apply both on a box-for-box basis and for all generic devices collectively. In our case, this also applies for all devices of any type earmarked for one application. Thus if 100 terminals for word processing were to be brought in within one fiscal year, each with a leasing cost of $100 per month together with DASD leasing for $2000, then clearly a formal financial analysis should be required. How this study can be carried out is illustrated in Chapter 3.

Yet suffice it to say at this point that the standards imposed on DP hardware should be the same as those used for other types of equipment and machinery throughout an organization. Thus a company's standard cost of capital as used by manufacturing, for instance, can be applied to data processing. The minimum return on investment or payback period used by distribution can also be applied to data processing. This requirement to standardize financial analysis becomes increasingly important as the amount of data processing hardware proliferates in various offices, departments, and divisions. The reason is simple. If an executive has one hundred dollars to invest in equipment and the manufacturing executive wants it for his operations while the director of management information systems (MIS) wants it for her device, the decision maker will have something approximating an apples-to-apples analysis from which to make a financial decision. From a DP point of view, in such a comparison, data processing more often than not can win because the ratio of cost to benefit of the highly technically advanced DP equipment often outpaces less advanced and more conventional machinery. Moreover, when hardware decisions are covered under the umbrella of a justified application, it is all the better, since it is the nature of DP applications to have very high return on investment and payback values compared to other projects, such as building construction and manufacturing machinery.

Any financial analysis should take into account that the cost of follow-on products will probably be less in data processing, which is usually the exception when analyzing industrial equipment. Thus for purposes of reporting on a company's assets in annual reports, since the cost of replacement is often included, either the cost of replacing old DP hardware or current equipment with follow-ons is usually taken into account in any formal financial analysis. However, auditors of company practices are finding increasingly that this kind of residual value analysis is not being done, despite various government regulations, so inevitably pressure will be brought to bear on the problem. Be aware of the issue and be prepared to factor it into any analysis of data processing hardware.

4. Require a Documented Statement of Costs and Technical Strategies and an Implementation Plan   Once a financial analysis has been completed and an option selected, it should be documented totally, taking into account the cost of the hardware in question, salaries of people being hired to use it, and the expense of developing the application programs that will run it. This document should also make a statement about the relative life of the hardware and when it might become obsolete and subject to replacement. In this way, financial management can ensure closer control over how accounting handles the equipment on the books. There is nothing more frustrating than buying a computer for use over five years and then to find out when you are about to replace it that the accounting department had it on the books for seven years because no one told the department to do otherwise. The same applies to depreciation methods. Assume that the accounting department will depreciate equipment on a straight-line basis over the longest period unless specifically told otherwise. Since even purchased DP equipment tends to be replaced more frequently than management originally forecasted, using alternative depreciation methods, such as double declining balance, invariably makes more sense. Remember that depreciation methods are not hard and fast; various methods can be negotiated with financial managers even after one has already been selected, because the U.S. government, for instance, will allow a change in the depreciation method employed on a device once in the life of that equipment within your organization. So, for example, if in a high-profit year you want to take more depreciation than was originally planned by switching depreciation methods, it is possible to do so if management agrees on the change.

Since depreciation strategies are so closely tied to the anticipated life of a particular device, the documented report on how a piece of hardware is to be acquired should also contain a statement about how long it will be within the company and what the basis of the estimate was at the time of the decision. Thus if management later wants to go back and measure the accuracy of the forecast (mainly for political reasons if someone is to be blamed for wanting to change equipment too early), it can be done. This document will also force serious consideration by everyone of all the key issues so that the final plan of action takes into account company financial strategies, the needs of a particular department requesting an application, and the realities of the DP technology in question.

Hints on Financial Strategies

If the four rules discussed above are followed, management stands a greater chance of understanding how it spends money on DP equipment and how better to control it. There are some other general rules of thumb that can also be applied in varying degrees in conjunction with the preceding four.

- As a general rule, if you think a piece of equipment is going to remain in the organization for more than two years, consider purchasing it; it may be less expensive than leasing, especially for terminals. For computers and other more expensive devices, the break-even point might be closer to three or four years, so apply the rule appropriately. The key is how long one intends to keep the equipment.

- Whatever you thought was the period you were going to keep the equipment will not in fact be the case. Terminals, DASD, and tape will be in your organization much longer than anyone originally thought, whereas computers of smaller size will often be replaced in less time than planned.

- When purchasing equipment, assume that newer technologies and follow-on product announcements will reduce the resale (residual) value of your equipment faster than you planned for. Price/value fall trends over the past 5, 10, or more years notwithstanding, the future is never the same as the past. Therefore, depreciate purchased equipment as fast as you can afford to or are allowed to by law, conventions, or company practices. If, when dumping equipment, you sell it at less than book value, you are in a no-win situation. On the other hand, if it is sold for more than its value on the books, thus resulting in a "profit," you are a genius.

- Never try to double-guess pricing strategies by vendors regarding their products. Given the dynamics of the industry, prices can go up and down very quickly, particularly purchase prices on computers. Such guesswork is popular with DP management but has about as much validity as betting at the dog tracks. Therefore, cost-justify equipment at the prices they were at when the acquisition decision was made. If there are price reductions later that you cannot take advantage of, do not cry in your soup, because there was nothing to be done about it. The same applies if a price increase comes along and you absorb it. If a number of projects are constantly in the works, some decisions will have lucky timing whereas others will not. The mistake that could be made is to attach an anticipated value to some hardware in cost justifying it (such as a price decrease before it gets installed)—because if you are wrong, the justification is off.

- Assume that equipment will not always go in on time or operate within the planned budget. Although this sounds much like Murphy's Law as applied to data processing, it is a reality. Therefore, apply our law, called "Fudge Economics," which states that those who cover themselves with extra toga run less risk of exposure. A few extra dollars in the budget in the range of 5% more per year would seem reasonable. This extra amount would take into account unforeseen overtime charges on rental equipment, transportation costs, unexpected additional maintenance fees, and other unforeseen charges for parts, people, and so on—and, of course, for inflation.

- Pay more attention to what a vendor and his or her company says about product direction than to self-appointed DP pundits writing in industry publications. The only caveat to this rule is: if a vendor's direction is out of line with the DP industry as a whole, look cross-eyed at the vendor and ask a lot of questions. For example, if a vendor says that memory on a particular intelligent terminal will probably be doubled or at least increased but the DP industry expects all intelligent terminals to quadruple in memory during the same period of time, be concerned. The reason for worry in this case might be that everyone knows that new releases of operating systems are requiring larger amounts of memory. This in fact was the case with computers throughout the 1970s. In 1970 alone, a large computer with 1 megabyte of memory was considered large except by vendors. By 1980, there were intelligent terminal systems installed with as much memory! Vendors found it cheaper to install more memory on computers than to reduce the size of operating systems. In 1970, the vendors knew this clearly but most DP managers did not. In short, be informed and remember that vendors are a useful source of information.

- A corollary to the foregoing rule is to try to acquire the latest technology available without seriously risking the possibility of reinventing the wheel for a vendor. Newer technology is usually cheaper. Older equipment is not, although ancient boxes are virtually given away (and for good reason, since nobody wants them). A case in point illustrates the issue. If you went into the marketplace in 1980 and acquired an IBM 155II computer on a two-year lease, it would cost about $5000 per month, whereas a newer 4341 would lease for $7500 per month. By the time you added $2000 per month maintenance on the 155 and an additional $1000 per month for electricity over what the 4341 would cost, the $5000 per month lease looks awful. Furthermore, the 4341 carries ITC with it, whereas the 155 would not. The only time that older technology makes sense is if it were installed for a short interim period while waiting for a more permanent, newer piece of equipment. Before we leave the subject of current technology, we should warn you not to go the other extreme and plan on installing hardware that someone anticipates will be announced, because more often than not, announcement dates slip.

- Assume that data processing personnel and most departmental managers in any part of an organization will do a poor job in identifying all the basic financial alternatives on major acquisitions. Therefore, make sure that someone who understands at least elementary financial analysis becomes involved so that decisions involving hundreds of thousands of dollars take into account such factors as company financial goals and objectives, basic hurdle rates, investment tax credit (ITC), pre- and post-tax cash outflows, various depreciation methods, and alternative time frames. Too often, even in well-run companies, these elementary factors are sublimated to politics or simply to "gut feelings" in decision making. Often this is even the case with computer acquisitions, where not even a simple capacity study is conducted. Is it any wonder that many companies acquire the wrong computer and are surprised when it has to be replaced so soon?

- Take advantage of a vendor's skill and experience in cost-justifying equipment when defining various financial alternatives. Even though vendors obviously take good care of their own company's interests, they are often excellent financial analysts who can apply your organization's criteria and conditions to help justify equipment. Their help can go far in quickly identifying several key financial alternatives worthy of management's attention. These people are particularly useful if they come from the major computer vendors because they constantly sell "financially" to upper management and thus have a clear understanding of how to cost out alternatives and then present the data in meaningful terms for decisions. Their efforts, however, do not absolve their customers from making the ultimate decision on what alternatives to consider or the values given to each. One other benefit of a vendor's help is that he or she can bring to bear on the analysis all the factors involving their company which you might overlook, such as one vendor passing on the ITC but another not, or in clarifying warranty periods on purchased equipment, which might save on maintenance expenses from one financial scenario to another.

- Keep the number of options limited to a predetermined amount. It is possible to come up with dozens of options, yet for all practical purposes most financial strategists suggest that for a reasonable decision to be made, four or five options is clearly adequate. Fifteen or even a hundred variations could be worked on before, but reduce them to five or fewer for the ultimate decision. Save the documentation on those that are rejected so that if there is any question later about the logic of the final decision, data will be available for reconstructing the decision-making process. Remember, simple common sense—spiced with a dash of financial acumen—is all that is required.

KEEPING TRACK OF WHAT AN ORGANIZATION HAS

So far in this chapter a great deal of material has been covered regarding the types of equipment an organization has, where it is used, who acquires it and controls its use, and who disposes of it. Thus in most organizations the question of how to keep track of all this hardware has become an important one for MIS directors, DP managers, and department heads. The remarks below are directed toward all three groups and their aim is better control over what is being used and at what cost. The comments and suggestions reflect basic steps commonly applied in many organizations today to track all manner of equipment—for both industrial and data processing—along with fleets of trucks, railway cars, or simply laboratory testing devices.

The primary concern that many managers have is in controlling the cost of equipment, which has been rising if for no other reason because more is being used. On the basis of cost, there are several general factors that must be taken into account in managing hardware effectively:

- Contractual obligations
- Economies of scale
- Maintenance responsibilities
- Efficiency of use
- Role in DP plans

Each of these presents unique problems and opportunities for management, and controls are essential. A brief review of each illustrates the methods of tracking data processing hardware.

Contractual Obligations

Nothing seems more confusing to more departments than contractual obligations on equipment. There are a variety of lease and purchase agreements to contend with, together with additional documents covering maintenance, software leases and support, others governing the environment in which equipment must reside, base agreements covering general relations between companies, and a raft of letters that are written covering various contractual issues. Such letters typically include discussion of invoice disputes, the movement of equipment from one location to another, maintenance, and removal or cancellation notices. Add to this large file the fact that a number of hardware vendors are often used within an organization, each with its own set of contracts and correspondence, and you begin to appreciate the complexity of managing contracts. If these files are not maintained properly, problems that arise can cause added expenditures and uncomfortable situations. Take as an example, a two-year lease that is due for renewal. Suppose the contract stipulated that if not notified within 30 days of the termination date of the base document, the device in question is switched from a lease price to a month-to-month rental charge, which is 10% higher than the old rate. If a manager did not know this and the leasing cost was $1000 per month, that person would be responsible for an additional $100 per month expenditure until a decision was made.

A more serious, yet common example is the lease that automatically renews itself if the vendor is not notified otherwise. Suppose, for instance, that a disk drive that leases for $1000 per month is renewed automatically for two years, yet the DP manager had planned to replace it four months later with a different unit. Now that person would face termination charges for canceling the contract, and the costs might run into thousands of dollars or possibly the monthly lease amount for the life of the contract. Either the sum is paid or the change in devices is not made. Proper management of the contract file could have avoided the problem.

The problem of managing such information can be solved quickly and simply. First, it seems logical that data processing management should have responsibility within an organization for keeping track of all DP equipment, regardless of whether or not the DP group has budgetary or management control over it. Step 1 then involves making a list of all devices within the organization. This list would include the device type, its serial number, where it is located, whose budget it comes under, if leased, and the date the lease ends. Figure 1-13 illustrates a sample form partially filled out that could serve as the basis for such a list for use in any organization. Note that simplicity is the key. The form should be treated as a journal and can have entries added when needed.

Who fills out this form and maintains all such forms in one file can vary from one organization to another. However, the initial inventory should be made by the DP department, since it is best qualified to recognize data processing equipment. Subsequently, such a list can be kept by the individual departments as long as the DP department has a copy of the list and is kept current at all times. Periodically, the journal should be reviewed to determine what contracts are coming up for renewal. Many companies actually computerize this report and simply print out periodically a list of all devices that are coming up soon (usually within 90 days) for contract renewal.

The DP department should also maintain a file on the configurations of the installed equipment, copies of the contracts governing their use, all

XYZ Company: Sales Division

Page ____

Device	Serial No.	Location	Budget	L, P, R	Date L Ends	Comments
3370 DIsk	56823	DP Dept.	DP #409	L	9/15/84	IBM auto. renewal
3278 CRT	11187	A/R Dept.	Accounting	R	Monthly	Q. Leasing Co.
9080 WP	W8732	Legal	Corporate	P	8/82	Fully depreciated by 8/82

L = Lease; P = Purchased; R = Rented

Figure 1-13. Sample log of installed equipment. Note that a form could be designed to include additional information (such as monthly cost) and have expanded room for comments.

correspondence involved, and any maintenance data that may have been gathered along the way. Invariably, a well-run file will also have a sample checklist of "to do's" filled out for the installation of a unit. Our chapter on installation management illustrates such checklists. Figures 1-14 and 1-15 illustrate typical documents that might be kept on each device.

The files can be of essentially two types. Typically, the best-organized

Problem Report Log

Device	I.D. No.	Person	Problem	Date
CRT	50122	Smith	No power	5/18/82

Figure 1-14. Sample form for logging problems.

Problem Report

Department: _____ Date: _____

Device type: _____Serial no. : _____

Problem description

_____

_____

_____

_____

_____

Submitted to: _____

Submitted by: _____

Telephone extension _____

Figure 1-15. Sample problem report form.

files will be folders either by device type (e.g., IBM 3270 CRTs and associated control units and printers) or by department. In some cases, individual folders are maintained by device with all the appropriate contracts, maintenance logs, letters, and so on, although that may not be necessary, as it could lead to redundancy of paper. However, many operations managers within a data processing department will maintain such records of all devices within the computer room. Because this type of data is often critical to the smooth operation of a data center, many are computerizing this information. For example, take the form illustrated in Figure 1-13. That report lends itself to computerization. A simple program could then be run periodically at scheduled times to produce lists of devices coming up for contract renewal by location, by date, by device type, or by vendor.

Such management tools have a number of uses. First, a report will allow management to consider replacing all devices of a certain type within the organization. Second, a strategy or policy regarding contracts can be developed once it is better understood what obligations exist now. Third, the information can be input for either next year's budget or for a chargeout system. Fourth, a review of leases to see if certain devices should be purchased (in order to save the organization money) makes sense. Fifth, major conversion plans involving the movement of equipment about could hardly be done without such reporting mechanisms in place.

In short, these records provide a vehicle for communications among departments, better plans, increased control over costs, and improved control over maintenance. A periodic review (should be carried out at least once each quarter, even if only for a few minutes) also allows management to inquire on a more formal basis if the equipment in question is still being used and if the organization is still obtaining benefits from these devices which justify their costs. For example, such reviews can help to identify quickly if there are terminals still in their original packing cases but for which the leasing fee is being paid, or a mini sitting in a laboratory that was closed six months ago, which could now be sold or transferred to another department.

Economies of Scale

By having a centralized data bank of information on all devices installed, it next becomes possible to take advantage of economies of scale. Some vendors will reduce the overall lease price of certain types of devices when the number of such units installed within a particular organization increases. For instance, some manufacturers of CRTs or minis or modems reduce lease prices per device by a fixed percentage every time the number of installed units increases by certain amounts (e.g., by 50). Thus if an intelligent terminal leases for $1000 for the first 10 units installed and the population grows to 50 units with a 2% reduction for every 10 new ones installed, the cost per unit could go down to $920 each (8% reduction), which, times 50, represents a savings of $4000 per month. Another typical example involves the $100 per month CRT for the first 50 installed, which then drops (say 5%) when additional units go in. In this instance the cost per device would drop to $95. The $5 savings times the original 100 CRTs is $500 per month, which more than pays for some additional terminals. Often these economies of scale are not possible unless a company tracks what it has installed, because many vendors do not since they may bill various departments individually across many states and thus not know that a discount should be activated.

Another common form of economies of scale involves quantity discounts on purchase. Suppose that a vendor is selling distributive processing units at 20% off the purchase price when five or more devices are bought within a year. To take advantage of such a discount, management would first have to understand how many units could be used (even replacing a mixed variety of others). Second, the cost of not taking advantage of the discount is made possible. For example, if a device sells for $10,000 and that of other vendors also sells for the same amount but the first has a quantity discount of 20%, one could either put in a sixth device in effect for free, or save $2000 per location times five, or $10,000.

Increasingly, quantity discounts are appearing in maintenance contracts. Usually, these arrangements call for maintenance requests to flow to one central location for transmittal to the vendor. Distributive terminals and their software provide a common example. Many vendors now charge less per terminal for maintenance if all service requests are centralized for analysis and possibly a repair by either one maintenance group or at first by a data processing department. Savings in maintenance charges can amount to as much as 50% of maintenance charges that otherwise would have been levied against each separate unit in the network.

Maintenance Responsibilities

Keeping track of equipment can also allow more simplified maintenance. If a problem develops in a particular type of device, repair instructions can go out quickly to all the units at the same time from one point of contact. For example, printers attached to CRTs might require some rewiring to prevent possible fires. The central DP location could ship out to each user of such printers the necessary wiring for local vendor maintenance personnel to change quickly. The type of handling is rapidly becoming common with microcode changes to intelligent devices scattered throughout the organization, ensuring that everyone obtains the same release of software simultaneously. Complaints about problems coming into one point could result in the identification of a pattern of problems, which could then be fixed. Suppose that CRTs develop a series of errors resulting in "garbage" letters on the screen. The solution might not be to send field engineering teams out to examine individual units but might involve a software problem at the host location's teleprocessing control unit—a problem that might not be identified if individual users simply called their local maintenance people.

Thus many companies are now finding it better to have a central point of contact (person, location, or telephone number). Moreover, two types of logs for these problems are being kept. First, most devices come with a manual in which users note problems. These comments are reviewed by the vendor's maintenance people when they come in to do periodic maintenance work on the device. Figure 1-16 illustrates a sample log, as does Figure 1-15.

The second type of log is developed by an organization to ensure that a central contact point is aware of problems. Such a reporting tool can be simple, possibly one page, that everyone is required to use in documenting all problems. The form could be filled out by the user or by the person at the central point. The form illustrated in Figure 1-17 suggests the type of information that should be collected and kept centrally. Use of such forms should apply equally to hardware, software, and applications. Periodically, the forms can be reviewed with vendor maintenance personnel, systems and programming staff management, and others to determine methods for reducing or eliminating problems. Often, such review sessions are held weekly.

Efficiency of Use

As the number of devices within an organization increases, communications among those who order and install devices, maintain contract files, and use the units tend to decrease. As the variety of devices and device locations expand, so does the complexity of any effort to manage hardware. Yet a structured form of communications with all users attacks the problem. By-products of an organized approach to understanding what is installed are many. The most common are:

- More efficient educational programs for new users of equipment
- Standardized step-by-step installation plans that are the result of time-tested experience within a particular organization
- Delivery and installation of units when needed, thus reducing costs, disruption of normal work, and frustrations

Perhaps the most common by-product of well-managed hardware (particularly for users) is the internal procedure manual. Every vendor provides some form of manual describing how devices are used. However, every organization uses these devices differently, for a variety of applications, with different ways to sign on to terminals, hours when certain units can be used, who to call for repairs, and disaster plans. For such issues, an internal procedure manual is imperative. Binders containing descriptions of widely used devices, instructions on how to use them, and the steps required to execute applications particular to an organization are typical parts of a procedure

LOG

MACHINE TYPE AND SERIAL

DATE	DESCRIPTION OF PROBLEM/ACTION TAKEN (DO NOT RECORD HOURS OR PART NUMBER)	EMPLOYEE INITIAL
◄FOLD HERE ━━━━━━━━━━━━━━━━━━━━━━━━━━━	┌FOLD HERE◄	
◄FOLD HERE◄ ━━━━━━━━━━━━━━━━━━━━━━━━	◄FOLD HERE◄	

Figure 1-16. Sample problem log. (Source: IBM Corporation, © 1975.)

41

PROBLEM REPORT

No.

For PROBLEM REPORTER: Fill in this section, keep last copy, and forward rest to Dept PC.

Name: _____ *Dept:* _____ *Ext:* _____ *Date:* _____

Machine/System used: *Description of problem:*

☐ TSO   _____
☐ IMS/VS   _____
☐ OS/VS1
☐ OS/VS2   _____
☐ S/370-155
☐ S/370-158   _____
☐ S/3

Supporting documentation attached:

☐ Hard copy of screen ☐ VTOC listing   ☐ Other—specify: _____
☐ Program listing   ☐ SEREP dump
☐ System dump   ☐   _____

Is this problem holding up your work?   Yes/No

For COORDINATOR: Keep last copy and send rest to problem solver.

Problem already reported: Yes/No—Report no.____Date: _____

Problem area: _____

Priority:___Deadline (bypass/solution): _____ *Assigned to:* _____ *Date:* _____

Priority:___Deadline (bypass/solution): _____ *Assigned to:* _____ *Date:* _____

Priority:___Deadline (bypass/solution): _____ *Assigned to:* _____ *Date:* _____

Solution accepted by: _____ *Date:* _____ *Closing code:* _____

For PROBLEM SOLVER: Keep last copy. Return a copy to Dept PC at each update.

Description of bypass: _____

Change request no.___submitted on:_____ Final: Yes/No   *Solution code:*

Change request no.___submitted on:_____ Final: Yes/No   _____

Information to users: on bypass   on solution

   —By coordinator when problem reported   ☐

   —By report to problem meeting   ☐   ☐

   — In newsletter _____   ☐   ☐

   —In handbook _____   ☐   ☐

Comments: _____
_____
_____

Figure 1-17. Example of a problem report form (Source: IBM Corporation, © 1976.)

42

manual and go far to ensure that devices will be used properly. Typical procedure manuals for CRTs may only have five or six pages, whereas those for minis and micros could run into hundreds of pages. Invariably, however, they all cover the same types of information:

- Description of the device being used
- How to use the units (sign-on procedures, commands, etc.)
- Applications accessed through this unit
- Procedures for reporting problems in software, applications, and hardware (including telephone numbers, names, addresses, and appropriate forms)
- Local maintenance personnel

In addition, each department using data processing equipment can have such a procedure manual containing additional information on such topics as:

- Inventory by device type and serial number installed
- Budgetary information on how much the department is paying for each unit monthly and to whom
- Copies of invoices, contracts, and maintenance logs
- Disaster plans

At a central point (such as a data processing department) sample procedure manuals are kept and updates shipped out to all users as needed. A central location could keep a log similar to those used in the departments, but more comprehensive, covering all departments. If this information is computerized, data processing management can generate bills for chargeout services on usage together with various reports by device type, lease termination date, and department or division, for whatever purpose deemed useful.

Budgetary Control

Budgetary information has long been a standard form of management control over hardware used in data processing. Figure 1-18 illustrates the kind of

Hardware Budget XYZ Company Data Center, 1984

Month: __March__

Device	Planned	Actual
Computer "X"	$10,000	$10,000
8 3370's	4,800	4,200
8 3420's	4,000	4,000
16 CRTs	1,300	1,600
Copier	500	500
16 Modems	800	820
TP controller	2,500	2,600
Totals	$23,900	$23,720

Figure 1-18. Sample monthly hardware budget. (This partial document can be used in the same format to show quarterly and annual statistics with totals.)

information that may be tracked within a data processing budget. First, this information may provide a basis for chargeouts by usage to other departments. Second, a quick glance at such numbers suggest whether certain items should be purchased or leased. Third, if a chargeout system is in place, the basis for next year's charges can be gleaned from a detailed hardware budget plan. The simplest form containing budgetary data in any data processing department is an invoice from a vendor and it can serve as the basis for developing any other hardware budget control document. This document is convenient only if all the installed equipment comes from one vendor. But if several vendors are supplying equipment, there are numerous invoices to track, making the need for a centralized inventory count by location conducted by one department all the more necessary.

Most organizations require their departments to keep copies of all invoices paid, together with intercompany debit and credit memos for audit purposes. Most organizations keep such files by departments rather than in a single file cabinet. More frequently today than ever before, data processing departments are conducting audits of equipment and invoices throughout their organizations to keep track of costs and to ensure that company procedures are being followed. Such procedures include ensuring that bills are paid on time, that the correct ones only are paid, that formal requests for capital expenditures are submitted, and that normal accounting practices are being adhered to by all.

Formal auditing is increasing because of legal requirements as much as out of any sense of better management. There are too many users, for instance, who acquire computer equipment under the guise of "testing devices" and expense out the purchase cost when, in fact, the company would want the units in question to be capitalized. If one device at $10,000 is financially mismanaged, an organization will probably not suffer, but what if ten departments and seven laboratories bring in micros at $10,000 each and expense them instead of capitalizing their cost? The effect on the income statement is definitely negative, eating into profits while violating accounting practices as well as tax laws.

Role in DP Plans

Accurate files on installed equipment avoid numerous problems for those preparing data processing plans, particularly in large organizations with dozens or hundreds of locations using equipment. With a known inventory, strategies can and are developed to provide for optimum purchase and lease plans for equipment, for capacity studies, for relocation of devices to those parts of the organization that need them, for the implementation of backup procedures in case of downtime on specific units (especially computers), or as a result of a serious disaster. Suppose that management wants to implement a distributive processing network to replace a number of antiquated applications, computers, or poorly managed data centers. Just to cost-justify such a major strategic direction and to determine real capacity requirements would necessitate knowing what the existing equipment costs and what termination charges would be involved as opposed to the cost of distributive devices, as well as understanding the use of these units. The financial analysis alone would be impossible without such elementary information. Centralizing data collection does involve encouraging distributive processing in many instances, the purchase of installed CRTs, the use of software application packages across the entire organization, and the establishment of network management teams within MIS departments, thereby reducing the costs of redundant and expensive data processing staffs.

Although it is not the purpose of this book to discuss planning in any detail, several general comments can be made about DP planning. It can be to see how to reduce or hold the line on hardware costs. It may involve the development of new applications. Also important, plans are developed to replace old hardware and software that are either no longer relevant or cost too much to operate. The latter is particularly the case in companies that still have 10- or 15-year-old computers with large numbers of applications that are no longer compatible with more modern hardware and software. Such a situation usually leads to duplicate staffs for maintenance of software on two systems, increased downtime on older devices, and complexity of management, since any change usually requires more work than with newer technology.

Thus the need to do more planning in data processing increases with time, and often and invariably it comes down to hardware issues. Where are they located, how much do they cost, and when can they be replaced and how? In most cases all formalized plans will include descriptions of hardware strategies with their costs. One common problem today that calls for planning is replacement of equipment, and this appears in most data processing plans.

Terminals that are purchased and charged out on the company's books in five years need to be looked at before the end of the fifth year to determine whether to keep them or plan for the expense of new ones. Computers on long-term leases coming up for renewal are the clearest example of managing plans and changes. An inventory count suggests shifting computers from division to division if that makes sense from the point of view of capacity and cost, or at least alerts management that different expenses are coming up with replacement units.

An increasingly common device to measure the movement of hardware is the "on-order report." For those companies that have many units on order from one or more vendors, the need for a report that shows what is on order is as important as documents illustrating what is installed. This kind of management tool is increasingly important because many vendors are beginning to place devices on rental charges x number of days after delivery. Moreover, more units are involved today than ever before. Thus the same

DP Hardware On-Order Report   As of (month):   March, 1984

Device	P.O. Number	Cost (dollars)	L, P, R	Dept.	Ship Date	Vendor	Budget Number	When Installed
Disk (1)	98765L	1,000	L	MIS	6/84	CDC	904	
CRTs (3)	9652, 3, 4	74 ea.	L	A/P	4/84	IBM	883	1 in 3/84
"X" CPU	12345	275,000	P	MIS	11/84	IBM	904	
Copier	XL873	1,000	R	Legal	5/84	Savin	234	
Modems (2)	4567, 8	50 ea.	L	Sales	3/84	ATT	345	3/84

Figure 1-19. Sample hardware on-order report. (This could also include a comments section, dates by day/month/year, and a management approval column.)

reasons that management has reports for installed equipment, also apply to on-order units.

Figure 1-19 shows what such a report might look like. With installed inventory reports, management has a fuller picture of what hardware is in or coming in and therefore what is available for use. On-order reports also have the benefit of allowing management to use vendor lead times to advantage because plans can be made in a rationale fashion based on demands, lead times, and capacity forecasts. Thus one can avoid the problem of discovering the immediate need for a particular device that has a six-month lead time. Installation plans can also grow out of such a report by making clear what devices are coming and when, so that management does not plan on doing too much within a certain period of time. For instance, if a computer is scheduled to be installed in April but 40 terminals are also scheduled for installation that month, it would probably make sense to either defer one project for a month or to accept delivery of all equipment but plan on installing some of it in May.

Companies should also establish guidelines for ordering equipment. The worst situation is where every department can and does order, which results in a hodgepodge of devices, incompatibility, wasted money, underutilized equipment, and rarely a capacity study and plan. Experience dictates which portion of the organization—typically the DP department—must pass judgment on the acquisition of new devices to ensure technical integrity, reasonableness of cost and function, and that the units in question conform to the master MIS plan, if one exists. Invariably in practice, this means that data processing shops within an organization do most of the ordering for themselves and user departments. However, many vendors deal directly with user management for such devices as word-processing units, micros, application minis, and time-sharing services. As organizations increase in size, so do the documented requirements that one must supply to control the acquisition of new equipment. Although each organization has to settle on policies that make sense to it, the elements involved are essentially the same. The following recommendations are made based on the experience of many companies:

(1) The DP group should be informed in writing a request for equipment. If the purchase value exceeds a certain amount, for example $5000, the DP manager must approve the request; if $10,000, an MIS director or a vice-president must also approve, and if over $75,000, corporate management must be included in the decision.

(2) The bigger the request in terms of dollars, the more formal should be the financial analysis that accompanies the request. If the request involves the use of contracts above a certain value, the legal department should perhaps become involved.

(3) If the DP department is being required to install the devices, they should approve them so as to acknowledge their responsibility in providing installation management and subsequent maintenance support for the equipment.

What seems reasonable for each layer of management to sign-off on today? Some general rules of thumb can be used. If a device is leased for two years or less at a total cost (leases, maintenance, transportation, etc.) of less than $1000 per month, the department head in conjunction with the DP department should be able to sign-off on the device. This amount would take into account all manner of terminals, disk, tape, and small printers and probably would not upset any budget or affect the company's books too much. For units that cost (monthly) over two years up to $3000, management immediately above the DP department might want to approve the request in conjunction with the DP department's acceptance. This limit would take into account minis, systems printers, and a variety of specialized DP equipment such as teleprocessing network control units, optical character readers (OCRs), memory bumps on computers, and even small central processing units. Above that amount, top management (divisional or corporate) probably should be involved to ensure that the following considerations have been taken into account:

- Financial alternatives (lease or purchase?)
- Impact on the company's books (tax, profits, expenses)
- Conformity with company business and DP plans (e.g., centralization or decentralization of DP)
- Conformity with the organization's "politics".

Most decision criteria involve all expenses: lease, purchase, maintenance, sales taxes, software, personnel, space, and anything else that might occur of a reasonable nature, such as transportation charges for equipment, additional electrical power, air conditioning, furniture, and labor costs. For additional terminals and peripherals, most such expenses are glossed over or are not relevant. Yet for computers they are invariably included in any analysis and usually in a formal report and presentation. In subsequent chapters examples of these considerations will illustrate the kind of data being looked at most frequently today.

CONCLUDING OBSERVATIONS

This chapter has identified where in an organization data processing equipment appears, the nature of the devices, the evolution of their function, what one might expect to see in the next several years, and some relative trends in costs and economics. It has been argued that better control over the use and cost of hardware can be made possible by the initial step of taking stock of what is installed and on order. Surprisingly, very few organizations have such elementary data conveniently at hand, yet without it, serious and costly mistakes can be made, capacities misunderstood, and, in effect, the efficient and smooth operation of data processing services disrupted. As a second step toward managing hardware, Chapter 2 addresses some of the fundamental issues involving capacity requirements and how to size an organization's hardware requirements.

Make no little plans; they have no
magic to stir men's blood.

Daniel H. Burnham

Too many companies spend too much money too soon on hardware that might not be right for them because the DP department does not do any capacity planning. This chapter illustrates how this is done and suggests where and how money can be saved by proper planning for additional equipment. The principles of capacity planning are reviewed for the types of decisions common to DP hardware today. Specific examples are used to illustrate the principles and to show what not to do. Finally, emphasis is placed on what can be done quickly, yet responsibly.

CHAPTER
TWO

Basic Principles of Capacity
Planning

Management is finding it more necessary than ever to understand how much power there is in its data processing hardware and what will be required in the future. A number of factors are making capacity planning a hot topic today. First, there is the increasing dependence on data processing and thus on its hardware. Second, with more hardware installed, the amount of money being spent is rising. Third, rapidly changing technologies together with differing ratios of cost to performance as new devices become available are forcing management to review constantly the worth of their installed base of devices. With hardware costs now running about one-third of a data processing budget for most organizations, the answer to better management of equipment can mean expenditures or savings of hundreds of thousands of dollars annually, even in small and medium-size companies. Decisions regarding the acquisition of additional hardware thus are coming under closer scrutiny, which in turn involves asking the simple question of how much work can be processed through a particular device. Others frame their concerns using different questions. What are the anticipated increases in work load for a machine for the period of time that management intends to keep it? What levels of service to users are necessary? How much will that cost? Is it worth it? These questions are being asked in a more formal manner than in years past and in a period when data processing is changing dramatically. Batch systems are being converted to on-line applications, and various options are becoming available more rapidly for both hardware and software configurations, all of which place enormous pressures on existing hardware resources.

The situation is at best chaotic to the untrained manager. Management is being asked constantly to consider computer upgrades, adding more peripheral equipment, changing software, and modifying or adding new applications. Word processors are mushrooming everywhere, and minis and micros are almost as common as the telephone. One of the best proven ways of trying to manage this incredible growth in hardware and systems involves capacity planning. It helps management understand and control change, directing it toward helping an organization on a timely basis, maximizing technological benefits, change, and costs rather than being pushed forward without any semblance of direction.

In dealing with hardware, three separate types of devices are involved in any form of measurement: the computer (with its memory), also called the central processing unit or simply CPU; various peripheral devices, such as tape and disk drives, controllers, printers, card input/output units; and an enormous variety of terminals, such as CRTs and teletypes.

The production system illustrated in Figure 2-1 suggests what a complete hardware configuration might look like in a small, simple shop. Note that the most significant component of the system is obviously also its heart: the computer. It remains the most expensive component of the system as well and thus the obvious topic of much attention by those wishing to do capacity studies and monitor work loads. The same applies for configurations of minis and micros, where the CPU portion actually represents an even higher proportion of the total costs of a system. The utilization of any CPU thus becomes a constant point of concern as whole operations staffs work to improve the utilization and availability of the central processor. Understanding what it does requires the continual attention of the entire data center, from the DP director down to the computer operator. By understanding how much "horsepower" there is and what portion of the available resource is being used to do current work, the demand for additional computer power can be judged sufficiently. If more is needed in the form of new

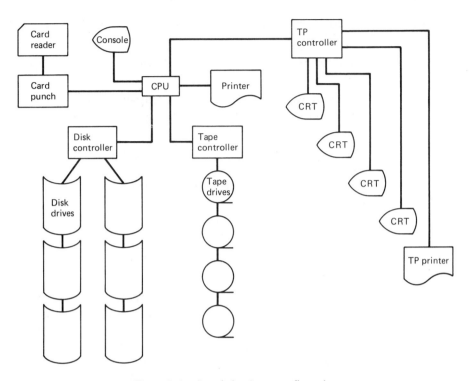

Figure 2-1. Sample hardware configuration.

or bigger upgrades, management will have time to plan for it, to cost-justify options, and to obtain necessary equipment on a timely basis by using capacity planning methods.

It is becoming an increasingly common practice in most data centers today to track CPU utilization and forecast demand from 6 to 24 months out in some fashion or another. By developing usage and demand forecasts on a time increment basis, management can also identify technical bottle-necks, fix them (see Chapter 5 on this), and then make additional acquisition decisions rationally. Users of the system are the people who drive its work-load characteristics and make demands for additional applications. DP management is thus constantly trying to double-guess its users and provide cost-effective hardware on a timely basis. This interrelationship between DP hardware capacity and user needs continually forces data processing management to question how much horsepower to have, how long commitments can be made on new equipment, and what has to be done to improve the performance of existing units. What is shocking is that frequently the DP department will attempt to answer these questions without even talking to users, let alone sharing with them responsibility for capacity planning.

Typical common concerns that emerge from the issue of capacity in all organizations include:

- Impact on response time when additional terminals are added to a network
- Effect of new acquisitions by the company, requiring the DP department to service new divisions quickly without deteriorating service to existing users
- When the existing CPU should be upgraded and for how long one should plan to keep it
- When additional memory must be added and how much, for how long, and at what price
- What effect changes to the computer will have on service performance
- What additional peripherals will be needed and when to support users, particularly in disk storage

Often, these familiar issues are faced as a reaction to a sudden change in conditions, such as a rapid deterioration in response time on the system because a group of new terminals were just added to the network or the company just acquired a new division that has to be serviced within 60 days. Not all DP managers have the organizational or managerial skills that can be applied ahead of time to plan logically for these kinds of contingencies. Frequently, therefore, capacity planning degenerates into an intuitive quick solution not using analytical techniques commonly available to improve the quality of planning. Constantly again, the consequences are evident of faulty quick decisions, made by management without solid planning. Machines run out of capacity, peripheral resources are severely constrained, existing devices are not used properly, tensions run high between users and data processing, and finally the work does not get done. It is a widely accepted maxim of data processing that the only constant in DP is change itself, yet frequently managers fail to manage change. Capacity planning provides a series of methods for managing change, offering more meaningful techniques for defining needs and options available to management. With serious capacity planning, management can have a better idea of what to do next, especially how best to use what is already installed.

The benefits of capacity planning and the consequences of no control affect an entire organization. For data processing, it strives to calm the organization instead of allowing chaos to reign. For non-DP management, capacity planning provides a warning system that additional resources will have to be planned for financially. Users can have a greater assurance that the work that gets done by DP personnel will be as responsive and timely as it is reasonable to expect and that cost-effective resources will be available when needed. If managing a resource is made easier for DP management, this benefit is evident all over the organization wherever hardware is installed. In short, the fundamental benefit of capacity planning is better management of an expensive and critical resource. How this can be done is the subject of this chapter.

WHAT IS CAPACITY PLANNING?

"Capacity planning" is one of those "buzz" terms circulating among data processing and business personnel, together with others, such as "word processing," "on-line," and "distributed processing." It is also one of the least understood of such terms and is hardly ever identified, so that everyone dealing with it within any enterprise is often thinking of a different definition, with little commonality across an organization. This babble of various meanings is made more difficult because even specialists within data processing cannot always agree on a single definition that meets everyone's needs. Regardless of the definition used, specialists all talk of capacity planning as a methodology or as various techniques that encompass a set of actions all geared to defining work-load characterizations, forecasting work loads, current and future performance, and availability of resources. They talk of it being a forecasting tool for future capacity requirements and frequently as a method of identifying what needs to be better tuned today. These various elements of any capacity planning effort will be reviewed below, defining what they are, how to execute them, and what benefits they offer. What must be kept in mind is that good and comprehensive capacity plans generally provide management with information in a number of areas that traditionally concern any organization. Briefly cataloged, they include:

- A description of a system's current performance. This includes utilization of individual and combined performance of all hardware and software.
- An analysis of the current work load's characteristics, which can then be the basis for forecasting future needs.
- A study of future work-load requirements and configurations necessary to support them.
- An analysis of response and/or turnaround time for various applications. A study of the time it takes a particular resource to do a set of tasks.
- A means for predicting the future performance of a configuration of hardware and software.
- An ongoing process for providing information about the system to management, so that there are no surprises and no degradation of services.

- A means of indicating clearly to non-DP management how well MIS managers run their departments. Ultimately, it quantifies the costs and benefits of competent DP management.

- A way to highlight the problems caused when users and DP personnel do not participate continually and jointly in capacity planning.

One common area of confusion should be cleared up before continuing our discussion of capacity planning. One has to understand the difference between the capacity of the computer and the capacity of the resource—an issue typically blurred, mixed, and always confused. A computer system incorporates all resources in a DP shop, of which the computer is only one part. Other components include peripherals, software, and people, as well as efficient management of all of these. Neither the computer nor the entire resource can be studied as part of the capacity planning process by itself or separately. Good capacity planning involves understanding the characteristics of each device or component and also the sum of their results. Specifically, capacity is determined by defining four critical parts of any data processing system:

(1) The system's availability
(2) Service levels provided to users
(3) Work-load characterizations
(4) Capacity and utilization of resources

Figure 2-2 lists the main components of capacity in a typical computer system. It illustrates major characteristics of the four points listed above. Notice that they include hardware and software characteristics and how they are managed and mixed together. Without such a blend it is impossible to arrive at an accurate view of capacity.

Another element of confusion should also be cleared up at this point: the issue of capacity planning and systems performance management. Systems performance management is an important part of capacity planning, in fact the main source of input into the process. In large installations and in many intermediate-size data centers, systems performance management is a daily activity. Data are collected constantly which become the basis for fine-tuning the system frequently. Although more will be said about tuning in Chapter 5, it is important here to understand that systems performance issues become the reasons for capacity planning. Systems performance management is thus primarily responsible for making the current configuration work well, whereas capacity planning is concerned with understanding what the resources are and what will be needed in the future.

Defining performance management is easier if three elements are kept in mind:

1. Performance management involves establishing objectives for the various work loads to be handled by a system. For instance, operations man-

Component	Example	General Definition
Availability of the system	Hardware: Total available hours less hours lost due to unscheduled IPLs, preventive maintenance, etc.	Best definition can be derived from users point of view: the total time during the 24-hour period that the user is able to process his or her work load
	Software: Total available hours less hours lost due to software failures, such as unscheduled IPLs	
Service-level objectives	Performance of the subsystems, which can be measured by response/ turnaround time	Service-level objectives, which relate to response-time objectives established by users; that is, the time between the entering of input to the system and the appearance of output; or in a batch environment, the turnaround time
Work load	Batch, on-line: transaction load for on-line, such as simple, intermediate, or complex activities: scheduling of work load depends on type of subsystem (such as TSO/IMS/CICS)	The characteristic of the type of work load processed through the system
Resource capacity/ utilization	Percent utilization of resources; average time spent in queue/queue size	This terminology defines the percentage of utilization of the individual resources and their combined performance; also how the utilization of one affects the user service objectives

Figure 2-2. Primary capacity components of a computer system.

agement might establish that the response time for simple on-line transactions should be 3 seconds each or that batch turnaround time shoud be 30 minutes. Finally, engineers designing on-line might be assured that the DP department will try to provide a 1-second response time on terminals. Comparing actual systems performance against these objectives provides a basis for future tuning.

2.   Performance management involves establishing priorities for types of jobs going through a system. Some tasks are more important than others and therefore should have a greater chance to use available resources. Establishing priorities thus enables the processing of the most critical work load during peak loads at a predetermined level of service. Level of service, particularly the consistency of that performance, is essential for users, especially those in an on-line environment. Any DP manager who has the misfortune of having a terminal in the office of the president of the company knows how important assuring consistent levels of predetermined service can be. On-line systems have the unfortunate characteristic of letting everyone know right away when the system is up, down, or just poorly managed.

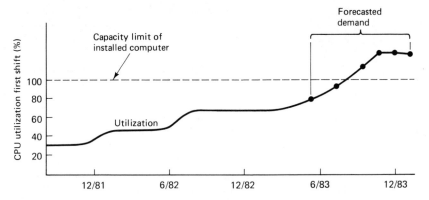

Figure 2-3. Sample computer utilization. By mid-1983 the computer would not be able to handle the work load.

3.   Performance management involves gathering data on the utilization of all the various components of a system. This exercise includes capturing information about the utilization of CPUs, channels, disks, printers, and so on, which are monitored continuously. These data are compared against work loads going through the system to record and understand changes in services, such as those caused when a new application is loaded onto the system. (See Figure 2-3.)

When managers first began to do capacity studies, they invariably thought that the collection and monitoring of systems performance data was in fact capacity planning, and so the studies were done only rarely, perhaps every several years. Today, an increasing number of managers are dissatisfied with that narrow approach. They argue that information about performance degrees must be correlated to various applications and to the forecasting of future work loads, and that it should be input to an analysis of the impact of additional work on the performance of an existing system. Finally, entire sets of interrelated data can serve as the basis for defining capacity requirements.

WHY CAPACITY PLANNING?

It may seem to the reader that by this point in the chapter the answer to the question of why there should be capacity planning is obvious enough. Yet in reality, in a number of common situations, capacity planning issues are not always appreciated. Five or 10 years ago, most data processing managers related performance management activities to capacity planning only when there was a problem, usually a constraint of resources. For instance, a fully loaded CPU, where utilization was very high, where work was just not being processed, or on-line and batch response times had deteriorated, would immediately initiate some sort of a capacity study. Perhaps heavy channel utilization or severe contention problems on the disk might trigger this flurry of activity. The solution was typically to alter the system's software or to add more computers, channels, disk, and so on, and that would be it, for the time, at least. But there was a political and business problem that inevitably emerged as a by-product of this panic planning.

Look at the very common example of the saturated CPU. Typically, performance degenerates slowly at first, accompanied by complaints from users, but as the work load increases, the problem grows dramatically, almost within days, to a severe crisis. Users complain to everyone that the DP department cannot get all its work done, the data processing department loses credibility, and the MIS director looks incompetent—but even worse, he is threatening the ability of the organization to function. Executives who know little or nothing about data processing become concerned almost at the same time, as users complain to them, but these general managers do not know what to do. The DP director now goes into high gear and announces that the department will perform a capacity study. The computer vendor is called in and probably overstaffs the situation, feeling that the account is in trouble if a solution is not found quickly; the top systems analyst and the operations manager go into monastic seclusion to do their study; and the rest of the world is kept in the dark. The current system is analyzed 10 different ways, reams of paper are produced, and fancy flip charts are prepared. The DP director then goes to executive management and says that he or she needs a new and bigger computer or more memory or something else that costs money and time. The fact that the old computer was brought in with the understanding that it was to be kept for five years and has only been installed for two creates its own obvious financial problems. The DP manager probably swore two years ago that it would last five and now wants to spend hundreds of thousands of dollars for a new one. Executive management, not having been prepared for this request, is caught off guard and feels trapped because it lacks the knowledge to challenge the DP manager's conclusion. Not to approve the new acquisition would threaten the vital functions of the organization, but to give in (its only alternative at this point) disturbs a number of budgets. There seems to be no choice since the vital functions of the company must not stop, regardless of where the money must come from or the effect that this lost budgetary resource would have on other business plans.

The scenario just described is so common as to lead this author to believe that it has happened at one time or another to every organization and to every DP manager. No one is a hero. The business undoubtedly suffers, the DP department loses credibility, users are upset and frustrated, and worst of all, it is very expensive. Yet it could all have been avoided.

In an attempt to learn from their past experiences, DP directors are therefore, for economic and political reasons, turning more frequently to capacity planning, making it an ongoing process within their departments. Politics and economics, more than technology or vendor lead times for delivery, are the real reasons why capacity planning has become so critical today. Without it, the risk of disaster is too great.

As the data processing industry began to concentrate on improving capacity planning, particularly in the 1970s, a number of elements emerged as critical to any effort and are now fairly common components of any study. These can be summarized as a catalog of those groups and individuals that should participate in one fashion or another in any serious capacity study.

Participants in Capacity Studies

- Data processing technical staff—includes systems programmers, who analyze operating systems; hardware specialists, who configure new equipment; software personnel, who judge the performance of various jobs and programs; and in large organizations, performance measurement specialists, who tie together various pieces of the DP department's capacity planning efforts.

- Operations—includes those individuals who actually operate the hardware and have the responsibility to define the work load, schedule jobs, track the utilization of all hardware resources, and determine how they are being used.

- User community—people in other departments who use data processing and thus can provide information about response time on terminals and levels of service objectives, and can articulate their additional requirements with costs and benefits.

- Application development staffs—the people who define and write new applications. These would include application programmers, who analyze current applications, forecast growth rates in software, and define expected performance of new applications within existing and planned hardware configurations.

- Data processing management—those individuals who ultimately carry the responsibility for selecting hardware and software options, order equipment, and ensure the integration of DP activities into the business plans of the whole organization.

In practice, this long list of people and functions is not terribly complex to manage. With a formal process, such a joint effort between DP personnel and users can define current work loads and configurations, make reasonable attempts at defining future requirements, select hardware configurations for these, and cost them out for management decisions. Requirements can be laid out over a period of years so that capital planning can be done, with the

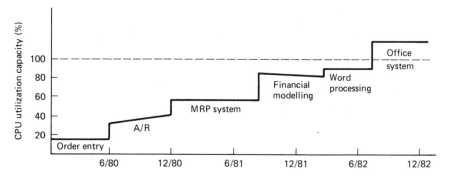

Figure 2-4. Capacity demand on installed CPU for planned projects. If systems go in as planned, CPU capacity will be exceeded in the third quarter of 1982.

DP department's input, for the entire corporation. Figure 2-4 illustrates, as an example, CPU requirements for the next several years for applications already approved. If management received financial options and a report on what would be loaded on the system in the future, reasonable decisions could be made to help the DP department do its job more effectively.

WHAT GETS PLANNED

Once management has decided that capacity planning is a good idea and mandates that it be done as an ongoing activity, the logical next question is: What gets studied? Although this question is answered differently within each organization, some common elements are evident both to users and to managerial and technical DP personnel. The question itself is part of the process of capacity planning, or more specifically, a number of issues must be addressed to answer the question. Briefly listed they are:

- What kinds of data must be collected in order to define the existing work load?
- What must be gathered to forecast future work loads and performance?
- What software and hardware tools are needed to help gather the information for capacity planning?
- How can these data be used to manage the DP center continuously in a better manner?
- What is a better manner?

These questions imply that the first step is to know what you have. More specifically, a department has to define what its current capacities are, how they are being used, and whether they can be made more efficient. With a better understanding of how each subsystem works within an overall system, fine tuning, rescheduling, or acquisition of additional resources becomes easier to define intelligently. These kinds of activities should be done with an eye toward supporting the overall mission of the DP department. Service to the user community is why data processing exists, and thus levels of service must be the benchmark against which all capacity planning is done. The capacity of a system, as viewed from this perspective, can be said to be the amount of time it takes to complete a job for a user. In scheduling work in a computer, for instance, the amount of time needed to do all the jobs is equal to the busy time of the CPU. In measuring this, the busy time is the capacity being utilized. Hence, if the busy time is the same as the scheduled time, the device is theoretically fully utilized. Any wait time—time that the system is not being utilized—becomes excess capacity waiting to be employed in the service of the user community. Theoretically, available capacity then is 100% and the busy time is expressed as a percentage of potential capacity. If a series of jobs running through a system take up 75% of the CPU, theoretically there is another 25% of busy time left for more work.

No system ever operates at 100% busy reality, except on freak occasions for a few seconds perhaps. Hence 75% of busy time might realistically be 100% utilization. There are too many variables preventing a computer, for instance, from operating at full capacity. Different input/output (I/O) speeds, a variable mix of jobs, the architectural characteristics of the operating system, and so on, all contribute to ensuring that it will be almost impossible to have 100% utilization at all times. Work loads change in the course of a day, for example, meaning that more processing may be done between 10 A.M. and 4 P.M. (peak load) than at 2 in the morning. Also, if utilization is too high, the system will degrade itself rapidly. For example, if channel utilization rises above 35% as a general rule, response time on the terminals will take longer since the CRTs must wait for data to travel along the crowded path to and from the disk, in much the same way that rush-hour traffic slows people going to and from home and work each day. Therefore, there are balances that are reached in which certain components in a system will have to operate at either higher or lower levels of utilization. The objective is to raise utilization across the entire system as much as possible as long as predetermined levels of service are not sacrificed. The benchmark remains the level of service necessary to satisfy user needs on a cost-effective basis. Such service levels are equated to response times on the terminals, turnaround time on batch jobs, amount of uptime for the combined software/hardware system in general, and even response time and turnaround by the DP staff in fixing software problems for individual users. Two types of components are measured: system capacity as a whole and individual hardware devices. Both must be examined by anyone doing serious capacity planning

Component	Indicators	Controllable Variables	Uncontrollable Variables
CPU	Utilization Average times of transactions in queue Average number of transactions in queue	SCP options Number of initiators Tasks Core allocation	Operator actions
I/O	EXCP count Channel utilization	Hardware configuration Volume configuration Placement of files	Unavailable devices sharing I/O Error recovery
TP: on-line	Response time Number of transactions/ time unit Time last request processed		Monthly, weekly, daily fluctuations Hourly fluctuations Software status
TP: RJE	Turnaround time Throughput Job size Job queue averages		Monthly, weekly, daily fluctuations Hourly fluctuations Software status
Operations			Number of operators Number of operator-caused errors Request-time delays

Figure 2-5. Subsystem variables. [Source: IBM, *Data Security and Data Processing* (White Plains, N.Y., 1974), III, Part 2, 207.]

in order to understand what resources are being used by the system. (See Figure 2-5.)

By system capacities as a whole, we usually mean response times, turn-around time, number of hours in a day when a system is available to users (hardware and software), amount of downtime due to software or hardware failures or maintenance, work load, and run times. In short, system capacity involves measuring user service requirements, availability, work loads, and resource capacities. In regard to hardware, typical devices that are measured for quality and quantity of performance are:

- CPU with storage
- CPU channels
- Control units
- Disk drives (DASD)
- Teleprocessing control units
- Other devices (especially printers)

Yet the performance of these components is meaningless unless standards are set based on existing work loads and the requirements of users. There are hours in the day, for instance in the morning after 9 A.M., when users will access certain applications more frequently (such as an order entry system) than they will in the afternoon. Thus a graph of on-line applications' usage would probably suggest that there is excess capacity that could be used at night but that it would do no good for users of the order entry system. On the other hand, batch work run in the morning might be moved to later hours as opposed to acquiring more computer power to satisfy response-time requirements in the morning. Thus availability standards—user needs—must be balanced against bottlenecks that can be eliminated, but only after understanding the current work load in the system.

Figure 2-6 illustrates cycle consumption in one day by application groups. Note that utilization varied a great deal in the 24-hour period and

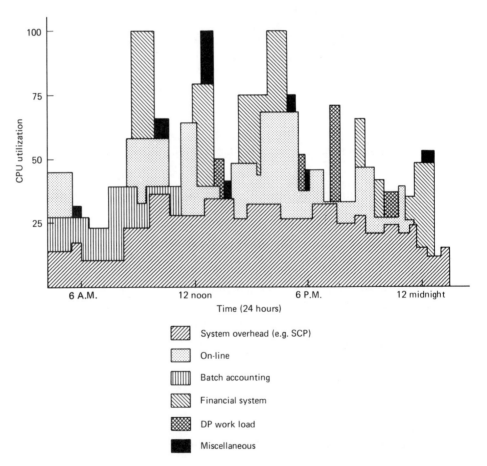

Figure 2-6. CPU utilization by application. This system is used on average above 40%.

that peak-load usage (during the daytime) was as much as this system could handle, whereas late evening usage was far lower. The problem with this load during the day is obvious. Perhaps some additional cycles could be allocated to the on-line systems if miscellaneous and DP center work were moved to later hours or to some period in the morning before 9 A.M. If not, the DP director of this installation would have to consider acquiring additional "horsepower" despite the fact that there is excess capacity in the late evening. The alternative would be degraded service to users.

One of the earliest steps in capacity planning involves establishing the current turnaround time for users and next, to determine if it is reasonable today. The same should be done with response time on the terminals (CRTs and RJE). Tinker with the existing system to improve throughput if existing levels of service are inadequate. Chart the effects of changes much as shown in Figure 2-6. If considering a larger computer, establish what the levels of response should be for users so that you can determine what has to be done in deciding on a new configuration that works. By this I mean that you must be in a position to understand how much more computer for x period of years you will need to maintain required service levels for existing applications and future ones planned for development during the life of the next computer. You may find that your initial thought about what size the next CPU should be changes dramatically. The same applies to peripherals, especially disk and printers.

DP directors experienced in changing computers always warn that in doing so you must provide the same level of service in the new machine (same terminal response time) as a minimum. If you improve it dramatically, only to slide back to old standards as new applications use up cycles, there will be a severe problem with users complaining about poor service. What happens is that they become used to the new, faster service levels and insist that they be maintained, even if this means that new applications cannot go on the system. This happens even though lower response levels would satisfy their needs. Therefore, by establishing with users what level of response and service should be provided, regardless of which system is installed, this problem is avoided. Also, most users will argue that it is more important that they receive consistent service than improved levels of performance which are erratic. This affects primarily on-line applications, where users become accustomed to the speed with which they perform, a rhythm of action that is interrupted together with their concentration if, for example, response time on the terminals varies widely from 2 to 4 seconds up to 15 to 20 seconds. Drastic changes in response time can also affect procedures in place within user departments and clearly affect the amount of work that can be completed. Experienced DP personnel learned long ago that if they install a faster computer, they can maintain previous levels of response time or improve it just a bit by throwing a cycle routine of some sort into the terminal software monitor which will delay response time by whatever

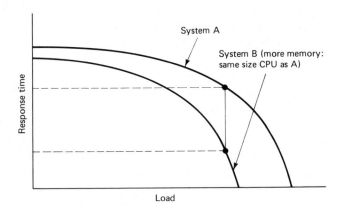

Figure 2-7. More memory clearly shows that additional work could be done by the same CPU.

amount is necessary, thus providing the user with fairly consistent service. As work loads on the CPU increase, the time-delaying code is changed or eliminated. (See Figures 2-7 and 2-8.)

There are ways of determining how response time can be changed in advance of making them. Although software issues are not the primary concern of this book, suffice it to know that queuing analysis, modeling, discrete simulations, and so on, using a variety of existing software tools (such as GPSS), can suggest performance levels against a theoretically established CPU (with thresholds of capacity defined) that can perform up to 100% of capacity. Although not completely accurate, they give more than a hint of possible performance given varying machine sizes. By forecasting such performance, potential bottlenecks can be identified with reasonable confidence and various capacity options developed together with their costs.

Once user requirements are better understood and the existing work load through a particular system is known, a DP department can begin the process of looking at the utilization of various components within a system.

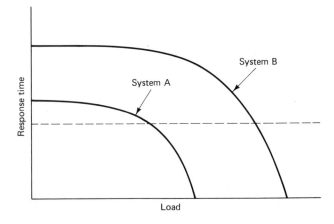

Figure 2-8. Same work-load run on two CPUs. CPU A responds in one-half the time of CPU B.

MEASURING CONSIDERATIONS FOR
VARIOUS DEVICES

Although CPU utilization is discussed further below, some basic elements of a configuration as a whole need to be reviewed next. Obviously, the most critical portion of a total configuration is the computer, that is, parts of the computer and its relations with various peripheral equipment.

Main Storage

Since main storage has a direct relationship with the performance of a processor and thus with its capacity, a system with major storage utilization problems will severely degrade a system, particularly the CPU as a whole. It is widely known that one of the fastest solutions to implement for a constrained system is to add more memory (also called *core*) to the computer. The importance of additional storage is suggested in Figure 2-9 for an actual situation. The vertical axis rises as response time improves while the horizontal axis shows increased work loads. Thus the more transactions that are loaded on a system, the poorer the response time. Increasing the memory available for these transactions improves response time proportionally. Each curve suggests an increasingly larger computer (more memory, too) and how it affects response time. The more memory you have, the easier it is to do more work with better overall response times. Dashed horizontal lines represent response-time levels below which this particular installation does not want to drop. The caveat to remember regarding memory, however, is that adding additional core beyond a certain point has a decreasing impact on

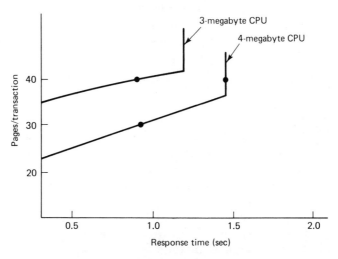

Figure 2-9. Effect of added memory on response time.

67

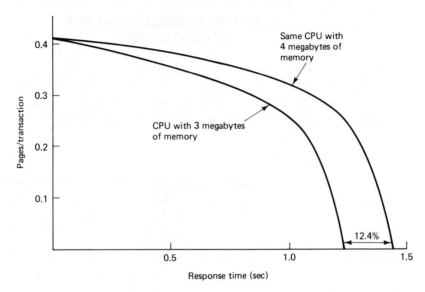

Figure 2-10. Same CPU as that of Figure 2-9. Here 12.4% more transactions with the same response times are possible.

improving performance because at some point there are just not enough processor cycles to keep memory busy. That is why you do not see small computers with billions of bytes of memory.

Figure 2-10 illustrates a case where a computer had an additional 1 megabyte of memory added to the system. The work load remained the same, as did the operating system and other peripheral equipment. In this case, an IBM 158 computer was capable of doing 14% more work with the additional memory overall, while 12.6% more work could be done at the same response-time levels as before for the terminal users. The difference in percentages was due to the fact that the disk in this specific configuration had already reached full levels of utilization before the additional memory was added. With faster DASD one could reasonably have expected better throughput percentages as a whole.

Channel Utilization

Channel utilization also has a direct impact on response time and can affect quite directly the level of service established for users. The rule of thumb is that as channel utilization increases, the service time for the devices attached to a particular channel increases as well. (See Figure 2-11.) Consider a channel as a highway between the computer and peripheral devices. If this road is overcrowded with data going to work at the CPU or back home to their DASD, the amount of time spent in commuting goes up dramatically,

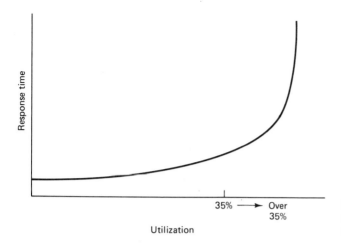

Response time

35% ——→ Over
35%

Utilization

Figure 2-11. Channel utilization pattern. As utilization exceeds 35%, a bottleneck forms quickly.

thus adding to the overall time that it takes a system to get data in, process them, and get them back out to terminals, printers, and disk drives. The same applies if there are multiple channels that service the same disk. Again, rules of thumb apply. If high response time for an application is needed (as for on-line systems), channels must be fast and their utilization must be kept low. Jobs with lower priorities or slower devices can be used with slower channels that have lower-priority access to the computer and can have higher percentages of utilization. Actual percentages vary widely from one computer size to another and from one job mix to another. Experience in a particular department suggests what reasonable levels are after they have been measured for several months. Thus knowing what makes sense in terms of channel utilization is yet another reason for identifying what your current work loads are, together with their impact on the total system, and for constantly tracking this kind of information.

In one instance, using large computers, it was found that utilization of any channel that had disk attached to it which rose to about 35% degraded the overall performance of the CPU and, from the users' point of view, slowed the response time at their terminals. This situation existed despite the fact that substantial amounts of memory and CPU cycles were available. The work was simply not getting into the computer fast enough when channel utilizations rose too high. Figure 2-12 illustrates the relationship between response time and channel utilization. In this example, response time was for a network of CRTs, not for batch work, and involved one channel with all the system's disk. Depending on the level of service, channel utilization may be acceptable above 35% or even 45%. If response times for terminals must be 2 to 3 seconds, for example, 45% or even 35% may be unacceptable, whereas another organization which allows response times of 5 to 7 seconds may find 50 to 60% channel utilization reasonable. Ulti-

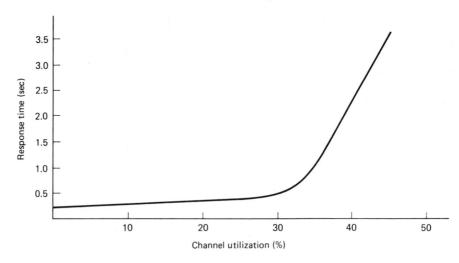

Figure 2-12.   Response time for CRTs versus disk channel utilization.

mately, it boils down to cost. Faster response time may mean more channels or a faster channel together with more DASD control units, all of which have costs associated with them.

I/O Contention, Control Units, Disk, and Printers

Other sensitive components of a system that directly affect performance and thus capacity are control units and their peripherals associated with channels. These can act both as bottlenecks to the system and as a drag on the computer. This is clearly illustrated every time someone replaces an existing computer with a faster one and fails to replace slower I/O with proportionally faster units and then complains that the new computer is not performing as touted by the vendor. Invariably, it is shown that the system is out of balance, because slower devices are just not going to keep up with the potential capability of the new and bigger computer. Heavy batch jobs that are primarily working with slow tape drives is perhaps the most common source of this problem, with disk very close behind. Occasionally, printers pose a problem; here the solution usually is to add more of them onto the system.

Because I/O contention is so frequently not understood, how it works is not applied as a means of either identifying usage or fine tuning. Yet this is a critical issue because poor performance here can cause severe degradation of service even when fast devices are attached to the CPU. The total amount of time that it takes to process I/O can be viewed as two activities: (1) the time spent in a queue or series of queues, and (2) the time taken to service a particular device. The second issue can include seek time on a disk drive searching for a record, rotational delay, and actual data transfer back to the channel and then up to the host computer. Longer times in a queue increases overall time for an I/O operation to be performed; therefore, more attention should be paid than ordinarily is to this portion of the time taken to complete a transaction. Such information is usually derived from software reports generated either by systems control programs or by specially written code designed to monitor capacity loads on computers. Better balancing of loads in the computer often reduces queue times for jobs. Yet before tampering with queues, one should take into consideration what is happening in a number of other areas:

- Contention within control units (especially those for disk drives)
- Disk arm contention (caused by too frequent access of same files or records on the same disk)
- Disk drive utilization
- Speed of tape drives (particularly relevant for long batch tape jobs)

Simply spreading disk work over larger spaces with more arms to read and write data over more strings with greater numbers of control units will reduce degradation bottlenecks, especially in shops with dozens or more of disk drives heavily used in on-line applications. Unfortunately, with tape drives, since tape-bound jobs are always accessing sequential files, the only solution is faster tape drives—but be careful not to overload the channel the tape drives are on; otherwise, the same problems evident with disk channels will pop up.

Since consistent response time for terminal users is essential, management frequently takes a close look at the problem of disk utilization, which can be monitored easily through the use of various DASD utilization programs. Although there are no general guidelines as to how much utilization is good or bad, because devices and applications vary too much, suffice it to say that like the CPU, 100% utilization is possible only theoretically. In reality it is far less than 100% and changing dynamically all day long. Some operations managers will argue, however, that disk utilization that exceeds 35% is simply asking for trouble in the form of degraded response time for all on-line jobs. This does not mean that the disk cannot be 100% full of data, just that access to that information must not be too frequent; and that level of frequency is a function of how fast the disk drives are. The faster they run, the more frequently they can be used, and consequently the higher the percent of utilization allowable. Most managers will play around with different levels of utilization to see what works most efficiently with their particular job mix. The key remains an understanding of which disks are slowing down the system and fixing the problem either by adding more disks or rearranging the files to reduce contention on the disk, control units, or channels to the host computer.

Printers also have capacity problems. Almost every computer system has at least one large printer attached to it via a slow channel to print the output of all its work. Information to be printed is stored temporarily in a print queue to be printed either on command from the console or as fast as the system's printer can get to it, usually in sequential order of print requests. As with other devices the amount of time that a printer takes to complete a job contributes to fast or slow turnaround time on a user-requested task. For example, if a print job remains in the queue for printing for 1 hour because other things are to be printed before it at that time of day, the amount of time in the queue adds to the overall turnaround time. Another job sent to the printer when it is not in use would be printed out right away. The second issue is printer speed. If a printer is rated at 600 lines per minute (lpm) but has to produce 800 lpm of work in a given hour, the work will not get done. The solution would be to install a faster printer, perhaps a 1000- to 1200-lpm machine, or a number of printers.

A further word about printers on a teleprocessing network. Much as channel speed and utilization factors can affect the performance of a host printer, the same can be said about printers at a remote site. We know that if the telephone line between the host and the remote printer is slow, the printer may not operate at rated speed. For example, a large systems printer with a rated speed of 1200 lpm will operate at only about one-third that speed with a 4800-baud telephone line. Why? The data to be printed simply are not getting to the printer fast enough. On the other hand, a 7200-baud line will drive a printer's speed up near 800 lpm, and a 9600-baud line will drive it even higher. Remember, as with other devices, there are theoretical and actual print speeds. The theoretical speed is the rated lpm value; actual speeds always fall below that. Print chain configurations can also affect performance. If a particular report uses a unique character which appears only four times on the print belt, every time that character has to be used, the belt has to loop around until it can position the correct charac-

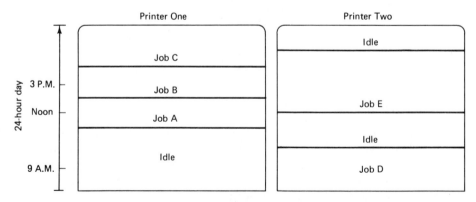

Figure 2-13.   Printer utilization: two systems printers.

ter above the paper before printing it. Therefore, changing print belts or avoiding certain infrequently available characters can dramatically improve printer performance, by as much as 20 to 50%. (See Figure 2-13.)

Terminals

Terminals are like animals in a zoo—they come in all shapes and sizes. These devices are made for various types of applications, using different kinds of teleprocessing disciplines, speeds, size, and technologies, with various requirements and ways of measuring performance. Despite all this variety, some general comments can be made about their use. All users as a rule perceive the quality of performance of a data center by what the response time and quality of the applications are on his or her terminal. That is their method of measuring what DP is doing for them. Ultimately, all equipment from the terminal back to the computer serves the purpose of maintaining a sustained level of response on all terminals. All other hardware components of the system are thus subservient to the terminal, merely supporting an acceptable level of response time or hindering it. Users rarely see other devices and could not care less about them. Figure 2-14 illustrates the potential number of technical "opportunities" that exist to cause bottlenecks in a network. Between software of various types (teleprocessing, network, system control, and application code) and various control units, I/O, and telephone lines, the chance for DP management to fail in providing consistent service is virtually guaranteed. Thus the process of reviewing bottlenecks, overloads within a system, and the need for additional capacity of one form or another remains an ongoing struggle in all DP shops.

In addition, uptimes vary constantly. Thus if a 99% uptime exists for the CPU, it is probably closer to 98% for teleprocessing control units, perhaps 90% for the modems and lines, and even less for various pieces of code. Obviously, from an elementary statistical point of view, the more variables in a system, the greater the chances are that something will not work sometime, thus driving down the *overall* availability of a system. Put another way, the greater the percent of availability of the system, the harder it will be to stay up and the more resources that will be needed. Thus an availability of 95% requires less perfect performance on the part of hardware and software and less backup hardware than for 96% availability, even less for 97%, and so on, keeping in mind that above 98% is virtually a dream. The resources required to increase the percent of availability grows almost geometrically and so do the costs. Thus the amount of resources needed to improve availability from say 85 to 90% is less than that required to take the system from 90 to 95%. Similarly, the resources required to go toward 100% would exceed those for a jump from 90% to 95%. Rarely do shops have to maintain availability much above 96 or 97%; therefore, the always existing capacity problem, be it ever so brief or long, is usually tolerable within certain ranges of cost and performance.

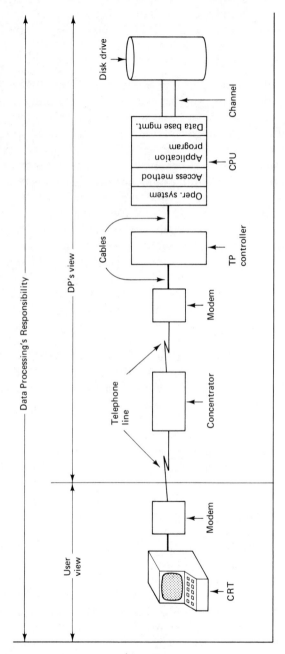

Figure 2-14. User and DP views of a network.

74

CAPACITY PLANNING TOOLS

Despite the enormous variety of potential issues and hardware units to track for both capacity planning and fine tuning, the job is not as difficult as it may first appear. A number of methods have been developed over the years to help, and a growing variety of specific hardware and software tools are available that can really assist. Many specialists will argue that much work remains to be done in the area of capacity planning and they complain that they do not have a sufficient number of tools with which to work. But these same people will then turn right around and offer a variety of ways to perform capacity studies. For practical purposes in day-to-day management of a computer installation, this kind of study can be done comfortably. Techniques range from rules of thumb and intuition to highly complex mathematical formulations of work-load forecasts and detailed hardware monitoring.

Good capacity planning begins with an assessment of the percentage of a particular application that occupies the resources of a system. Tools that help to do this make it possible to cluster types of applications (e.g., batch, on-line, teleprocessing, system overhead, etc.) so that management can later balance work loads to increase yield of performance from a system. By tracking the needs for hardware resources by groups or individual users, managers develop better ideas about what hardware is needed and when. Moreover, how much resource a particular subsystem uses can also be revealing. Thus many managers in small or intermediate-size shops fail to realize what a large percentage of their overhead is taken by system control programs, especially in the case of micros and minis, where this might account for over 40% of capacity (CPU cycles). Also, what kind of operating system can affect capacity? Thus using IBM's small mainframe operating system (DOS/VSE) in a 3033 will always show low CPU utilization simply because the operating system cannot handle as many tasks as the computer can. On the other hand, using a large system control program (SCP) of IBM's, such as MVS, which is meant for the 3033, on a small computer (such as on a small 4300) would show CPU utilization to be inordinately high compared to DOS/VSE because of the extra-size overhead. In reality, you would not even be able to put such a large SCP in such a small computer.

In using tools, particularly software, there is a certain amount of overhead associated with such packages that must be factored out of the total utilization. For example, if a performance analyzer is known to use up to 3% of the CPU's capacity just to run, when it reports that the computer is being used at 59%, either the package must deduct 3% to provide a true utilization (i.e., 56% when the monitor is not used) or you have to do so with the output to bring it in line. The only time this should not be done is if the monitor is always installed and running as part of the DP department's own overhead of operations application programs. It is because of this overhead that some specialists talk about capture ratios and deviations in reporting quality for capacity monitors. Do not let this hyperbole scare you away from using such tools, because overhead variables are easily factored out of most packages automatically before you see their output.

The kinds of data that software monitors capture for purposes of capacity studies should include the following elements:

- CPU utilization
- Channel utilization
- Control unit, disk, tape, and other I/O utilizations
- Software utilization (subsystems, applications)
- Number of transactions over time (per hour, day, month, quarter)
- Total number of transaction by day and type
- Response time by terminal and transaction type (such as inquiries versus updates)
- Execute channel program instructions (EXCP) by type of transactions and quantity
- Paging rates
- Memory utilizations
- Deactivation of partitions
- Utilization by partitions
- Telephone-line error rates and types

Although various packages will define a multitude of issues using numerous terms and points of measurement, the list above covers the essential data that can be acquired easily. Properly read and analyzed, these indicate hardware and software utilization in the major components of a hardware system both over time and by application or subsystem.

Some monitors will also check the activity of a particular subsystem. For example, the IBM CICS Performance Analyzer II will monitor all CICS transactions right down to the terminal being used or the types of transactions being performed, whereas a more generalized type of monitor might review the performance of the CPU in which CICS resides in one partition. Regardless of what tool is used, any monitor is utilized best when the results are broken down by subsystem, such as utilization due to batch work or on-line, and over specific periods of time, as by shift. Some DP departments have an ideal environment in that they carry the analysis to the point of defining which application, department, or individual is using what percentage of the system. Although that is a capacity planner's dream, it is often not worth the extra effort to break down the costs and overhead that way unless it is part of a chargeout system designed to allocate costs by utilization. (See Figure 2-15.)

Software Tool	Vendor	Reports
RMF	IBM	CPU utilization, work loads, channel and I/O usage, paging rates, page/swap data set activities
SVSPT	IBM	CPU and memory utilizations, channel and disk usage, job activities, other I/O usage, basic system characteristics, summary data
VS1 and DOS/VSE PT	IBM	CPU utilization—as a whole and by partition, channel usage, memory usage, I/O device reports, partition deactivations, basic system characteristics, summary data
CICS/VS PAII	IBM	Transaction summary, quantity and type by system and by user, DL/1 counters and clocks
IMS Log Tape Analysis	IBM	CPU utilization, DB updates, exception reporting, message queues and resource usages
APO	Boole & Babbage	Program usage by total paging, memory utilization, CPU elapse times
SPARK	Burroughs	Core availability percentages, overlay activities, CPU, I/O, and ready queue rates
BEST/1	BGS Systems	Work load characterization, response-time profiles, CPU throughput, CPU utilization, disk response times
Value Computer Scheduling System	Value Computing, Inc.	CPU utilization and availability, averaged program CPU usage, memory and tape usage, partition maps

Figure 2-15. Some of the reporting functions of software utilization packages available on various systems; it is by no means a complete or thorough list, however. Note that each of these packages measures basically the same types of hardware activities.

The use of software and hardware monitors will produce an abundance of statistical data, indeed too much. There is hardly a package on the market today that does not give more statistics than necessary. Although this extra information is good to have if there is a specific performance problem to resolve, it is not necessary for capacity forecasting. Remember, experience shows that keeping the number of variables to be tracked to a few basic ones —track disk utilization, load on the CPU channels, percent of computer processor utilization, paging rates, and overall response time for the major software applications—keeps the capacity planning process simple. If a problem is flagged by any of these, the minutia presented by such packages can provide operations with the additional detail that might be needed to improve hardware performance. If you complicate the process, you drown in detail, missing the trees for the forest. Thus a shop with hundreds of disk or tape drives should worry less about individual device performance than about overall channel utilization and pathing to the I/O. Shops with high paging rates should worry about additional memory more than about the percentage of disk being utilized. In short, sacrifice exactness to the possible nth degree for a more reasonable and easier task of monitoring general trends. Break a problem down to measurable components only.

Selection of tools and methods of measurement are in large part a function of who has to hear the good word on performance and how big the staff is to bear the message. In large installations, there usually is a capacity planning group with a manager reporting to the MIS director on the utilization of all hardware and software. The group personnel talk to systems people regularly about fine tuning, and the MIS director constantly updates management on the performance of all systems. In small or intermediate-size shops, various software tools are used frequently (maybe even weekly) by one or two systems personnel to do the same, and in the smallest installations it is usually done only when a vendor is trying to prove scientifically that the customer should buy a different system. Regardless of the size of the department, capacity planning of some sort should go on all the time. The benefits are usually seen on an almost daily basis.

Operations can better understand how its resources are being expended and thus warn upper-level management when new equipment is needed. They can also schedule work loads better, to improve response time and throughput. Software or systems people can better utilize and fine tune software (particularly useful here are teleprocessing monitors and code to improve application programs), again to improve response and turnaround time. The MIS director learns when he or she is running out of resources, so that there will be time to find additional cost-effective hardware and sell the need for its acquisition to upper-level management. For executives it provides a clearer understanding of when an MIS director intends to dip into the cash register or why users are satisfied or unhappy with their data processing services (and their productivity levels). With a large computer still costing over $1 million, such an early warning system is essential for any organization, especially medium-size companies with annual capital budgets of only a few million dollars for the entire organization.

Methods of Forecasting

Capacity planning is not simply keeping track of what is going on today. For most managers it is even more important to forecast what will be needed in the short- and long-term future. The fundamental technique for forecasting boils down to comparing the requirements of a proposed new system against what an existing system is taking today. Utilization figures abound in the DP industry about how much, for instance, an inquiry will take versus an update transaction, x lines of Cobol versus x lines of Fortran code, and so on—all predicting and comparing against past history. There is no known more accurate method for forecasting in the industry today. Although various schemes are constantly being concocted, articles with frighteningly complex mathematical equations offered, and packages with insuperable amounts of output sold, the basic methodology remains the same.

The fundamental problem that all shops must overcome, therefore, is to try and identify how the current work load runs. Even with the use of packages, it is difficult and time consuming to establish what percentages of the various resources are going to batch systems, on-line, first and second shifts, and so on, but such evaluations are critical to an understanding of current and future requirements. Without them, capacity planning lacks credibility. Despite these frustrations, various methods for measuring capacity have evolved over the years which have proven useful. They include:

- Rules of thumb, intuition, "experience"
- Formal linear analysis methodologies
- Queuing systems
- Discrete simulation models
- Simulated benchmarks (CPU and networks)
- Real benchmarks

The expense in time and effort runs from the least, rules of thumb, to the costliest, using full benchmarks (particularly useful with overstaffed departments with nothing better to do). Most data processing departments find that the most useful tools involve a combination of intuition, simulation models (particularly for networks and teleprocessing applications), and linear analysis, but all rely heavily on the use of software to capture data about existing usage. (See Figure 2-16.)

Rules of thumb are based on the experience of managers with a particular mix of applications and hardware; often this is considered the best form of capacity planning and also the worst. It works well when the commitment, based on the results, is for only a short period of time (such as one or even possibly two years for a computer acquisition), but it declines in value over time. Linear analysis, although more formal, may not in fact increase the accuracy of the conclusions because there is an implied constancy of growth in usage inherent in any mathematical smoothing of data. Queuing theories hold a greater potential benefit provided that the analyst understands the true interaction of hardware performance factors with those of software. When such a sincere understanding exists, this method becomes a complex

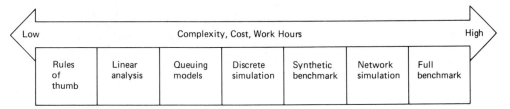

Figure 2-16. Spectrum of techniques for analyzing hardware/software performance. [Source: L. Bronner, "Overview of the Capacity Planning Process for Production Data Processing," *IBM Systems Journal*, 19, No. 1 (1980): 20; IBM Corporation, ©1980.]

mathematical approach that few departments can afford to use. Simulation models are easier, especially for teleprocessing, since the number of potential transactions on a particular size network is fairly simple to develop and good packages are available to reflect performance. You simply plug in the data they require and let them run, or even better, they tap the system for their own statistics. Even a generalized modeling package originally designed for non-DP uses in economics or sociology or electronics (such as GPSS) can easily be used for such an analysis. Benchmarks themselves are time consuming and a nuisance. They involve taking the entire work load or a portion of it off one CPU and putting it on another, complete with all necessary software. It is easiest to do with batch loads but is almost impossible with on-line systems. Regardless of how it is done, this method takes up a great deal of time, and although the results are clearly more precise and real than with any other method, the detail may be more than that needed to forecast requirements for new power. In general, modeling systems are inherently weakened by the fact that not all factors affecting output are understood or fed into the model for consideration. Obviously, there are exceptions, and when they exist, they are magnificent. Yet this author's experience dictates that capacity tracking packages, together with both known differences in speed and size of hardware on the one hand, and rough guidelines on transactions types and their rates on the other, suggest faster and just as valid conclusions without the headaches and time-consuming work involved with mathematical modeling or actual benchmarks. (See Figure 2-17.)

There are some specific techniques either widely in use or becoming increasingly fashionable that can be briefly defined. Invariably, they involve a method and a software package; all require constant attention and ultimately reporting of results to both DP and general management.

Type	Benefits	Disadvantages

Hardware	No hardware overhead
	Simultaneous measurement
	  of activities
	Works on any CPU
	Very accurate
		Expensive to lease/buy
		Complicated to install and use
		Does not measure specific
		  activities by system, application,
		  partition, disk, or tape
		Limited attachability of probes
		Can damage hardware
		Easy to dislodge off CPU
		Can take hardware overhead

Software	Good source of data
	  on various types of hardware
	  usage, applications,
	  operating systems, data sets
	Fast to install, flexible
	  to use
	Easy to install and use,
	  accurate readings possible
		Does not fully measure SCP
		  activities that have priority
		  over most monitors
		Simultaneous measurement of
		  activities not always possible

Figure 2-17. Hardware and software monitor options. As the chart suggests, most users find software tools easier to work with and their output more relevant.

One approach, developed at AT&T is called by their specialists a "demand capacity chart." It measures available resources against what is used. It has, as with most capacity methodologies, the purpose of holding down costs while providing predefined levels of service to users. Theoretical levels of potential capacity (usually provided by the manufacturer of the hardware) are discounted by experiential factors to allow for realistically available resources, as presented by the actual mix of hardware and software in a particular department. Once this is done, trends in utilization and availability of resources are tracked on a monthly basis. Average response and turn-around times are measured, with capacity needed against use. Usage is based on CPU, disk, tape, and key applications and software subsystems. Thus if the practical utilization of a CPU is 60% and a software monitor indicated that 45% was used during the first shift, 15% capacity remains. Similar logic is applied to key peripheral devices (such as disk, tape, and printers). Charts similar to Figure 2-18 are then created for each major hardware resource and each is tracked separately.

The benefits for management of such a method are obvious. First, the

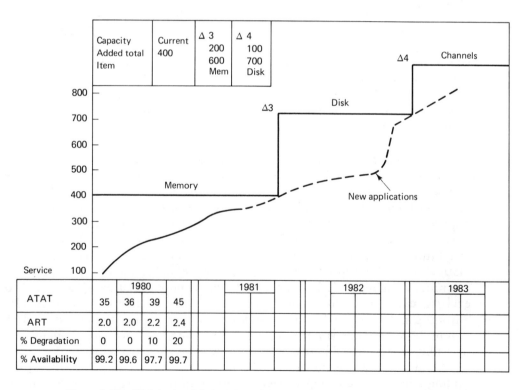

Figure 2-18. Slightly simplified version of the AT&T demand capacity chart. [Source: J.M. Jenkins, "Measuring System Capacity," *EDP Performance Review*, 5, No. 4 (April 1977): 2; Applied Computer Research, Phoenix, Ariz., ©1977.]

RMF Reports	SVSPT Reports	VSIPT Reports
CPU activity	CPU and channels	CPU utilization by partition
Work-load activity	Job activity	Channel utilization
Channel activity	Real main storage	I/O device report
I/O device activity	Direct-access devices	Real main storage
Paging activity	Non-direct-access devices	Basic system profile
Page/swap data set activity	Basic system profile	Summary
	Overall activity	

Figure 2-19. Recommended base measurement reports. Sample data obtainable using IBM software packages. [Source: L. Bronner, "Overview of the Capacity Planning Process for Production Data Processing," *IBM Systems Journal,* 19, No. 1 (1980): 17. Reprinted with permission from IBM Corporation, © 1980.]

output (a chart) is easy for all managers to understand, regardless of their knowledge of data processing. Second, it becomes an early warning system to DP management that it needs to find additional hardware. Third, fine-tuning activities are tracked and compared against previous performance to measure the effectiveness of any actions taken to improve system through-put.

A variation of this method is presented in a variety of IBM software packages, such as DOS/VSE PT, CICS/VS PA II, SMF, SVSPT, and VS1 PT. These track utilization by CPU, partitions, channels, disk, memory, paging, I/O activity, thrashing, and so on, presenting the data by period of time measured. This can then be graphed over time in a linear fashion similar to the AT&T method, indicating a set of conclusions. The benefits are similar to those of the AT&T method. The clear advantage over the earlier technique is that these cover software and hardware performance and by subsystems. (See Figure 2-19.)

Yet another technique used in many large data centers is a program or technique called USAGE, originally developed by IBM Canada. It is a process of identifying current usage of a computer system by application or business unit and then using that information to guide forecasting of future resource requirements. It relies heavily on SMF data captured automatically from the operating system around the clock for one month and then analyzed to project future demands. It takes into account the peculiarities of systems information normally captured by the SCP while marrying business plans to resource availability. It has the benefit of being rational and fairly easy to execute and to continue using as a normal part of systems management. Its output can be graphed in time series charts much like that illustrated in Figure 2-18 and thus is understandable by managers who have to make buy decisions on additional hardware but know little about data processing.

An increasingly fashionable technique for presenting data, and ultimately findings, involves reducing capacity information to a Kiviat figure. This is essentially a circle with a radius and an axis growing from the center, each representing a portion of the time associated with a particular axis. Figure

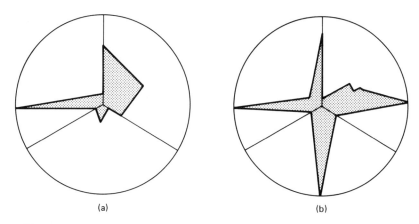

Figure 2-20. These sample Kiviat graphs illustrate two different situations: (a) a heavily utilized CPU but with light use of channels; possibly indicating a CPU-bound system; (b) a balanced system where utilization is high for both CPU and channels.

2-20a and b illustrate what Kiviat figures look like. A shows a computer with CPU utilization far exceeding that of its channels. B suggests a fully utilized system, in which both the processor and its channels were busy 100% of the time when this measurement was made. Once familiar with these charts, they show graphically potential bottlenecks and heavily utilized resources. Pictured over time, they also offer trend analyses of utilization.

Hardware monitors also exist. These are essentially hardware probes physically attached to key signal points in the computer. They measure the number of events and their duration over time at particular points by recording the on and off electrical impulses as they pass across certain areas of the computer's processor, memory, or channels. These are actual indicators of utilization. They are often complicated to install and just provide raw horse-power usage with no correlation to what software was running unless operations management keeps a manual track of applications being processed at the time the monitor was operative. In other words, they measure an impulse without corollating it to a business-related task. It can be used to monitor a portion of a system, such as the CPU or only a channel, and today they are used more frequently by personnel responsible for debugging hardware problems than for capacity identification. The reason for this is simple; software-capacity analyzers are easier to use and more comprehensive.

Regardless of whether a department uses hardware or software tools, or methods of measuring utilization and demand, they all help management qualify the effectiveness and efficiency of a processor and its associated peripherals. By effectiveness we mean how useful the system is to a user (example: excellent response time versus degraded service), not the efficient use of the equipment. Thus good response time might be bought by never

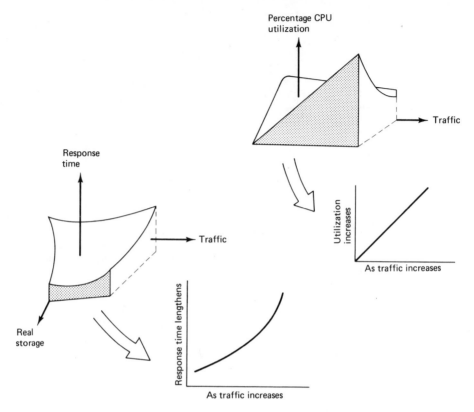

Figure 2-21. Relationship of utilization of CPU and response time as volume of transactions grows.

utilizing the CPU more than 30%. Efficiency stresses high utilization of re-sources regardless of the quality of efficiency for the user. Thus a system might be shown to be 85% utilized (good use of the resource), but the response time on the terminals might be 25 seconds! Obviously, a balance must always be struck between these two elements. (See Figure 2-21.)

Network Analyzers

Analyzing hardware and software in the teleprocessing network of any organization always presents unique problems and issues separate and apart from those discussed above, which concerned only computers of all sizes and their peripherals. Network capacity studies are done in essentially two ways. The first involves counting the number of transactions going from the host computer out to the terminals and the response time. This can be done either through canned software that various teleprocessing vendors sell (such as IBM with its CICS PA II or Network Performance Analyzer) or with

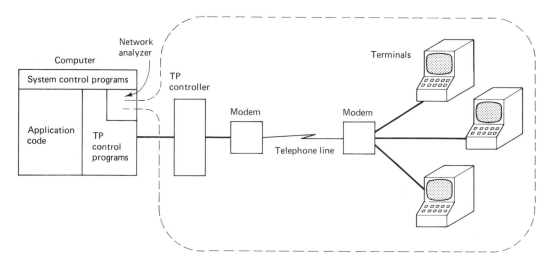

Figure 2-22. Portion of a computer system measured by a network analyzer.

various homegrown programs. Such code resides on the host or a front-end processor and contributes to an understanding of what the main computer's utilization is since most teleprocessing access method code and monitors for terminals remain in the host processor. (See Figure 2-22.)

A second approach involves modeling and monitoring a network that would involve not only on-line interactive applications (such as those clocked by the first method) but would also track remote job entry (RJE) batch transmissions as well. Typical network analyzers provide data to identify performance degradations, indicate possible fine-tuning options, and help determine future capacity loads and, obviously, requirements. Such data can be viewed from a terminal in a real-time environment or can be captured in batch for review later. The kind of data captured by a typical package would include the following elements:

- Multiple network resources
- Message rates on each line: actual response time as against required levels of turnaround performance
- Exception messages from the network when overloaded
- Communications miniprocessor utilization statistics
- Buffer utilization
- Slowdown percentages
- Message traffic information regarding rates, percent of resources utilized, and statistics on messages sent and received
- Line control data showing line utilizations, byte rates, polling activity, errors, error messages sent, and bytes sent and received

Some packages also allow modeling whereby a teleprocessing specialist can query the system regarding response time and resources required. For example, suppose that the specialist wants to find out what will happen to the utilization on a specific line if 10 additional CRTs are added to it. A normal modeling package, when told that there would be an additional 10 CRTs with x number of average transactions each per hour at a specified line speed, could easily provide data on what the teleprocessing controller's utilization would increase by, what the response time would be on the terminals, and how much the line would be loaded. Armed with such data, the specialist could determine if the controller has enough capacity (cycles, memory, or ports) to handle the extra volume of work, whether the response time would degrade so much that a faster or second line would be required and at what cost, and whether or not the host computer might encounter higher utilization as a result of the extra load and, if so, how much. If additional resources are then needed, their cost can be calculated. Thus management could argue that 10 additional CRTs will cost x amount if performance (such as response time) is to remain the same as today and y amount if we can tolerate a certain specified amount of degraded service.

Invariably, insufficient network capacity management takes place. CRTs proliferate throughout a network faster than anyone would think. Most MIS directors have only a rough idea as to how many are installed, and most teleprocessing specialists can only guess. CRTs keep coming in, one here, two there, and so on, rapidly eroding an organization's network resources with little warning of problems ahead. If any capacity planning is done, it is usually with the host computer—that multimillion-dollar box—rarely with the network, which in fact may have a total dollar value exceeding that of the host computer. A small network of only 100 CRTs with associated printers and controllers could have a purchase value of nearly $1 million (based on 100 CRTs, 35 printers, 5 control units, a teleprocessing controller, and a full complement of modems). Yet network management is coming into its own. It is a complex and growing field that is attracting increasing attention. Dozens of books have already appeared on the subject, consultants are teaching courses on teleprocessing management, and the major vendors of products for this area are developing programs and methods to control teleprocessing. Suffice it to understand here that there is a great deal of information that can be captured and applied to understanding capacity usage, forecasting, and fine tuning. It is increasingly evident that teleprocessing management is essential as the percentage of total DP resources devoted to networks increases. Distributed processing and on-line applications in the past five years alone have surpassed batch work. Often, hardware budget dollars expended on terminals and lines exceeds that which is spent annually on computers and peripherals. Some organizations spend hundreds of thousands of dollars each month just on line charges and even more for the hardware, but only a fraction of that on the host computer. Thus in viewing capacity for hardware, data processing can no longer overlook network management. For many, the greatest cost control and efficiency may lie in this area, not in the easier-to-manage host computer.

HOW TO GET STARTED

Armed with a conceptual overview of capacity planning, the next logical question is how to conduct such a study and make it an ongoing activity. The first step is to recognize that operations, systems, and applications personnel must contribute to the effort. Operations can monitor the hardware, systems the basic operating systems control programs, and the application people the types of transactions and their frequency. Working together they can combine their knowledge of hardware, subsystems, and applications to define standards (such as required response time) and do an intelligent job of forecasting and handling tuning resources. This process must also involve key user groups because they can help define what, for example, is a necessary response-time average for terminals, how many new users there will be, and what applications must come on stream next year and in subsequent years. Forecasting without their input becomes a guessing game with about as much reliability. In a large data center there may be a permanent capacity planning department working constantly with DP and user personnel. In medium-size shops it might be a part-time task with sporadic (monthly or quarterly) meetings to review efforts. In small organizations one person several times each year might undertake the task.

In a medium-size department (say, with a staff of 30 to 40 people) someone should have primary responsibility for the ongoing effort and work with those within the DP department who have the necessary skills. This person would typically be the technical support manager or the head of operations. A second person should be designated as a backup. Complete and sensible documentation of all studies must be preserved. In a large shop, the backup is usually there as well as documentation of all efforts. In either case, there must be continuity regardless of who is doing the work. The problem remains with the small department, where capacity planning is a stranger or a rare visitor, in which case documentation is poor or nonexistent, and skills chronically weak.

Increasingly, non-DP management is gaining an appreciation for the value of capacity planning and of providing resources from DP for this kind of activity. In exchange, upper-level management is expecting better tuned and thus better utilized hardware with more cost-effective efficiency. Within DP itself, management should recognize that without capacity planning as an important activity, a number of problems will simply never go away: running out of computer power, frequent variations in response time with associated user complaints, longer turnaround time on jobs, and embarrassment in going back to management for yet more equipment without forewarning.

In companies and organizations where capacity planning is an efficient process, management will argue that this activity integrates the concerted efforts of a number of people and elements:

- Executive management
- DP management

- Technical personnel
- Users
- Hardware and software
- Forecasting tools (modeling, data collection, work-load characterization, capacity software)

Each of these elements calls for understanding by those involved in the process. The net effect is that a series of common events typically take place. Figure 2-23 illustrates a common cycle.

Successful efforts invariably are characterized by centralization of all information and its communication in relevant formats to DP management, users, and executives. Typically, the kind of information that is captured involves current and forecasted work loads on key pieces of equipment by

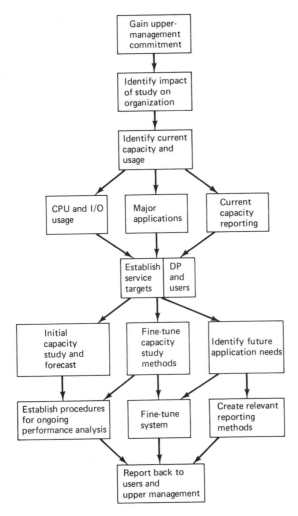

Figure 2-23. Flowchart of sample activities for a capacity study effort.

month or quarter, historical data on past performance, and reports on current day-to-day activities (such as this morning's response time on the CRTs). Once a capacity planning process is initiated it becomes an ongoing one with information going to those responsible for fine-tuning hardware and software, other data being fed to DP management on utilization, and yet more projections to management on anticipated requirements.

Case Study: Was the Computer Out of Capacity?

To illustrate some of the issues and by-products of a capacity study involving one situation at one time, examining what one company did is instructive. A large data center decided to review the utilization of its CPUs, memory, and channels. The study was conducted primarily to identify the causes of intermittent performance degradations experienced at the host data center. As a result of this study, the DP department concluded that both computers were memory constrained and that the operating system could better perform if the I/O configurations were redesigned (as a result of looking at the utilization of peripherals). The data center clearly stated in its final report that its objectives for the study were (1) "to establish an acceptable framework for ongoing analysis and tuning of system performance," and (2) "to evaluate the current environment and make recommendations for stabilizing systems performance." What was done was to capture data from the system control program (in this case MVS) using a Resource Measurement Facility (RMF) which was part of the operating system, covering one shift during the day for two weeks, and collecting information from the two systems every 15 minutes.

The group involved looked at three areas of potential problems:

- Saturated CPU with high utilization
- I/O contention, particularly on the disk and on main memory
- Work-load management

Taking the performance data drawn off the host computers, the study group concluded that CPU cycles were not a constraining factor since utilization ranged from 30 to 50% on the first system, with peaks of 65 and 70%. On the second CPU, utilization varied from 20 to 55% with peaks at 60%. Clearly, the problem was not here. Figure 2-24 shows the actual utilization data presented to management in the final report.

| | System 1 | | System 2 | |
Date	Avg. of Peaks	Avg./Day	Avg. of Peaks	Avg./Day
4/9	39	36	43	34
4/10	48	41	52	38
4/11	47	40	53	39
4/12	44	39	45	36
4/13*	45	37	—	—

*Good Friday—holiday

Figure 2-24. CPU utilizations by system (%).

	System 1			System 2	
Date	Avg. of Peaks	Avg./Day		Avg. of Peaks	Avg./Day
4/9	62	53		53	37
4/10	64	56		38	28
4/11	55	45		34	24
4/12	43	38		27	20
4/13*	20	16		—	—

*Good Friday-holiday

Figure 2-25. Paging rate per second by system (paging being the total number of pages in and out of memory).

	System 1	System 2
Date	Avg./Day	Avg./Day
4/9	39	21
4/10	42	18
4/11	34	13
4/12	28	10
4/13*	10	—

Figure 2-26. Page fault rate per second.

Next, memory utilization was examined for the same period. These data were expressed in terms of paging rates in and out of memory. Paging rates varied widely during the course of the day and across both computers. (See Figures 2-25 and 2-26.) The page fault rate per second is important because there is a high correlation between this rate and response time on all on-line systems. Page fault rate measures the sum of nonswap pages in and out of the system and hence, together with actual paging rates, it truly a measure of memory utilization. Since the most important factor influencing the paging rate in memory is the multiprogramming level or number of address spaces in storage, the capacity study team looked at memory from this point of view. For each of the two systems these data (Figure 2-27) suggested that on average there were 13.9 starter tasks, of which 13.7 were active and being executed in the computer. It was important to calculate this information because any increase in the number of starter tasks or in the amount of work in those tasks would reduce the amount of available real storage for use in

	System 1					System 2				
Type	Max.	Avg.		Max.	Avg.	Max.	Avg.		Max.	Avg.
Batch	9	6	In ready	8	0.5	13	12.1	In ready	7	0.9
STC	16	13.9	In	18	13.7	16	12.8	In	22	18.6
TSO	—	—		—	—	—	—		—	—

Figure 2-27. System address space analysis. In system 1, an average of 13.9 starter tasks occurs, with 13.7 active and executing. Further increases reduce the real storage available for allocation to batch, slowing down batch work.

batch jobs. In turn, therefore, the batch applications would suffer degraded performance together with the on-line systems.

The next area of review was I/O utilization. Specifically, the team looked at average channel utilization data. For the size of computers installed, utilization should have been about 35% for disk. In these systems utilization of key channels went above 40%, thereby documenting that there existed a contention problem of some severity. They then calculated the device service time. So as to ensure that there was no misunderstanding when reporting the results to DP management, the group defined service time via Figure 2-29. Then, relying on the data shown in Figure 2-28, they concluded that the average amount of time needed to service an on-line request was 84 milliseconds (ms). Device service time was 42 ms for the same period. For the kind of disk installed (in this case IBM 3330s and 3350s), nonpaging volumes would be expected to range between 25 and 40 ms, respectively, for acceptable response times. Clearly, there was a problem with disk. The math to calculate the information that led to this conclusion was fairly simple to perform.

average time to service a request

$$= \frac{\% \text{ of device busy} + \text{average queue length} \times \text{RMF time interval}}{\text{device activity count}}$$

$$= \frac{0.6014 + 0.59 \times (15 \times 60)}{12{,}723}$$

$$= \frac{1.1914 \times 900}{12{,}723}$$

$$= 84 \text{ ms}$$

average time per device access

$$= \frac{\% \text{ of device busy} \times \text{RMF time interval}}{\text{device activity count}}$$

$$= \frac{0.6014 \times 900}{12{,}723}$$

$$= 42 \text{ ms}$$

In presenting these results to management with DP, the three individuals doing the capacity study recommended the following:

(1) Ongoing capacity planning had to be performed relying heavily on RMF data to measure system availability.

(2) Paging rates had to be monitored more frequently since they affect all processing in all systems in all CPUs.

Date: 4/11 Time: 15:45 to 16:00

			System 1			System 2		
1. CPU utilization:			35.76			55.1		
	System 1 Channles	System 2 Peaks	% Channel Busy	% Channel Busy and CPU Wait	Ratio (%)	% Channel Busy	% Channel Busy and CPU Wait	Ratio (%)
2. I/O channel busy	0							
	1		0.00	0.00	0.00		0.00	0.00
	2		15.58	11.07	71		4.28	45
	3		12.24	8.18	67		7.45	49
	4	40%	5.01	3.17	63	33.02	20.57	62
	5	56%	8.07	3.34	41	43.97	23.18	52
	6							
	7		6.01	4.12	68	1.22	0.44	36
	8		14.08	9.74	69	9.78	4.28	43
	9		13.08	8.18	62	15.68	6.56	41
	A		12.19	9.40	77	15.56	8.45	54
	B	50%	0.22	0.17	77	46.58	25.79	55
	C	40%	5.62	4.01	71	25.13	13.56	53
	D		12.52	9.85	78	14.73	7.00	47
	E		0.00	0.00	0	1.72	0.61	35
	F		3.45	2.17	62	0.61	0.33	54

	System 1	System 2
Three busiest devices	251 SIPAG 1, 45.08% 362 XXXX, 53.48% LMF (SIPAGO), 66.11%	363 WK3021, 60.14% 42D YYYY3, 52.92% 42E WK3020, 53.42%
Average time (ms) to service a request	73	84
Average time (ms) per device access	50	42
3. Storage Page fault rate, per second	46.53	16
Paging rate, per second	63	26
4. Swaps Long wait	13	10
Detected wait	96	95
Unilateral	15	49
Exchange	27	5
Enqueue exchange	—	8
Total swaps work load	85	109
Total ended transactions	32	45
Swap ended transaction ratio	2.65 : 1	2.42 : 1
Total swaps, including performance group = 0	System 1 = 151	System 2 = 167

5. System address space analysis

Type	Max.	Avg.		Max.	Avg.	Max.	Avg.		Max.	Avg.
Batch	9	6.0	In ready	8	0.5	13	12.1	In ready	7	0.9
STC	16	13.9	In	18	13.7	16	12.8	In	22	18.6
TSO		0								

Figure 2-28. Channel utilization date for case study, giving details on activity within both systems.

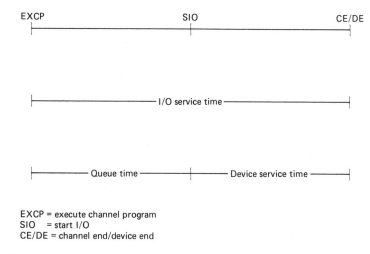

EXCP = execute channel program
SIO = start I/O
CE/DE = channel end/device end

Figure 2-29. Schematic definition of device service time used in the case study.

(3) Channel utilization had to be kept below 35% to improve service by reallocating work loads on specific channels.

(4) Since the high device service time could be caused by control units, arm contention, or channel utilization, the work load had to be rebalanced by relocating data sets on the disk, moving heavily utilized disk drives to other control units, and possibly adding an additional disk control unit.

It had been obvious at the start of this study that memory was a problem. Rules of thumb, intuition, and experience all pointed to this. And indeed memory was heavily utilized. Yet by conducting this study, it became equally clear that perhaps a greater part of the problem was not in memory, and that before running out and buying more memory, redistributing the work load on the disk and channels might improve the situation sufficiently to avoid that additional expense. Even the acquisition of another disk control unit would have been less expensive. After that was done and the results analyzed in the same way as in the initial study, management could make a more intelligent decision about the acquisition of more memory. Not only was a needless expense put off at this time, but management was actively forewarned that it would have to be made and could thus begin planning either the replacement of these CPUs or the acquisition of memory, costing out options and selling their requests to executives. There were no surprises and the data center illustrated that it was in control. Three people working part time for several weeks did the study. As a result of this learning experience, an ongoing effort is in place today in this shop which takes less time to do than it did initially. It now becomes possible to learn quickly if the computer is out of capacity and when.

Case Study: Consolidation of Data Centers

Perhaps the most complicated form of capacity study is that which involves consolidating the work of a number of computers into a single, larger unit. Often conducted with magic, mirrors, and lots of intuition, the potential for disastrous miscalculations is virtually guaranteed. Although measuring current work loads on all existing systems and then translating them into comparable work loads on other centralized systems to determine capacity requirements is a time-consuming technique, the effort is essential. In this case, 10 people participated in the study, which required several months to complete.

The average CPU utilization was approximately 65% at the start of the study on the main computer during prime shift. During the second and third shifts it varied from 40 to 50%. To determine accurately the computer requirements and the impact of various locations on the main computer, work loads were identified (batch and on-line) for the key computers. The main host was an IBM 370/158. The largest computer to be consolidated was a 370/135, which the team equated at 17.5% of the 158. For other locations, since data were not always available in any quantity, surveys and various reports were used as the basis for the team's analysis. And because there were a variety of computers involved, index points were established for these. These index points were developed by calculating the CPU resource demand to process required work load based on known CPU utilizations and the requirements for overhead on the operating systems. Figure 2-30 shows the team's hardware plan based on work load. Lines 1 and 2 illustrate the correlation between index points and time for production work with required CPU power at the end of the consolidation. Note that line 1 represents the average and line 2 the peak work load during the first shift. Line 3 includes both production and test work with an early start because computer power would be needed in the initial phases of consolidation. Line 4 suggests the computer requirements, with an anticipated growth rate of 7% assumed for the first year and 17% for each of the following three years. The reason for a four-year window was to match the length of time that management had set (for financial reasons) to keep installed the computer system eventually selected for the consolidation.

Examining the data presented in Figure 2-30 suggested that the present 158 would be fully utilized by the middle of the first year and assumed no growth in application work. Additional computer requirements for the short term were needed (such as a 158 AP at the time, a 168, or a 3033).

The presentation to DP management included a consideration of support for these conclusions by offering large amounts of information backing the recommendations that additional power be acquired. Using the 135 system as an example, the team illustrated the calculations of work load as it would look on the 158. The math they used is applicable to any computer system work load when comparing one CPU to another, usually within the same family of computers (such as the same vendor's) or compatible models.

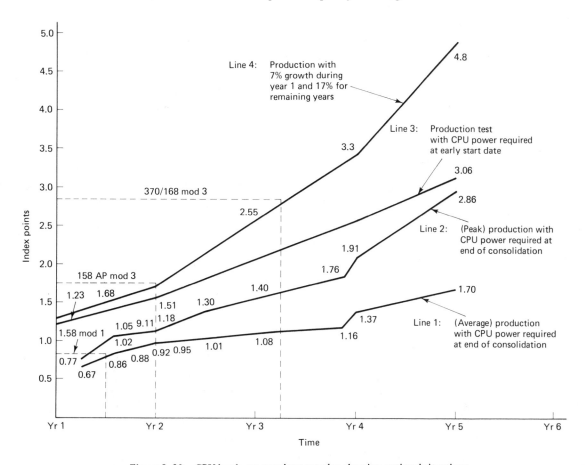

Figure 2-30. CPU hardware requirement plan showing optional situations.

average daily transactions on

$$158 \text{ computer} = 30{,}000$$

$$\text{CPU time} = 2 \text{ hours (7200 seconds)}$$

Hence

$$\text{time to process one transaction} = \frac{7200}{30{,}000} = \frac{0.24 \text{ second}}{\text{CPU time}}$$

$$\text{elapsed time} = 24 \text{ hours}$$

Hence

$$\text{arrival rate of transactions} = \frac{30{,}000}{(14 \times 60 \times 60)} = \frac{0.6 \text{ transaction}}{\text{second}}$$

Assuming

$$\text{peak rate} = 2 \times 0.6 = \frac{1.2 \text{ transactions}}{\text{second}}$$

$$\text{utilization of the } 158 = \text{arrival rate} \times \text{service time}$$

$$= 1.2 \times 0.24 = 0.28$$

$$= 28\%$$

For the 135, the daily transaction rate was 1/3 of 30,000; hence the 135 teleprocessing work load = 28/3 = 9% of the 158 computer. The total 135 work load (batch and on-line) was, therefore, assuming 60% utilization of the present 135 (based on the software monitor results):

$$= \frac{0.149 \times 100}{0.85} \; (0.85 = \text{of a } 158)$$

$$= 17.52\% \text{ of a } 158$$

Conclusion: the total 135 work load was 17.52% of the 158, of which 9% was on-line work providing the same response times.

Since a variety of CPUs were being consolidated, the impact of all their work loads on the mainframe had to be measured by index points. Machine instruction performance (MIP) rates for all of the machines were taken from published reports (vendor and industry) and a table created by the team by which to measure the "horsepower" of one system against another. In this particular case the following was the table based on the consolidation of a group of computers scattered about the organization.

Index point table

158 Model 1	0.85
158 Model 3	1.0
158 AP Model 1	1.5
158 AP Model 3	1.7
168 Model 3	2.7
168 AP Model 3	4.6
3033	4.6
3033 (+ enhanced software)	5.3

For the purposes of this particular study the team considered their index numbers as 100% utilization: index points = MIPs.

The team prepared some extensive charts showing the various locations and what hardware they had installed before the consolidation, together with planned consolidation conversion dates. (See Figures 2-31 and 2-32.)

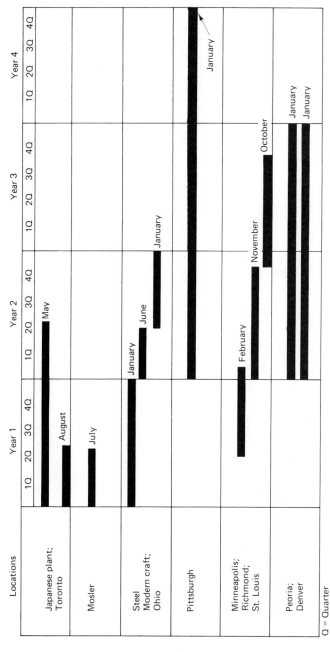

Figure 2-31. Consolidation plan showing which locations would be absorbed, when, and how long the task should take.

Q = Quarter

Location	System Type	Memory Size	Conv. Date End	SCPTO MUS	MIP Rate	Utilization		Index Points		Cum. Index		Conv. Date Start	Cum. Index Reqd.	Line in Fig. 2-30
						Peak	Avg.	Peak	Avg.	Peak	Avg.			
N.J. data center	158	2m		1.2	0.85	75	65	0.765	0.66	0.77	0.67			
Mosler	135	512K	7/1	1.4	0.18	100	80	0.25	0.20	1.02	0.86	10/0		
Toronto	360/20	8/1		1.5	0.03	60	40	0.03	0.02	1.05	0.88	10/0		
Modern craft	3/10	64K	1/2	1.7	0.05	75	50	0.06	0.04	1.11	0.92	11/0	1.25	1
Ohio	NCR 200	64K	2/2	1.5	0.09	50	25	0.07	0.03	1.18	0.95	6/1	1.30	
Japanese plants	3/10 qty. 3, 360/20		6/2	1.7	0.18	40	20	0.12	0.06	1.30	1.01	10/0	1.17	
Richmond	360/40	124K	11/2	1/5	0/09	75	50	0.10	0.07	1.40	1.08	1/2	1/40	
Steel	3/10	24K	1/3	1.7	0.05	40	20	0.03	0.01	1.43	1.09	6/2	1.54	2
Eng. system	Various							0.23		1.66		6/2	1.77	
St. Lous	3/15	96K	10/3	1.7	0.08	75	50	0.10	0.07	1.76	1.16	11/2	1.87	
Peoria	GE 435 qty. 2	32K	1/4	1.5	0.12	100	80	0.18	0.14	1.94	1.30	1/2	1.45	
Denver	HIS 1200	65K	1/4	1.5	0.09	75	50	0.10	0.07	2.04	1.37	1/2	1.45	3
Pitts-burg	UN 9070	1m	1/5	1.2	0.34	95	80	0.39	0.35	2.43	1.70	1/2	1.51	
Arts dept.	Minis							0.43		2.86			3.06	

Figure 2-32. Hardware to be consolidated by location.

There were some additional assumptions and definitions given to management which took into account the close correlation between hardware and software. The first involved changing a number of operating systems to MVS (the central-site SCP). The team created relative requirements or weights for each of the various operating systems' needs to translate into MVS power to support the various work loads. They also took into consideration, therefore, a number of different operating system architectures. For example, if an IBM System 3 were to be converted to a disk operating system (DOS) environment, they calculated the overhead due to the operating system at about 15%, with the use of the software vendor's technicians providing such input. For other operating systems, the team jointly arrived at figures for use in working up their work loads. Note that these are not hard and fast and can vary from company to company. These also happen to be for operating systems in releases that the reader may not find installed today. Therefore, if doing such a study, you would still have to create your own table based on current overheads. For this case study the data reached were as follows:

System 3 to DOS	0.15
DOS to DOS/VS	0.10
DOS/VS to VS1	0.15
VS1 to MVS	0.20

The study group assumed that for normal commercial job mixes the ratio from VS1 to MVS would be about 1:1, but because precise data on all the computer systems were not obtainable, they fudged the numbers to provide some buffer, used a factor of 1:1.2, and then reformatted the data into a matrix chart (Figure 2-33).

Because the System 3 was the most unique system involved with the least comparable operating system compared to the others, including MVS, an additional set of calculations were made to establish what the conversion from the 3 to MVS would entail. The ratio was arrived at in the following manner:

$$1.15 + \frac{10\%(1.15)}{A} + \frac{15\%(A)}{B} + 20\%(B)$$

$$= 1.15 + 0.115 = 1.26 + 15\%(1.26) = 0.189 + 20\%(1.44) = 28$$

$$= 1.26 + 0.189 + 0.28 = 1.72$$

Type	DOS	DOS/VS	VS1	MVS
System 3	1.15	1.26	1.44	1.72
DOS	X	1.10	1.26	1.51
DOS/VS	X	X	1.15	1.38
VS1	X	X	X	1.20
MVS	X	X	X	X

Figure 2-33. Relative requirements of one SCP against another.

		Index Points		Cumulative	
Steps	Location	Peak	Average	Peak	Average
Step 1 (present)	N.J. Data Center	0.765	0.663	0.77	0.67
Step 2 (3rd qtr, yr 1)	Mosler	0.25	0.20	1.02	0.86
	Toronto	0.03	0.02	1.05	0.88
Step 3 (4th qtr, yr 1)	Moderncraft	0.06	0.04	1.11	0.92
	Ohio	0.07	0.03	1.18	0.95
Step 4 (2nd qtr, yr 2)	Japanese Plants	0.12	0.06	1.30	1.01
Step 5 (4th qtr, yr 2)	Richmond	0.10	0.07	1.40	1.08
	Steel	0.03	0.01	1.43	1.09
	Eng. Systems	0.23			
Step 6 (4th qtr, yr 3)	St. Louis	0.10	0.07	1.76	1.16
	Peoria	0.18	0.14	1.94	1.30
	Denver	0.10	0.07	2.04	1.37
Step 7 (4th qtr, yr 4)	Pittsburgh	0.39	0.33	2.43	1.70

Figure 2-34. Increments of additional work in terms of system capacity required as each step of the consolidation is taken.

The capacity planning team defined the index point as a measure to calculate demand for CPU resources needed to process a defined work load, which in turn was based on existing utilization and overhead of operating systems. In equation form it looked like this:

$$\text{index point} = \text{loading factor} \times \text{MIP rates} \times \text{peak/average utilization}$$

Cumulative index points were based on consolidation end dates. These data were then converted into Figure 2-34 to show a conversion plan. Figure 2-34 was qualified more specifically on several points as well to avoid criticism of the data arrived at by either non-DP management or managers within the MIS department itself. Loading factors for system control programs converted to MVS for all locations with CPUs other than IBM systems were considered as if they were DOS-to-MVS conversions. Necessary conversion work on MVS itself was included in the analysis. Data from line 3 of Figure 2-30 had production and test with an early start date considered as cumulative index points for consolidation up through the first year. Growth for early testing was added in the following manner. On 1/1/78, the index points from Figure 2-30 were 1.51. The total number of personnel required was 40. Following their assumption, one analyst used up 0.005 MIP; hence 40 yielded 0.005 × 40, or 0.2 MIP. Figure 2-30, line 3, was given a peak value based on the peak for line 2 + 0.2 MIP = 0.2, for a figure of 3.06. In the same chart, line 4 showed the growth in index points as stated before:

$$\text{base point } (1/78) = 1.51$$
$$7\% \text{ growth} = 1.51 + 7\%(1.51)$$
$$= 1.62$$

When all these data were taken together and summarized, the formal conclusion reached was that the current host system (158) would be fully utilized by the middle of 1977, assuming no additional growth. Thus to maintain good service levels and optimize usage of the hardware, the team recommended two specific alternatives: (1) install a 158 AP interim to taking delivery on a 3033, or (2) install a 168 Model 3 interim to a 3033. The 158 AP or 168 should be chosen on the basis of when the 3033 could be delivered. At the time the study was conducted, lead time for delivery of the larger processor was over 18 months. In reviewing the situation with management, the DP department was able to forecast that the 158 AP would be fully utilized by early 1978 and thus was only a reasonable alternative if the 3033 could be installed in the first quarter of 1978. Otherwise, the second option would be necessary, as it could carry the data center through the entire period of the consolidation but not beyond it. Armed with such data, DP management in this case obtained permission to plan for a 3033, especially after the savings by consolidation had been worked out in similar detail. After obtaining a delivery date on the 3033, a decision was made to acquire the 168 as much for financial reasons as for practical ones; management did not want to keep moving CPUs in and out of the data center while converting smaller shops to theirs.

SPECIAL CONSIDERATIONS WITH CAPACITY PLANNING

A number of considerations in capacity planning have been suggested throughout this chapter which might conveniently be brought together in summary form. Capacity planning continues to be a topic that causes considerable controversy both in DP literature and in actual day-to-day situations. It is controversial for a number of reasons. At best, it leaves much to be desired. We know, for example, how to measure work loads in large computers, but hardly anything about how to do so in minis and micros that have architectures different from traditional computers. If the architecture for a particular mini or micro is similar, then techniques used in medium-size to large data centers are applicable. Second, analyzing work loads by application is often a long and tedious job that comes up with imprecise results since the application and job streams are dynamic, changing from day to day and hour to hour in all departments. Third, it can be expensive in staff time required during a period when the cost of hardware is falling so fast that it becomes tempting to acquire the next-larger device rather than going through the bother of a capacity study, especially with micros, minis, and distributed intelligent terminals with cycles and memory. These are invariably planned for replacement every two years or so anyway.

Users also have their complaints. They argue that work-load management is irrelevant because they are not allowed to define what DP resources they want or can use; only data processing management does this. Users do not know what future work loads they will want to bring to the data center, let alone what the amount of processing on existing systems will be even a month from now unless executive management forces them to sit down and think, work, and commit themselves to quantified opinions. Or, users will argue that the DP department is doing a fine job, so why rock the boat with new studies or methods that take up everyone's time. This last point is fine as long as the DP department has substantial capacity, but it becomes a disaster when capacity is slim or a chargeout system is imposed on users.

We have already seen how financially, even with declining costs of hardware, the lack of capacity planning can hurt an organization. Broken contracts are very expensive and the only way to make a commitment to a particular device is to know realistically how long one can live with it. Users billed for their usage of a data center's resources should be the first to demand formal capacity and tuning studies as a means of holding the line on rising costs. That they do not is probably true of all organizations to their detriment, because then the only pressure on data processing to be more efficient is the embarrassment an MIS director might want to avoid when going to management with a surprise request for more capacity.

No one seems to be sympathetic to the DP director when response time, disk capacity, or computer availability create a problem. It is then the DP director's fault or responsibility, and clearly many conclude that the director does not know what he or she is doing or would not have gotten them all into such a pickle. Since a considerable portion of any DP manager's job (whether an operations manager or a DP director) is spent putting out fires, reacting to user complaints, and responding to pressures to produce more lines of code or install additional applications and terminals, capacity studies provide an effective tool by which the manager can gain some control over data processing events while improving service all around. In short, capacity planning increases the amount of time available to DP management to do its job—running data centers and installing equipment, applications, and code—in a dynamic environment riddled with hostility. It is not a panacea but clearly a weapon, a tool, and a means out of an otherwise difficult situation.

Capacity studies allow organizations to shift responsibility for cost-justifying equipment and applications to the persons in the organization who ultimately know best why these are needed and what they are worth: the users. Typically, a user will want an additional terminal or submit a request for an application without having any conception of the costs involved, let alone their quantified benefits. With numerous similar requests on his or her desk, the DP director frequently will make choices based on limited resources, possibly electing to help one portion of the organization over another for political or personal reasons rather than for business causes and possibly in direct conflict with the general business plan of the organization. Capacity planning allows the DP department to force general management to participate in the allocation of data processing resources by imposing on users the discipline of forecasting needs, justifying costs and benefits with the DP department, and to provide referral services if multiple requests cannot be satisfied simultaneously. This last factor alone is often the most important reason for a DP director to preach the gospel of capacity planning. For executives, in turn, it provides a means of controlling a technology they do not understand by funneling its energies toward supporting their business plan and not that of the DP department.

Capacity planning, like other DP activities, has fostered its own folklore wisdom and rules of thumb, each with its element of truth. Some of the more commonly heard are:

- Any capacity plan that is complete is already out of date.
- No capacity plan is ever correct.
- Most capacity plans help fine-tune systems more than cause systems growth.
- All hardware and software can be measured with a capacity planning effort.
- Most capacity plans underestimate resource requirements by at least 25%.
- Available hardware capacity will always be used up faster than forecasted.
- The longer the projection into time of capacity, the more inaccurate the conclusions will be.
- Capacity plans are most accurate for CPUs that cover about two years, disk for six months, teleprocessing networks for three months, and applications for three to six months.
- Capacity planning is not hard to do, just time consuming.
- Capacity planning is an art, not a science.
- Most capacity plans take too many details into account.
- Without capacity planning all equipment costs more.
- With capacity planning all equipment still costs more.
- Without capacity planning all software performs poorly.

- Increased work loads are directly proportional to poor performance without capacity planning.
- Non-DP management is more apt to agree with data processing when capacity planning buttresses an argument.
- Common sense armed with a few data go a long way.

These quips of wisdom drawn from various data processing managers and non-DP executives suggest a blend of the Peter Principle and Murphy's Law, with the underlying negative assumption that capacity is a necessary nuisance for self-protection and improved productivity. They imply that it offers additional control in what might otherwise be a chaotic environment where change is truly the only constant and where reality is a loaded form of panic.

In summary, a number of factors should be remembered when implementing effective capacity planning:

- It is critical that top management be committed to support capacity planning efforts and apply the right resources to do the job.
- Define what the current capacity planning functions and reports are (if any) before initiating any new ones.
- Account for as much hardware utilization as possible by cycles, memory, channels, subsystems, applications, and users.
- Establish service-level objectives with users for those things that are important to both users and DP personnel (such as response and turnaround times, and quality of outputs).
- Establish service levels relevant to the DP department (such as quality of inputs to systems and feedback on anticipated needs by users).
- Make an initial attempt at forecasting and capacity planning as a means of expanding your understanding of local needs and concerns while learning what the process is all about.
- Develop parameters for defining what future workloads will entail in capacity (such as transaction types, requirements for batch versus on-line applications, file sizes, terminals).
- Translate these kinds of future requirements into terms established when you defined current work loads and utilization levels.
- Establish procedures for tracking performance and forecasts over time on a continuous basis (weekly, monthly, or quarterly—whichever makes sense for your installation).
- Create standard reporting tools (such as routine reports) that managers become familiar with and can compare against earlier ones.
- All reports should reflect summary information on each of the major

elements monitored (hardware utilization, work-load characterization, network and terminal loads, response times, etc.).

- Share the results of your efforts with upper-level management and users on a regular basis.

Although other guidelines could be added, it suffices to remember that capacity planning is an integral part of hardware management. Without it, the topics discussed in other chapters of this book cannot be appreciated or correctly implemented.

Never invest your money in anything that eats or needs repaint-
ing.

Billy Rose

People are trapped into poor financial strategies with regard to data process-ing hardware more often than in any other sector of the DP industry. This chapter shows you how you can possibly save your organization millions of dollars by using some simple, commonsense tactics that take into account your needs as well as changes in technology. First we review purchase versus lease considerations, including case studies. Next, we define commonly at-tractive financial strategies. We conclude with proven ways of maximizing investment in hardware.

CHAPTER
THREE

Cost Justification
of Hardware

Although the cost of individual pieces of data processing hardware is declining, the amount of equipment being installed in an organization is not. It is not uncommon today for hundreds of devices to be installed within a company in the course of a year. Therefore, the total amount of money being spent on hardware is actually going up faster than inflation and in many companies far surpasses the growth in expenditures for other types of industrial equipment. It is thus understandable that many managers feel increased pressure to cost-justify data processing hardware in the traditional accounting and financial manner, much as others have always had to do for manufacturing equipment or new buildings. Moreover, if properly done, such exercises can save an organization considerable sums of money. Although the subject of financial analysis is worthy of a book of its own, this chapter illustrates some of the basic elements that can be used to cost out hardware using simple, yet practical techniques commonly applied in many organizations today. At a minimum, the reader will learn enough about the process to be able to conduct intelligent conversations regarding hardware with financial and general management personnel.

PURCHASE VERSUS LEASE ISSUES

Invariably, an acquisition decision involves whether to purchase or lease devices. The issue frequently affects which units should be installed as well as from what vendor. The question becomes acute when it involves such expensive items as computers (otherwise known as mainframes, hosts, or CPUs) or large quantities or peripherals. There are certain traditional kinds of situations in which an organization finds leasing more attractive than purchase, whereas other classic circumstances dictate the opposite. In brief, one leases if the period over which the device is to be kept is less than four years. Leasing is also attractive if there is fear that technical obsolescence will reduce the value of your equipment. In addition, if working capital or credit is not available, purchasing is not an attractive option. Lease payments are level with limits set on price increases as a rule, and the risk of ownership remains with the vendor. It is often easier to change hardware, and with less cost, if it is leased rather than purchased. Many managers feel that they obtain better service and attention from a vendor if equipment is leased because they feel that the manufacturer then has a stake in making sure that the devices remain installed. And, of course, a company that leases does not have to worry about residual values, or perhaps insurance or financing the lease.

On the other hand, however, there are some disadvantages to leasing. First, it may not be the least expensive way to finance a device. Since lease payments are expensible items on an organization's tax returns, capital and depreciation rules do not apply. Expenses have to be absorbed and accounted for in the year they take place and so cannot be spread out over periods when the cash flow may have already stopped. For instance, if a device is purchased in year 1 and paid in full, the amount could be spread over five, six, or more years, thus appearing on the books in year 1 as less expenditure than it really was, whereas with a lease over five years, money leaves the organization each year.

The disadvantages of leases are the benefits of purchase in most instances. The longer a unit is to remain installed, the more attractive it becomes to purchase it. Residual value (leftover value when the device is removed from the organization and possibly sold secondhand) goes to the purchaser. Thus the owner can sell the equipment at the end of the depreciation period, when it is no longer needed, for some residual value and obtain a profit or at least try to match the amount left undepreciated. For example, if a device is purchased for $100,000, depreciated over five years down to 10% (rcsidual value of $10,000), and sold in year 6 for $11,000, a profit of $1000 has been realized. In a lease, the owner of the machine—not you—would have the opportunity to make that profit.

In a purchase arrangement, costs are fixed; there is no risk of lease or rental payment increases. Even the value of purchased equipment can be calculated, since data processing equipment is understood fairly well in today's marketplace. It is considered a valuable investment with known risks. Despite occasional press reports about specific situations where gross miscalculation of values took place, values are tied to the availability of current and newly announced technologies. Thus forecasts for demand are fairly sound and made easier by the fact that the demand for hardware still exceeds the manufacturing capacity of all computer vendors.

Depending on the terms of a purchase, there is considerable flexibility in how devices are acquired and financed. In the United States, purchasers of equipment also benefit from the investment tax credit (ITC), which is a direct subtraction from tax payments to the government based on a certain percentage of the purchase price of the equipment. The ITC can be extremely attractive with large computers. For example, a CPU purchased for $1 million and kept for more than five years would have an ITC of approximately $60,000, which could be deducted from the tax bill for that year. Obviously, therefore, the value of $60,000 after taxes is greater than $60,000 worth of tax deductions. In short, it makes the $1 million computer less expensive. (See Figure 3-1.)

Purchase may not always be attractive, however. The commitment is longer than to a lease and thus a better set of plans have to be in place for

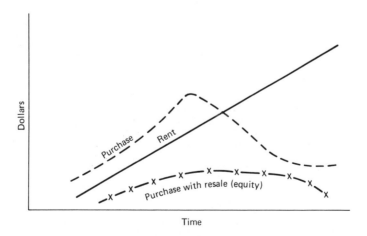

Figure 3-1. Cumulative after-tax cash outflow (same situation: three financial alternatives).

the device because as a rule it will stay in the organization longer. If a residual value plays an important part in the cost justification of a unit, its decline over time can represent a risk that should be well understood.

Despite the pros and cons regarding leases and purchases, companies lean in one direction or another if the following general conditions exist:

With a Lease

- When capital is not available for the transaction
- When the obligation must be a fairly short one (usually less than four years)
- When costs must be understood for the life of the installation and remain at a specified level
- When service leverage against a vendor is deemed important
- When long-term planning is difficult or impossible to conduct
- When residual values are not identifiable or are considered irrelevant to the analysis

Thus companies that have too much debt already, have few or no long-term data processing plans, feel that the cost of capital is too high (as we saw in 1981), or feel that their purchase money would be better spent elsewhere will simply lease hardware. Yet because the purchase of hardware is often one of the most attractive investments a company can make compared to other possibilities, purchases are often made.

The kinds of conditions that typically lead management to opt for a purchase include:

With a Purchase

- When capital funds can help reduce some long-term operating expenses (usually done in a year of good cash flow)
- When an organization expects many years' worth of service from a particular device
- When the probability of taking advantage of high residual values is possible (usually the case if you install and purchase early in the life of the technology)
- When tax benefits such as ITC and depreciation are attractive
- When purchase conforms to predetermined company policy concerning the acquisition of equipment
- When the acquisition is deemed a solid business investment
- When the cost of capital (interest charges on borrowed money) is less than about 15% (for current purchase prices)

One of the keys to a sound purchase decision is having a realistic idea about how long the device will be used and for what purpose. Next, having the necessary capital available with which to make the purchase becomes essential. Thus richer organizations may do more purchasing (if they wish) than can be done by less fluid companies. Wealthier companies are often better run anyway and have more data processing plans in place, which allows them to exercise the option of purchasing more frequently, thereby better controlling hardware costs.

Economic Considerations

In recent years, several economic conditions have directly influenced purchase and lease decisions. Each in its own way continues to affect such thinking as well. The following factors represent a short catalog of the most important influences on financial strategies:

- High cost of capital (ranging from a low of 9% to over 25% in the past five years)
- High inflation rates throughout the industrialized world, resulting in increased cost of money, uncertain residual values in certain instances, and possible fiscal uncertainties for many organizations
- Changing technologies, resulting in faster introductions of newer devices at better cost/performance ratios than ever before
- Trend of many vendors toward unbundling or breaking out the cost of software and maintenance from lease and purchase prices of equipment, leading to a more complex analysis of total costs for hardware
- Lack of sufficient number of technical personnel to maximize the use of equipment
- Sharp increase in the cost of technical personnel
- Changing opinions about data processing strategies as new and different products become available (centralization versus decentralization or distributive processing)

Each of these factors typically affects a decision in both financial and planning terms. For example, look at the impact of high interest rates. If a device is purchased at 15% interest over seven years, the total cost in hard money is about twice what the vendor charged for the equipment. If that interest rate is closer to 30% (and it was for some companies in 1980), you can see what that does to pushing up the total cost of purchasing. Thus all kinds of questions get asked. If the cost of capital is about to go up again, is it better to buy quickly now? Is it cheaper to lease to avoid maintenance charges, or better to buy and pay them? Can I find reasonably priced personnel to take advantage of these new technologies? Or do I place a premium

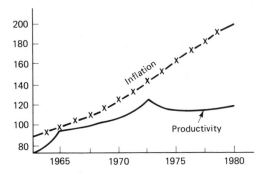

Figure 3-2. Productivity versus inflation in the United States. (Inflation based on Consumer Price Index; productivity drawn from Index of Output per Person/Hour in Private Business; 1967 = 100 annual average.)

on devices that can be operated by non-DP people or from a host data center? How expensive is moving to new devices versus sticking to things our staff is already familiar with? Is my organization going to continue having high enough sales to justify the order entry application for which this new computer is being leased or purchased? Such questions are real and come up repeatedly in discussions of financing acquisitions of data processing hardware. Yet there are no simple answers to any of these questions. Each situation requires special attention, but the key point is that these questions should be asked and answered in some fashion rather than making hardware decisions arbitrarily.

Perhaps the most important factor, however, that forces management to look at machines is productivity. As Figure 3-2 shows, people productivity has declined or gone up only slightly while inflation has continued to march always upward. At the same time, hardware costs have actually been dropping. This has resulted in greater use of equipment, and when its functional productivity is measured against people's (via computerized applications), the pressure to install more hardware continues.

Strategic Considerations

The issues mentioned above are raised with all manner of equipment, from micros and minis to full-sized computers to data entry units to distributed intelligent terminals. Since management wants to reduce a number of possible options to just several from which to make a final decision (e.g., four scenarios), a number of specific issues will affect any set of plans. The following concerns and questions should be visited each time a collection of options is defined for decision making:

- How long will the device in question remain in the organization?
- What method of depreciation of a purchase should be used?
- What are the lease and purchase prices of the equipment?
- How much ITC is involved; who gets it (us or the vendor); will it pass to us or a broker; will the vendor pass it on in a lease?

- How and when would the asset be sold off or simply thrown away (with a zero residual value)?

- What is the impact of all taxes (local, state, and federal) on my options?

- What expenses are incurred for transportation, maintenance, physical site preparation, travel, and education?

- Should sales taxes be carried on the books as expenses, capital outlays, or be folded into a lease?

- What are the termination charges should the lease contract be aborted early?

- What is a reasonable salvage value (residual) that can be factored into the cost of equipment and might be realized when it finally is exercised by the sale of the hardware?

These questions are not impossible to answer, and within any organization there are several reliable sources for answers. The first source is the vendor in question, who can articulate the costs of lease and purchase, maintenance, education, transportation, termination charges, and installation fees. Data processing personnel, through their general understanding of the industry and its product cycles, can work with vendors to establish the length of time that a particular device might reasonably be expected to stay within an organization, work up reasonable residual values, and identify the effort required to dispose of the asset at the end of its useful life. Analysts in the financial department would be in a position to determine tax considerations and the impact of an acquisition on tax, profit, and budget books. Although discussion of each of the foregoing factors could warrant a book of its own, suffice it to say that each of these factors should be weighed. The examples of financial analysis below illustrate the process.

Checklist of Do's and Don'ts in Financial Analysis. Typically, organizations without much experience in analyzing the costs of data processing make a number of mistakes that are easy to avoid.

1. Make financial planning a *joint* effort among management, DP, and finance. Otherwise, a purchase decision could be made to be amortized over four years and actually be depreciated over seven years, because accounting was not informed of the strategy signed off on, causing expensive problems later when the asset is to be disposed of with its book value greater than its market sale price.

2. Do not be greedy by pushing off into the future the cost of equipment through straight-line depreciation over too long a period of time. Depreciate purchases as quickly as you can afford to and if in a tight year, depreciate on a straight-line basis but make sure to switch depreciation over

to double declining balance in the second or third year. Otherwise, the asset is valued too high on the books.

3.   If acquiring secondhand older technology, be especially sensitive to the costs of the contract and to the greater expenses of maintenance over newer technologies.

4.   If new applications are to be developed for which equipment is being leased or purchased, go through the formal exercise of justifying these new functions in quantifiable terms. This will provide greater financial flexibility when costing hardware.

5.   If user departmental managers are to be charged for hardware, they should participate in acquisition planning since they will have to live with the results of the approved game plan; otherwise, they may protest and not comply.

Some Sample Cases

There are several classic situations that confront management when acquiring computers and peripheral equipment. Typically, in regard to computers, formal financial analysis may be conducted on alternative financial methods of acquisition. These involve leases from a vendor, outright purchase, or leasing from a third party. The situations below suggest the kind of effort that should be expended in order to tailor scenarios to your own organization.

Purchase versus Lease: Trends and Case   With today's technology, the number of dollars involved in either a lease or purchase situation has declined sharply from the level of 5 or 10 years ago. A second trend has been toward reducing the ratio of lease to purchase prices by vendors. Ten years ago, for example, a lease-to-purchase ratio of 1:48, that is, purchase equal to 48 times the monthly lease price, was very common. Today the ratios range from 1:28 to 1:40, making purchase attractive at a time when the cost of money (interest rates) fluctuates upward more frequently than it did a decade ago. Purchase versus lease analyses thus remain useful exercises.

The fundamental question concerns how long a piece of equipment is expected to stay within an organization. If, for instance, a computer is expected to remain only a short time, leasing becomes more attractive (typically less than three years). If this computer were to stay longer, purchase usually is less expensive. The key, then, is to identify the break-even point, the point where purchase becomes less expensive than having continued to lease. Break-even points are usually measured in months or fractions of years. Although formulas vary, they all have essentially the same ingredients:

$$\text{break-even (months)} = \frac{\text{purchase price} - \text{warranty} - \text{accruals (if any)}}{\text{monthly lease charge} - \text{maintenance costs}}$$

Simply illustrated: the $100,000 purchase price on a computer less $6000 worth of free maintenance during the first year (total) divided by the $3000 monthly lease price less the monthly maintenance cost of $500 if the computer was purchased (paid after the warranty period was over) would yield a break-even point of 36 months. The answer thus suggests that purchasing the computer makes sense if it is to remain installed in the organization for more than 36 months. If for a shorter period, leasing it would make more sense provided that the lease contract was drawn up for three or less years. Moreover, if the tax benefit of ITC is subtracted from the cost of the computer on the top half of the break-even equation, the break-even point is actually several months shorter. Depending on how many factors you want to include in your formula, the break-even equation is basically the same. Other factors, such as one-time purchase or lease expenses, simply make the formula extend farther to the right of the = sign.

A more complete financial analysis illustrates how an organization looks at the numbers. As a sample example, assume a computer to be used for five years, leasing for $3000 per month and purchasable for $800,000. Monthly maintenance is paid on purchased equipment after the first year of warranty at a rate of $3300 per month but not on leased equipment. In our case the ITC passes to the organization. If purchased at 16% cost of capital over 60 months with a final residual value of 10% arrived at through double-declining-balance depreciation, the other factors included are 46% federal tax, 6% state income tax, and 5% sales tax. In this case the organization has also decided that if it purchased the equipment, its sales tax (on the purchase) would be capitalized, that is, spread out over five years on its books. Its insurance would be one-fourth of 1% of the purchase price. It was also decided that the acquisition of this computer would save $183,000 per year in other expenses avoided over the first four years. Figure 3-3 shows how the numbers would look for purchase and lease before and after tax deductions were accounted for. Note that the cash flows were extended out annually over five years so that management could see where and when its expenditures would come.

Figure 3-4 shows the differences between lease and purchase and adds a present-value factor of 25% to discount the money involved. In Figures 3-3 and 3-4 note also that the negative numbers are actually cash inflows. Thus in Figure 3-3 the cumulative before-tax cash outflow if purchased was $632,226, yet after tax deductions were taken, a cash inflow of $7063 was realized. If leased, the cash outflow before taxes was $1,126,500; after tax deductions were taken, it was down to $211,376. Thus in this situation, if the computer were kept for five years, it would be cheaper to buy.

What if the computer were purchased and sold off earlier than five years? Several things would be done. First, a portion of the ITC would have to be paid back to the government. Yet if a larger computer were then brought which also had ITC, the tax benefit may actually be greater during the year in which the devices were swapped. Second, the residual value of the com-

If purchased:	80–81	81–82	82–83	83–84	84–85	85–86
Before taxes: Principal	87,614	134,311	157,449	184,573	216,370	39,525
Interest	96,230	110,815	87,677	60,553	28,756	1,330
Total payment	183,845	245,126	245,126	245,126	245,126	40,854
Maintenance	20,790	41,580	41,580	41,580	41,580	6,930
Insurance	150	200	200	200	200	33
ITC	−36,000	0	0	0	0	0
Other benefits	−183,000	−183,000	−183,000	−183,000	0	0
Total outflow	−14,215	103,906	103,906	103,906	286,906	47,818
Cumulative		89,691	193,597	297,503	584,409	632,226
Tax deductions (exp.)						
Depreciation	252,000	235,200	141,120	84,672	36,792	4.144
Deduct. expenses	81,170	152,595	129,457	102,333	70,536	8,293
Total expenses	333,170	387,795	270,577	187,005	107,328	12,437
(less at 0.4924%)	164,053	190,950	133,232	92,081	52,849	6,124
Tax impact	164,053	190,950	133,232	92,081	52,849	6,124
After-tax cash flow						
Cash outflow	−14,215	103,906	103,906	103,906	286,906	47,818
Subtract deduct.	164,053	190,950	133,232	92,081	52,849	6,124
After-tax cash	−1728,268	−87,044	−29,326	11,825	234,057	41,694
Cumulative		−265,312	−294,638	−282,813	−48,756	−7,063
If leased:						
Before tax	283,500	378,000	378,000	378,000	378,000	63,000
After-tax cash	−39,095	8,873	8,873	8,873	191,873	31,979
Cumulative		−30,222	−21,349	−12,476	179,397	211,376

Figure 3-3. Sample cash flow (purchase vs. lease—before and after tax).

puter on the books could have been too low, which means that when sold at a higher value, a small profit could have been made. Some companies actually look at the financial implications involved in selling off an asset earlier and plan on replacing it with other devices simply because it is less expensive than living with the unit for five years.

The point is that various scenarios can be constructed quickly to suggest what alternatives would cost and which are more attractive. Executives can then decide, for example, to lease the equipment now because the cost of money is too high in a year of poor sales, but with the understanding that purchase of the installed computer would be purchased next year. Or management could determine that such an acquisition would make more sense when the cost of capital dropped to 15%. Typically, in companies where cash and credit are in short supply, leasing with the option to buy (usually with accruals from a portion of the rent paid up to that moment of purchase) can be applied toward converting a lease to a purchase. Thus some computer companies allow their customers to buy installed equipment at a discount of up to 50% of the normal purchase price, depending on how long the device was installed. Such discounts are usually figured monthly, earned

Date: Purchase minus Lease	80-81	81-82	82-83	83-84	84-85	85-86
Before-tax outflow						
If purchased	−14,215	103,906	103,906	103,906	286,906	47,818
If leased	100,500	195,000	195,000	195,000	378,000	63,000
Delta between them	−114,715	−91,094	−91,094	−91,094	−91,094	−15,182
Cumulative		−205,809	−296,903	−387,997	−479,091	−494,274
After-tax outflow						
If purchased	−178,268	−87,044	−29,326	11,825	234,057	41,694
If leased	−39,095	8,873	8,873	8,873	191,873	31,979
Delta between them	−139,173	−95,917	−38,199	2,952	42,184	9,715
Cumulative		−235,090	−273,289	−273,337	−228,153	−21,439
25% present value						
After-tax cash flow	−126,279	−72,573	−23,380	1,037	15,764	3,243
Cumulative		−198,852	−222,232	−221,195	−205,431	−202,188

Figure 3–4. Sample cash flow difference between purchase and lease. (Remember: minus numbers indicate a desirable result because they represent money coming in as a result of an investment.)

cumulatively as a percentage of the total purchase price (usually about 50 to 60%), with about 40 to 60% of the monthly lease going toward accruals.

Leasing Arrangements: Trends and Case   Leasing arrangements for equipment are of essentially two types. The first is the lease offered by the manufacturer of data processing equipment (Honeywell, IBM, etc.), which their customers accept as is. They are operating leases and thus their costs are expensed annually by you the customer. The cost of carrying the inventory of leased equipment is borne by the vendor as part of its title of ownership. These leases typically range from one to four years, have accrual and purchase options, include certain limitations on price increases for the life of the lease, and may or may not pass ITC to the customer. Termination charges are imposed for breaking the lease; these are usually articulated in detail and thus the potential added expense is identified. Sometimes maintenance is covered in such leases, whereas in other circumstances it is an additional expense to the user of the equipment and covered by other agreements. It is typically the vendor lease that is measured against the option of simply purchasing equipment outright.

A more complicated type of lease that is still quite popular involves either a third-party financing a purchase lease-back or one in which an organization will buy the equipment and arrange its lease back to itself through a bank, investment group, or leasing company, in which case, knowing how that transaction is performed is important as a means of quantifying the cost of such an option. The best way to describe the process is to price a sample lease. (See Figure 3-5.)

Rent/Lease Checklist (Annual Costs)

	Option 1	Option 2	Option 3
1. Price for configuration			
a. Model	____	____	____
b. Control unit(s)	____	____	____
2. Minimum/maximum lease	____	____	____
3. Delivery dates	____	____	____
4. Interim costs	____	____	____
5. Termination charges			
a. When (by year)	____	____	____
b. Costs	____	____	____
c. Special provisions	____	____	____
6. Upgrade costs			
a. For features	____	____	____
b. For models	____	____	____
7. Downgrade costs			
a. For features	____	____	____
b. For models	____	____	____
8. ITC			
a. Amount	____	____	____
b. Which year earned	____	____	____
9. State property tax	____	____	____
10. Maintenance			
a. Your costs	____	____	____
b. Vendor	____	____	____
11. Purchase accruals			
a. Term	____	____	____
b. Percent	____	____	____
12. Transportaton cost	____	____	____
13. Installation expense	____	____	____
14. Power and air conditioning	____	____	____
15. Cables and supplies	____	____	____
16. Software support			
a. Operating system	____	____	____
b. Application	____	____	____
c. Product	____	____	____
17. Other expenses	____	____	____
18. Total period cost	____	____	____

Figure 3-5. Sample rent/lease costing form.

Assume that a particular computer will have a purchase price of $540,700 and that the cost of capital is 16% to cover a lease of 84 months, with ITC passing to the lessor. The residual value in this instance has been set at 20%. A specific set of steps are now taken.

First, the equipment purchase price of $540,700 is used to subtract from its pretax ITC, which in this case is $108,139, as determined by the tax laws, which state that for this category of equipment one can take 10% of after-tax dollars from the purchase price, leaving an actual gross purchase price of $432,560.

Second, this purchase amount must now be adjusted to take into account residual value remaining at the end of the 84 months. Since it is a future benefit, it will be discounted. For this case the reasonable amount of 12% was selected to apply against the 20% residual value. The formula for this is usually:

residual value % $\times$ present-value factor (drawn from a standard table)
= discount residual value %

Going to a standard table, we take 0.20 X 0.452 = 0.09. Now take the formula: gross amount less adjusted residual = net amount. In our case, this means taking $432,560 – ($540,700 X 0.09) = $383,900, which becomes the amount on which to figure the lease.

Third, to determine the monthly payment, take the net amount ($383,900) and the interest rate to be used (16%) to calculate the monthly payment required to liquidate this purchase price over 84 months. The formula used is:

net amount X annuity factor (drawn from a standard table)
= monthly payment

In this case the arithmetic is: $383,900 X 0.01960 = $7524 each month for the lease. Charts and tables help make the math simple, as does a hand calculator, but they are also confusing. The tables used above, for instance, are the same as those used by real estate dealers in determining house mortgages or used by banks. If you think of the calculation in those terms, the thought process becomes simpler to understand, because third-party leases typically are full-payout instruments that require complete amortization of the original purchase price. Use tables when possible, as they save time and reduce the calculations to a few minutes. Thus we looked for 16% on an annuity chart until we came to 84; the point where the two figures crossed was the 0.01960 factor used above in the calculations.

Now, armed with the amount of $7524 per month, we could add the cost of maintenance of the equipment and arrive at the total cash outflow for the computer. In this instance, maintenance was an additional $1000, bringing the total to $8524. As a good rule of thumb, tax deductions on expenses will cut the after-tax cash outflow to half the amount, or roughly $4260 per month on the company's books, although the data processing department will actually have paid out over $8000 per month.

Be aware that variations in any factor will affect the final amount. Sensitive factors such as time, amounts, or percentages have a significant influence on the numbers. The longer the period of time involved in the analysis, the lower the monthly pretax cash outflow should be. The same applies to lower interest rates or higher residual values. The shorter the period in question, the higher will be the numbers, but so too should be the residual values. Typically with computers, residual values should decline at between ½ and 1% of the original purchase price, with counting beginning when that generation of technology first was shipped by a manufacturer. Thus, applying this rule of thumb, a computer purchased for $500,000 and installed at the start of its generation (such as installing an IBM 370/138 in March 1977, when some of the earliest computers of this class were sent to customers) suggests that if sold two years later one might expect to find the market price about 24% less than the original price, or about $373,000. In effect, then, this computer would have cost the original owner about $127,000 (the difference in the two prices) plus any maintenance and interest charges incurred. If the total worked out to about $5000 per month (pretax) plus maintenance and interest, the after-tax cash outflow would have been quite low.

The calculations above indicate possibilities and rules of thumb, with assumptions that should be carefully weighed each time an analysis is done since circumstances keep changing. Yet it is obvious that certain kinds of variables should be kept in mind when analyzing financial alternatives.

Checklist of Key Variables

 (1) Length of time device will be kept
 (2) Length of time for each financial case
 (3) Interest rates and length of time they will be operative
 (4) Costs before and after taxes
 (5) Purchase price
 (6) Maintenance charges
 (7) Other expenses (ongoing and one-time)
 (8) Residual values
 (9) Discount factors
 (10) Benefits involving cash coming in or not going out (cost avoidance)
 (11) Legal terms and conditions of contracts, loans

Trends to Keep in Mind

Some general comments about trends currently evident in data processing hardware transactions help establish the value of various strategies illustrated above. The ITC makes the purchase of any equipment less expensive, and it appears that the U.S. Congress will not revoke that incentive in the immediate future because it encourages the acquisition of industrial equipment manufactured in the United States. Various tax incentives in Europe provide similar incentives. A second trend is the continuous flow of new equipment and technologies into the market, making some organizations leery of purchasing for that reason alone. However, with purchase prices declining, break-even with leasing is also shrinking, often hovering around three to four years, which matches the distance in time generally evident between the availability of current technology and newly anticipated ones.

Thus making a sincere effort to look at both leases and purchases remains a necessary exercise for smart financial planning. Smaller computers, such as micros, are usually available only for purchase, thus their amortization is predetermined by the fact that they cannot be leased. Because micros are undergoing significant change, with anticipated improvements in price performance, they should be purchased and depreciated rapidly (use double-declining-balance methods if possible, since they cause depreciation to occur quickly), while with larger minis and mainframes various alternatives can reasonably be considered. Remember that as a rough general rule, the larger the "horsepower" of a computer, the higher the percent of residual value it can be expected to have. So with small devices plan on minimal residual or salvage values. As programs and applications increasingly require more and more computer power, devices that we consider of a comfortable size today will within a few years be considered small and thus have fewer marketable features. This traditionally happens with the smallest members of a computer family and invariably within five to seven years. There is no evidence to suggest that this pattern will change in the immediate future. Some vendors have addressed this issue by providing owners of small computers with the capability of upgrading in the field the cycles and memory in their computers, thereby also ensuring that they will be obsoleted less quickly and that their residual values will remain stronger for a longer period of time.

The increasing population of used computer equipment means that more attention will be paid to this option over newer devices. There are several basic factors that companies look at when comparing new to older devices. To be sure, older units lease and sell for less because much of their original value has been amortized and discounted. In looking at such equipment, remember that maintenance costs are often higher than for newer devices, as are costs for electricity and air conditioning. Also, these units may lack certain features or not support more modern devices that may be of value to your organization. Also, certain software may not run on older units. On the other hand, they may be purchasable at lower rates, and in the case of extremely old units (IBM 360s and early members of the 370s, for example) may be acquired for just a few thousand dollars per month. Just remember that there are no bargains in data processing because demand still outstrips supply of equipment. One must look at the *total* cost of equipment to determine the difference between price (what a vendor charges for a device) and cost (the total cost required to operate it).

FINANCIAL STRATEGIES AND HOW THEY CAN SERVE AN ORGANIZATION

The comments made above lead to a more fundamental question: How can the acquisition of data processing hardware support the financial strategies of an organization? This question grows in importance as the amount of cash spent on such equipment rises each year.

Methodology

Organizations experienced in making judgments about industrial equipment invariably follow a methodology that is as relevant to computer acquisitions as it is to manufacturing machines, process control devices, or other indus-

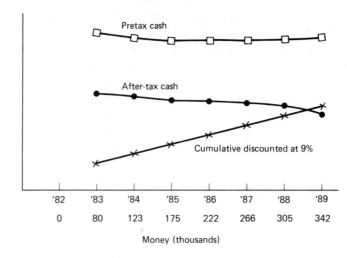

	'82	'83	'84	'85	'86	'87	'88	'89
	0	80	123	175	222	266	305	342

Money (thousands)

Figure 3-6. Relative impact of a lease decision from a number of points of view.

trial hardware. The process essentially involves developing several scenarios or options for the acquisition of hardware. These options range in quantity from as few as two to over ten, but in practice three or four make sense. Typical scenarios might include purchase outright from a vendor with the intent to keep for x number of years; lease over the same period of time; third-party lease-back; and lease with purchase later during the life of a lease contract. Other sets of scenarios might involve products from several different vendors. Thus option 1 might be to acquire x equipment from Honeywell; option 2, similar capacity from IBM; and option 3, equipment from Univac. A third set of options common in many organizations involve the way data can be processed. Thus a first option might involve establishing a stand-alone data center in a division to process its own work, a second to do the same at a corporate data center, a third to use a service bureau, and a fourth a combination of the first two. (See Figure 3-6.)

Second, once general options have been identified, the costs and benefits of each have to be developed. Typically, this involves four kinds of data:

1.   The actual pretax and posttax costs for an option, which would include the lease and/or purchase of equipment, maintenance, transportation, salaries, physical planning and site preparation, costs of software and training, and any other relevant expenditures directly associated with a particular scenario.

2.   The actual cash savings that would result from implementing a strategy. For example, if you were to set up your own computer and no longer communicate your work to a corporate data center, there would be a cash savings in telephone-line costs which would disappear together with

other expenses related to teleprocessing equipment no longer needed. Perhaps certain people would also no longer be required and could be transferred to other budgets.

3.   Soft cash savings which are identifiable and thus cannot be relegated to the nebulous world of "intangibles." Using the case of centralization versus decentralization, if you set up your own data center, any charges made to your division by the corporate data center for the use of central-site computers would disappear, thus saving the division some internal budgetary expenses. Since this cash flow is an internal transfer of budget amounts— "funny money"— and does not reflect a savings in hard cash flowing out of the total organization to other companies, it is not as valuable a savings because its elimination does not flow down in hard dollars as a benefit to the profit line. In fact, it could result in additional overhead at the corporate data center because a portion of its expenses could no longer flow out to be shared by the division. Yet the internal savings would be relevant to the division trying to set up its own data center.

4.   The last set of benefits involve cataloging those factors that have value but which managers are reluctant to quantify. These include a vast collection of circumstances that might typically be called "control," "ease of use," "convenience," "better morale," and "improved customer service"—in short, those benefits that would probably result in some fashion or another but are either not worth trying to quantify or simply do not lend themselves to exact measurement.

Once armed with documented scenarios, management is in a position to weigh the relative merits of each. Economics plays a critical influence in any decision, but so does politics. The latter influence can involve making sure that scenarios reflect the prejudices of particular individuals or organizations, but it can also mean making certain that the options support the overall strategies of an organization. Executive management and frequently upper middle management at this point are looking for a synthesis of financial thought that comes down to two basic factors. The first is to have the data processing options translated into such things as return on investment and payback so that a data processing proposal for investment of money can be compared to other proposals from the same organization for other projects: manufacturing expansion, additional sales personnel, research and development equipment. The second factor involves identifying what the impact of a data processing (or other) expenditure would be on the profit and loss statement, income statement, general ledger, and ultimately on the public books of the organization.

These are ways in which management formalizes any analysis of a project to ensure that it conforms to the objectives of the organization as a whole. Thus specific elements should be kept in mind when matching scenarios against company-wide guidelines and in the actual definition of the costs and benefits of options:

- Corporate financial hurdle rates (Is the minimum return on investment required being met?)

- Corporate policies (For example, is purchase allowed for equipment valued above or below a specified dollar amount?)

- Decision levels (If expensive enough, will the decision have to be made by the board of directors or just an executive vice-president? Who do you want to make the decision?)

- Data processing direction (Is the organization committed to a distributive processing plan? If so, does your proposal support or contradict this strategy?)

- Changes in the organization (Do you want to upgrade the computer installed in a division which management plans to close later this year?)

- Control issues (If control over data processing resides in one part of the organization, will your option threaten that control?)

- Documentation standards (Have your options been documented for decision making as required by specific company rules? Have the correct forms been filled out properly?)

- Management support (Have the key decision makers and the people who influence them been convinced to consider favorably the options in question?)

- Industry direction (Does a particular scenario take advantage of DP industry trends or those of the industry of which your company is a part?)

Although the list could be expanded considerably, these nine elements are traditionally the most important in influencing the development of various scenarios and thus should be kept in mind.

Relevant Issues in the 1980s

Any methodology for creating options in acquiring hardware has to take into account the types of factors mentioned in Chapter 1. Several major issues will influence decision making in the immediate future, and thus their potential costs and benefits should be briefly identified.

1.   *Centralization versus Decentralization.* This issue, perhaps the oldest concern of data processing strategists, has cycles of popularity in data processing. In the 1960s and 1970s, the costs of computers and the staffs required to operate and maintain them often dictated that the economies of scale clearly favored large central-site data processing. Standard arguments in

favor of this approach included economies of scale for mainframes, multiple uses of peripherals around the clock, the critical mass of expertise in people who would not have to be duplicated in various smaller data centers, and complexity of programming and systems maintenance. Counterclaims in favor of decentralization included local control over data processing, ease of use, relevant local applications, economies of scale (again), and a sense of progressive management of business.

In the past several years, however, several developments in the data processing industry have ensured that the struggle over centralization and decentralization will become more intense, with decentralization probably winning this time. Hardware costs have continued to drop for all devices from terminals through large mainframes, covering the entire spectrum of available equipment. Second, the complexity of programming and of systems programs has continued to decline as vendors bring out better operating systems targeted for use by individuals with less technical expertise than ever before, together with the continued spread in the use of high-level languages (e.g., APL, BASIC, and PL/1) by non-DP professionals. Systems are becoming easier to use and maintain, thereby increasing the possibility that fewer high-priced systems analysts and their management would be needed. Another factor is the availability today of larger quantities of application packages, which require little technical expertise to install, maintain, and use. In large part, these developments explain why many departments will acquire computing power without even contacting their data processing departments, using instead dedicated minis for specific tasks such as order processing, billing, or inventory control, and micros for financial modeling or engineering using Fortran or BASIC. (See Figure 3-7.)

Applications	Word processing
	Electronic mail systems
	Manufacturing
	Engineering graphics
	Text processing
Hardware configurations	Terminal networks
	Mainframes, minis, micros
	Distributive processing
	Application terminals
	Home computer systems
Software systems	Bigger/more comprehensive
	Operating systems
	On-line monitors
	Data bases
	Application packages
	Teleprocessing software
Technologies	Miniaturization
	Denser chips
	Lasers
	Magnetic bubbles
	Josephson devices

Figure 3-7. DP trends of the 1980s.

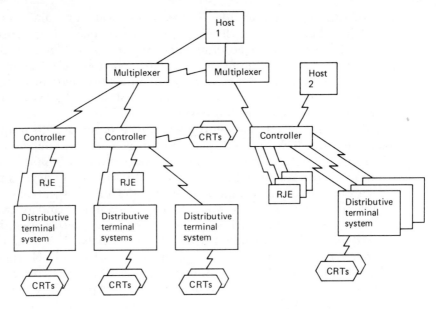

Figure 3-8. Sample distributive processing network. (Note: A variety of functions and machines are possible in such a top-down, integrated concept.)

The nature of hardware continues to change. Manufacturers of data processing equipment are selling more and better distributive systems than they did even two or three years ago. Intelligent terminals with memory and disk as well as more application code and an incredible growth in telecommunications capability has made it possible to distribute computing power at various levels of sophistication to all portions of an organization and at reasonable prices. Thus increasingly, it makes more sense to centralize only those functions that are required for corporate accounting and finance or which require massive quantities of large computing power, such as for engineers doing on-line design work or for financial analysts modeling the entire accounting and budgeting process of a company. Localizing applications that are unique to a division (such as manufacturing systems, order entry, local budgeting, and local programming) are an increasingly common phenomenon and account for the large increase and popularity with minis and micros, together with more rationale integrated networks with intelligent terminals that communicate across various portions of an organization. (See Figure 3-8.)

2. *Marriage of Software and Hardware.* As the costs of data processing personnel and clerical help increases while that of hardware declines, the economics and practicality of using more data processing will actually speed up, especially in application areas not really utilized in the past, such as word processing. Part of the ease of moving in this direction comes from simpler use of hardware. The single greatest cause of increased ease of use came from

the incorporation into hardware through microcode and software control of more functions that previously had to be performed by individuals. The first step in this direction was selling hardware with prewritten application code, such as that used by microprocessors to drive a papermaking machine or a metal press. Then came microcode (known also as *firmware*), which took many pieces of code from systems control programs or that originally had to be written by programmers using the system and making them part of the machine. For example, ten years ago a computer operator might have been required to tell the computer what job to run each time a task was to be performed. Today, whole series of jobs can be loaded in at one time and will run one right after the other or run simultaneously in various partitions without operator intervention. Another common type of development is the capability provided by firmware for a computer or other device to try and complete a job stream automatically after there had been some type of hardware failures, often without even notifying a human being that there had been a temporary problem. Logging these problems for later analysis either by field engineering personnel responsible for the upkeep of the equipment or for software persons to correct later is also part of the current trend in software developments for hardware use.

3. *Maintenance Activities.* Increasingly, equipment has fewer moving parts, less bulk, fewer pounds of iron, fewer feet of cables, and fewer screws and bolts to rust. Mechanical activities are increasingly being taken over by chips, which are becoming so inexpensive that several are frequently installed within a device where only one is necessary, so that if one fails an alternate does the job. This means that:

- Machines break down less frequently.
- Maintenance is often automated into the equipment itself.
- Vendor maintenance can, to a certain extent, be carried out remotely over telephone lines without visiting the device.

Thus hardware more frequently has diagnostic capability to identify its own problems. Maintenance personnel in another location can communicate with the device over telephone lines to determine problems and repair methods. In short, the general evolution of hardware and thus the ease of maintenance is clearly leading to increased reliability. Users can become more dependent on these devices to perform their normal daily work functions without as much fear of downtime on the equipment as true even five or ten years ago. This is not to suggest that hardware does not fail; it simply means that today's technology is doing it less frequently, and thus more groups within an organization can rely on devices secure in the knowledge that maintenance is actually improving. (See Figure 3-9.) And this is coming at a time when many vendors are looking for ways to automate maintenance and thus cut back on labor-intensive field engineering activities!

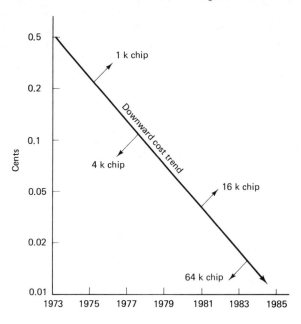

Figure 3-9. Trend in cost per bit at the chip level.

4. *Application Equipment.* Increasingly today, devices assigned to specific applications are appearing in the market which are cost effective and easy to use. Designed for a specific purpose, they make certain applications possible. Banking terminals that take deposits and issue money serve as one example. Word processing is perhaps the most obvious illustration. Industrial terminals that can tolerate acid heavy air in paper mills, dust particles in steel mills, and jolts in hot warehouses are common. Unique devices that have magnetic card strip readers and printers for distribution centers and as security units for buildings are also encouraging the use of more data processing hardware in a distributive fashion either with local micros, minis, or mainframes or through control of central-site computers. The ease of use frequently comes from application code written by a vendor marked concurrently with more reliable hardware. The net result is the availability of an increasing number and variety of units which are the by-product of computerized technology.

Changing Methods of Justification

Traditional issues of justification which have taken into account only the cost of capital, the purchase price of a device, its resale value, depreciation, and vendor maintenance are no longer accepted as covering the total spectrum of issues requiring analysis for any financial case. Cost performance and wider use of equipment, with their economies of scale, are only part of the story. More attention is paid today than ever before to other concerns, such as the amount of energy consumption, pollution, and the use of units in parts of the organization never before exposed to data processing. Each of these topics has rapidly altered the whole perspective on the process of justification. The introduction, for example, of IBM's 4300 series of computers together with those of other vendors, clearly suggested that justification of equipment would change if for no other reason than because the manufacturers were selling the devices differently, putting financial cases together with new factors strange to more classical situations. Thus the way older equipment was looked at also evolved if for no other reason than as a means of measuring what aging technology cost as compared to newer products. Identifying the *total* costs of one versus the other in new ways became relevant. Some examples illustrate current factors now becoming more common in any financial analysis.

For one thing, the cost of maintenance has gone down sharply with the latest technologies. A number of factors have accounted for this, and since they will continue to affect such expenses, they are worth listing:

- Decline in the number of mechanical parts in any given machine
- Increase in the use of chips to replace mechanical functions
- Expanded use of microcode to do problem determination and by-pass troubles
- Greater use of data banks with vast quantities of information on the troubles and problems of a particular device type
- Better diagnostic tools available to field engineers and user personnel

The relative value of such developments can quickly be illustrated. An IBM 370/145 might have cost $2000 per month to maintain in the late 1970s, while an IBM 4341 in the 1980s could cost as little as about $500 per month and yet cover a device that was much more powerful than the 145 and with four times the memory.

Some maintenance charges could be avoided by going to faster technologies. Thus if you have a computer operating three shifts, with maintenance on all of them, a faster device could perform the same amount of work in 18 hours rather than in 24 and would thus save on at least one shift of maintenance, dramatically so if you move from the technology sold in the 1970s to that of the 1980s. Maintenance costs on backup units could be reduced simply because today's devices probably do not warrant the costs.

The improved uptime suggests yet another area of justification. For example, if order entry clerks must work overtime each day that the computer to which their terminals are attached goes down, the dollar amount in overtime can be saved with more reliable equipment. The number of incidents in a year may be fewer than a dozen on older technologies, but the actual cash outflow can still be severe. If, for instance, an unscheduled downtime incident forces one dozen clerks to work an extra 2 hours per month at $7 per hour each, downtime costs $7 X 2 hours = $14 X 12 clerks = $168 per month X 12 months = $2016 per year, of what was probably unbudgeted money. Manufacturing plants that cannot receive their materials requirement plan (MRP) runs, or even worse the shop orders for the day, because the computer was down all night, wind up paying workers who do none of the anticipated work, resulting in tens of thousands of dollars in lost productivity. How many plant managers can afford that kind of an episode and still produce products profitably?

Energy Conservation

Energy costs can be a major source of savings. Computerized technology require electricity for two things: to run the device itself and for air conditioning. Although more will be said about energy in later chapters, the cost implications are relevant for review now. The 1980s technology uses anywhere from 50 to 80% less electricity than that of the 1960s or 1970s. This generalization applies as much to computers as to disks and terminals. In fact, old disk drives introduced in the early to mid-1960s use as much energy as some computers that were being installed in the mid-1970s. Smaller devices with fewer moving parts require decreasing amounts of electricity and put out less heat (fewer Btus), calling for less air conditioning. It also means they can more often be installed in normal office environments.

Looking at some samples illustrates the dramatic evolutions. A 4341 computer uses 80% fewer kilovolt-amperes (kVA) than a 360 Model 65. To quantify what savings can be gained, first calculate the number of kVA used by a particular device or configuration. Multiply the total kVA by 0.85 to translate your data into kilowatts, which is what electrical companies use to determine charges for electrical usage. Multiply the kW by the number of hours the system is running, then times the cost per kilowatthour (kWh) to establish a cost. Do the same for the proposed configuration and simply subtract the two totals to arrive at the potential savings per month. To make the exercise accurate, use vendor-supplied kVA and call your local electrical company for their rates on kWh (measured in the United States in cents and in most European countries as fractions of the metric currency). The entire process takes only a few minutes.

Suppose that a computer uses 40 kVa. Then 40 kVA × 0.85 = 34 kW × 200 hours (monthly use of our hypothetical device) = 5800 kWh per month. This total kWh × 16 cents/kWh rate (from the local electrical company charged to industrial customers near where one of the authors lives) = $928 per month in electricity to run the computer. Now add the costs of air conditioning (which in this case ran another $250 per month) and you arrive at a major cost consideration in any financial analysis. This is particularly so when you extend your cash flow out several years because of the rapid rise in the cost of electricity (15% was a common amount in many American communities in 1980 alone), suggesting that any equipment that uses 50% less would be most attractive.

Space savings can become another element. Newer equipment is simply much smaller than earlier units. A like-for-like function may in fact take less than 50% of the space required before. In more traditional computer system configurations, for example, whole refrigerator-sized units were required as tape and disk control units, power generators for computers, and stand-alone teleprocessing controllers, not to mention other teleprocessing equipment. A variety of currently available computers incorporate under their covers many of the functions originally performed by control units and in computers that take up only a bit more floor space than a large desk! Thus a number of possible scenarios are evident together with cash implications. If a data center is expanding rapidly, the acquisition of new devices may result in the avoidance of costs in expanding the computer room, implying savings of over $100 per square foot. New computer rooms for distributive processing may not have to be built at all (with typical savings ranging from $10,000 to over $100,000), since many devices can now operate in normal office environments. Units that do not require special conditions include most terminals, many micros and minis, some mainframes, intelligent devices with memory and cycles, and most new tape and disk drives. The decline in the construction of new computer rooms, or avoiding the expansion of existing ones with the associated expenses of more air conditioning, results in considerable savings. (See Figure 3–10.)

Outside time-sharing expenses can be looked at in fresh ways today. If the opportunity exists to take advantage of newer technologies over those of several years ago, identify what outside time-sharing expenses your organization has today and determine how much of that could come in-house assum-

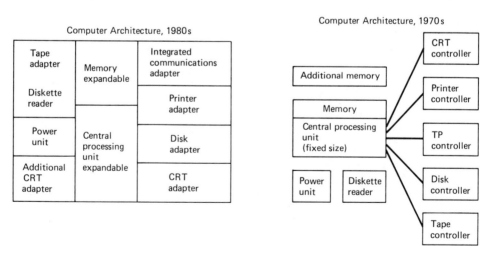

Figure 3-10. Computer architecture of the 1980s versus that of the 1970s. (Note: the trend toward integration of functions handled separately in the 1970s into newer mainframes as part of the computer in the 1980s.)

ing that hardware and software costs were not a problem. Then examine the costs of today's hardware for the amount of equipment it would take to support the time sharing brought in. There will be surprises for all involved in many cases. Just within the past three years the sharp cost declines in computing power of a size that could absorb a particular organization's outside time-sharing load has made it possible to consider alternatives not thought to be feasible earlier. Vendors who could not provide a big enough computer before at a cost-effective price are now identifying marketing opportunities for them, which become ways for you to save money.

Today it is possible, for example, to have a powerful computer system (with large amounts of disk, two tape drives, a raft of software, and on-line computing) for less than $10,000 per month which would have cost—for the same capability and capacity—$40,000 per month five years ago. At $40,000 very few organizations feel they have enough potential outside time sharing to go through the exercise of trying to bring it in-house. At $10,000

Summary of Monthly Budget Costs

	Present System	Option 1	Option 2
Lease/budget charge for deprec. (computer and peripherals)	$	$	$
Energy			
Electricity for hardware	$	$	$
Air conditioning	$	$	$
Maintenance on hardware			
First shift	$	$	$
Second shift	$	$	$
Third shift	$	$	$
Weekends	$	$	$
Idle personnel at downtime (__hr at $___/hr)	$		
Other expenses	$		
Space (avoidable expansion)	−$	−$	−$
Personnel			
First shift (__at $__/month)	$	$	$
Second shift (__at $__/month)	$	$	$
Third shift (__at $__/month)	$	$	$
Other (__at $__/month)	$	$	$
Taxes (type_____)	$	$	$
Insurance	$	$	$
Systems software cost	$	$	$
Systems software maintenance	$	$	$
Outside time sharing coming In	−$	−$	−$
Application benefits	−$	−$	−$
Grand totals (pretax)			

Note: Present all sums as dollar amounts per month before tax/finance taken into account. Resale of equipment should be entered in benefit row under "application benefits."

Figure 3-11. Sample form for collecting total costs of three options.

per month, single time-sharing users or departments could have dedicated systems, save money over current time-sharing expenses, and have additional capacity for even more computing without necessarily adding any more costs.

Figure 3-11 is a sample form that could be used as a model for creating one in your organization to help collect quickly the costs of existing computing as compared to some newer option. This or a variation relevant to your institution can quickly call attention to the need to review periodically what a system *really* costs in light of continued availability of better hardware at more attractive prices and as netted against the rising cost of people. Such an exercise can also be conducted to measure the true costs of current systems against third-party offers for much older and seemingly less expensive hardware.

Although the methodology implied by Figure 3-11 is relevant for all types of data processing hardware, the cash impact is most striking with mainframes and current disk and least so with micros and terminals. Since some minis will cost thousands of dollars per month, the formal exercise of costing them out in detail is usually a worthwhile one.

INPUT/OUTPUT DEVICES AND TERMINALS

Primary focus in this chapter so far has been on computers, since they still represent the single most expensive piece of data processing hardware. Yet most of the comments made about computers are relevant for other types of I/O equipment, including all classes of terminals and associated teleprocessing devices, along with the discussions about financial analysis. But with the cost of computers, minis, and micros dropping, the percentages of total hardware costs for peripherals and terminals are going up. Thus a total hardware system that in the 1970s might have leased for $40,000 per month might have consisted of about $20,000 for mainframe and the rest for peripheral devices. Today the same computing power would probably result in a cash flow of some $5000 for the computer and another $10,000 for peripherals and software. Chargeable code (such as the operating system) that cost nothing or little in the 1970s could today account for a third of the total system charge. Thus acquisition and costing strategies for noncomputer equipment is important to develop, especially since many companies are only just beginning to realize that their money is being spent in ways far different than those of even five years ago.

In Chapter 1 some general comments about trends in hardware were made that are worth reviewing briefly here. It was suggested that the variety of terminals was increasing together with their function and cost, although, like other data processing equipment, its expense (both lease and purchase amounts) was declining per unit. It was also argued that classical elements of a system, such as disk and tape drives, would grow in usage and thus in number installed, but that their costs would continue downward on a box-for-box basis, dramatically so for disk. The question to be answered now is what such trends suggest to companies trying to maximize price/performance on a timely basis.

Disks

Increasingly, data processing management is coming to the conclusion that a variety of data storage medium are required in their data centers. The cost to store a word of information in machine-readable form varies by device type, on those that are leased versus purchased, from diskette to disk to tape, and in mass memory units. Therefore, management is being frequently called upon to establish general guidelines on what types of data will be stored on which devices. One of the by-products of such policy setting should be a set of financial strategies that call for opinions about how long certain devices will remain in the organization and how they will be used.

Most of the major publications in the data processing world have at one time or another carried articles about the hierarchies of data storage, and vendors of disk and tape drives have also made presentations to their customers about similar subjects. It is becoming a finely defined exercise in large companies to create a strategy for storage. Thus the subject is worth a chapter or more of a book. Suffice it here to make a general statement as to how they affect financial game planning. Batch jobs are traditionally tied to tape and disk usage, while backup for long-term storage continues to be on tape. With the introduction of mass storage devices that hold billions of bytes of data, the cost of tape medium becomes more questionable with each new DASD announcement by major vendors.

On-line work (which in most shops is increasingly the majority of the work load) is always disk oriented. But the choice is between removable disk and fixed devices. Fixed units (whose packs cannot be removed from the drive) are less expensive per byte and consequently are being installed more frequently than ever before. A by-product of this trend is the increased practice of leaving more data on-line all the time rather than removing packs when others wish to use the drive. With more on-line systems being used, DP management is being given little choice but to leave data up on disk more often anyway. This trend eliminates the confusion of keeping track of what packs are up at any given moment and also reduces the number of personnel required to staff a data center because less human effort is spent with disk.

Thus companies with dozens of disk drives working over several shifts per day could probably move to nonremovable units, save on personnel cost and effort (at 1980's salary levels that is not an insignificant benefit), and saving on the cost of DASD while even increasing their capacities. The savings of one person alone is probably worth $1500 per month in total costs. For that kind of money a company could acquire on-line storage for more than 500 million bytes of data! Think of how many on-line systems could be supported by that with their benefits to the organization overall. Also, a shift to fixed units can save easily 20% of the cost of leased disk with removable disk drives while also saving on the cost of expensive disk packs.

Essentially, there are two issues to address if DASD is to be expensed properly. First, what will the units be used for? If primarily for small batch jobs, perhaps removable units used heavily with tape might make sense. If the volume of these jobs is not anticipated to increase sharply over the next few years, purchase of these units probably makes sense even in light of new technologies available, although a comparison of both should be made. Active, on-line applications suggest that fixed medium becomes the more attractive option for a number of reasons:

- Fixed devices have more capacity.
- Data must be available all the time.
- Data centers just cannot be interrupted by the hassle of switching packs all the time.
- The fixed units are more reliable performers and are less apt to break down than are the older units.
- They are cheaper than removable units.

Moreover, if the amount of data that must be kept on-line keeps increasing sharply (and it is in most companies), management will probably opt for leases while taking advantage of new technologies as they are introduced. Smart managers will learn to run shops with two or more types of technologies, some of them leased and others purchased, thereby in fact developing a hierarchy of storage medium and policies governing their use.

A second essential issue involving DASD inevitably comes down to measuring the cost of storing one piece of information in any of a variety of possible configurations. Typically, the bottom denominator conveniently used by many is the cost per 1 million bytes of data. Although the permutations are varied, the 1 million byte yardstick seems fairly common and thus is often used in financial cases. Measuring the costs of one configuration over another is not a difficult thing to do either.

Suppose it has been determined that a data center must store on-line an average of 800 million bytes of data (not a large amount these days) and over a period of five years (for purposes of building financial cases). Vendor A has suggested that you lease a DASD, each spindle of which stores 70 million bytes and leases for $900 per month for every set of two spindles. That means having 11 spindles (probably 12, since most come in pairs) at a total cost of $5400 per month. Add to this some expense for disk packs, at least 12 and probably more, since you would want backup packs. These little devices may cost $80 per month each. But even leaving them out of the analysis for the moment, the drives alone would result in a cost of $6.75

per million bytes. If these same devices were purchased when they were installed and kept for five years, the costs would be different. Assume that a purchase versus lease analysis was made and that instead of costing $5400 per month, the financial analyst has done all the correct arithmetic. Now the cost is down to $4000 per month. Now the cost of 1 million bytes of storage would be about $5.00 plus whatever expense would be for the disk packs.

Now vendor B comes along and proposes a newer technology that could support the required amount of data on fewer devices (fixed pack) at a lease price of $3800 per month. Purchase would obviously bring that number down lower. Now in either situation proposed by vendor B, the cost per million bytes has gone down even more and this time there is no additional charge for disk packs. Also, in all probability, the configuration would probably allow for more then 800,000 million bytes of storage. The difference in scenarios just described essentially illustrates the technology sold in the late 1970s and that now being made available to DP management.

Yet there can be disadvantages in each proposal, which unfortunately does not always make it easier to rush out and acquire one type of unit over another. For example, if the newer devices can only work off a new computer, the financial analysis requires that one consider replacing the main-frame—not a bad idea if the better half of your costs are in peripherals anyway. Control units provide another situation with gray factors. If vendors A and B each required control units in addition to their disk costs, the cost per million bytes goes up, probably substantially. It is quite possible that vendor A's control unit might only support its proposed disk drives, while vendor B's could allow attachment not only of the new technology but also a second string which could be older technology, probably purchased a while back and planned for continued use for a few more years (in all probability with some depreciation left to take place). Furthermore, vendor B's control unit might have some diagnostic capabilities not in vendor A's box which could improve uptime and identify problems on the mainframe's channel to the disk drives.

Thus a little common sense, some financial analysis, and a few technical questions asked can save a lot of problems and lead quickly to a sensible strategy. In any situation, however, make sure that the following factors have been considered thoroughly:

- Age of the technology(ies) involved
- Control units and their functions
- Anticipated growth requirements for DASD
- Current limitations due to technical features (e.g., compatibility with installed DASD)
- Conversion costs
- Current contractual and financial obligations

Applying the suggestions made earlier in this chapter to the financial aspects of DASD acquisitions, together with keeping the foregoing six issues in mind, will lead to clearer thinking about the role and cost of disk in your organization.

Tape Drives

Increasingly, the amount of tape work is declining as a total percentage of a data center's costs. Even the length of running time for major batch jobs (such as payroll or MRP for manufacturing) is being reduced as much of this work is shifted over to DASD. At some point, disk storage will become far less expensive than tape, but the next few years at least will continue to see widespread use of tape drives. It is being relegated more, however, to backup functions. Thus demand for tape technology is leveling off and may account for the relatively few technological developments in tape over the past few years compared to what has happened in disk. Yet this is not to say there have been no interesting developments. Tape drives can be acquired that run from a slow 80 kilobytes to those easily ten times as fast and units that pack data on tape from a density of 800 bits per inch (bpi) to 6250 bpi. As computers become faster, the need for faster tape drives grows while the slower units are being relegated to such configurations as remote intelligent terminals as backup for disk or to minis and micros that do not require high-speed devices. A number of other advances have been apparent just within the past several years that match trends with other devices:

- Smaller boxes taking up less space
- Units requiring less electricity and air conditioning, thus reducing operating costs
- Fewer moving parts, thereby simplifying maintenance while reducing the chance of downtime
- Shrinking lease and purchase prices

Measuring the value of one tape drive over another is often easier than with disk. The unit of measurement is not how many bytes of data are stored on tape drives (since storage is done on tapes and not on drives) but rather by how many units (drives) are needed to run a series of jobs concurrently on a computer. Operations managers are becoming smarter in their use of resources. One of the more common strategies today is to run concurrently as few jobs as possible that require tape. Thus if two jobs each needing two tape drives ran concurrently, four drives would be required. Yet the same jobs run at different times would reduce the need for drives in half. Properly balanced work loads in the computer can actually decrease the need for tape drives.

Because there is less technological change with tape drives, simple lease versus purchase type of analyses often suggest that the purchase of installed

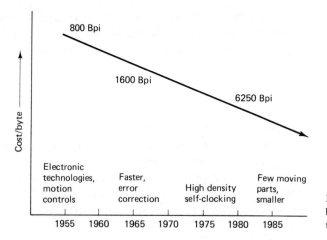

Figure 3-12. Trend in cost to store 1 byte of data on tape over time on ½-inch tape.

units or of new ones when they are attached to your configuration makes sense, especially is they are to be in the organization for four years or more. The break-even between lease and purchase tends to be longer than with other devices, simply reflecting the purchase/lease ratios of devices priced out by vendors in the 1970s. (See Figure 3-12.)

Terminals

Terminals vary so much and their population is growing so fast that any general comments about financial strategies are difficult to develop and deserve a page of qualifiers and disclaimers. Yet there are some general comments worth mentioning, some rules of thumb that continue to have relevance in the 1980s and grew out of the experiences of the 1970s.

1.   CRTs (monochrome or color) will probably stay in your organization longer than anyone originally thought. Thus it would, in many cases, pay to purchase these units and treat them much like typewriters. As such applications as word processing and user on-line programming increase along with more traditional terminal-based uses of the computer, the demand for terminals will ensure that there will be a need for them somewhere. In fact, some marginally justifiable projects may develop into sound business proposals precisely because already installed purchased terminals, which now cost less per month than leased units, could be used for such applications. New terminals could then be assigned to applications that are easier to justify. Although maintenance costs (as a percent of overall purchase or lease expense) remain high compared to those of nonterminal equipment, they are worth it in locations that have few terminals and thus need to use every device possible. Those locations that have extra units might be able to avoid having to spend money for monthly maintenance contracts, paying instead for service when needed, especially if the units are very reliable in the first place.

2.   CRT control units are undergoing radical technological changes as vendors increasingly add diagnostic capability to them, providing for increased throughput performance on higher-speed lines, SNA/SDLC teleprocessing support, the ability to use new devices, terminals, and color CRTs, and attachment to recently introduced intelligent processors and micros. Thus with such volatility, in the past two years alone, many organizations have turned over many of the old control units, replacing them with newer devices, with many being leased. The question of purchase or lease remains tied to the more fundamental issue of how long a unit is planned to be installed.

3.   Intelligent terminal systems (including processors, terminals, printers, card I/O, etc.) should be looked at much like data center computers and peripherals. Going through purchase versus lease options makes good practical sense, particularly since there are an increasing variety of vendor and leasing options for financing the cost of these units. Some of the more recent offerings include quantity discounts on purchase and lease, expanded use of rental accruals, and upgrade capability to larger units within a lease. What many of these arrangements have done is to encourage management to distribute applications of a common type across ever-expanding networks with commonality of equipment. Thus using intelligent systems or minis to put the same set of applications in a dozen warehouses within one company as one application looks more attractive in this kind of environment than ever before. Of course, to take full advantage of the technology now available for this kind of data processing and to maximize the yield on terms and conditions designed for such environments, there is a premium placed on good planning with a solid strategy in place for distributive processing in three areas: hardware, software, and applications. Without that, costs will be high, confusion the norm, and there will be serious application problems for all.

4.   Make sure that any intelligent RJE or processor-based system supports high-speed Bysnch and/or SNA line speeds. Increasingly, devices are becoming faster. Thus units that support speeds of 7200 or 9600 baud or faster are more likely to be in use in the years to come than those running at 2400 or 4800 baud. The resale value of purchased equipment will be pushed downward if the items in question operate on slower lines. Moreover, those excluded from such current disciplines as SNA networks will also be less attractive because they cannot take full advantage of more modern telecommunications technologies rich in function. Other competing line disciplines will also demand greater capability in the area of teleprocessing functions of terminals, copiers, and so on.

5.   Given a choice between acquiring older technology and the newer, opt for the latter if at all possible, for the same reasons as for a computer. They are less expensive than older ones (usually about 25% or more over

predecessors as a rough rule of thumb) and have a host of new functions that increase productivity in programming or in application richness. Again, the logic is much the same as for a new computer over older ones.

6.   With distributive intelligent terminals, make sure that the vendor can support these units with maintenance personnel located near each of your potential sites. Nothing can be worse than buying a bunch of devices from a salesperson in New York for installation in rural parts of the country, only to find out later that the maintenance personnel operate primarily out of far-away major cities and thus take too long to get to your terminals. Make sure that your vendor has a strategy in place to support migration from earlier generations of devices and has a software plan so that the programs you write for these units today will not have to be scrapped several years from now and rewritten. Remember, programming, whether for a computer or an intelligent terminal, should not simply be a one-time expense but must increasingly be treated as an investment because of the substantial cost it entails.

7.   Finally, develop a rational company-wide strategy for the use of terminals so that questions of compatibility across networks and devices can be addressed, issues concerning line costs examined, and data security properly handled. Point seven has been the subject of many books by itself. Suffice it to say here, however, that with integrated networks supporting multiple devices and types of terminals, hanging off shared lines with complex TP software controlling them, costs can be cut sharply or held down to controllable levels with the use of some common sense and a degree of organization.

INSTANT FINANCIAL ANALYSIS

Since management is being asked increasingly to perform at least some elementary financial analysis on the acquisition of peripherals, a quick method should be employed which takes little time and can be done with minimal effort. After such a first attempt at the numbers, more detailed analysis can be prepared if appropriate and with some scenarios in mind that the initial math suggested would be beneficial. We have already seen how to determine break-even on a purchase versus lease situation. Since many devices are purchased, a cash flow analysis spread over the life of the device in your organization, including the tax impact, is needed next. Figure 3-13 illustrates a simple formula that factors taxes, depreciation, and cash flow. In fact, a worksheet with fill-in blanks could be drawn up and distributed to all those who would have a need to cost out hardware, whether data processing or other. Such forms, when completed, can be kept on file as a partial record of the financial logic for why and how a device was required.

Figure 3-14 illustrates the output of an analysis on the purchase of CRTs

1.   Cost to lease equipment per year
2.   Depreciation — total cost ⑪ ÷ estimated life at
     1/2 year first year and full years thereafter
3.   Investment tac credit __% × cost ⑪
4.   Income before taxes ① − ② − ③ = ④
5.   Tax at statutory rate ④ × 0.50 = ⑤
6.   Net income ④ − ⑤ = ⑥
7.   Add depreciation ②
8.   Cash in ⑥ − ⑦ = ⑧
9.   Cash out: cost of maintenance
10. Cash flow ⑧ − ⑨ = ⑩
11. Original cost of investment
12. Balance ⑩ − ⑪ = ⑫

Figure 3-13. Formula   for   hardware
financial analysis.

using the formula. In this case the life of the investment was four years. Federal and state taxes were combined to reach the 50% figure shown, and depreciation was a simple straight line. It is important to lay out the results across each year so that if a particular budget is to be charged, it will be done in appropriate amounts annually. Moreover, since accounting people will want to total the depreciation of this project together with all others to come up with the gross annual depreciation amount for tax and public books, the exercise has to be conducted anyway. Better that it be done initially by someone who knows the costs of the units than to find out later that through some misunderstanding, your department was charged the expense of full purchase this year. It happens all the time. Moreover, if straight-line depreciation makes the project too costly, you at least know to go through more formal math to find alternative depreciation methods that reduce the cost at those times during the life of the device when you can least afford expenses.

There is usually no need to develop an instant financial analysis on the rental or lease of equipment because that is simply a hard cash outflow out of this year's budget, of which 46% is deductible from U.S. federal taxes as a business expense. The data, in short, are straightforward and only need

	Year			
	1	2	3	4
Savings	23,856	23,856	23,856	23,856
Depreciation (4 yr)	3,626	7,252	7,252	7,252
Investment tax credit	-	-	-	-
Income before taxes	20,230	16,604	16,604	16,604
Tax @ 50%	10,114	8,302	8,302	8,302
Net income	10,116	8,302	8,302	8,302
Depreciation	3,626	7,252	7,252	7,252
Cash in	13,742	15,554	15,554	15,554
Cash out (maintenance)	2,796	2,796	2,796	2,796
Cash flow	10,946	12,758	12,758	12,758
Cost of investment	29,012	-	-	-
Balance	(18,066)	12,758	12,758	12,758

Figure 3-14. Financial analysis of installed CRTs purchased (dollars); see Figure 3-13.

financial manipulation if they are part of a project for some application that involves balancing the costs of doing it against some anticipated benefits or capital appropriation. However, since all organizations want to track what the total cash amount of their contractual obligations are, especially publicly held companies which have to report all their commitments, departments signing contracts for leases would have to keep a total of their obligations—reporting that is usually done as part of the normal budget process. If it is not, a simple log or file with all hardware contracts should be kept from which running totals on contracts can be added up quickly for this year, next year, and so on, and only when needed.

SOFTWARE INFLUENCES ON HARDWARE COSTS

In the past two years alone, a dramatic shift has taken place in the total cost of in-house computing for intermediate-size systems. Vendors have separated the cost of software (mainly systems control programs) and maintenance from the lease and purchase of hardware. Similar patterns of financing minis is evident and is also apparent with large computer systems. But clearly this trend is most evident in intermediate-size computer installations, where the percent of expense for software and maintenance is the highest. The smaller the computer system, the greater the portion of total cost that goes toward the mainframe, while in large shops with banks of peripherals the percent of expense going toward mainframes is less. Software costs and maintenance are usually tagged to a mainframe, and thus in smaller shops they are the greatest. A few examples illustrate the impact and are presented to make it patently clear that a new pattern of DP expenses is emerging that will have to be understood and budgeted for in the years to come.

    Take as an example one computer, a printer, a card reader, a card punch, four disk drives, a disk control unit, four tape drives, a tape drive control unit, ten CRTs, their control unit, and a small printer for the programmers. In our case, the computer leases for $7000 per month, all the other hardware for $15,560. The software to run in this system (systems control program; compilers for RPG, Cobol, BASIC, and APL; sort/merge, a fast copy package, and a data base manager together with CICS/VS and no application program packages) comes to a total of $4000. Software maintenance totals an additional $1000, and second and third shift maintenance on the computer adds another $400 per month. Thus our totals are:

Computer lease	$ 7,000
Peripherals lease	15,560
Software lease	4,000
Software maintenance	1,000
Hardware maintenance	400
Total system cost	$27,960 (pretax)

Of the total of $27,960, hardware represented 80% of all expenses, software roughly 14%, and maintenance 6%. Two years ago the more typical ratio would have been 90% hardware and close to 10% for software, with no maintenance charges on either leased hardware or on software (or very little). The same raw computer power two years ago would have cost a great deal more, too. The computer (today's technology at $7000) would have leased for about $19,000 per month.

The example detailed above was a real situation (as of this writing) and had gone through the classic evolution from more expensive computer power to less costly power and saw a shift described above in the number of dollars spent on hardware out to the software portions of the budget. In that particular installation, DP management has now created a separate line item within the budget for systems software and maintenance and another for application packages—symbols of the changing economics of the data processing industry.

The pattern can be further identified by illustrating a slightly larger DP shop. Take the same software as above, the next-size-larger computer, and twice the number of DASD. The numbers falling out of that budget are:

Computer lease	$25,000	
Peripherals lease	19,812	
Software lease	4,000	
Software maintenance	1,300	(tied to size of computer)
Hardware maintenance	1,500	
Total system cost	$51,612	(pretax)

Of this total, all hardware represented about 87% of the expense, software roughly 8%, and all maintenance 5%. Note that the larger system had a higher percent of costs still associated with hardware but that software was not a minor cost. If software occupies the degree of importance in the budget in the larger shop as it does today in smaller ones, a considerable amount of money will be diverted from equipment to software in the immediate future. The key point to keep in mind is that software and maintenance costs are increasing as a percent of the total costs of running a system and that therefore, when determining the costs of hardware, attention should also be focused on these other expenses. No longer can we look at a computer lease tag and exclaim: "Wow, only $7000 a month!" That is too myopic a view today. The total cost of the computer, software, and maintenance still makes the system far more attractive than equivalent power and software of the 1970s, but to understand true costs, each component must be seen simultaneously. (See Figure 3-15.)

Increasingly, data processing budgets have seen hardware costs decline as percentages of all expenses, while new categories have been identified and expanded on—software maintenance, charges for leasing system control programs, maintenance on hardware leases, different types of distributive equipment leases—making it necessary to educate management on the shift-

	Smaller System Costs (%)	Larger System Costs (%)	Degree of Change (%)
Computer lease	25	48	+23
Peripherals	56	38	−18
Software lease	14	8	−6
Software maintenance	4	3	−1
Hardware maintenance	1	3	+2
	100	100	

Figure 3-15. Percent differences in the cost of various systems from a small to a larger system, with percent differences of the larger over the smaller systems.

ing trends in budget dollars. At the same time, the number of software packages that could be purchased and thus be amortized exactly like hardware has also gone up. Thus it is becoming possible to treat software financially much like any industrial equipment. Clearly, then, the shift in the ratio of the total cost of hardware to software represents one of the most fundamental changes in the economics of data processing to appear in the past three years. Books dealing with software management and cost control already discuss the kinds of issues being treated in this volume. Because the shift is relatively new, it is too early to chart the relative cost of hardware and software in relation to each other. But the trend is clear and unmistakable. Therefore, when cost-justifying hardware, new questions must be asked. For the sake of convenience we have grouped them together in a checklist.

Checklist of Hardware Justification Questions

(1) What are the hardware maintenance costs for lease/purchased equipment?

(2) What are the software lease prices and maintenance charges?

(3) Do software costs end after a certain period of time if purchased (if leased), and if so, by how much and when?

(4) What are the terms and conditions of maintenance and lease contracts for both hardware and software?

(5) What, if any, are the installation charges?

(6) What price increase provisions are there in hardware, software, and maintenance contracts?

(7) If I change the computer in my configuration, do my software lease and maintenance expenses change also? If so, by how much? And does that extend the life of any existing contract?

(8) Will the tax law allow my organization to take the ITC on software? (This may become a relevant issue in the years to come, although not at the time of this writing.)

(9) If I have multiple computers within a data processing center or distributed off a host much like intelligent terminals, do I pay for

the extra copies of the software used? Are there any discounts involved? How is maintenance charged and handled for such an environment?

(10)   If I have multiple computer systems, do hardware maintenance costs change for the second, third, or more mainframes?

(11)   What provisions are there for quantity discounts on lease or purchase of other equipment?

In short, many of the questions traditionally asked about hardware must be modified to include the whole issue of software expenses which in the past might have been looked at separately from considerations regarding equipment.

CONCLUDING SUGGESTIONS

In this chapter we have emphasized how hardware justification can be performed while taking advantage of recent trends in price/performance within the range of new products. There are some points to keep in mind constantly, however, regardless of changing technologies or costs. First, since most organizations grossly underestimate their capacity requirements, more attention must be paid to the issue. Quantum jumps in capacity of all types is more the norm than atypical. Linear growth really does not take place if for no other reason than computers and related peripherals can usually be upgraded only in quantum fashion. Therefore, justification must account for the realities of capacity growth and their associated increased or decreased costs. It is not uncommon, for instance, to see computer power growing in companies by 40% each year rather than by the 10 to 15% that many still plan for. Terminals represent another area of miscalculation. Very few organizations have as many CRTs as they need and thus they are constantly waiting for delivery. This underestimation also goes far toward explaining why so many vendors have developed enormous lead times on CRTs—their customers try to acquire terminals in spurts rather than planning needs and ordering in a more rational, even fashion. Disk requirements present another source of gross miscalculation, perhaps the worst, because capacity in this area is probably the least understood. Clearly, any organization that does not have a strategic plan for its on-line data storage requirements will spend money foolishly and, more serious, may not have enough capacity when it is needed. On-line applications can deteriorate as a consequence; so can completion of new services from data processing. Therefore, determine how long you want to stay with a particular generation of technology, how it will be used, and look at a number of financial scenarios with which to pay for these units.

Never before in the history of data processing has there been so much flexibility regarding contractual obligations on hardware. Prior to the 1980s, for example, computer commitments had to be for a minimum of four years and in many instances ranged up to seven and ten years, which placed a tremendous burden on management to do a good job in capacity planning. In some cases, as managers got toward the end of a long lease, application growth was inhibited even when the services were cost-justified simply because of a lease. Talk about a tail wagging a dog! Today, computer contracts are typically two-year commitments with some four-year arrangements still evident. Peripherals are universally leased at two-year terms, whereas purchases involve three- and four-year periods. In short, there is greater flexibility to change devices, but at the same time, the need for capacity planning and a DP hardware strategy remains an acute requirement because so much money is being spent on so many pieces of equipment. Micros and minis are primarily still sold as "purchase-only" items, which therefore require a more traditional commitment such as we would have made in the 1960s and 1970s. Yet newer devices with more program support, often dedicated to some specific application, make decisions in this area still reasonable to arrive at and in fact will increasingly be made as more units appear on the market.

Strange and wonderful devices are coming onto the market that were simply science fiction five and ten years ago. These include laser printers, optical scanning devices, magnetic card readers and printers, bubble memory disk, fiber optics, and computers with incredible capacities built into denser chips. Thus the pressure for flexibility will continue to be evident in many acquisition strategies. The use of such new devices will grow along with specialized units for use in word processing, electronic mail, more automated manufacturing facilities, and in telecommunications. Since there is a trend toward shorter leases, management will find it easy contractually to try many of these new technologies at a fairly low cost. However, to capitalize properly on these new pieces of equipment, organization-wide plans for their use will have to be drawn up together with the justification for new applications.

For instance, electronic mail applications are useless within one department and make sense only if used by the entire organization, thereby cutting down sharply on paperwork and postal expenses. Developing an inventory control system using magnetic stripe readers and printers for one warehouse does not make as much sense financially either as installing the application in all the warehouses and tying them together into a central data base for consolidation reporting to management or as a means of communicating to various locations what inventory is available, where, at any given time, especially if this is carried to its logical and practical conclusion of being tied into an order entry and allocation system. Each of these examples imply a commitment that lasts for years beyond normal contractual obligations on equipment and in fact determines the way an organization will function. Traditional capacity planning, DP strategic planning, and ultimately financial planning remain critical in the acquisition and use of data processing hardware.

Once it has been determined what devices to use and how many, and the necessary cost justification completed, the next area of concern is its proper installation. Chapter 4 deals with this critical issue, showing how best to accomplish this without upsetting cost expectations or plans for the use of hardware.

Damn the torpedoes—full speed ahead!

David G. Farragut

Nothing is more frustrating or so reflects poor management as an inferior hardware installation. This chapter spells out in detail how to configure equipment, manage the development of an installation plan that an organization can live with, and select systems which assure that what is proposed will actually run. It also describes how to avoid problems and cost overruns by having DP personnel and users work together. Finally, comments applicable to most types of installation activity are presented.

CHAPTER FOUR

Installing Equipment

Increasingly, the number of devices being installed in any organization is expanding, placing more pressure on all involved to manage the installation process better. Today, responsibility for making sure that equipment goes in properly is being shared more often by DP departments *and* users. Hardware is being placed in every type of office and building, while the variety of units involved is multiplying, therefore requiring the skills and managerial authority of a variety of people. Vendors are constantly introducing new products into their markets which no longer require technical personnel to install, at the same time that data centers continue to add more devices to support their major applications. It is not unusual today, for example, to see a company with annual sales of about $500 million, and active in data processing, installing a minimum of several devices per week or doubling the traffic on a teleprocessing network in the course of a year. Thus, more than ever before, the question of how best to install equipment efficiently is being asked, and not just by vendors and DP managers; general management and user department heads are involved today. Thus the need exists for a manager's primer on how to manage the installation process. For without effective management of this growing activity, the potential costs due to poorly run installations can grow. This chapter is not intended as a technical dissertation on how to hook up cables, nor is it a training manual on operating equipment. Rather, it discusses how to manage the resources that are required and responsible for installing equipment in a smooth and cost-effective manner. If anything, equipment is becoming easier to install; the problem addressed below is how to install more of it, properly, than ever before.

CONFIGURING HARDWARE

Because of the enormous variety of hardware products available today, each with numerous possible configurations of features, sizes, and functions, it is imperative to pay close attention to defining exactly what is needed. A number of issues are always involved:

- Function
- Interface with other devices
- Financial considerations
- Physical planning
- Usage

Each of these topics in one fashion or another must be addressed when configuring hardware, whether it is merely a terminal or an entire computer system. The process is exactly the same in either extreme.

Clearly, the first and most obvious consideration is function. What will the device be used for? Often, detailed consideration of this issue is lacking, with the result that hardware comes in incapable of performing to expectations. Some simple yet common examples illustrate the problem. A company decides that it wants to use the APL programming language on-line in engineering, runs out and acquires a compiler, and tells the engineers to use the existing terminals in their department. Most manufacturers of CRTs, however, specifically require different features on both their terminals and control units to support APL. The keyboards are different because they must support APL characters. Another organization decides to use Fortran on their computer, tries to install it, and finds that the code will not work because no one checked the computer's configuration to see if it had the floating-point feature. A very common error is installing a printer that cannot produce reports at the speed with which they are needed. Also popular with careless individuals is trying to install hardware not supported by a particular operating system. This problem is often seen with disk drives. Equally widespread is the one in which someone tries to add some peripheral equipment to a particular computer that is not compatible or supported on their mainframe. This mistake is usually seen when management tries to add newer peripheral devices on older computers. Such stories and examples could be listed for pages, but suffice it to state that whenever a major software or hardware change is contemplated, reconfigure all the equipment involved to make sure that everything works within a system and thus the way you intended.

A second reason for configuring equipment properly is related to the availability of hardware and its associated costs. For example, in the case of the APL CRT, the relatively inexpensive features required to support the language may take three months to get from the vendor. Therefore, some planning is required to make sure that APL is installed at the time when the appropriate features are available to you. Costs are also involved. If the APL software arrived in June and immediately went on rent, whereas the hardware features did not arrive until September, the code would be paid for over several months without even being used. Multiplied by a number of such poorly coordinated incidents within any organization, and you will quickly find thousands of dollars being wasted needlessly.

Configuring equipment is a relatively simple process. It involves understanding what the devices are to be used for, making sure that they have the capacity to do the amount of work required of them, and then sitting down with the appropriate vendor to identify all the features needed on a particular unit. Do this for every device involved. Figure 4-1 illustrates a sample

Unit	Model/Feature	Description	Quantity	Lease
3274	B01	Control unit	1	$466
	6901	TP adapter type A1	1	29
	7802	TP adapter type B1	1	35
	9885	208-V non-lock plug	1	NC
				$530
3278	002	Display station	15	855
	1090	Audible alarm	15	30
	4627	EDCDIC typewriter key	15	225
	4690	Numeric lock	15	NC
	9082	EBCDIC character set	15	NC
	9550	Attach to 3274-1B	15	NC
	9891	120-V non-lock plug	15	NC
				$1110
3288	002	Printer—120 lines per minute	2	734
	4450	Forms stand	2	NC
	9089	EBCDIC character set	2	NC
	9881	115-V non-lock plug	2	NC
	9944	Cross error print	2	NC
				$734
		Hardware totals 2-year lease		$2374

NC – no charge

Figure 4-1. Sample configuration of CRTs and printers at the XYZ Corporation, showing features. Prices are samples only and do not reflect official IBM prices. (Reprinted with the permission of IBM Corporation.)

configuration that might come out of such a planning session. Notice that the specific models of the devices are identified with all their features. It is also possible now to obtain an exact price for the lease, purchase, and maintenance of these units. Many vendors have automated this process to ensure that all prerequisites are identified, which is particularly necessary for equipment that must integrate into larger systems. Yet this does not mean that the configuration is correct because there may be some optional features that someone wants which the vendor is not aware of, such as light pens on CRTs, different colors on computers, or alternative power requirements. Therefore, the process of configuring a system or one piece of equipment should be a joint process between the vendor and the customer. This is particularly necessary where large numbers of equipment are involved. Figure 4-2 shows a configuration for a small computer system with peripherals. Notice that there are a large number of features that must be discussed before this configuration could be completed.

To make sure that all the major elements of a configuration are reviewed,

Unit	Model/Feature	Description	Quantity	Lease	Purchase
4331	J01	Processor: 1048 kilobytes	1	$1,895	$76,100
	9063	Blue covers		NC	NC
	9902	208-V ac 60-cycle 1-phase	1	NC	NC
	1421	Block multiplexer channel	1	117	4,620
	1901	CTRL store exp-display/print	1	136	5,355
	2001	Adapter expansion	1	28	1,275
	3201	DASD adapter	1	96	3,780
	5248	Byte multiplexer channel	1	94	3,695
	7851	3340 direct attachment	1	NC	NC
	8701	ECPS: VM/370	1	NC	NC
				$2,366	$94,825
3278	A02	Display console	1	74	2,680
	9880	120-V lock plug	1	NC	NC
	4634	Operator console keyboard	1	29	1,080
	9606	System attachment-4331	1	NC	NC
				103	3,760
3203	005	Printer—1,200 lines per minute	1	1,405	38,320
	9903	208-V ac 60-cycle, 3-phase	1	NC	NC
	9190	Diagnostic tool kit	1	NC	NC
				$1,405	$38,320
3340	A02	DASD	1	1,050	37,800
	9043	Blue covers		NC	NC
	9903	208-V ac 60-cycle 3-phase	1	NC	NC
	6202	Rotational pos. sensing	1	23	907
	9606	System attachment 4331	1	NC	NC
				$1,073	$38,707
		Hardware totals 2-year lease		$4,947	$175,612

NC – no charge

Figure 4-2. Sample configuration of a small system, showing features. Prices are samples only and do not reflect official IBM prices. (Reprinted with the permission of IBM Corporation.)

keep in mind the following:

Checklist of Configuration Requirements

(1) Memory or model required (usually based on capacity requirements)
(2) Quantity (how many are needed, and how many can be connected together within one system)
(3) Electrical features (115 V, 208 V, or 230 V)
(4) Features for future expansion (based on planned requirements)
(5) Features required to support specific pieces of software (such as operating systems, languages)
(6) Maintenance support features desired by vendor's field engineers

In addition to configuring devices, a number of other issues are always present. These deal with the environment in which the equipment is to operate. These may be summarized as follows:

Checklist of Hardware Physical Planning Requirements

(1) Cables (which ones, how many, what lengths)
(2) Air conditioning and power in rooms where equipment is to be installed (more and where)
(3) Strength and type of floors to support DP equipment
(4) Modems (also known as data sets) for equipment in a teleprocessing network (terminals, distributed processing; how many, which ones, and where)
(5) Furniture required for terminals, tape racks, operators (how many and where)
(6) Physical security for hardware (doors, walls, locks)
(7) Power plugs and wall sockets (they vary for DP equipment; some are locking plugs, others are not)
(8) Physical layout of the equipment (enough space?)

Invariably, someone will forget to identify what cables are needed for some machine to hook up to another and thus will fail to order them. The result is that hardware is delivered and cannot be installed until calls are made on vendors, or a check is made of local warehouses for extras, or some are borrowed from another company in the area. Modems for teleprocessing and their associated telephone lines are often overlooked also. Typically, it takes a minimum of a month to obtain telephone lines and modems and at least two weeks for cables. Thus each of these items should be ordered at least two months before hardware is delivered. Power requirements and varying wall sockets also appear as a common oversight in many installations, yet these also require at least ten days to correct.

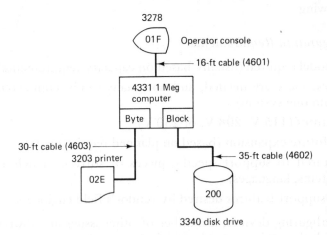

Figure 4-3. Sample layout of a small computer configuration, showing how devices will attach to each other, device addresses for operating system, length of cable, and cable group (ID) numbers.

Figure 4-3 illustrates how a sample configuration of equipment is to be connected, and Figure 4-4 shows a room layout for those units. Note that these documents were the output of a formal configuration, such as that illustrated in Figure 4-2, and should always be done. There are three steps involved in preparing this elementary documentation:

(1)   Configure the hardware needed with all features.

(2)   Diagram how each of the devices will interface with other units, specifying device addresses, cables, and cable lengths.

(3)   Draw a floor plan showing where equipment will be positioned, showing the space necessary to open all panels, ensuring that there will be room for field engineers to perform maintenance.

In well-organized data processing departments, several sets of configurations, diagrams, and floor plans will exist to indicate how the hardware environment will change over the next several years, indicating such things as where additional DASD might go. This is usually a part of a normal disaster plan, particularly if the plan calls for a temporary data center to be established in another predesignated room. All of this extra work is extremely useful in defining the requirements for floor space, air conditioning, power, and correctly timing changes in hardware and rooms, and quickly flags any major problems that might otherwise go undetected. Some obvious ones include not having cables long enough or the correct ones, insufficient memory on a teleprocessing controller to support additional terminals, insufficient power outlets for more equipment in convenient locations, or the wrong features, making it impossible to hook some devices to others.

Where one sees a formal three-step approach, such as was just described, is when a major system is to be installed. One common scenario requiring such a formal approach is the replacement of the first computer with a second interim to a third within a short period of time. Another is the addi-

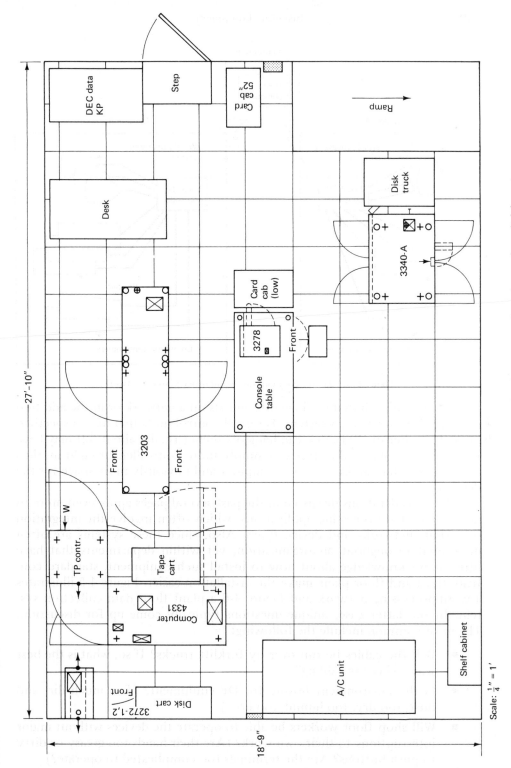

Figure 4–4. Sample physical layout of devices showing access paths and space for units' doors to open.

159

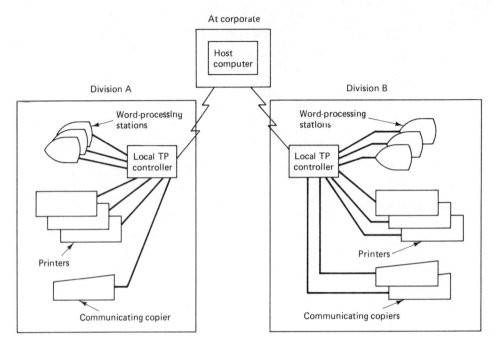

Figure 4-5. Sample configuration of an office systems network.

tion of more distributed intelligent terminals on a network or in the addition of more disk drives on a system. Terminal control units that have a specified limited number of CRTs that can hang off them (usually about 32) may have to be replaced with other types or simply more controllers brought in, thus requiring channel addresses on a computer and obviously more space for the devices.

The considerations discussed in the past several pages apply even more to new distributed processing applications, which often involve the integration of various networks and device types. Also, since these systems are often duplicated throughout an organization, yet within departments that have little or no knowledge about how to install such equipment, standard configurations and floor plans make the installation easier. Figure 4-5 illustrates a word-processing network and Figure 4-6 a plant floor data collection system. In the latter case, unique questions typically come up for discussion. The most common include the following:

- Will the cables be run over by forklift trucks? If so, what is the best way to lay the cabling?

- Is the environment hostile for DP equipment? (Too much dirt and dust, too dry, too humid, too hot?)

- Will shop floor workers be able to operate the devices without major interruptions to their own work? (Are their hands too greasy or dirty to push buttons? Are the terminals too complicated to operate?)

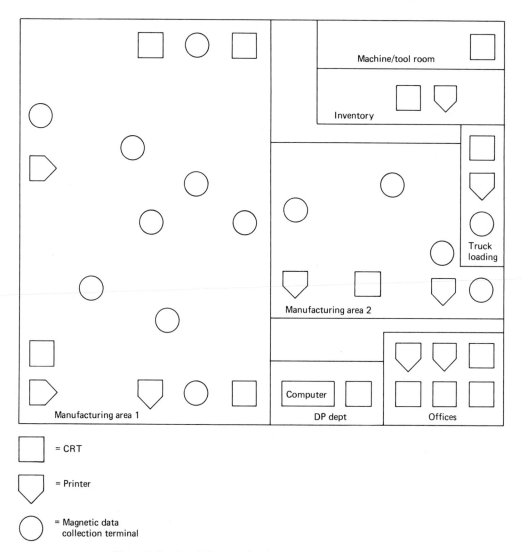

Figure 4-6. Sample layout of a plant hardware network with a local data center.

- How will the equipment be positioned so as not to interrupt the normal functioning of plant equipment?
- Does it violate any local building, fire, or electrical codes? (How about insurance and union requirements?)

In office systems similar environmental questions come up for discussion and resolution. The most common include where the most convenient place is to position devices, how many, who should have them, where must cables be installed and outlets, and what kind of furniture will be needed consistent with the decor of the rooms. If telecommunicating copiers are used, are special telephone lines required together with modems or telephones next to the devices? How and when should these items be installed, and who in the office will be the focal point for complaints or coordination? Office systems force additional pressure on those managing the installation of equipment, because these devices are often very close to—maybe only feet away from—upper-level managers and executives who will be quick to notice if the job is not well done. At least in installing equipment in the DP department, a poor job can be hidden from executives, but can they in an office environment?

Increasingly in the past two or three years, vendors have been placing more responsibility on the shoulders of their customers to develop configurations that are appropriate and are forcing them to take more initiative in developing and carrying out their installation. Still, however, in reality both groups work closely together to arrive at configurations that make sense and which are correctly priced. Nonetheless, a trend toward greater user responsibility is evident. Thus in many situations both have developed procedures for configuring equipment, policies that make sense to each. Usually, with a formal proposal, a vendor will provide a documented configuration of equipment. If the proposal has been well prepared, discussions between customer and vendor prior to the development of the configuration and boiler-plate document will ensure a reasonably well done configuration that accurately reflects features and prices. Yet even after the proposal has been accepted, inevitable changes arise out of joint discussions. One should remember that only a small proportion of all DP equipment ordered is as a result of a proposal. A great deal of ordering comes from simple volume growth. Thus hardware is often ordered and delivered without going through a formal proposal effort. Although this process saves time for both the vendor and the customer, the requirement for a configuration jointly agreed to remains. Only if each understands the needs of the other very well can this be a smooth process.

If additional terminals are being ordered which are configured like others already installed in a particular company, a vendor will probably pull out of the files an old configuration frequently used before and simply place the order. The same is often done with additional DASD and tape drives. Printers usually occasion some discussion because of varying printing requirements. However, all intelligent devices going into new sectors of an organization and computers should be totally reconfigured each time to make sure that they are perfect for where they are going. Failure to do so might result in installing incompatible devices and probably at some cost not anticipated. Moreover, some user manager might refuse to take delivery of a configuration he or she is unfamiliar with. If the manager who is to receive DP equipment is unfamiliar with data processing, he or she will have a tendency to adhere strictly to the set of instructions received from the MIS department and reject anything that looks unfamiliar. In short, attention to detail by vendors and those ordering DP equipment makes good business sense.

Things to Do When Ordering Equipment

1. Jointly discuss possible configurations of equipment and involve users of those devices. This admonition is particularly important for users outside the DP department who might have special requirements not known to MIS personnel, such as engineers requiring special keyboards on their CRTs.

2. If a vendor has a computerized configuration program, have that run so that all required features are identified together with their costs.

3. When configuring additional equipment to be put on a controller, computer, or intelligent terminal system, reconfigure everything (both installed items and all new devices) to see if any features have to be added to or taken off specific pieces of equipment already installed. This is often necessary with some peripherals when changing from older to newer computers and on terminal control units that may require additional ports. A reconfiguration will also help identify quickly if it is not possible to add additional devices, for example on a particular network or on a specific string of peripherals belonging to a particular computer system.

4. If lead time is critical and equipment must be brought in quickly, identify which features or pieces of hardware may cause your delivery schedule to be longer than desired so that alternative configurations can be developed. A common example of the problem is a newly announced DASD which will not be available for 18 months to two years, thereby pushing the installation of an entire computer system out for the same period of time. In such a case the computer and all the other peripherals might take less than a year to get except for that particular type of DASD. In such a situation, using other currently available disk drives interim to the newer devices might result in an entire computer system being delivered from the manufacturer much earlier.

5. When configuring multiple devices, make sure that contractual obligations on all units are understood. It is quite possible that a particular vendor's lease may be for two years for one device, while for another in the same system it may be three or more years. If the requirement is that no device have a lease of over two years, then those that are offered with longer terms should not even be configured in this instance. Another common type of problem frequently seen is when an installed system is modified with little attention being paid to contractual obligations. Take as an example an intelligent terminal system consisting of a mini or micro with a separate controller for terminals. Everything is on a two-year lease when data processing decides that in order to hang different terminals off the system, the controller must be removed and replaced with a different one. Technically, there is no problem except for the fact that contractually, someone is either going to have to

pay for the remaining lease money or a heavy termination charge on the old control unit. Perhaps the solution lies in transferring the unit to another part of the organization; it is then simply a matter of cost versus benefits.

DEVELOPING INSTALLATION PLANS AND INSTALLING EQUIPMENT

Once equipment has been configured, appropriate management has signed off on its use, costs, and benefits, and it has been ordered and a delivery date has been received from the vendor, plans can be finalized for the installation of the hardware. Invariably, at this time some nebulous plans are in existence, but rarely detailed and concrete plans that take into account such fundamental elements as:

- Software development
- Physical planning
- Operator training
- Use and maintenance procedures

Yet the period from when a decision is to made to acquire hardware to the time the hardware is installed successfully should be one during which necessary plans are drawn up. This process should take place to one degree or another regardless of whether the project is an entire computer system or a simple additional terminal. In either extreme the types of concerns involved are essentially the same.

The first step is to make a list of all the activities that must take place to ensure a smooth implementation. Depending on the complexity of the project, such a meeting may or may not include the vendor, but usually it does with all the people who will be involved in the installation in attendance. These are the people who in effect make up the list of "to do's." The group draws up a written list of all the necessary activities, sorts them in the order that they must be completed, and sets up target dates for their completion. If a major installation is to take place, the list will be longer than for the installation of a few terminals or disk drive. Yet in either case, the plan should be documented and checkpoint meetings held before the installation to ensure that all tasks are completed and problems identified (and overcome).

Stepping through the installation of a computer system illustrates the procedure. A data processing department is about to install a computer with peripherals and to generate an operating system with a few applications. A staff already exists and a system has been ordered. Now comes the first planning session. Attending this meeting would be DP management, software and operations and from the vendor's side marketing, systems engineering, and field engineers. After identifying the list of tasks to be accomplished, a form such as the one illustrated in Figure 4-7 might be used to catalog them.

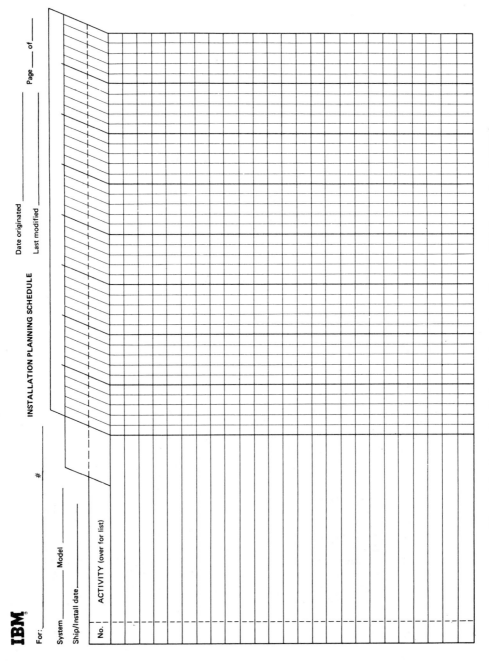

Figure 4-7. Sample installation task input form. (Source: IBM Corporation © 1975.)

Activities that would be identified in this kind of a situation include:

- Education of staff
- Ordering of software
- Physical site preparation
- Application design and writing
- File layout plans
- Ordering of supplies such as paper, ribbons, disk packs, and tapes
- Periodic checkpoint meetings
- Establishment of documentation standards for operations
- Periodic review meetings with users
- Conversion of old programs and existing files
- Testing of software and hardware (on-site or elsewhere)
- Actual installation plans
- Post-installation reviews

Any good plan of action would list the activities required in several lists in order of:

- Chronology
- Phase or project
- Person

Task	Time (hr)	Who	Target Date
Meeting with vendor software service	1/2	XYZ/vendor	5/15
Hire additional programmer	1	Howard	5/15
Determine which access method to use	1	Jim/Bill	5/15
Run programs through conversion aid	2	Jim	5/15
Operating systems class	5	Jim/Bill	5/15–5/19
Access methods class	2	Jim/Bill	5/20–5/21
Meeting with vendor hardware service	1/2	XYZ/vendor	5/22
Operating system installation class	3	Jim	5/23–5/26
Complete computer site preparation		XYZ	5/28
Install computer	2	Vendor	6/1
General operating system	2	Jim/Bill/vendor	6/5
Convert 150 tapes	3	Jim/Joe	6/6
Establish tape files on disk	2	Jim/Joe	6/8
Review software/hardware status	1	XYZ/vendor	6/9
Test and debug 15 programs	20	Jim/Joe/Bill	7/21
Convert/test/parallel welfare system (10 programs)	40	New hire	7/29
Install additional disk	1	Vendor	8/1
Install 6 CRTs	1	Vendor	8/3
Review status of conversion	1	XYZ/vendor	8/4
Parallel test additional programs	5	Jim/Joe	8/9
Post installation hardware review	1	XYZ/vendor	8/10

Figure 4–8. Sample computer installation activity list. Actions are listed chronologically, with the amount of time required to complete them in units of days and by whom the actions are to be performed.

Figure 4-8 illustrates a page from a plan that listed events chronologically. Note that both software and hardware events were listed conveniently so that as they were done, the manager in charge of the installation could check off the events. Figure 4-9 shows some activities by phase, in this instance the

Task	Time (hr)	Who	Target Date
Meeting with vendor hardware service	1/2	XYZ/vendor	5/22
Complete computer site preparation		XYZ	5/28
Install computer	2	XYZ	6/1
Review hardware status	1	XYZ/vendor	6/9
Install additional disk	1	Vendor	8/1
Install 6 CRTs	1	Vendor	8/3
Post-installation hardware review	1	XYZ/vendor	8/10

Figure 4-9. Sample hardware installation activity list (drawn from fuller list in Figure 4-8).

hardware installation portion. In our case when it was actually done, the phases included:

- Computer installation
- Software implementation
- Education plan
- Program conversion plan
- On-line system implementation

Figure 4-10 suggested the kinds of events required for program conversion and Figure 4-11 showed the actions required by one individual. Such a list should be made up for each person, and as revisions are made to the plans, everyone involved should receive them. Some managers will go the extra step of having a project file in machine-readable form that is updated after

Task	Time (hr)	Who	Target Date
Call users of conversion program	—	Jim	4/21
Setup time on computer for conversion and compules	—	Bill	5/2
Stripe out old code and rewrite access code and recompile (15 programs)	5	Jim	5/8-5/12
Run programs through conversion aid and compile on new computer	2	Jim	5/15
Convert 150 tapes	3	Jim/Joe	6/6-6/8
Establish test files on disk	2	Jim	6/8
Test and debug 15 programs	20	Jim/Joe/Bill	7/21
Parallel systems test	5	Jim/Joe	7/28
Convert/test/parallel welfare System (10 programs)	40	New hire	7/29

Figure 4-10. Program conversion activity list: sample list of actions required to complete software conversion to new computer system.

Task	Time (hr)	Target Date
Determine print train layout	—	4/21
Order disk packs	—	4/21
Complete computer physical planning/ air conditioning/power requirements	1	5/1
Determine location of six CRTs	—	5/1
Order additional keypunch for peakload	—	5/1
Confirm computer and CRT cable requirements with vendor	—	5/2
Order carriage control tapes	—	5/8
Hands on computer time at vendor's data center	2	5/9–5/10
Operating systems class	5	5/15–5/19
Meeting with vendor's hardware service	1/2	5/22
Install software	1	6/6
Convert 150 tapes	3	6/8
Parallel test of 15 programs	5	7/28

Figure 4-11. Activity list for Joe Smith: sample list of actions required of one person to complete conversion to new computer system.

each meeting to reflect the latest actions. The use of such common tools as PERT charts or homegrown lists have proven useful. Figure 4-12 is a simple example of one used in installing an IBM 4331 system replacing a 370/115. Armed with such plans, it then becomes easier to install complex systems. It also points out possible problems such as the potential concern on the part of a vendor in making sure that he or she has trained people to help install specific types of devices.

The process can be illustrated yet another way by using something as simple as installing new terminals to replace older ones within a company's division. In this situation, only minor software changes were required. The plan was to exchange 20 CRTs along with six printers and one control unit. Both the modem and telephone lines remained the same. Figure 4-13 illustrates a plan of action drawn up for this operation. If not prepared in advance, the chances of the new terminals arriving at the division without any warning probably are great, with double rental (on the old and new) costs taking place. Users would have been confused, frustrated, and their managers mad, especially if the new terminals cost more than the older ones and were not accounted for in their budgets.

Software Considerations

Although software changes in any installation plan can have as many variations as there are companies and devices, there are some general issues to watch out for and to be addressed head on:

- Addresses of all terminals and peripherals in software
- Appropriate releases of operating systems
- File layout and conversion from one type of DASD to another

4331 AND DOS/VSE CONVERSION SCHEDULE   12/18/79

COMPL DATE	START TIME	TASK	RESPON PERSON
121779		ORDER DOS/VSE SYSTEM IPO/E	RM
122179		FINALIZE ROOM LAYOUT FOR 4331 & I/O	RM, JG
122879		VERIFY ADEQUACY OF A/C UNIT FOR 4331	RM
122879		CHECK IBM CABLE ORDER FOR 4331 & I/O	RM
122879		ESTABLISH ELECTRICAL NEEDS AND ORDER CHANGES	RM
010280		ORDER 50 TAPES, 6250 BPI	JG
011480	1330	PRE-INSTALLATION MEETING W/IBM	RM, JG, DC
011880		RECEIVE DOX/VSE SYSTEM IPO/E	RM
011880		CONVERT ISAM/SEQ FILES TO VSAM	DC, RH
012580		ESTABLISH I/O UNIT ADDRESSES FOR 4331	DC, JG
012580		ESTABLISH SYSGEN OPTIONS FOR D)S/VSE, REL 2	DC, JG
012580		ESTABLISH SYSGEN OPTIONS FOR POWER/VSE	DC, JG
020180		SYSGEN OF DOS/VSE, REL 2 AT IBM, APPROX 6 HRS	DC
020280		TEST SYSGEN OF DOS/VSE ON 370/115	DC, JG
020280		SYSGEN OF POWER/VSE ON-SITE	DC, JG
021480		TEST OF BATCH & CICS PROGRAMS AGAINST DOS/VSE	DC, JG
021480		LAST DAY OF PRODUCTION BEFORE CONVERSION	JG
021580	0700	POWER SHUT DOWN	JG
021580	0700	DISCONNECT 3505, 3525, 3410, 3411, 3115 & REMOVE FRM ROOM	JG, ALL
021580	0700	DISCONNECT 3203 FROM 370/115 CONSOLE	IBM
021580	0730	VACUUM FLOOR & REMOVE CABLES FRM UNDER NEW 3203 POST	JG, ALL
021580	0800	MOVE 3203 TO NEW POSITION	JG, ALL
021580	0800	UPGRADE OF 3203 FROM MDL 2 TO 5, HRS	IBM
021580	0800	FEATURE CHANGES ON 3272, 3340	IBM
021580	1000	VACUUM SUBFLOOR, REMOVE EXTRA CABLES	JG, ALL
021580	1200	LUNCH BREAK	
021580	1300	MOVE NEW UNITS INTO ROOM & PLACE IN POSITION	JG, ALL
021580	1500	UNPACK & CABLE NEW UNITS - 4331, 3420S, 3803, 2520 AND CABLE EXISTING UNITS - 3340, 3272, 3203	IBM
021580	1800	TEST TOTAL SYSTEM HARDWARE	IBM
021680	0800	BRING-UP DOX/VSE, REL 2 POWER/VSE & COMMENCE TESTING	DC, JG
021880	0800	TEST CICS, RUN DAILY JOB STREAMS	DC, JG
022380	0800	SYSGEN OF DOS/VSE, REL 3 ON-SITE ON 4331	DC, JG
022980		TEST OF BATCH & CICS PRGMS AGAINST DOS/VSE, REL 3	DC, JG
023080		CICS 1.3 → 1.5 COMPILES (2 DAYS)	DC, JG

CONTINGENCIES

1. IF 4331 IS NOT OPERATIONAL FROM A HARDWARE STANDPOINT BY 2400 ON 02/17, A DECISION TO RE-INSTALL THE 370/115 WILL HAVE TO BE MADE.
2. IF DOS/VSE & POWER/VSE ARE NOT OPERATIONAL AND PRELIMNARY TESTS COMPLETED BY 2400 ON 02/18, A DECISION WILL HAVE TO BE MADE TO BRING-UP DOS/VSE, REL - 34.

Figure 4-12. Sample computer printout of action items to complete installation of computer system.

- Conversion of files from one file access method to a required new one
- Conversion of old application programs to newer or different forms
- Migration of an older operating system to a newer or modified release
- Addition of new application or system software (very common today

IBM

INSTALLATION PLANNING SCHEDULE

For: OLD CRTS TO NEW CRTS   #

System CRTS   Model DIVISION A
Ship/Install date 9/15

Date originated 5/20
Last modified 12/1

Page 1 of 1

P = PLANNED   D = DATE DONE

No.	ACTIVITY (over for list)		
JIM	1	PROPOSE CRT CHANGE	
JIM	2	ORDER 40 CRTS, 6 PRINTERS	
BILL	3	DIVISION SIGN OF ON CHANGE	
BOB	4	ORDER INSTALLATION MANUAL	
MIKE	5	PLAN TP SOFTWARE CHANGES	
JIM	6	PLAN INSTALLATION W/VENDOR	
MIKE	7	ORDER NEW CABLES	
JIM	8	CANCEL INSTALLED CRTS	
VENDOR	9	DELIVER DEVICES TO DIV.	
BOB	10	DISTRIBUTE AROUND BLDG	
MIKE	11	GEN. DISKETTE ON CONTROLLER	
MIKE	12	WEEKEND HOOK UP, TAKE DOWN OLD CRTS	
BOB	13	DELIVER USER MANUALS	
BOB	14	PACK UP OLD DEVICES	
ALL	15	POST INSTALLATION REVIEW	

Figure 4-13. Sample installation plan completed and fully filled out to end of installation. Project involved replacing older CRTs with newer ones along with some printers.

170

are new diagnostic programs to help users and vendors do hardware tests and troubleshooting)

Often these software issues, if not handled completely, will reduce the odds of installing hardware on time regardless of how good and detailed the planning is on physical site preparation and hardware hookup.

Physical Planning Considerations

Several types of issues come up under this general topic, ranging from the actual layout of the room in which equipment is to be installed to such other concerns as where to put peripherals in other parts of the building and access to the area at installation time. The following list of locations should be visited and discussed in some detail during any review of physical site preparations.

Checklist of Physical Site Preparation

(1) Floor space and weight of devices

(2) Power required: type and number of electrical outlets

(3) Air conditioning: number of Btu generated by all devices and number of tons of air conditioning required to overcome them

(4) Physical security involving doors, combination locks, fire prevention and extinguishers, alarms, and lighting

(5) File, card, and disk storage

(6) Cabling for all computerized devices

(7) Furniture for all personnel, racks for tape and disk, console tables, and racks for manuals

There are some additional guidelines that experience shows to be relevant in most physical planning. The vast majority of computer devices are still used in machine (or computer) rooms with special reinforced raised flooring which allow for storage of cabling and room for cold air to flow from the air-conditioning ducts. For distributed processing devices, some minis, and most micros, which are often all located in normal office environments, weight is not a problem, as these devices rarely weigh more than 400 to 600 pounds. But check to make sure. Power for computers are usually 208- and 230-V three- or four-phase lines, whereas terminals and many distributed systems today are usually 115 V, as in our homes. Some computer system peripherals are 115 V, such as console CRTs, so make sure that a sufficient number of the right kind of outlets are available.

Air conditioning, although becoming less of an issue as newer devices replace hotter older ones, is still a consideration. When adding significant amounts of equipment to a room, have the vendor identify how many Btu (British thermal units—the measure of heat generated in an hour) the

devices in total will create. Then determine how many tons of air conditioning currently feed the room. As a general rule of thumb, 12,000 Btu can be
cooled down to about 69°F with 1 ton of air conditioning. Thus a computer room generating 400,000 Btu would need about 33 tons of air conditioning just for hardware. As another general rule of thumb, one should add
another 25% of air conditioning (or Btu) to account for body heat generated
by operators and by lights in the room. Typically, additional air conditioning
is not required for devices which are installed in offices as part of office
systems or distributed processing, since they were designed for that kind of
environment. But check anyway, especially if the office in which they are
to be installed has few or no air-conditioning ducts nearby. Also, industry-
hardened terminals sold for use in factories do not require additional air
conditioning, but there are limits to everything, so the admonition to check
remains.

Fire prevention essentially involves having a fire-retardant gas extinguish-
ing system installed to smother flames. Some DP shops still use water sprin-
klers, which are not recommended since water damages computer equipment,
often beyond repair. A leaking pipe dripping into peripherals can cause
shortages, loss of data, shock operators, and the destruction of very expensive units. Remember also that should a gas system kick on in combination
with an activated sprinkler, the room will cloud up immediately with a white
fog so thick that you cannot see your hand in front of your face. Thus
people can be injured as they bump and stumble around trying to get out
fast. Have one or the other system but not both, and if possible have no
water at all.

Storage near computerized equipment for cards, paper, tapes, and disk
is not simply for convenience. Since data are often stored on these media,
the question is one of security. Lose that information (especially if they are
backup files) and you have destroyed an important asset of an organization.
Beyond the question of theft, destruction, or malicious behavior or even
convenience is the issue of temperature tempering. If paper—especially cards
—are stored at about 80 to 85°F but must be used at 67°F and probably with
a shift downward of 20% in humidity, the cards might become stuck together or stuck in either a card reader or printer. Ideally, all paper items
should be at the same temperature and humidity as both the room in which
they are used and the equipment. Extremes in temperature with tape sometimes cause a loss of data or a data check, so variations in degrees should be
held at a minimum. The same applies to disk packs that experience radical
changes in temperature. In fact, one argument many vendors use when
selling nonremovable disk drives is precisely that their units are environmentally sealed to prevent dust, extremes of humidity, or temperature changes
from interfering with the performance of the units.

Cabling between devices can present some problems. As a good policy,
draw on paper which devices will attach to what, and define the distance
between them, thereby leading to a good estimate of how much cabling is

required. Remember that cabling must go down from one device, over to another, and then back up to where the other end will be attached. Therefore, if the distance between two units is 35 feet, for example, the cable has to be longer, perhaps 40 or more feet. Assume that you need a length greater than the distance measured, even if only a couple of extra feet. Remember also that cabling changes with devices. The tendency today is toward smaller, lighter cabling, so it is quite possible that your cabling requirements may change dramatically with new equipment.

Pay attention to where cabling is to be placed. Earlier in this chapter, reference was made to making sure that cabling in a plant does not get in the way of forklifts—but add to that trucks, carts, and overhead cranes. In an office environment the concern will be about whether cabling should be under the carpet, run in the walls like electrical wiring, or in the ceiling dropping down to the device. In a computer room, cabling is invariably placed under the floor. Should cabling be run from one room to another or under the ground from one building to another, make sure that it does not run parallel and close to powerful electrical wiring. An ideal distance apart is about 6 feet [to prevent any interference in the flow of electrical impulses (data) across the cabling].

In some states insurance companies require the cabling attached to major pieces of computer equipment be via locking plugs. Figure 4-14 shows a drawing of locking and nonlocking plugs for attachment into a wall electrical outlet. Local ordinances may require similar locking devices for distributed or office systems. In general, either type of plug is readily available from both computer vendors (hence the need for a detailed configuration) and any well-stocked electrical supply company.

At times, furniture is another consideration. For example, with increasing use of CRTs for consoles on computers which are detached from the mainframe (unlike in years past), the need exists for a table on which to place the terminal, manuals, and so on. Tables for CRTs in user departments are similar to those needed for typewriters, but a bit wider and deeper. Tape storage racks are specialized because the tapes are stored in an upright posi-

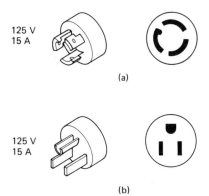

125 V
15 A

(a)

125 V
15 A

(b)

Figure 4-14. Examples of (a) locking, and (b) nonlocking plugs. (Source: IBM Corporation, © 1979.)

tion hung from the bottom side of shelves off hooks rather than the way in which we store books. Tapes are never stored on their sides for more than a few days at a time, because the tape itself will begin to warp and sag, preventing the tape drive from reading or writing all data accurately.

Installation Procedures

Once physical planning has been completed, education plans have been put in place, and everyone is ready for the arrival of equipment, the next step is the actual installation. Regardless of whether the vendor or your organization does the installing, preinstallation planning meetings should be held to ensure that everything is ready. Such topics for discussion at this time include electrical supplies, furniture, space, cabling, and any software work necessary. This is usually a period several weeks before the equipment arrives and is a good time to schedule people and time for the actual hookup. It is also during this period that final decisions are made about how equipment will be pulled out, other equipment modified, and new equipment installed.

These kinds of details should encompass several important subjects:

- Backup
- Testing
- Cutover

Backup is insurance in case something goes wrong. What if the equipment that arrives is configured incorrectly? What if something does not work and therefore cannot go live as planned? In short, the possibility of a problem always exists. Therefore, some backup plans should be made. Typically, these might be as simple as relying on the previous equipment for another few days or just waiting until the new devices are operational. If a computer is being replaced and some of the peripherals rebuilt to operate with a new host, backup is another matter. No longer can the old computer be easily hooked up again if there is a problem. In such a case, arrangements should be made in advance to operate critical applications (such as payroll) on another computer system compatible with the one being changed, either at another data center within the same organization or at a nearby company. Often, well-run data processing departments will have, as part of their disaster plans, backup that can be used when converting over to different equipment.

Testing procedures also vary a great deal, but time and effort should be allocated for this activity before putting new equipment into production. Some simple time-tested suggestions are in order.

Testing Recommendations

(1) Test new software for new equipment at another data center or on a different system prior to the arrival of new hardware so that known programming problems are resolved in advance.

(2) If the equipment coming in is new technology, either go to a vendor's data center or to another organization that has the particular hardware installed and practice using it.

(3) Once your equipment is installed, regardless of type or quantity, allocate time to test it and run it through its paces so that operators can become familiar with it and all software can be checked out against it.

(4) As for terminals, a few hours of testing is usually more than adequate. With a computer, plan on at least one day, and for a whole system, at least two days.

Cutover is simply dropping dependence on previously installed equipment and using the newly acquired devices. As insurance, keep the older hardware physically nearby for a few days in case some unanticipated problems arise. This may mean paying double rental, but the price is worth it just for peace of mind. If already budgeted for, and a problem arises, management will not be surprised. For instance, many companies will keep an older computer around for two extra weeks, and terminals and disk drives for a few days. Similar patterns of behavior are evident with users of minis and micros. In converting over to different types of disk drives, often one string of the older units will be kept for weeks or months as a gradual phaseover to the new devices takes place. In short, push-pull or going "cold turkey" with equipment is not usually dangerous as long as planning has been sound and the older devices are kept for a short while.

Shakedown and Availability

All data processing equipment usually has what field engineers call a "shakedown" period. Equipment is quality-checked at the plant of manufacture and again at installation time, often with the use of a variety of diagnostic aids. Yet in travel, movement around the room, and so on, parts can be jiggled loose, wiring pinched or broken, logic boards cracked or found to be faulty. Thus it is quite possible that for a number of days or even weeks after installation, intermittent or known problems may arise, causing irritating amounts of downtime. Management and users should be aware that this possibility exists and expect it. In general, whole computer systems may experience shakedown problems for weeks (obviously the larger the number of units installed, the greater the chance of problems), while less complex devices such as terminals may experience none. Well-run field engineering maintenance teams usually have a good idea of what this period is, which devices may cause concern, and plan to allocate extra repair time for an installation's new equipment. Experienced DP managers invariably have a collection of others' experiences to guide them in establishing their own shakedown time. Curiously enough, most problems occur within the first week of operation and are quickly fixed.

The reliability of hardware is increasing for most vendors, thus reducing both installation and shakedown time. This is particularly the case with equipment being installed in non-DP departments, such as industrial or office terminals, distributed intelligence, and some forms of teleprocessing. With the trend toward less mechanical devices, smaller units, and greater use of chips, repair time is shrinking together with the number of installation problems common during the 1960s and 1970s.

Installation plans tend to follow some familiar patterns. For a planned, properly organized network of distributed processing using the same kinds of devices, wise managers will bring into a data center a fully configured pilot system. They will write the programs later to be used, install the hardware, work out any "bugs," and plan the installation of exact or similar systems throughout the company in a phased approach. For very large networks the typical strategy is to create a "swat" team, whose sole purpose is to develop applications and install them according to a predesignated schedule. Such a team might arrive at a location a week before equipment is to be installed, train local users, install the hardware over a weekend, test, and if everything is fine, go live with it on Monday. Such teams might include either a representative of the vendor whose equipment is going in, traveling with the team or drawn from a local office. The addition of terminals to a network where a base system already exists often does not require such a team, just commonsense planning and communication from the central site.

Installation of computers replacing older ones are best done over a weekend, so that the system can be put in when the organization least needs it. A well-run operation should result in a computer being installed easily over two or three days. Responsible vendors will work around the clock if necessary and over a weekend or holiday to make that happen. As a general rule, the only time that working over a weekend or holiday is not necessary is if an additional computer is being installed, in which case that can be done more leisurely during the week. Testing can be done either during the week or on a weekend. Either way, one should obtain from the vendor installing the devices an estimate of how long the installation should take and plan accordingly.

Special Considerations in Hardware Installations

Invariably, a number of little issues become big problems during installation if not anticipated in advance. The best known of these are the following:

1. If installing over a weekend, will the building be open to the vendor's people? Is a guard needed? If so, make sure that someone is there or that the people involved have keys to the building and combinations to open secure doors.

2.   If new or additional power was installed for equipment coming in, is there an electrician handy in case of unforeseen complications? At least have your electrician's name and telephone number convenient and make sure that individual is aware that his or her services may be required over the weekend. Also make sure that the local power company has no plans to do maintenance or some other work that day on your street, cutting off all electrical power just when needed.

3.   Is power shut off in the building late at night or over the weekend? If so, make sure that it is left on.

4.   Do the field engineers know how to use the telephone system? If not, make sure that they are informed, for example, if they have to dial 9 or 90 to make outside calls. If they need parts or additional help, they may have to telephone warehouses or their managers.

5.   If people are going to work around the clock under the pressure of time, the question of food, soft drinks, and coffee becomes relevant. Either identify local restaurants that can provide these, or at least have a coffee pot handy.

6.   With the installation of any equipment, regardless of quantity or type, always have an employee familiar with DP or this equipment present. Some vendors will not install hardware (e.g., over a weekend) without an employee of the company or organization accepting the devices being present. For more than just security reasons, questions or problems may come up that require an employee to help.

7.   Since good communications and proper organization will avoid many problems, make sure that the manager in charge of the department in which the equipment is being installed is available, at least by telephone. Field engineers should at least have the manager's home telephone number in case a problem arises that requires a decision. If the devices are being installed outside the DP department, the home phone number of someone responsible from the data processing side of the house should also be convenient. Conversely, the whereabouts of managers responsible for the installation should be made available to all involved.

8.   Discuss the availability of parts necessary for the installation and make sure that if not stocked at your location they are at a nearby parts center run by the vendor. More time is lost trying to locate parts than any of us care to think about. Too frequently, someone discovers over a weekend that some part is missing and a day is lost while replacements are located, invariably in a warehouse on the other side of the country. This can be a problem, particularly with newly introduced equipment which may have been installed in your area only recently and for which parts might still be

scarce. A little joint planning with the vendor will reduce this possibility considerably.

9.   Each of the eight comments just made applies equally to installations at data centers, plants and offices, and in small and large teleprocessing networks. One further note: if a number of vendors are involved in an installation, the need for careful planning which takes into account each of the suggestions made in this chapter becomes even more imperative, since only the user or DP management has ultimate control and responsibility for coordinating among various groups.

Special Considerations in Distributed Processing

An additional set of comments needs to be made about distributed processing. With the sharp increase in the number of devices and networks outside DP departments, the need to manage this complexity has grown. The formula that seems to be evolving into the most effective management of such environments is centralized maintenance strategy. Essentially, this means that users will make known any problems to one individual at the central site driving the network. This strategy has made the maintenance of large and small networks a great deal easier in the past few years. Moreover, vendors have also applied this same approach to maintenance. Working with the person or team in charge of a network at a central site, they review and adopt all software fixes, general hardware engineering changes, and review network problems jointly. For instance, a user in Denver, when he or she runs into a problem, would have a telephone number to dial to the host location, say in Chicago. The data center at Chicago would determine if it has to fix the problem or if the vendor is to fix it. If the vendor, the contact would be made at Chicago, where diagnostics might be run remotely and, if necessary, someone could be dispatched from an office in Denver to work on the machine. Such an approach has reduced the cost of maintenance sharply while keeping control over networks in a responsive fashion. Patterns of problems are also easier to identify earlier, thus leading to more preventive maintenance before crises occur.

There has been a trend in just the past five years toward greater reliance on built-in diagnostics in hardware, which has had a dramatic impact on uptime. Many vendors of both computers and terminals have engineered into their products self-diagnostic aids (usually packaged as part of the microcode, firmware in chips, or in microprocessors) that will tell maintenance personnel quickly and accurately what is wrong with the equipment and, in some cases, what replaceable parts to bring from the parts warehouse. Another facet of this trend has been to provide for remote diagnostic capability whereby a field engineer, say in Chicago, has access to the console on a crippled computer in Dallas and can determine what systems software or hardware problems exist, using remote diagnostic tools. Similar facilities are increasingly becoming available and more comprehensive for network managers at data centers. This development reduces maintenance time because of its speed and accuracy. It also makes it possible for pertinent individuals to take advantage of major maintenance data bases which are continuously capturing a large amount of data about problems and repairs throughout the country, while reducing the requirement that users understand how equipment operates for "experts" everywhere.

Developments in diagnostics have also made it possible for users to install their own equipment rather than rely on the vendor. CRTs, for example, are often so loaded with built-in diagnostics that a non-DP person can unpack these devices, plug in the wall, connect to a network, run diagnostics, and test all without any technical background. This is also happening with intelligent minis and terminals. A very widely used example of this is the IBM 8100 terminal system, which has terminals, disk, computer power, tape capability, and telecommunications.

SYSTEMS ASSURANCE

Systems assurance is the process by which management tracks in a formal manner all the activities that must take place in order to ensure a smooth installation of equipment or software. Many vendors have internal systems assurance procedures to make sure that their products have a better than reasonable chance of being installed on a timely and efficient basis and will be used properly. An increasing number of companies and government agencies are also instituting formal procedures for the same reasons. The process varies only in detail, as the general exercise is common across all types of equipment. Much of it simply is the organization and documentation of the actions that must take place. Many of the components of any systems assurance procedure have been discussed already in this chapter. Putting the process in some logic order is necessary to understand how it is done.

The first step in any systems assurance is to document what hardware is to be installed, to which other devices it (they) will be connected, when, and how. Thus the initial effort is in making sure that the technical feasibility of any plan exists. If problems occur where there is a concern as to whether or not a configuration is possible, problems can be resolved at this early stage. Typically, this point is when equipment is being configured or ordered, often with considerable time in which to alter configurations, obtain necessary sign-offs, and identify the costs involved.

Traditionally, the output of such an exercise is the detailed feature-by-feature, box-by-box configuration of the devices to be installed. Other documents that typically accompany such a configuration would be a migration plan detailing not only what units are to be installed but what other hardware projects planned over the next year or two will affect this system. This allows for problems to be identified, and hopefully some solutions put in place, early in the cycle of events. A short example of such a problem might be a plan that calls for more terminals on a controller over the next 18 months than the device will support, causing these plans to be changed to include the installation of a second controller when needed. Typically, such a plan would include a list of applications to be developed with the equipment. Such a plan should be jointly arrived at between the vendor (or vendors) and their customers, so that each has an opportunity to access the technical feasibility of the project and to understand their specific roles. (See Figure 4-15.)

Invariably, after an initial systems assurance meeting, a list of action items is generated, requiring more work before plans are completed. Such a list of "to do's" should have completion dates and a second meeting scheduled to review a detailed documented plan of action that will also include, in addition to finalized hardware and software configurations, such information as conversion and implementation plans together with the names of specific individuals assigned to them. This is also a good time to have a backup or recovery plan that takes into account procedures, who does what and where, and all sign-offs or agreements arrived at. For instance, if another company's data center is to serve as backup, the file should contain an exchange of letters by the two DP managers involved identifying the specific understanding they have. Although this sounds very legalistic, per-

Item	Date	Comments
Install 370/138	12/79	Interim CPU
Install disk	1/80	for A/R
Change tape model	2/80	
Add two-channel switch on TP CU	2/80	To talk to two computers
Install 4341	5/80	Release 138
Install 40 CRTs (Division A)	6/80	Replaces older CRTs
Additional disk	9/80	Volume growth
Install mini in Division B	11/80	Labor reporting system
Add memory on 4341	3/81	
Discontinue card reader	3/81	
Replace 370/145 with second 4341	6/81	
Install new printer, disk	6/81	
Install new TP controller	6/81	Vendor thinks too much going in in 6/81; urges TP in 7/81
Replace all disks with new devices	10/81	
Add additional tape drives	12/81–3/82	

Figure 4-15. Sample hardware master plan. (Note: such a plan does not have to be detailed; only a general outline is needed at this point.)

sonnel turnover is often the case between the start of a planning cycle and the completion of an installation, so that a documented trail has to exist to help inform any new people joining the project in midstream.

An area that causes considerable problems because of the number of individuals and locations involved is teleprocessing. A minimum of four groups are involved in any such installation:

(1)   DP service personnel

(2)   Telephone company people

(3)   Hardware vendors

(4)   Users

Thus a number of questions requiring coordination come up, placing a premium on organization. These issues include coordinating the delivery of hardware, modems, and telephone lines to the correct locations on time. It involves making sure that user management is in agreement and is part of the plans that DP people draw up. The question of central versus remote hardware and software maintenance must be resolved. Again, it is primarily a question of who will do what. Someone will have to ask such questions as: Have all the vendor's branch offices involved been notified? Have all user departments been notified also and are they part of the planning process? Who is going to pay for all of this? The questions and issues just raised are usually resolved quickly and the process is typically not terribly complex— but only if there is good common sense and planned leadership.

As installation time comes closer, physical site preparations must be documented, understood, and completed in time. Common issues involve electrical and air-conditioning work, completion of rooms and buildings, receipt of a certificate of occupancy from municipal building authorities, and furniture and hardware scheduled properly to come in *after* physical sites have been completed. Too often, it happens in the reverse order because of faulty estimates of construction time needed or delays in obtaining telephone lines and modems, or gaining necessary sign-offs from local building inspectors or even electrical outlets from your internal maintenance people.

Each of the situations just described above can be managed better through the use of normal project management practices. Figure 4-16 illustrates a simple form that can be used at each step of the way to identify what remains to be done. Notice that the key elements are what has to be done, by whom, when, and its status should it not be completed by a particular target date or meeting. A great deal of detail is not needed. What would be useful are minutes of meetings reporting details and who was in attendance. In some organizations, each systems assurance meeting requires formal sign-offs that actions taken so far are approved and that subsequent plans are technically feasible. This is a particularly useful exercise to use in distributed systems, where remote sites are required to accept configurations and applications. It avoids many fights and political problems later when

Action Plans and Comments

Name _____ Date _____

| REVIEW DATE | ON | ACTION PLAN DESCRIPTION / COMMENTS | ACTION PLAN | | | STATUS |
			RESPONSIBLE PARTY FOR ACTION ITEM	TARGET COMPLETION DATE	FOLLOWUP DATE	

Figure 4-16. Sample list of action items report. (Source: IBM Corporation, © 1979.)

182

management might otherwise reject equipment, blaming others for not bringing them into the planning phases. Paper reduces finger pointing.

So far, two major groups of systems assurance activities have been reviewed—definition of an installation and detailed plans. A third phase with its own set of issues involves management of the software and hardware. Logs for recording outages and problems, documented plans for changes in hardware and software, others cataloging the results of joint customer/vendor meetings, maintenance actions, along with analyses of component failure impact studies, outages, and methods for measuring availability (subjects covered in some detail in Chapters 2 and 5) are all important. Various audit tools and management controls typically are part and parcel of a good systems assurance procedure, as are data security practices that go beyond simply having a lock on the computer room door. Each of these items has been the subject of many articles, books, and seminars and has become common practice in many organizations today. Suffice it to mention here, however, that they make up part of the systems assurance process to ensure that plans can and are implemented smoothly.

A fourth and too often improperly managed facet involves identifying what resources and people will be needed to ensure a reasonably good installation. The major components of this stage of action can be cataloged as follows:

- Who (by name) will do what and when
- How much of each person's time will be needed and allocated for the task
- Education plans put in place, classes scheduled
- Similar questions resolved on the vendor's side of the house
- Risks involved identified and minimized (such as lack of training or availability of equipment arriving on time—what impact will they have on the project?)
- Formal, written agreements defining who is responsible, particularly when it involves several departments and/or companies

Finally, and perhaps most important, everyone should be in relative agreement concerning what benefits and performance are to be obtained from the equipment. This process goes far toward eliminating false hopes, faulty marketing, misunderstandings, and fights among vendors, departments, and managers. The key elements of such expectations and possible contingencies include the following:

- What is the hardware going to cost, and how is it to be acquired (e.g., by purchase or lease)?
- How much is the equipment expected to be operational (i.e., not down), what will be its operating speed (throughput), response time

on networks, ease of use, serviceability, and convenience of installation, and how reliable is it?

- What delivery schedules for everything are expected, and are the ones received acceptable and tied into the installation plans?
- What things could go wrong, and to what degree do they threaten a smooth installation?

The last issue does not really require a crystal ball. The most common factors that play havoc with plans are changes in management or business conditions, or loss of key technical personnel. Others might be availability of either software or hardware when needed, completion of a physical site, or some other factor unique to a particular organization.

In each instance some assessment of risk is necessary. In most installations each of the issues just raised can be dispensed with quickly; less frequently, there are serious problems that require constant monitoring to remain contained. In summary, the important elements of a complete systems assurance cycle are:

(1)   General installation plans

(2)   Detailed installation plans

(3)   Management of hardware and software

(4)   Identification of resources and responsibilities

(5)   Anticipated benefits, performance, and problems

Many vendors will conduct their systems assurances for major software and hardware installations either with or without their customers. Often output from these sessions guides vendors in their joint planning with customers. Many of the elements discussed in the preceding pages represents a formal structure of review meetings within, for example, IBM and other large computer product manufacturers, where even system assurance forms are filled out by attendees with questions on each of the five major elements. Such practices are rapidly spreading to users of data processing equipment, as a method of controlling change. In the first chapter it was mentioned that the number of new devices coming into an organization is growing faster than ever. When one sees on-line storage growing on an average of 45 to 50% nationwide annually in the United States, for instance, or terminals being installed by the hundreds of thousands each year, the need for a formal change management technique such as the one described above becomes essential to hold back chaos and cost.

The financial savings can be substantial. Take, as a small example, a company that has annual sales of just over $500,000,000 and which spends about 2% of this on data processing, or $10,000,000. And suppose that one-third of the DP expenditure goes toward hardware ($3.3 million in leases) and that a third of this equipment is replaced each year with newer or different units. The amount changed is equal to about $1.1 million's worth. Now if the devices coming in this year were put on a rental basis by the vendor on a specified target date and half of the equipment went into production one week late (a conservative amount of time, since much equipment goes in many weeks late), the amount paid on rental for uninstalled gear could equal about $10,500. All of that money was spent unproductively.

Terminals are particularly subject to late installation. An example illustrates the financial problem. Going from one set of terminals to another with an overlap of several weeks involving 40 CRTs each leasing for $70 per month in exchange for 40 going out (at $90 per month each) is a lot of activity. Suppose that an overlap of three weeks occurs because nobody installed the 40 new CRTs which the vendor has now put on a rental basis because they were customer-installed units. Here is the cost of the late installation:

$$40 \text{ CRTs} \times \$52.50 \text{ (3 weeks' rent)} = \$2100 \text{ wasted}$$

Multiply this poor performance by a half dozen such situations within an organization and a lot of money is wasted, not to mention the possible loss of benefits for untimely installation of applications, frustrations with management, and confusion on the part of users. Yet there is probably not a single organization today that has avoided this kind of a situation (buried in someone's budget and probably without anyone's knowledge).

Involvement of Non-DP Personnel

Since equipment is increasingly being installed by non-DP departments away from their company's data processing personnel, the involvement of non-technical personnel in hardware installation planning is rising. Vendors are marketing directly to engineers (who are buying minis and time sharing), office managers (who are acquiring a variety of office systems), and plant managers (who are installing shop floor data collection and scheduling systems). Often, the DP department finds out about these transactions long after the equipment has been installed or just as some problem arises that now has to be fixed by data processing personnel. It is not unusual, for instance, for a DP manager to attend a routine management staff meeting chaired by an executive to hear a status report by another manager (in engineering, for example) describing among his many projects the installation of a mini for drafting and design equal in power or cost to the company's main computer. What a shock for the DP director, not to mention an invasion of his or her empire!

Besides the obvious concern that his or her monopoly is falling apart (which it is), there remains the more serious problem of the compatibility of systems and their costs. These themes have been the subject of dozens of books and hundreds of articles in the past several years. But from the point of view of installing hardware, the fact remains that a growing proportion of this kind of activity is taking place outside the confines of the traditional

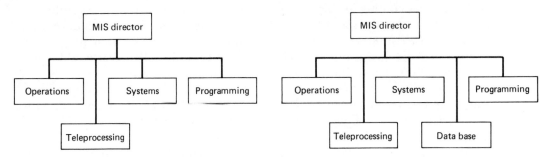

Figure 4-17. Sample organization charts reflecting common structures developed during the 1970s.

data processing department. Consequently, many companies are now redefining a DP manager's job to include all information systems, often renaming the position "MIS Director." One of the by-products of this change has been to concentrate more resources within the DP department for working with users in the installation of applications. Earlier signs of this were the creation of teleprocessing network coordinators followed by managers for teleprocessing, and most recently, the establishment of data base groups with their managers. (See Figure 4-17.)

Now yet another managerial arm is becoming evident in larger organizations and no doubt soon will appear in smaller ones. This involves the establishment of a group responsible for coordinating the installation of specific software and hardware throughout an organization, often establishing guidelines for acquisitions and standards or at least keeping track of specific developments. Managers of such groups have been variously called Project Leader, Manager of Plans, or (more chic) MIS Coordinator. Some are still called Technical Support Manager, although increasingly they are devoting all their time to main computer systems software. Whether they are considered staffers who are always concerning themselves with your business, or "bean counters," auditing activities, they suggest that the initiative for installing new data processing equipment is shifting from DP departments to its users. (See Figure 4-18.)

From the point of view of managing the process, some coordination must take place if equipment is to go in properly and in a cost-effective manner. The usual prescriptions for any project apply equally here and can be summarized as:

- Gaining user management sign-off on all configurations, software, and plans
- Defining in writing responsibilities for each in an installation, the use of equipment, and its maintenance
- Checkpointing jointly through meetings the status of all projects

In addition, since companies in some cases have nationwide contracts with vendors, giving them economies of scale for software and hardware products,

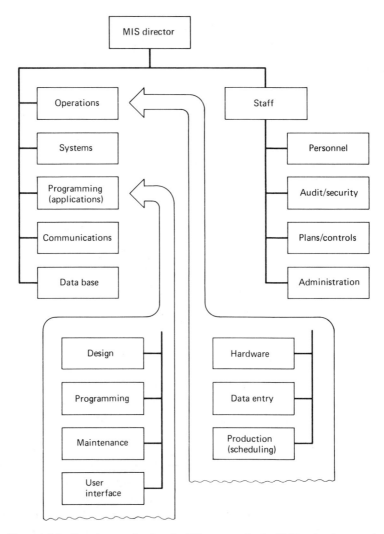

Figure 4-18. Sample organization for DP common in the 1980s, showing organizational functions in operations and applications.

educating users about what is available within an organization is thus cost effective. Letting them know what equipment is on order and their delivery dates in case, for instance, some department needs extra terminals or printers becomes a real service. Educating user management on DP trends often leads to new ideas about networking, cost-effective applications, and new equipment of real benefit, and creates the necessary understanding for the real complexities of data processing. A true appreciation of central-site problems and what DP personnel have to go through to support users, together with a better sense of what non-DP personnel want, is thus possible without a complex bureaucracy rife with political intrigue.

Such communications also allow for better balancing of work loads on networks, better coordination with telephone companies and with vendors of widely used devices (such as minis and terminals within the organization), and the consolidation of expensive service bureau work on computers that have additional unused capacity—typical of what is happening increasingly in companies and government agencies today. One other reality must be kept in mind as well: it is usually user management that has to pay for the equipment installed in their departments and out of their budgets, which often gives them real veto power over the installation of hardware. As the data processing industry has clearly learned, these managers are not hesitating to spend substantial sums on data processing equipment.

ROLE OF USERS IN DATA PROCESSING

In addition to the obvious role that users of data processing have in the planning and installation of equipment is the equally important role they play in using these devices. Here some specific suggestions will be made to improve the coordination of diagnostic activities with maintenance to ensure a higher degree of hardware availability regardless of where it is installed. The assumption made below is that some central-site data processing organization will have the final responsibility for all hardware's functioning within any network. Many of the suggestions made below are, however, equally applicable to those users who have independent minis and micros that do not communicate with any other part of the organization. But because the trend is toward integrated networks of commercial, financial, engineering, plant, and office systems, the problems of maintenance and installation are broad and affect a large percentage of any organization.

But first a little history. During the 1960s and 1970s, data processing departments usually took the initiative in establishing distributive processing throughout an organization, often designing, justifying, and implementing systems with only minor involvement by users. Where user involvement did occur, it came as a rule in the design and justification phases. Once the application in question was installed, data processing continued to carry the primary burden for maintaining the system. Any hardware or software bugs were the responsibility of data processing to fix, rarely the user's. Various departments would submit requests for program changes, and occasionally hardware requirements (such as for more terminals), but hardly more. This situation was fine as long as the number of users scattered about the organization and their applications remained small. But as the explosion in the number of on-line distributed processing grew in the second half of the 1970s, the old approach began failing and rapidly. The number of requests for programs, changes to existing ones, maintenance on hardware, and the addition of more or newer devices all became bottlenecked in data processing. DP staffs meanwhile grew rapidly in size, but it seemed never to be fast

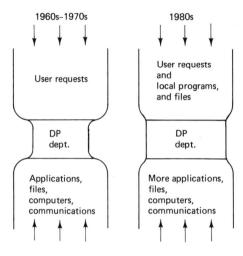

Figure 4-19. DP environment over the last 30 years. Note that placing more data processing in user departments reduces the bottleneck syndrome, thereby increasing MIS services.

enough. Hence the perception spread in many organizations that the MIS group was not responsive or efficient. (See Figure 4-19.)

Software developments during the 1960s, and especially in the 1970s, pointed to a possible solution to this growing problem because they provided users (both DP-trained and not) with the capability of doing their own programming, making changes to existing applications, and updating files without going through any particular individual within data processing. We saw the expansion in the use of such higher-level languages as APL, BASIC, and PL/1 together with the availability of hundreds of interactive software packages. These allowed DP management simply to make available sufficient computing power and disk storage, together with enough terminals and printers scattered about the organization so that users could get on the system whenever they wanted without going through the DP department.

Along with these developments in software came others in hardware. We saw the introduction of equipment that was easier to install and now find it common for much distributive processing equipment installable by users without any involvement on the part of DP personnel or vendors. Hand in glove with this development came better built-in diagnostics on terminals, minis, micros, and disk drives, so that users could determine quickly what problems they had with hardware and possibly how to correct them—again without involving DP personnel all the time.

Industry as a whole today faces a different problem to solve—how to manage data processing in this kind of environment. The potential for confusion is great, DP departments feel circumvented and therefore threatened, DP vendors call on all levels of an organization and across every department, and users are buying more equipment than ever. In fact, vendors cannot make their products fast enough, the demand is so great. Networks are becoming more diverse, large, and complex, with the potential risk of companies failing to perform their functions due to increased dependence on the

DP department rising rapidly if not properly managed. Thus the question many executives are asking themselves today is how to continue some centralized DP supervision over a growing complex of data processing without constricting the growth of automated services. The answer increasingly evident in industry lies in two areas: the organization of data processing departments and the role of users.

Already mentioned in this chapter is the changing organizational structure of DP catering to a larger number of users and teleprocessing networks. The objective is to eliminate the bottleneck by integrating into user departments some of the functions previously performed by the DP department. (See Figure 4-20.) Essentially, this shifting of responsibilities means placing

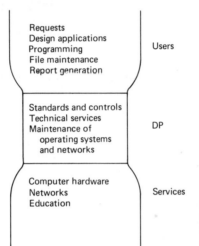

Requests
Design applications
Programming
File maintenance
Report generation   Users

Standards and controls
Technical services
Maintenance of
    operating systems
    and networks   DP

Computer hardware
Networks
Education   Services

Figure 4-20. Changes in DP functions in last few years. Note the shift of application design, programming, and file maintenance to users, with DP playing a supporting role (see also Figure 4-19).

greater emphasis on users participating in the following areas:

- Design and coding of applications
- Maintaining their own data bases physically resident in their departments or on a centralized computer
- Making sure that their hardware conforms to an organization-wide set of teleprocessing and equipment standards
- Placing more responsibilities on the shoulders of user management to perform first-level software and hardware troubleshooting
- Providing clearly specified centralized points of contact within DP for major problems and for fast resolution

In short, more than ever before a trend toward distributing the responsibility for a system's integrity is not only necessary but is clearly evident.

Dozens of books have been written on the design of systems and on project planning which talk about sharing responsibility for system design. Little is said about hardware installation and maintenance in these. In previous portions of this chapter suggestions were made about installation activities. Some additional comments are necessary on maintenance as they apply to users. A number of practices evident in American industry, for instance, are proving relevant and are relatively simple to apply across an entire organization.

Acquisition of Hardware

Any acquisition of hardware by a user department which will plug into an existing network within the organization should be approved by the DP department, which has to maintain the larger system. Thus, if a department wishes to add terminals, which device gets installed and when should be mutually decided upon, with the DP manager having ultimate veto power if there are technical difficulties. Costs for such devices would in all probability be charged out to the users. For stand-alone devices, the DP department should (depending on company philosophy) either at least be informed or should participate in a technical feasibility and selection process. Since such systems are expensive and departments become heavily dependent on them, clear lines of responsibility for programming and maintenance of these should be spelled out in advance so that there are no recriminations later.

By at least informing DP personnel of a department's intentions, moreover, opportunities for cost savings are possible. For example, suppose that a particular department wishes to acquire a mini to do engineering work under Fortran. It is quite possible that the central DP department may support Fortran on its computer and thus need only provide a CRT and printer for a user department—a far less expensive solution than buying a mini. Or it is quite possible that another department no longer needs a mini that it has which does support Fortran and that it was about to sell the mini. A simple transfer from one department to another might be more practical. And there is always the possibility of a department taking advantage of a quantity purchase discount within the entire organization.

Maintenance of Hardware

A number of specific practices have been shown to work effectively in reporting downtime on terminals and networks. The best managed networks typically have for each terminal or user several items:

- A procedure book describing how to use the device, commands necessary to access a particular application, and usually a manual from the equipment manufacturer describing its components and configuration

- A file at the host location on every device, giving its teleprocessing address, detailed configuration, location, and log of previous performance problems

- A log that users have available at the device in which to record problems, when they developed, when they were fixed and by whom
- A series of management reports within the DP department on system problems to guide personnel in improving the quality of applications and networks and which can become the basis of periodic status reports to users and their managers
- An information card taped to the device listing its network address, serial number, and telephone number ("hot line") to call network managers

Perhaps the most visible tool is the user complaint log. Figure 4-21 illustrates one example, but any with similar types of information can be developed. It should be a form that can be sent to the DP department with a copy to remain locally. In some organizations, such information is kept on-line and can be entered through another terminal nearby, describing problems on any device (which is fine as long as the telephone line is not down).

DP management is increasingly developing a series of reports to catalog and help track problems and fixes for users. They thus help develop awareness of problems and contribute to resolutions. Typical reports that any network manager should have include:

- Change report, which describes what software and hardware changes have been made since the last report, listing which were planned and those that were not
- Problem status report, which describes what problems exist, how many, which were resolved, and which and how many remain open since the last report was generated
- Statistical report, which describes in more detail the number of problems by types and is particularly useful in large networks involving hundreds of devices of various types
- Analysis of trends report, which describes the number of incidents reported over a longer period of time than other reports for such items as downtime on lines, specific types of equipment, software, and applications (usually relevant if issued quarterly with comparative data for earlier periods)
- Down time report, which describes which devices failed to perform and is usually relevant if issued weekly and daily if a lot of hardware is involved

Most of the reports mentioned above could be produced on a weekly basis, although any trends report should be less frequently generated. It is good politics to share some of the output of these reports with user management, particularly when there is one large problem causing a number of smaller ones, which is being fixed but would take time. A common example of this is downtime on the main computer caused by insufficient capacity,

IBM® 8775 Display Terminal   Problem Report Form

TERMINAL IDENTIFICATION	PROCESSOR IDENTIFICATION
— Serial No.	— Machine Type . . . .
— TPC No.	— Machine Serial No. . . . . .
DATE AND TIME	
REPORTED BY	LOCATION . . . .

1   Record all the symbols that are displayed in the operator information area of the failing terminal.

2   Record the Section Number of the Problem Determination Guide and state the step where you detected the failure.

3   Is your terminal data-link attached?

4   Is the keyboard failing?

5   If the keyboard is failing, fill in the appropriate keyboard section below or overleaf.

Typewriter Keyboard and EBCDIC Typewriter Keyboard

Mark all failing keys.   ☐ All keys fail.   ☐ All character keys fail.

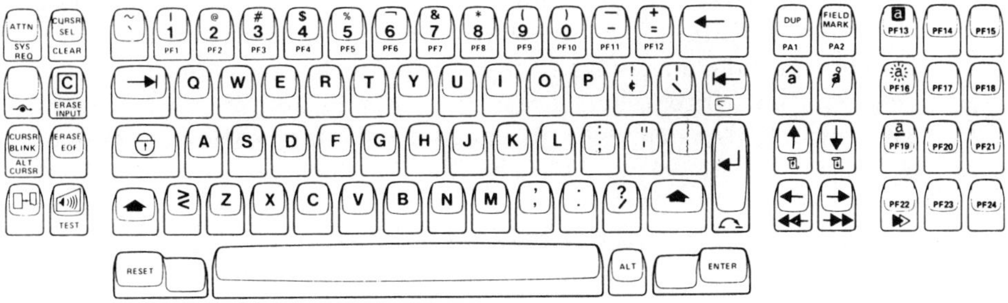

Figure 4-21.   Sample complaint log for users of CRTs. (Source: IBM Corporation, © 1979.)

193

which is being fixed by replacement with a larger mainframe due to be installed in three months. Knowing that fact makes it possible to come up with interim solutions, such as temporarily scheduling different departments on a network in staggered loads, and could be accomplished with few complaints. (See Figure 4-22.) Users would recognize that the situation is only temporary.

If a number of problems persist and users complain about service in general, monthly meetings with appropriate middle management to review what concerns remain and how they are being handled are in order together with follow-up documented minutes of these meetings. A written action plan to fix problems should also be the output of such meetings and thus can serve as an audit trail to keep track of what was committed to in any meeting. If a problem coordinator for users exists in a data processing department, it would make sense to give that person a terminal for logging problems and concerns as they are reported. This input can then become the raw data feeding a computerized reporting system generating the five types of reports listed above. Most departments already track operational problems within a computer room (mainly in the form of I/O error reports and console logs), but the other reports could just as easily be generated by the system. These reports then serve as descriptions of existing problems that are known and are quantified, chapter and verse. Random generalized criticisms by users go away and are thus replaced by specifics—real protection for the DP department from unfair attacks!

For users with stand-alone systems independent of a centralized DP function, similar approaches are recommended. Keep a documented problem log and a telephone number handy to call a vendor for help and repairs, and review problems on a scheduled basis within the department and if need be, with a vendor's maintenance personnel. The same kinds of reports discussed before make sense to generate in this environment as well and can guide management in evaluating the quality of any given piece of hardware against anticipated performance while quantifying the nature of support from data processing. Without such ammunition, no manager can reasonably expect to demand better service from data processing or to justify replacing equipment.

In summary, users should become more involved in problem determination and resolution, and every effort has to be made by data processing management to take advantage of those devices that have diagnostic and recovery features built into them. These two sets of actions go a long way toward ensuring a higher degree of uptime and reliability of any equipment.

POST-INSTALLATION ACTIVITIES

Just as good software managers will come back to their users days, weeks, and months after a new application has been installed to see what else can be done to improve things, so too should this be done with hardware. The

```
PROBLEM REPORT                                                    No. 794


Reported by/Recorded by:    Dept./Area              Ext.      Date/time submitted

Type of problem/routed to:  Attached evidence   System No.:   Operating system:
  [ ] Hardware                [ ] Sysmsg                       [ ] O/S  [ ] DOS  [ ] Other [ ]
            Vendor                                     Type of dump taken:
  [ ] Software                [ ] Dump _____               [ ] Standalone # _____
                                      type
  [ ] Operations              [ ] Compile         [ ] O/S    [ ] Logrec   [ ] DAR PR O/S

  [ ] Standards               [ ] Program Output  [ ] DOS    [ ] SEREP    [ ] VTOC List [ ] Other ____

  [ ] User Liason             [ ] Console Message  Down Code:  Time System went down _____
                                                               Time Vendor notified _____
  [ ] Programming             [ ] Other _____              Time System up (re-IPL) _____
                                        Specify

If Hardware problem:        If software problem:

DEVICE TYPE _____         MACHINE [ ] WAIT (indicate bytes 0-7) [ ][ ][ ][ ][ ][ ][ ][ ]
DEVICE ADDRESS _____
DISK MOD. # _____         STATUS: [ ] SYSTEM   [ ] MANUAL    [ ] TEST     [ ] LOAD
DISK BANK # _____         FILL OUT PROGRAM/SYSTEM LOOPS:
VOLUME SERIAL NOS.          1.          2.          3.          4.
_____ or _____           5.          6.          7.          8.
 tape      disk            9.          10.         11.         12.

DESCRIPTION OF PROBLEM: _____
_____
_____
_____
_____

                                                                     Date
Shift Supervisor name:         Date:      Problem Report cordinator:  received:

Assigned to: _____      Date _____  Action taken _____
                               Date _____  Forwarded to _____

Assigned to _____       Date _____  Action taken _____
_____                   Date _____  Forwarded to _____


Problem Resolution: _____
_____
_____
_____
_____
_____

Resolved by: _____      Date _____  Code _____  RCR # _____
Recorded by Coordinator/date _____  Fix/change schedule _____
```

Figure 4-22. Sample problem report log. (Source: IBM Poughkeepsie Systems Center Technical Bulletin (June 1975), p. 45, Poughkeepsie, N.Y.)

post-installation review is something that can be held a week, month or even six months after the event, depending on the sophistication of the equipment. For a computer system, it should be held a few days after its installation, again after one or two months, and probably again after six months. Subsequently, any discussions usually center around the two issues of capacity and ongoing maintenance. In the case of reviews held a week or a month after installation, the original documentation used at systems assurance time should be examined

- To make sure that everything that was supposed to happen did happen
- To learn from actual experience what did not happen and why.

For instance, perhaps estimates of the time required to install a certain type of terminal were too low—an important conclusion to reach if others are to be installed later. It is thus as much a learning exercise as it is a means of cleaning up loose ends of unfinished business.

Typical issues that come up at post-installation reviews include identifying what features or parts were missing at installation time (e.g., kick strips on printers, wrong color on the cover of a disk drive, and so on), review of configuration and performance (should a system's printer be moved to another channel to speed up teleprocessing controllers currently sharing the same path?), and to review what can be done to correct performance problems. Perhaps reconfiguring what devices should be on any particular channel, or relocating heavily used data across a number of disk drives, or the addition of a microcode feature can improve throughput. Perhaps the issue at hand is the physical layout of devices in a room, making it inconvenient for operators to move about. Cables are often the wrong size, and the correct lengths can be determined and ordered in such a meeting. In short, gatherings of this sort can clean up leftover details while organizing everyone's thoughts about why something was or was not installed properly.

Such meetings should be held between data processing personnel and vendor's representatives, but they should also be conducted by management within an organization involved in an installation. Thus managers representing departments that recently hooked up to a network with the DP department should review how it went and what problems remain. Often, user management will raise the question of how to obtain additional terminals and printers or more disk capacity for their distributed minis and micros. Thus these sessions often become a planning tool for further fine tuning of systems and their hardware.

Fine-Tuning Suggestions

Software managers learned a long time ago that no matter how much planning and preparation goes into the development of an application, changes will have to be made after installation to overcome unanticipated problems.

The same applies to hardware, particularly if work loads and circumstances change. Much like post-installation reviews, periodic meetings to discuss fine-tuning hardware are essential, even if equipment has been installed for years. Initiative should be taken by either DP management or users and should be conducted at least twice each year. Properly handled, the following topics would ordinarily come up for discussion in one form or another:

- Quality of operations of all hardware
- Quality of operations of all software
- Quality of performance by all user personnel
- Quality and kind of maintenance given the equipment
- Impending contractual decisions (e.g., renewal of lease contracts versus purchasing)
- Other problems and concerns

While such meetings can become complaint sessions if not strongly controlled and kept on a positive plane, they are essential. Thus one person might feel that his or her biggest problem is glare on a CRT screen, which is easily fixed by putting an inexpensive shield on its surface. Another might complain that a printer is too slow, which is easily fixed by installing a faster one. A third might complain that a vendor's maintenance team takes too long to respond to a call for help. Perhaps a meeting with the vendor can fix the problem; otherwise, you fix the vendor by changing equipment. Other concerns less easily addressed may involve the need for more support personnel in DP or the lack of data accuracy being put into a system by users.

Since personnel in user departments change constantly, the possibility of an increasing number of people not adhering to preestablished procedures for using equipment increases as time passes. Therefore, in such a meeting the question of ongoing training for new people can be faced and a plan developed. Tactics can be explored for replacing equipment with more or different devices, thus leading to a sensible and jointly arrived at opinion about what to do with leases and proposals for purchase. (See Figure 4-23.)

Obtaining better performance out of installed equipment is as much a function of what applications are being used as when. A good suggestion is to have users and those who developed or have to maintain software meet periodically to exchange views about their shared systems. This then becomes a good opportunity to have formal presentations on new releases of application software packages, new features available for hardware, and new equipment announcements. An excellent source of information for improving performance on hardware never utilized enough is the vendor whose equipment is the subject of discussion. Nobody will know better the inner workings of the equipment. Manufacturers build, improve, and maintain hardware and have the broader experience of seeing what many companies are doing with their products. These experiences can be shared with your organization. Examples abound. For instance, experience in operating new computers

Functions	DP Department	User Departments
Application Justification		X
Application Requirements	X	X
Application design	X	X
Application programming	X	
Hardware selection	X	
Hardware installation	X	X
Hardware maintenance	X	
Hardware changes	X	
Controls & secuirty	X	X
Data integrity		X
Plans	X	X
Education	X	X

Figure 4-23. Primary responsibilities for data processing activities today. Note that in some cases both departments are responsible for a particular functional area.

from one organization to another can influence decisions about how much peripheral equipment can really be connected to the mainframe and how best to do it. The actual use of terminals by clerks can often be improved by seeing what other companies are doing, as an illustration, in the development of operational manuals and in-house education. Sharing these kinds of information can come by way of the vendor introducing one of his or her customers to another or simply by relating experiences. The point to remember is that vendors can be more useful to you than just selling you equipment.

An extension of this is the user group. In the United States, for example, users of certain types of hardware and software periodically meet and exchange experiences. GUIDE and SHARE are two such organizations that come to mind; each has committees dedicated to specialized software and hardware whose members all use them. DP managers in specific industries also get together to discuss specialized software and hardware. Thus management in paper companies will meet to discuss plant terminals and paper-related applications, while a manufacturer's association will discuss machine loading and work-in-process code. Within many companies, users of particular systems do meet periodically to share experiences and to funnel suggestions for improvements back to user and data processing management.

CONCLUDING SUGGESTIONS

In this chapter we have covered a great deal of ground by discussing various installation activities. The problems associated with configuring hardware, system-assuring it, developing installation plans, and making sure hardware is installed, together with a review of common concerns about the role of data processing personnel and users and in fine-tuning systems, represent serious and time-consuming activities. Yet the essential theme and thus the basis for any practical advice is that you make sure that everyone involved in an installation communicates with the others in a practical and organized way. Make sure of what you want, how it will go in, and review the results. Document each step (since there are so many confusing ones) and track progress. The same advice applies as much to data processing hardware as it does to manufacturing machinery, fleets of trucks, or to the construction of new plants. If you forget that simple fact, the management of data processing hardware will remain the mysterious activity that it is not.

If we do not lay out ourselves in the service of mankind, whom should we serve?

Abigail Adams

This chapter deals with the all-important issue of hardware availability and how to make sure that the equipment you have is running when you want it to run and as efficiently as possible. It illustrates management principles that are applicable to all types of hardware, especially to computers and their peripheral devices, as well as being cost effective. Managing change and problems, which is always perplexing for most organizations, is discussed in detail, as are specific tools to run data processing smoothly. The benefits to an organization of each of these functions are also reviewed in detail.

CHAPTER
FIVE

Managing Hardware Availability

If equipment does not work when it is supposed to, the justification for such devices goes away. As the complexity of configurations has increased, together with dependence on them, a whole new intensified concern grew in the 1960s and 1970s for an issue called availability. The term *availability* refers to the body of methods and procedures involved in making equipment and software stay running on a timely basis, providing anticipated and desired levels of service. It is a combination of vendor maintenance activities and an organization's own management of hardware resources. Variations of this concern emerge frequently under such labels as "uptime," "response time," "processing speed," "downtime," "fine tuning," and "timeliness," among others. These phrases clearly suggest an organization-wide concern

203

with improving the efficiency and usability of hardware. Although most of the effort involved in improving availability is directed toward the computer itself, in reality it is a delicate balance of resources across all types of hardware and software making up a particular system.

This chapter defines briefly many of the primary issues involved when managing availability of hardware, describing proven methods for maintaining high levels of service across an entire configuration. The emphasis is on showing managers what issues they must focus on in guiding the technical personnel who are actually responsible for ensuring the smooth working of equipment and systems. Some of the topics mentioned below have already been touched on in previous chapters—the impact of better quality technology, capacity planning, and the scheduling of jobs—and others will be reviewed.

The first step in defining availability, and how it can be achieved, is to distinguish among various terms. *Availability* is viewed as the amount of resource that a user of data processing has rather than the amount of time a particular device is operational. As suggested in Chapter 2, if a computer is turned on and operational 99% of the time but the user on a CRT has access to it only 72% of the time, availability is far less than what DP operational management might suggest. Our user would argue that the service level is terrible and rightfully so, because 28% of the time the computer is unavailable. Therefore, availability should be considered as the amount of time, quantity of resource, and speed of service that a user receives. Part of the definition of availability thus also includes establishing standards and managing to them. If, for instance, the on-line system should be up from 8:30 A.M. to 5:30 P.M., anything less than that is poor service—poor availability. A second example: if 5-second response time on the CRTs is the target and, in fact, it is 3 seconds, availability exceeds minimum standards, but if it were 10 seconds, clearly a problem would exist.

Availability is a broad term which describes the effort at maintaining an entire system. Another concept that is commonly confused with availability but is nonetheless linked to it is the familiar phrase *fine tuning*. Fine tuning is the art and science of increasing the amount of work that can be processed through a particular configuration by improving the efficiency of a system or any of its components. This is done by eliminating bottlenecks in a configuration that prevent the overall system from doing more work or faster. Fine tuning is not, as many people still believe, a method for increasing resources. You can only do that by installing bigger computers or more peripherals. Fine tuning is in fact a trade-off of resources. For instance, suppose that response time on the terminals degrades to the point where something has to be done. A DP department can use its capacity planning tools to find the bottleneck (if there is one). In our situation a common one is a disk channel that is heavily utilized. Fine tuning would probably involve shifting files to another channel already on the system, thereby removing contention on the disk channel and possibly relocating files on the disk drives themselves to reduce arm contention. Channel utilization would drop, disk usage increase across a number of drives, and CPU utilization would probably go up as more work comes into the computer not now constrained by the channel. The net result in this case is a better balanced use of resources across the entire configuration, improving response time for the users.

The important lesson is that fine tuning is a part of the process of providing availability. A second set of activities that accomplishes the same objective is the art and science of capacity planning, already discussed in Chapter 2. Both go together to make it possible to have better utilization of equipment and therefore a more cost-effective set of management practices applied to hardware resources. To this end it becomes important to marry hardware to software while linking management precepts as well into an overall coordinated plan for preserving acceptable levels of equipment performance.

INTRODUCTION TO AVAILABILITY MANAGEMENT

No device needs more management to ensure adequate and efficient use of its power than the computer, whether a large CPU or a small micro. Most efforts at availability management and fine tuning thus involve the computer, the primary topic of discussion for the next few pages. It is the one component that dominates any configuration, and often it is the most expensive part. The hardware issues involved include memory and cycle utilizations, I/O usage, software, and data activities. Each in its own way influences the overall availability of the entire system.

Memory and Cycles

As suggested in Chapter 2, memory plays a critical role in availability and in the overall quality of a system's performance. When looking at a computer, one has always to determine whether or not to increase or decrease utilization of either the memory or the speed of the processing. More work going through the machine will require more cycles and memory. More partitions drive up memory usage, while fewer partitions with expanded work loads can do the same. Multiprogramming, involving the use of many partitions concurrently, drives up memory utilization very quickly. As more partitions are added, more I/O to support these jobs is needed. Without this additional hardware, memory usage declines as the overall system is not properly used. This situation can be likened to a lawn mower choked with too much grass. It is fairly well understood today, given current types of technology, that availability declines exponentially as either memory or cycles are overused. Those levels or points of degradation vary from one type of configuration to another and are best defined as part of a capacity planning effort.

The perfectly balanced system which has no CPU waiting (all I/O is being used at reasonable levels) probably does not exist. If there is not enough I/O, cycle utilization shoots up for overhead, making less CPU time available for processing user jobs. This is caused primarily by an increased overhead for I/O queuing, not to mention the limited amounts of peripherals and channels with which to move data in and out of the system.

Many techniques have been developed over the years for balancing loads. Some are part of the operating system provided by the manufacturer of the computer, others are canned packages, and some are homegrown. A few are terribly complicated mathematical queuing methods which often prove to increase overhead themselves or are too complicated for the normal computer center to use realistically. In most cases, such methods are best left to the development labs inventing new computers and software. Yet there are certain steps that any data center can take. As a good rule of thumb, remember that as you increase the speed of a computer, you should increase the speed of all highly used I/O devices. Therefore, do not put slow disk drives on an extremely fast computer. CPU vendors can suggest which devices are most suitable in providing a balanced hardware configuration. For example, putting a slow tape drive originally designed for an IBM 370/115 computer on a large 4341 in a shop that has a great number of time-consuming tape-bound jobs guarantees a built-in bottleneck that simply will not go away. Tinkering with the jobs, their programs, and schedules will not help. The first step then in improving and preserving acceptable levels of availability involves making sure that the access speeds of all I/O devices are appropriate for the computer installed. Failure to do so ensures that the performance of memory and cycles on the computer will be impaired.

Hardware balancing is of particular concern in a multiprogramming environment, where I/O is continually being accessed while various jobs are running concurrently. Utilization of all channels, access devices (such as on disk), and cycles in the CPU to manage these activities are active and will grow exponentially, even geometrically, in this kind of an environment. This is complicated even further by the fact that multiprogramming increases the amount of CPU and memory utilization unless, of course, I/O is so slow that the system in general cannot get the work out effectively.

Reducing the number of I/Os, that is, the amount of traveling to and from peripheral equipment, is another method used to improve computer availability. More buffers, for instance, can be set up to handle larger amounts of work, yet these drive up utilization of memory and thus can bring you more quickly to a point where the situation can present its own bottleneck. In that case, your system would require either more memory or a larger processor. Blocking and deblocking of files and jobs also costs in increased cycle overhead, but are useful techniques to use if data are not coming into the system fast enough. Playing with these can help. If you have a great deal of spare memory, blocking and deblocking can be a method for bringing larger chunks of data into a system. On the other hand, this memory might better be used for multiprogramming more effectively if your blocks are bigger than the average size of a job's program (as would be the case with very small computers). There are no general rules of thumb regarding blocking impacts on systems because they vary too much from one configuration of hardware and software to another. What data centers do is constantly vary them as work loads change, thereby finding in an interactive fashion what improves throughput the best.

Other techniques used to improve the quality of data manipulation and job execution through a computer include blocking of logical records and files together and compacting and decompacting data (also called *encoding*). Each drives up cycle utilization but maximizes channel usage. So if your channel utilization is too high and for the CPU too low, with yet more work to process, these two techniques are worth trying. The same applies to memory. They help bring more work into the computer and can be used to drive up cycle or memory utilization or to push one or the other down. Since memory costs are dropping faster than for any other hardware component, it makes sense to push up memory usage, even adding more memory to a system, as a means of improving the performance of other devices. Using larger blocks of memory to house greater amounts of data for jobs is clearly an attractive and easy trick to use. Storing tables for large number-crunching applications in memory saves having to waste cycles to calculate data needed repeatedly and thus can help hold down CPU cycle usage, not to mention pushdown channel traffic. The most extreme technique calls for storing data entirely in real storage, which reduces the need for peripheral storage, particularly disk, if there is not enough on the system.

Each of the methods outlined above has its own financial implications. Take the last example as a case in point. If a manager has the choice of putting 1 megabyte of data in real storage or in disk, the cost can be compared. If 1 megabyte of storage on the computer costs $15,000 while the same amount on disk is $10,000, then clearly it is less expensive to acquire more disk rather than another bump in memory. If a computer has excess channels but not enough memory, it would also probably be cheaper to acquire more disk, place them on a free channel, and just bring into the CPU those data that are needed at a particular time. However, this should not be done so much that cycle utilization rises too fast, thereby slowing the speed with which jobs are completed. Again, everything has its costs and trade-offs in performance. All resources—costs, hardware, software— must be balanced one against the other.

Impact of System Software on Computers

Several well-understood characteristics of any system will affect the overall performance of a computer. These typically include multiprogramming, paging, and thrashing. *Multiprogramming* is the process of running various jobs at the same time. As usage of a particular job (or partition) increases, the total amount of resources available to other concurrent users declines. Hence most data processing centers will assign priorities of resources to various jobs so that the most important are given processing capabilities first (scheduling). But at some point in a heavily utilized machine, an increasing number of users are simply not given any resources, or too few, by the system. As Figure 5-1 suggests, when the number of jobs increases, the amount of resources available decreases, usually proportionally at first, then later geometrically. Put another way, as the amount of resources required to execute high-priority jobs goes up, the amount of availability for other users goes down, sometimes quite dramatically.

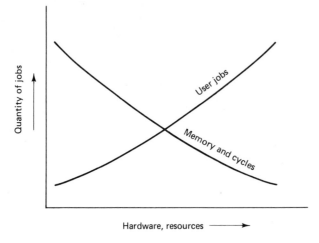

Figure 5-1. Multiprogramming effects on a computer.

On the other hand, with a proper balance of CPU, memory, and I/O (especially disk) utilization, multiprogramming can actually improve overall system throughput or availability. Memory remains active, there are enough cycles to do the work, and disks are properly operating to support the demands of the computer. From a user's point of view, jobs either take longer or shorter to run, response time on the terminals goes up or down, jobs in the print queue are printed quickly or later, batch work is turned around now or the next day. Thus in assessing whether to push more work to memory, cycles, or disk, measure the effect on the user's turnaround time.

Paging rates are dear to the hearts of most systems personnel. To them paging has a folk wisdom around it that says how the system is performing overall. Paging is essentially the process of bringing blocks (pages) of data into real memory for use by the computer. It is a dialogue or passage of information from memory to channels, then to disk or tape. This traffic is measured in the number of chunks of data (pages) that come and go through the system per second. Each page is of a certain size, that is, it equals a certain number of bytes of information, the exact amount varying from one manufacturer of systems control programs to another but generally about 4000 bytes each. Over the years, various calculations have been made to establish what reasonable paging rates are given the size of various computers and are spoken of in terms of pages per second for different types of CPUs and peripheral configurations. These are usually available from vendors on an individual basis and emerge out of years of experience with a particular data center. As a general rule of thumb, as paging rates go up, so does CPU utilization (the overhead to manage traffic), together with channel usage and I/O seeks and writes. That is why paging rates are such useful guides for systems personnel charged with the responsibility of preserving acceptable levels of availability. Paging systems in themselves are useful because they help improve the overall performance of a computer (e.g., faster response times), because they help to provide the data needed at any given time to perform a specific job.

Thrashing is a by-product of this kind of environment when an extreme is reached in unbalanced resources. Remember, paging ensures that the needed data are always brought into memory on a timely basis. Multiprogramming is the method of ensuring that the maximum number of processor cycles can reasonably be used. However, if both are abused, thrashing occurs. This phenomenon manifests itself when the system spends as much resource in doing a multiprogramming job as it might in a monoprogramming environment. Systems personnel liken the process to a situation when the number of I/Os being done exceeds, in terms of overhead, the amount of user jobs being performed. It is also the point when the computer overhead goes up faster than the amount of jobs (their overhead) being given to the CPU to execute. This situation results in a declining amount of user work being completed, and long before an expansion in the amount of time it takes to complete jobs. At some extreme point, jobs are just not completed. In short, thrashing is caused by too much of a good thing.

Thrashing is a common problem in highly utilized systems and commonly leads to yet another problem, commonly known as *deactivation*. In a highly advanced form of computer architecture, the operating system has the capability of, in effect, turning off users or partitions (deactivating them) when there simply is not enough resource to go around and still be able to complete the most critical jobs. Thrashing is often the signal that the system uses as the start of deactivation. By this time either memory or cycles are being used for overhead, far out of proportion to what they might be in a larger system doing the same set of jobs.

All shops at one time or another will experience heavy paging rates, thrashing, and deactivation. The objective is to keep these at a minimum by balancing the load on the system, rescheduling batch work out of prime shift when peak load demands usually exist from on-line systems. However, if these problems persist, particularly after attempts have been made to fine tune everything, it may be time to make your computer salesperson happy by acquiring more hardware. If a proper job has been done on capacity planning, the problems would be seen coming long in advance and hardware changes could thus be properly scheduled.

But many people miss the obvious. Everything must be in balance. Memory must balance with cycles and with peripherals. Multiprogramming, paging, swapping systems, and so on, have an invisible relationship that changes from configuration to configuration but which is quickly identifiable to system personnel using the techniques described in Chapter 2. Understanding which portion of a system to fine tune and thereby to improve overall system availability then becomes a fairly simple process. Although it is fundamentally a process of trial and error done on an ongoing basis as jobs change and capacity requirements need to be identified, it is in practice normal, comfortable, and accurate.

Fine-Tuning Techniques

Other methods are available for improving the performance of a system and thus in making availability better. One of the most frequently used, as a result of capacity planning, is rescheduling. Although this was discussed briefly in Chapter 2, some additional points are worth keeping in mind. Too often in a system, the amount of work being processed during peak-load times is far out of proportion to other times and much need not be processed when the system is so heavily utilized. Thus managers seek to level their work loads as much as possible to improve overall systems performance. (See Figure 5-2.) Batch jobs being run during peak-load periods might be pushed to earlier or later hours or shifts. One on-line system may be allowed to be on the air only in the morning, another only in the afternoon. As on-line systems proliferate, peak loading becomes a critical concern.

In a purely batch environment, almost perfect leveling is even realistically possible but not in an on-line environment, where everyone comes to

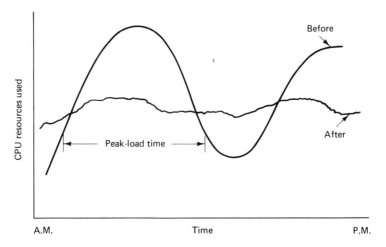

Figure 5-2. Peak loads and leveling. The objective is to level the work as much as possible within reason.

work in the user community at about 8:30 in the morning and leaves at 5 in the afternoon. Peak loads tend to go from 9 to 12 and from 1:30 to 4. They start out shorter, for instance 9 to 11, then expand to 12, 1 to 4, and get more intense as the number of users in these periods increases. Most DP managers fail to track properly the evolution of peak utilization. They keep loading on more work and installing more CRTs everywhere without tracking the impact of these actions on the system. Even more sloppily, they add terminals and do not track how many active users there are on a system during peak loads, yet they might even have software installed that at the flick of an on-line command could give them such data.

Active users are a concern that clearly needs attention. For example, suppose that 100 terminals are installed. As a good rule of thumb that is often violated, a DP manager can expect 25% of all installed CRTs to be active and in use at any given time during peak load. So if 100 are installed, 25 could be expected to be in use during the day. If each CRT uses 1.5% of the CPU, then during peak load these terminals are absorbing 37.5% of the system. When that population creeps to 200 CRTs, about 75% of the system must now be dedicated to the on-line community or a bigger CPU has to be installed. The first step taken is usually to reschedule batch work into night shifts to meet the additional requirements for cycles, memory, and disk without buying more resource.

How often has anyone suggested reviewing all the jobs being done on a system to see if they should be executed at all? This is rarely done. Yet there are jobs being run on probably all mainframes that do not need to be, or as frequently, or at the time currently scheduled. A periodic audit of all jobs, done say once a year, will invariably reveal this kind of problem, which left uncorrected, forces down the quality of availability. There are, for example, reports being printed that are never read, probably because they are too long or could be printed once a week instead of every day. Producing exception reports instead of fully detailed documents also cuts down on overhead, yet provides more relevant, easier-to-use reports. Eliminating excess printing, for instance, can make more printing capability available for more relevant, time-dependent print jobs while not burdening the computer with superfluous work.

Other techniques, involving retiring inefficient application code poorly written in the first place, could be the subject of an entire book. The point is, however, that there are programs around in all shops which take up too many resources or are too slow. Changing operating systems by going to releases that are more efficient and with shorter data paths can improve availability from 5% to as much as 15% without altering job streams, reconfiguring hardware, or retraining users. Using more efficient sort/merge packages (which in many systems account for about 40% of all processing) can have a dramatic effect on availability. Using different languages to program jobs can also be very helpful. Languages such as APL and PL/1 are often more efficient and therefore faster to process than COBOL jobs.

There are many instructions that take only two lines of APL to write which in COBOL require ten. You shorten the amount of time to write a program while reducing the time to process in a computer. Clearly, there are both hardware and software productivity considerations here to be kept in mind when selecting what languages and operating systems to use.

Objectives of Availability Tuning

Up to this point we have been discussing the relationship of various components and the impact they have on each other. Keeping those elements in mind, there are some general goals on availability that should be established as targets for any department. Setting specific goals gives meaning and direction to those charged with the responsibility of maintaining some sort of availability. Since these would naturally vary from one organization to another, it is more meaningful to catalog the areas that should have targets:

- Strive for a stable operating system with minimum of software problems (such as broken code, bugs, etc.).
- Strive for a relatively clean set of application programs that also have a minimum number of software problems.
- Strive for a balance in the use of the key hardware components of a configuration by never having one resource extremely over- or under-utilized.
- Draw on the hardware manufacturer's guidelines for what constitutes overutilization as a means of defining specific goals in any balancing effort.
- Take capacity planning data and use them to identify where bottlenecks exist in the system and as a means of measuring the results of fine-tuning efforts.
- Establish specific performance objectives with users (such as CRT response time, turnaround time on batch jobs, printing, etc.), so that any tuning activity is directed toward meeting those specific objectives.
- Remember that there will also be a fine-tuning effort necessary to maintain changing levels of required availability. In short, the process never ends.

Typically, more tuning is required than normal when (1) a new major piece of hardware is installed or (2) when the number of users or jobs has taken a dramatic jump up in utilization. The first condition is always caused by the fact that all the prognostication in the world will never be a complete substitute for running jobs on your machine. When a new computer is installed, for example, the work load will perform differently than as forecasted, so adjustments have to be made. Also, new equipment calls for another learning process as operational personnel familiarize themselves with the new and different equipment in their own specific environment. As new and major applications go on the system, an intense period of tuning usually takes place in order to fold in the additional work load within existing requirements, thereby minimizing the effects of declining availability. Any application that adds 10% or more to the work load can be expected to require such activity. Generally speaking, anything less will probably not have a dramatic impact on a system unless it is highly utilized already.

Technically speaking, there are a number of specific objectives in tuning to improve availability that go beyond the general recommendations just made. These include:

- Reduce bottlenecks or gaps in the usage of all system resources.
- Reduce inefficient use of resources (both hardware and software, particularly disk and on-line programs).
- Level out or balance the utilization of all resources across the entire system (especially channels).
- Improve computer throughput without adding too many resources by making sure that paging rates are kept low, deactivation is never allowed, and thrashing is kept to a minimum.
- Reduce or hold the line on CRT response time and maintain this consistently.
- Offload to other portions of a system or network jobs and activities being performed by those portions of the hardware being overworked (from one disk channel to another, for example).

If these fail to provide adequate availability, you can always acquire more disk, memory, or a bigger computer.

In general, tuning objectives are most frequently defined by focusing on both capacity issues (as discussed in Chapter 2) and throughput. The latter involves every piece of hardware in a system but is applicable most frequently to the CPU and critical channels. By this, one usually means getting the most amount of work done (through the system) in any given period of time, usually within a 24-hour segment. Such performance is frequently graphed (e.g., the amount of time to do x job today versus previously). Figure 5-3 suggests three situations. In line 1, there is good throughput versus resources expended and thus little fine tuning is probably possible. Lines 2 and 3 suggest opportunities for improvement because the amounts of work being done here are dependent on the performance of specific hardware (such as memory, cycles, disk seeks, etc.).

As hinted at in the figure, the possibility of overtuning exists and should be avoided. The DP manager who brags that he or she has 4-second response time for CRTs, with a CPU utilized at 99%, is probably guilty of spending more time, money, and effort at tuning than is worthwhile. For example, the

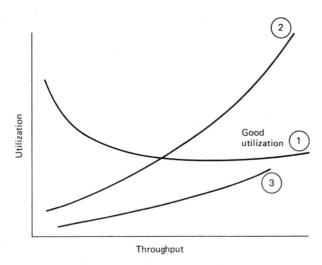

Figure 5-3. Throughput utilization versus resource utilization.

author once saw this exact situation with a 99% utilized CPU. The DP manager in this particular case had two systems analysts dedicated to tuning at a cost of $7800 per month (their salaries and benefits). The same hardware availability could have been achieved by upgrading the system to the next-size computer with more memory and for a cost of $4300 per month. This manager could thus have saved his organization $3800 or left open the option of using the systems people for other cost-effective projects, such as application development. Clearly, he had stretched the technical capabilities of the hardware to its limits but had shown poor business judgment.

Yet even on a more technical note, overtuning can have disastrous effects on availability. The lack of flexibility in resource availability within a system when something goes wrong will quickly degrade overall performance. For instance, the absence of some slack in memory can cause major degradation in response time when there is a slight, unanticipated increase in the requirement for memory, which in a less-tuned system would be provided by the computer without having any effect on users. Also, if your calculations on usage are off by even a little, you may be the cause of degraded response time, severe thrashing, and even possible deactivation of applications in which little or nothing gets done. Therefore, give a system some slack, a buffer against unanticipated work loads, and balance the increased cost of systems maintenance against the declining expense of hardware. Many operations managers generally consider a computer as running flat out when it is about 70% utilized, channels at 55%, and printers, disks, and tapes when utilized more than 75%. They find that it is smarter to throw more memory or disk at a problem than to do the more exciting job of tuning the system technically. In the end, fine tuning should be a combination of technical expertise being used, yet managed with business prudence.

WHAT IS PROBLEM MANAGEMENT?

Regardless of tuning procedures, all systems remain dynamic because they constantly change. Change itself is thus a major cause of declining availability. Therefore, tuning in itself is not enough to counter the forces at work on any system. Just as soon as a configuration is fine tuned and the users settle back into a comfortable routine, a new application goes on that affects everyone. More terminals cause degraded response time, or additional disk pushes up utilization on channels, and so on, forcing a new look at tuning. Therefore, in addition to normal tuning activities, data processing management finds it necessary to initiate formal procedures for managing problems and changes. Some of these were described in Chapter 4 and are applicable in providing adequate levels of availability. The most obvious is planning the installation of a computer quickly and at a time when most users are off the system, such as on the weekend or at night. But that is the exception, because most installations rarely change their computers and do not daily add peripherals. So a method to account for normal ongoing problem management becomes an essential part of controlling hardware in a cost-effective manner.

The first step taken in problem management is to establish a method of reporting concerns. This is essential particularly as the number of users relying on data processing increases, since they are the people in any organization who know the least about computers. Therefore, one must develop a method for reporting problems in terms understood by them, yet relevant to data processing, because it is only at that point when someone can look for a solution and thereby restore availability. Second, together with a reporting mechanism comes the opportunity to take too long to fix the problem as it is defined, too long to find the correct person to fix it, and too long to identify and apply a solution. Pressures on DP can be enormous, particularly if the whole system is down with hundreds of users unable to process work and all screaming to know when they can go back to work. Another element of problem management involves avoiding these crises by tracking changes to the system, hardware, software, and applications. If a specific change caused a problem, appropriate documentation can thus be available for quick analysis and hopefully will suggest a fast solution.

Often one individual is assigned the responsibility for tracking changes—a change coordinator—to whom DP management goes at a time of crisis and who works with hardware and software operational personnel to ensure that a solution is found. Another tactic profitably employed today is scheduling changes so as not to inconvenience users, thereby not taking away availability from other departments. Such a person should track all problems and changes over time to provide management with the kind of information necessary to improve the reaction and solution development process while shortening the amount of time needed to fix problems. Without this complicated activity being so monitored, availability will suffer.

A formal problem management procedure has proven cost benefits for any organization. Essentially, such a procedure involves increasing the availability of systems, lowering the costs of hardware and software for both the organization in general and users specifically, and improving productivity by driving down the total amount of personnel costs dedicated to maintenance functions. Figure 5-4 suggests areas of cost typical in most organizations and where quantifiable benefits may be found by having a problem

Effort	*Benefit*
Reporting a problem	Easy if reporting to only one point
Executing a bypass	Moderate but faster than no solution
Determining the significance of a problem	Cheaper if a problem coordinator does this
Effort and time to enforce procedures	Faster problem identification and resolution
Bringing all problem solvers together	Dramatic cost reduction in problem resolution
Effort and time to solve problems	Major cost savings on resolution and maintenance activity
Effort to test solutions	Significant reduction in rerun, lost time, disasters, maintenance
Effort to make change and to document reschedules	Moderate benefits, primarily in time; preserves controls
Effort at backups	Significant if a disaster hits the data center

Figure 5-4. Efforts and benefits of a good change control system.

management system in place. Other benefits which are not as easily quantifiable but which contribute directly to increased availability and usage of hardware include:

- A diminished number of crises because procedures will contain problems before they get worse.

- Increased control over operations in general because of better reporting procedures.

- Reduced user dissatisfaction because users are kept better informed about availability, the DP department's services to them, problems, and resolutions.

- Faster reporting of problems because properly defined procedures will increase the probability of problems being defined properly and quickly and put on the desk of those best qualified to fix them.

- Redundancy of changes are avoided through better coordination and reporting.

- More deadlines are met through better understanding of problems anticipated and overcome.

- Reduced maintenance activity because better systems and reporting minimize potential problems that call for additional repair work.

- Better utilization of hardware through decreased need for job reruns, testing, and catchup work.

- Better availability since productivity of systems, hardware, and people in both user and DP departments has been shown to be possible with better problem management techniques.

Large data centers today generally have problem management procedures in place. They have proven to be all that they promised. Increasingly, such methods are being employed in medium-sized data centers and in smaller shops simply because the dependence on data processing has increased to a point where such organizations can no longer live without them.

The Process Defined

The process is essentially quite simple. First, someone has to perceive that there is a problem and sets up a hot line or desk that users can come to for help. Now a user determines that something is wrong and goes to one person to relay the concern and its characteristics. The problem coordinator takes down the information, asks appropriate questions, and tracks the problem until it is finally resolved. This person also makes sure that the problem lands on the desk of whoever should solve it. The individual resolving the problem comes up with an answer and documents the solution, which must then be audited for impact on hardware and software performance. Once approved, it is applied. (See Figure 5-5.) Periodically, a review of problems is held with management to identify patterns of concerns and to implement procedures to improve the daily availability of the system. Depending on the size

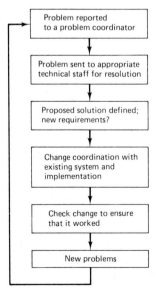

Figure 5-5. Change management process.

of installation, the problem coordinator and the change coordinator might be the same person, or various individuals might operate a "hot desk" much like a complaint department in a large retail store.

An early step in setting up such a procedure for handling problems is to define what the requirements are for your organization, followed by the development of plans to implement procedures. Finally, the department must create a reporting mechanism to keep track of events for purposes of future better management of availability of hardware and software. It is absolutely imperative that this third step be rigorously employed; otherwise, you do not learn from your mistakes or those of others. One person can either head up the installation phase of such a program or do it all himself or herself, reporting directly to the DP or MIS director. A number of questions must be answered in the planning stages:

- Who currently handles DP problems and changes?
- How do they do this today?
- Where are the bottlenecks and other problem areas?
- Where should the problem coordinator or individual handling a "hot line" fit into the DP department's organizational structure?
- To whom should that person report?
- How much responsibility and what type should be placed in this function?
- What documents should be used to support problem definition and crisis management?
- Are there other tools that will be needed?
- What reports should be developed to document trends in problems and resolutions?
- What methods should be employed in managing this functional area?

These all involve a myriad of questions about how detailed reports should be, how often management must review the operations of systems management, how these must be applied to capacity planning and fine tuning, as well as concerns about who should carry out this responsibility and how to get the users to cooperate. Surely the current system of having users either call the DP manager directly or the computer room cannot be continued as problems and users increase in number. What is most exciting is that this approach really works.

Reporting a Problem

To fix a hardware or software problem, it must first be reported to data processing with its characteristics identified in sufficient detail to permit resolution. This can be done by having a standard form to report problems on and by training users and DP personnel on how to document their concerns. Users of data processing should have a fast and simple way to do this, with a minimal amount of training or bother. They should be able to identify their concerns on a document, have a telephone number to call (usually printed on the CRT), and be prepared to answer certain types of questions. The same applies to the DP department. Figure 5-6 illustrates a sample problem reporting form, suggesting the type of information that must be collected. Note that this form allows the DP department to create an audit trail on what was done by whom, which later management can assess and thereby determine the quality of the DP department's response to problems. Notice that it does not require an enormous amount of detail, so it can be filled out quickly, yet provide enough information to start the process of problem resolution.

The question of who should handle such a function is critical. Because most problems coming in will start out as a complaint about an application not working, in general the individual should have a software background. Second, this person should be patient, understanding, polite, and not become harried by the existence of so many problems. Operations should keep that person informed about anticipated or actual hardware and systems problems so that as users call in, they can be given some news. The manager handling problem management probably should have a software background but can be an operations manager. Clearly, both software and hardware managers should jointly set up the procedures in the beginning and share in the periodic reviews. Various members of the DP department's software and operations staffs can take turn answering telephones, provided that they meet the requirements just described. Rotation also forces members of the staff to deal with users and causes them to see what goes on outside the monastic walls of DP.

Coordinating Resolutions

Once identified, the problem has to be put in front of an individual who could possibly fix it. This could be a software specialist, an operations manager, a hardware operator, a teleprocessing specialist—whoever. The individual selected to fix a problem can come from a list available to the problem coordinator based on skills, or the problem can be passed to a manager, who then assigns it immediately to someone. The process of taking a call on a problem also involves identifying a possible solution and once a solution has been determined, getting back to the user with bypass information or a resolution. The problem coordinator or the person fixing the problem should also establish a deadline for the solution so that users can plan around the breakdown. The documents flowing from such a dialogue form an audit trail and consist of a problem determination report, logs, minutes of meetings with key personnel, and reviews after major problems or clusters of them to see how things might have been handled more efficiently.

Figure 5-7 illustrates the problem reported in Figure 5-6, but this time with the second section filled in, indicating the first step toward resolution

PROBLEM REPORT

NO.

0093

For **PROBLEM REPORTER:** Fill in this section, keep last copy, and forward rest to Dept PC.

Name: Eva Smith _____ *Dept:* Accounts *Ext:* 412 *Date:* 760102

Machine/System used:

☒ TSO
☐ IMS/VS
☐ OS/VS1
☐ OS/VS2
☐ S/370-155
☐ S/370-158
☐ S/3

Description of problem:

Tried to copy lines from beginning to end
of dataset. When I scrolled, I got
Abend ØC4.

_____

_____

Supporting documentation attached:

☐ Hard copy of screen ☐ VTOC listing ☐ Other—specify: _____
☐ Program listing   ☐ SEREP dump
☒ System dump   ☐   _____

Is this problem holding up your work? Yes/No

For **COORDINATOR:** Keep last copy and send rest to problem solver.

Problem already reported: Yes/No—Report no.____Date: _____

Problem area: _____

Priority:___ Deadline (bypass /solution): _____ *Assigned to:* _____ *Date:* _____

Priority:___ Deadline (bypass /solution): _____ *Assigned to:* _____ *Date:* _____

Priority:___ Deadline (bypass/solution): _____ *Assigned to:* _____ *Date:* _____

Solution accepted by: _____ *Date:* _____ *Closing code:* _____

For **PROBLEM SOLVER:** Keep last copy. Return a copy to Dept PC at each update.

Description of bypass: _____

_____

Change request no.___submitted on:_____ Final: Yes/No   *Solution code:*

Change request no.___submitted on:_____ Final: Yes/No   _____

Information to users: on bypass   on solution

  —By coordinator when problem reported   ☐

  —By report to problem meeting   ☐   ☐

  – In newsletter _____   ☐   ☐

  —In handbook _____   ☐   ☐

Comments: _____

_____

_____

Figure 5–6. Sample problem report form. (Source: IBM Corporation, © 1976.)

PROBLEM REPORT

NO.

For PROBLEM REPORTER: Fill in this section, keep last copy, and forward rest to Dept PC.

Name: Eva Smith   *Dept:* Accounts *Ext:* 412 *Date:* 760102

Machine/System used: *Description of problem:*

☒ TSO   Tried to copy lines from beginning to end
☐ IMS/VS   of dataset. When I scrolled, I got
☐ OS/VS1
☐ OS/VS2   Abend ØC4.
☐ S/370-155
☐ S/370-158
☐ S/3

Supporting documentation attached:

☒ Hard copy of screen   ☒ VTOC listing   ☐ Other—specify: _____
☐ Program listing   ☐ SEREP dump
☒ System dump   ☐   _____

Is this problem holding up your work? Yes/No

For COORDINATOR: Keep last copy and send rest to problem solver.

Problem already reported: Yes/No Report no.____Date: _____

Problem area: TSO SPF edit

Priority: 4 *Deadline (bypass /solution):* 76020 *Assigned to:* TSO Support *Date:* 76 0115

*Priority:*___*Deadline (bypass /solution):* _____ *Assigned to:*_____ *Date:*_____

*Priority:*___*Deadline (bypass/solution):* _____ *Assigned to:*_____ *Date:*_____

Solution accepted by: _____ *Date:* _____ *Closing code:* _____

For PROBLEM SOLVER: Keep last copy. Return a copy to Dept PC at each update.

Description of bypass: _____

_____

*Change request no.*___*submitted on:*_____ *Final:* Yes/No   *Solution code:*

*Change request no.*___*submitted on:*_____ *Final:* Yes/No

Information to users: on bypass   on solution

  —By coordinator when problem reported   ☐
  —By report to problem meeting   ☐   ☐
  - In newsletter _____   ☐   ☐
  —In handbook _____   ☐   ☐

Comments: _____

_____

_____

Figure 5-7. Sample problem report. (Source: IBM Corporation, © 1976.)

221

Problem Log

Source			Problem		Signficance		Solution			
Number	Date	Source	Subject	New?	1 to 5	Deadline	Assigned To	Assigned Date	Solution	Closed
98	0102	Smith/AC	TSO	Yes	3	0202	Ralph	0115	0202	0203
99	0103	Jones/Sales	CRT # 50111 broken	No	5	0204	Mary	0116	0207	0207

Open Problem Report   Week/ending 5/17/82

Operations	5
TP	6
Development group 1	15
Financial dev. group	4
Data base manager	3
Total this week	33

Figure 5-8. Sample problem report control sheets.

of the problem. This document allows for a check against past problems to see if there is a solution already available, appropriate documentation, and in-house talent to implement the solution. A follow-up telephone call to the user might be necessary to obtain more details, which can also be accounted for on this sheet. It is also important to know how critical the problem is to the user because that information lets DP management know whether or not resources have to be pulled away from something else. Thus if a CRT malfunctions in a department that has 30 other CRTs, the problem is not severe. On the other hand, if an RJE station breaks down just as it is beginning to print payroll checks, the problem is critical.

In addition to reporting specific incidents, a log should be kept of incoming problems for later review. Individual problems are unique, but collectively they may document a more fundamental problem, such as the steady decline in response time, availability of batch partitions, slow decline in available disk space, or chronic teleprocessing line problems, and thus can be input to either fine tuning or capacity planning, both of which support the mission of maintaining adequate levels of availability. Logs do not have to be very detailed or complicated to fill out; Figure 5-8 illustrates a simple approach designed for fast use.

Solving a Problem

Now that the problem report exists, it should go to the individual assigned to fix the problem with whatever documentation the individual at the "hot desk" collected. This problem solver has the responsibility for updating a change log, indicating what he or she wanted to do, so that management can approve the solution. Diagnosis of the problem would be detailed and technical. The appropriate technical people would be consulted and a documented solution proposed. Figure 5-9 illustrates the original problem form now filled in with comments by the person assigned to fix the problem.

As with any other software or hardware change within the DP department, a formal request should be made. The form used as a vehicle for this transaction should be the same as the one users and the department fill out for other, normal application work and should not be a special form used just to identify hot problems; there are too many forms around anyway, so do not add another. As with any form, however, a definition of the problem or request for a change should be sufficient to make it possible for management to understand. (See Figure 5-10.) This document, once the proposed change has been approved, can go to whoever is responsible for making the change. Thus a full record of what happened is prepared quickly and easily and preserved. Along with a log similar to the problem log already referred to, anyone can keep up with the changes made in an organized manner, using a change log that probably already exists rather than approaching difficulties as a panic event.

Managing Systems Management

In any installation, what was just described would normally happen many times each day with varying degrees of severity. If the process is to be more than simply a smooth and efficient way of fixing specific problems, management must also review these files to determine if there is a pattern of behavior, if there are problems not readily seen that require attention as a means of reducing the overall number of incidents, and as a way of being able to measure the quality of availability. The process is clearly a linking of software and hardware considerations. There are tools and techniques commonly in use today which help management in general to manage problems beyond the individual crises.

For management to react intelligently, it needs to have certain types of information which can only be properly gathered in a disciplined fashion if DP personnel are required to prepare certain reports periodically. These should cover reporting on the status of problems, changes, and on hardware and software availability. The objective is to take crisis events, that is, nonroutine occurrences, and treat them in a normal fashion thereby reducing their potential damage and expense. And for many of the same reasons outlined in Chapter 4, a review of detailed documentation allows management to rebound more quickly from a problem situation.

In problems analysis, management should look for trends. Are terminals going down more often today than last year? What is happening to key applications; are there more problems than before? Are certain types of hardware

PROBLEM REPORT

NO.

For PROBLEM REPORTER: Fill in this section, keep last copy, and forward rest to Dept PC.

Name: _Eva Smith_ *Dept:* _Accounts_ *Ext:* _412_ *Date:* _760102_

Machine/System used: *Description of problem:*

☒ TSO _Tried to copy lines from beginning to end_
☐ IMS/VS _of dataset. When I scrolled, I got_
☐ OS/VS1 _Abend 0C4._
☐ OS/VS2
☐ S/370-155
☐ S/370-158
☐ S/3

Supporting documentation attached:

☒ Hard copy of screen   ☒ VTOC listing   ☐ Other—specify: _____
☐ Program listing   ☐ SEREP dump
☒ System dump   ☐

Is this problem holding up your work? Yes/No (circled No)

For COORDINATOR: Keep last copy and send rest to problem solver.

Problem already reported: Yes/No (circled No) Report no.____ Date: _____

Problem area: _TSO SPF edit_

Priority: _4_ Deadline (bypass /solution): _76022_ Assigned to: _TSO Support_ Date: _76 0115_

Priority: _5_ Deadline (bypass /solution): _✓_ Assigned to: _"_ Date: _76 0124_

*Priority:*___ Deadline (bypass/solution): _____ Assigned to:_____ Date:_____

Solution accepted by: _____ Date: _____ Closing code: _____

For PROBLEM SOLVER: Keep last copy. Return a copy to Dept PC at each update.

Description of bypass: _Only happens when scrolling full page or more. Use_
half page instead

Change request no. _45_ submitted on: _160408_ Final: Yes/No (No)   Solution code:
VEN

Change request no.___ submitted on:_____ Final: Yes/No

Information to users: *on bypass*   *on solution*

—By coordinator when problem reported   ☒
—By report to problem meeting   ☐   ☐
- In newsletter _____   ☐   ☐
—In handbook _____   ☐   ☐

Comments: _Referred to vendor, solution rec'd in zap 02 of_
_760321._

Figure 5-9. Sample problem report. (Source: IBM Corporation, © 1976.)

224

CHANGE REQUEST   No.   0045

For REQUESTER: Fill in this section, keep last copy, and forward rest to Change Coordinator.

Name: John Marshall   *Dept:* TSO Supp   *Ext:* 225   *Date:* 76-04-08

Affected element:	*Type of change:*	*Description:*
TSO SPF	Monthly run	Zaps

Reason for change: *Comments:*

☒ Solution to problem _____

☐ New requirements _____

☐ Other _____

Dependencies:

This change must be implemented before/after/with: _____

Supporting documentation: List of Zaps

Who will be affected?   *In what way?*

TSO Users   New parameters to TEST command

Who has budgetary responsibility?

Name: John Marshall   *Dept:* TSOS   *J. Marshall* 76-04-08

(Signature and date when change approved)

For COORDINATOR: Keep last copy and send rest to change implementer.

Agreement required from: *Received:*   *Agreement required from:*   *Received:*

_____   _____   _____   _____

_____   _____   _____   _____

Change scheduled for: _____   *Date:* _____

For CHANGE IMPLEMENTER: Keep last copy and return rest to Change Coordinator.

Change implemented on: _____   *Signature:* _____

Comments: _____

Figure 5-10. Sample change request form. (Source: IBM Corporation, © 1976.)

Weekly Problem Summary Report   For Week Ending _____

		Severity			
Software	*Number*	*1*	*2*	*3*	*4*
Open from last week	_____	__	__	__	__	__
New problems	_____	__	__	__	__	__
Problems solved	_____	__	__	__	__	__
Waiting for solution	_____	__	__	__	__	__
Waiting for APAR	_____	__	__	__	__	__
Operations					
Open from last week	_____	__	__	__	__	__
New problems	_____	__	__	__	__	__
Problems solved	_____	__	__	__	__	__
Waiting for solution	_____	__	__	__	__	__
Unscheduled IPL's	_____	__	__	__	__	__
Number of reruns	_____	__	__	__	__	__
Hardware (hours)		Comments			
Downtime on CPU	_____	_____
Downtime on disk	_____	_____
Downtime on tape	_____	_____
Downtime on printers	_____	_____
Downtime on CRTs	_____	_____
Downtime other	_____	_____

Figure 5-11. Sample weekly problem status report.

malfunctioning more often now than before? (See Figure 5-11.) How fast was the department in a position to recover, and why? Or, why not? (See Figure 5-12.) Regarding hardware, actual downtime should be clocked very strictly by device type. Figure 5-13 shows one installation's downtime for an entire system (CPU, peripherals, software). (See also Figure 5-14.)

Management should also document meetings on various types of problems so as to track them. Minutes of meetings should not state who said

Weekly and Year-to-Date
Systems Problem Report   Date _____

Problem	This Week	Year to Date
CPU	4	75
Tape	9	99
Disk	13	110
Printer	2	15
TP controller	0	3
Card I/O	2	19
Operator errors	10	1109
Reruns	10	1300
Lost output	1	64
Incomplete output	3	87
Space allocation	5	100
Application	30	700
Systems	3	110
Data base	2	22
JCL	2	45
Procedures	10	111
Other	3	330
Total	114	4299

Figure 5-12. Sample weekly systems problem report.

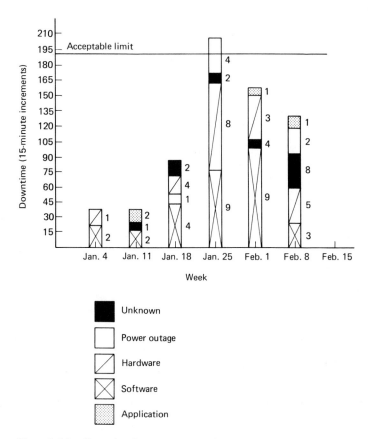

Figure 5-13. Chart showing system downtime by type. Numbers indicate occurrences.

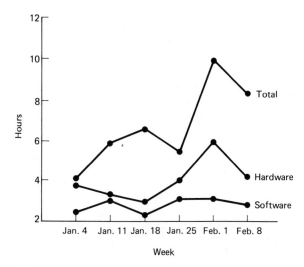

Figure 5-14. Summary of system outage by week and hours.

227

XYZ Meeting with Magic Software Incorporated   2/15/82

Attending: _XYZ_: R. Jones, P. Smith, J. Gonzalez

            Magic: R, Marbel, R. Levy

Subject: Status of A/R package

I.   Closed

      1.   Unable to copy vendor file.
           Was caused by faulty file label. Correct procedure outlined
           in new procedure manual received at meeting. Closed 2/10/82.

      2.   Redundant customer number list. Was caused by broken code
           in file module. APAR submitted; fix installed 2/8/82.

II.   Open

      1.   Password message 2115.
           Magic doing problem determination; not completed; priority 2.
      2.   Insufficient number of user manuals delivered. Magic has
           ordered 10; expects them delivered by 3/1/82. Priority 5.
      3.   Release 3.
           It was determined that support for Release 2 would continue
           until June; therefore, Release 3 would be installed by 5/15/82.
           Priority 1.
      4.   Magic asked for reference accounts using Release 3. Deadline
           4/1/82. Priority 4.

Submitted by,

R. Jones

Figure 5-15. Sample minutes of meeting lasting two hours.

what to whom but simply what the problems were, what was done to fix them, and what remains as open issues. These meetings should also be used to define criteria for fixing problems. (See Figure 5-15.) Figure 5-16 illustrates the output of one such meeting, illustrating the kind of information that must be captured on paper. This simple guideline was developed by

Severity	Type	Performance Objective
1	System goes down	Fix within 24 hours
2	Subsystem crashes	Fix within 24 hours
3	Slows critical application	Fix within 3 days or before next run time
4	Impacts testing	Fix within 5 days
5	Miscellaneous	Fix within 4 weeks

Figure 5-16. Sample of problem severity standards for use by users and DP with target dates for resolution known by both groups.

looking at a month's worth of problem logs to establish what was obtainable and how. The comments made in this chapter apply to all forms of hardware, whether on a central host, a mini, a terminal, or a process controller. The elements of good management for availability remain the same across all configurations and circumstances.

    Fortunately for most organizations, the elementary rudiments of an information system with which to manage better availability are already in place. Most operating systems on computers today generate various types of usage data, error listings, and hardware utilization statistics. Many DP departments have chargeout systems in place which already cause additional data on usage by software package and application to be generated. Those departments that do serious capacity planning have yet additional information to draw on. Finally, almost every data processing department has logs which the operators fill out routinely on such topics as:

- Operator errors
- Unscheduled and scheduled initial program loads (IPLs)
- Hardware malfunctions, fixes, and vendor maintenance response time
- Usage of tape, disk, and printers
- Software outage errors

These kinds of information serve as the foundation for good systems management.

AVAILABILITY AND HARDWARE MAINTENANCE

So far discussion in this chapter has focused on such issues as the best use of installed equipment, and other chapters have reviewed when hardware should be changed and what might be used. Everything so far has dealt with what DP and user personnel within an organization can do to have the right equipment, at a reasonable cost, being used in an efficient manner. Another link in our hardware chain is the actual maintenance of hardware when it physically breaks down. Similarly, the whole issue of broken code which must be fixed by a vendor requires attention. Thus the entire topic of relations with the manufacturers of your equipment and software is critical if the procedures and controls discussed in this book are to work well, because understanding how primary vendors maintain equipment and software goes far toward ensuring that your installation is properly supported. The objective is two-fold: first, to make vendors support your installation the way it has to be, and second, to make sure that your plans and procedures are not fundamentally in conflict with theirs.

Vendor maintenance has become an overnight issue that in the past rarely got any attention because in just the past two years there have been some fundamental changes instituted in the way DP manufacturers have decided to support their products. Not since the 1950s have such changes taken place. Yet the reasons for these are not hard to find. As suggested in Chapter 1, the cost of hardware has plummeted in the past several years for two reasons: improving technologies and changing methods of maintenance. One goes with the other. As new technologies evolved, the amount of maintenance required declined and at a time when maintenance (a highly labor intensive activity) was going up sharply in cost. The latter condition forced all major vendors to develop new ways of managing maintenance. Moreover, as the industry grew dramatically with thousands of new computers being installed and millions of terminals, the old ways simply would not work, especially in an era when dependence on data processing's availability was sharply on the rise. Today, no major vendor supports its customers the same way as in the 1970s or as late as about 1980–1981. New methods are the rule, and the patterns already evident will be expanded. Appreciating these developments makes it easier for data processing departments to take advantage of them as part of their overall program for managing hardware.

Central-Site Maintenance

Vendor maintenance practices cover essentially three types of activities:

- Mainframe hardware
- Peripherals and terminals
- Software of all types

Each is rapidly undergoing dramatic changes in support. The least fundamental of these changes regards large computers and their immediate peripherals (tape and disk drives, systems printers, etc.); nonetheless, even here changes are discernible. Just in the past three or four years, new computers and peripherals that are smaller and have fewer parts have reached the market. There are fewer mechanical (moving) components, since an increasing number of functions are being taken over by microcode or chips, neither of which physically moves and is therefore never repaired, only replaced. Equivalent-powered devices from the late 1960s and early 1970s had thousands of feet or more of internal cabling and wiring, dozens more moving parts, were usually a third larger in size and weight, and broke down more often. Maintenance of these devices required at least one-third more maintenance activity on the part of computer vendors than do current technologies. The proof is evident everywhere. Notice what is being charged today for maintenance compared to years earlier. Although the cost per hour has continued to rise, the overall costs decreased since the number of hours that had to be spent maintaining equipment declined. Thus a machine that cost $2000 per month to maintain in 1974 might, in today's equivalent technology, only cost $500. Vendors are not giving away maintenance today; it is just that technology is currently better, thus requiring fewer repairs.

Repair incidents are down per unit. There are fewer parts to fix and those that do break down are simply replaced quickly, often with fairly inexpensive components. Logic boards that cost $50,000 ten years ago cost thousands less today. The result of all this is that the breakdown incidence will probably continue to decline, together with the amount of field engineering coverage needed per device.

Another change that has come about as a direct by-product of this new technology is a decline in the amount of preventive maintenance necessary. As highly mechanical parts disappear from a configuration, so does the need for preventive maintenance. Tape drives and printers will require this kind of effort, but not disk (now with their nonremovable packs) or most computers, minis, micros, and intelligent terminals. Hence the requirement to turn a whole system over to the field engineers weekly or bimonthly for preventive maintenance is beginning to disappear. This means that systems are more available to users.

When equipment does break down, two other trends become evident. Diagnostic tools are improving each year, resulting in faster identification of a problem and, therefore, quicker resolution. These diagnostic capabilities are resident in built-in trouble identification chips in a machine or resident on microcode that logs recoverable problems and gathers data on nonrecoverable crises. There are many troubles which machines today can recover from that they could not years ago, and thus do not require immediate maintenance attention. Also, maintenance personnel are increasingly being given new, more sophisticated diagnostic tools which require less skill on the part of personnel to use. New micro- and miniprocessors now have hand-calculator-size devices that step maintenance personnel through a total and rapid set of diagnostics on a system; this is far more accurate diagnostic work than simply taking an educated guess followed by trial-and-error repairs.

Another characteristic of maintenance, already hinted at, is the throw-away philosophy. Essentially the argument is that if a part does not work, do not try to fix it (this cannot be done if it is a chip anyway); simply replace it. Many vendors have discovered that with some of the emerging technologies, it is less expensive to replace a board or a cable than to repair the item. And with an increasing amount of hardware coming out on logic boards anyway, these cannot be fixed in the field.

A different characteristic of central-site maintenance that is increasingly obvious is that different pieces of hardware now form the weakest link in a total configuration from those that were weakest several years ago. In the mid-1970s, an operations manager looking at the incidence of downtime in a configuration would probably have been able to document the argument that the computer, disk drives, and printers went down most often. Today printers and tape drives provide the greatest amount of trouble, whereas computers and disk drives do not, because they have had the greatest number of technological improvements. Thus operations personnel tracking downtime need to be sensitive to the fact that certain devices today go down more often than others and as new devices come to the market, they should consider replacing older mechanical units. Without that thought in mind, the overall availability of a system is threatened. The only other practical alternative would be to install redundant peripherals to serve as backup for units that are highly prone to breakdown.

Repair Center Maintenance

The greatest change in hardware maintenance has come with a host of new products introduced in the past two to three years, primarily lightweight CRTs, printers, modems, and control units. This strategy basically calls for users of certain types of devices to bring them to a repair center when they malfunction. They are then fixed immediately or are left for maintenance and are picked up later. This kind of maintenance provides the least cost per unit of time spent on repairs, since the manufacturer spends no time traveling to and from accounts. Second, they can enjoy a higher level of productivity, with specialists working only on a select set of devices. Maintenance can be done faster because such repair centers are also a parts depot; thus no time is usually lost running up and down the road obtaining components for broken machines. For users the net result is faster turnaround time on repairs.

This approach first became evident outside of data processing with cameras, later with small appliances, and then with typewriter repairs, all of which proved it to be highly productive for all concerned. Now we notice its expansion into data processing, particularly with CRTs, tabletop printers, and portable desktop computers. In some instances these repair functions are also housed in the same building as a computer store selling the types of devices being maintained there for both commercial and consumer customers. This practice is becoming widespread across the entire industry from the large manufacturers, such as IBM, with repair centers and now computer stores, down to the highly specialized single-product companies. The cost for everyone is also fairly low, even though it means that a user may have on hand backup CRTs and other equipment to be used to fill in for devices that are at a repair shop. Thus a CRT selling for $1300 subject to repair shop maintenance is cheap and repairs are easily justified compared to the more traditional device for which maintenance personnel came out to work on it but which had to be purchased for about $3000 each.

The repair center process just described represents a long step in the direction of what many DP industry specialists forecast as eventually becoming "throwaway" technology. If costs continue to drop in the next ten years in proportion to what they did in the past decade, it may well be cheaper to throw away a small CRT than to fix it. Science fiction? This author thinks not. Most readers have probably participated in this phenomenon already by throwing away or simply ignoring a hand calculator that no longer works—and that is a microcomputer!

Software Maintenance

Since hardware availability is so desperately linked to the proper functioning of system and application programs, how these are being maintained by their manufacturers is also an essential issue in any discussion of equipment. It used to be that if a vendor's code malfunctioned, the DP department would call for a systems engineer to come down, look at the software, read dumps, go back to the office, work on a solution, and finally bring the solution out to the computer center. That system worked well for many years, but today two problems exist that border on the intolerable. First, the process became too slow given today's increased requirements for availability. Problems must be identified faster and fixed sooner. Second, the use of large armies of software maintenance personnel became too expensive at a time when the people required to do this kind of work could not be hired and trained fast enough. To have continued in this manner would have spelled long-term disaster for any major software house; therefore, new, more productive methods of maintenance were needed.

By about 1981, new methods were emerging that in various pilot programs in the late 1970s had clearly proven to be both faster and less expensive to implement. These essentially called for a three-pronged attack on the problem. First, data center personnel with a broken code situation involving SCPs and major software packages were given a national hot line that they could call. Specialists at the other end of the line would query the DP caller about the problem, and search an on-line data base for a solution which could then either be given over the telephone or be mailed out quickly. Studies have shown that over 65% of all problems reported could be resolved over the telephone without waiting for hours while a software maintenance specialist came out and ran diagnostics. If an immediate solution did not exist or the problem could not be described in sufficient detail over the telephone, then either another specialist could get on the phone and work on the problem or a specialist could be dispatched to the troubled data center as in years gone by.

Clearly, this method of maintaining software was less expensive for both customer and vendor. It offers more skill for a particular problem on a timely basis. In short, it is a faster way to resolve problems. This method has been applied primarily for broken code, software problems, and for planning. Since the hot line specialists know what the current set of common problems are, what many data centers do today is call in and find out if there are any points to watch out for just before installing new programs or a new release of software. This activity saves a great deal of time by avoiding problems at the data center. For vendors, it also makes possible a form of preventive maintenance that can avoid problems with customers later. Today, almost every major software vendor does initial problem determination and a considerable portion of maintenance in this manner. Usually available around the clock, seven days a week, data centers can perform maintenance whenever they want rather during normal business hours. The only real exception to this procedure are the specialized or small software houses that either cannot afford such a program or charge enough for their products so that there is no need for it. Typically, these would include application vendors and those who develop software for micros and minis. (See Figure 5-17.)

A second prong involves a system engineering hot line that can be called at a local vendor's branch office. Using a similar approach, systems engineers answer telephones and provide advice on how to use software. They can also offer specific suggestions on installing and maintaining packages. This is par-

Type of Problem	Type of Maintenance
Broken code	Field engineering hot line
Application usage	Systems engineering hot line
Code installation	Systems engineering hot line
	Systmes engineering data center
System hardware failure	Field engineering branch office
Major component failure	Field engineering branch office
Minor component failure	Vendor repair centers
Personnel problem	Vendor education centers
Vendor relations	Vendor branch management
User concern (application)	DP department
User problem (all types)	DP problem coordinator
User hardware failures	DP problem coordinator

Figure 5-17. Types of DP maintenance functions and who handles them today.

ticularly evident involving the use of application software (complex accounting, financial, and manufacturing systems, for example), where broken code is not so much the problem as how best to use them. Poor documentation of technical packages (such as teleprocessing monitors and data base managers) generate their own set of problems, which often are best resolved through a call to the local systems engineering hot line. Such services are usually available between one and two shifts during the week and frequently are staffed with people who also have an intimate knowledge of their customer's specific environment, having spent time out at the data centers as systems engineers in the field prior to hot lines being installed. That will change as fewer vendor personnel call on data centers, but in the meantime during the adjustment period, there are fewer strangers involved.

Many of the benefits noted with broken-code hot lines are evident with local calls. Response to problems is also more rapid than in the past because technical personnel are usually at their phones instead of out at an account. Specialists can concentrate on specific types of problems and have greater skills since they handle more of the same types of situations than in the past.

The third prong involves an education program run by systems engineers on a local level using a mini data center complete with classrooms to support their customers. They conduct walkthroughs on generating various types of programs, installation classes, sales presentations on products, maintenance seminars, fine-tuning lectures, and offer hands-on capability through customer support centers at local branch offices. Thus users of software and hardware can plan installations more efficiently, establish practical maintenance procedures, and gain experience by using equipment and software located nearby even before they are installed within their organization. The benefit to vendors is that customers come to them in groups for such services as mass selling, education, and servicing, thereby improving the marketing and support people's productivity. Customers deal with specialists and meet other users, and so can have an exchange of views and experiences. In short, it has been proven to increase the productivity of both vendors and customers. Ultimately, in practice, the availability of all systems goes up because of faster, better quality performance.

Preventive Maintenance Strategies

Given the changing nature of maintenance being provided by DP vendors, it is imperative that MIS management include these developments in their overall maintenance practices to ensure even higher levels of consistent availability. A number of techniques exist that have proven to meet this continuing challenge for service and performance.

First, there is no substitute for using well-educated, skilled software and hardware operations personnel in a data center. That requirement has not disappeared. If anything, such personnel are more important than ever, because vendors no longer will hang around data centers looking for problems or holding someone's hand. There is no time left for this anymore. Therefore, training personnel in such topics as systems management, network management, capacity planning, problem determination, tuning, and systems generation is critical. Where it is not done, things go wrong more often than they should and availability is always the casualty first.

Second, preventive maintenance of software must be a routine practice. Hardware is not breaking down as often as in the past, but software continues to do so. Therefore, just as in the past operations managers would dedicate a morning each week to hardware maintenance, that approach must now be applied to software. The amount of time dedicated to this activity will vary from shop to shop depending on what is installed. Yet with maintenance possible today on major systems on-line and while the computer system is still up and usable by other departments, this is not a difficult procedure to initiate. If anything, users find the system denied to them less frequently than in the past, when hardware maintenance called for equipment to be taken off the air. Also, users prefer to have scheduled lockouts rather than unanticipated downtime. If a department knows, for example, that the applications it uses will never be available on Friday afternoons, it can plan around it. What is unacceptable to users is when the system is denied them, usually at a time that it is absolutely the most inconvenient and disastrous for them.

Third, operations must track patterns of failures and downtime that directly reduce availability in different areas than in the past. Hardware does not do the kind of damage that it did years ago, but software still does. Therefore, the same methods employed to track the causes of unscheduled IPLs, downtime, and so on, for hardware must be imposed on software. This also means that users with no knowledge of data processing will have to report failures in software in exactly the same manner as they did for hardware, possibly using hot lines to vendors or, preferably, to a central point of problem control within the organization's data processing department.

Fourth, with the cost of hardware declining, the issue of redundancy of equipment can be considered more often. If you find that terminals of a particular type break down and have to be taken to a repair center, keep extras around to backfill. If the system performs poorly because memory is too heavily utilized, add more; it is very inexpensive. Disk space is also cheap. More modern terminals with storage and processing capability also make it possible to distribute function and redundancy as well as backup. The benefits are clear. For example, rather than dedicating an expensive systems person full time to purge and relocate machine-readable files, add more disk and thereby use your expensive person for more productive work. CPU channels can be added inexpensively to computers in less than two hours, so why let a bottleneck in this area hold back quality availability? With additional data paths to the computer now costing almost the same as a CRT, anything less is foolish. In short, when facing an availability issue, consider the cost of solving the problem with hardware instead of people. You will be surprised how often it is less expensive, quicker, and more effective to put more equipment on a system instead of personnel who are probably overworked already.

A MEASUREMENT TOOL: OUTAGE ANALYSIS

Outage analysis, commonly called *component failure impact analysis,* is one of the most useful methods available to management in data processing today. It is also one of the easiest to implement and use in addressing almost all facets of the issue of availability. Basically, it is a grid chart that shows what software and hardware a system or user depends on. It details the effects on users when any key component is malfunctioning. In most shops it has as its purpose to highlight the impact of a malfunction on overall availability and thus causes management to focus on recovery procedures and backup before they are needed, and when a disaster exists, draws attention to those links in the chain that need fixing the fastest. The quicker a problem is fixed, the sooner availability is returned to users. A good outage analysis will drive the kind of disaster planning outlined in Chapter 8, and will help define and justify additional backup hardware to support specific availability and capacity requirements as described in Chapter 2 and elsewhere. It helps identify recurring areas of performance exposure and where management should concentrate maintenance activities. In other words, it offers a disciplined way of describing the cost of each weak link in your configuration chain, made up of a combined software and hardware environment. It is as applicable to a centralized data center as to a highly decentralized distributed processing environment. It is not dependent on a particular type of hardware or software, either.

   Without employing an impact outage analysis tool it becomes nearly impossible to provide for responsible availability management and, as described in Chapter 8, can have deadly consequences for most organizations today, regardless of size. One cannot stress too strongly how valuable and essential it is to perform component failure impact analyses as an ongoing process in all installations. (See Figure 5-18.)

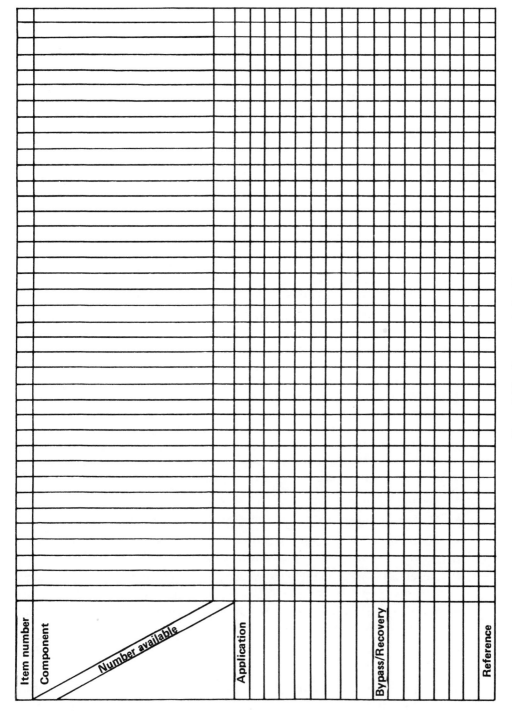

Figure 5-18. Outage analysis grid.

In addition to helping recover from problems more quickly, such an exercise helps evaluate the design of systems and alternative configurations of both hardware and software, to identify weak points and critical paths through any system that might otherwise seem stable, and to help justify additional programs and equipment to maintain availability in certain critical situations. In short, the objective is always to recover from a problem as quickly as possible and to plan the best we can. This tool goes further than most in supporting both goals.

How to Start

Three basic steps must be taken:

(1) Decide to do such an analysis and gather the necessary data.

(2) Do the actual analysis and produce a grid of applications, hardware, and software.

(3) Maintain the grid and do any of the things that suggested themselves during the analysis phase.

The first step involves identifying the applications, software, and hardware that must be examined, establishing business and technical priorities about the value or criticalness of various elements. Next, pull these data together and form the kinds of grids illustrated in Chapter 8, and finally, keep the grid up to date. It should be incorporated into normal daily operations and into the disaster plan. Periodically review it for accuracy and relevance to the business needs of the organization.

One of the earliest steps has also got to be setting availability objectives against which applications, software, and hardware can be measured. In addition to the examples listed earlier in this chapter, here are some that are commonly discussed during an outage analysis:

- Having hardware available (up) 97% of the time
- Having the teleprocessing monitor up 95% of the time
- Maintaining a 4-second response time on commercial CRTs, a 1-second response time on engineering design CRTs
- Never allowing channels to exceed 55% utilization during peak-load periods
- Ensuring that the order entry system is up at all times, even if the system is operating in degraded condition
- Establishing how maintenance can be done concurrently with users still on the system

Such an analysis can usually be done by as few as three people initially, invariably all from data processing, provided that they can interview key users to identify the most important applications for the organization. These people should include a representative from systems, another from applications, and a third from operations, and should have the right to consult user and DP management to ensure that a correct list of priorities is drawn up. The amount of time it will take to pull such a study together ranges from a few days full time to several weeks, with the greatest amount of effort being spent on analyzing data for inclusion on a grid.

The kinds of specific information that such a team needs to develop the grid must include the following:

- A list of the most important applications run at the data center(s) in order of greatest priority, with the most important at the top
- Full and detailed configurations of all equipment installed, down to a list of features and a configuration diagram
- A list or chart describing disk requirement for major application files (see Figure 5-19 for an example)
- A similar list describing applications, illustrating what hardware is used by which applications, including alternative hardware paths to perform major functions (see Figure 5-20 for an example)
- A chart illustrating maintenance components, essential to indicate what tools and hardware are necessary to repair applications, software, and hardware (see Figure 5-21 for an example)

Volume identification:	DOS/VSRES	DOS/VSRES	AA 111	BB 111	CICS 101	CICS 102	ETSS 103	LIB 222	BAS 1C335	APL 444	WORK 45	WORK 46	WORK 47
Model:	1	1	11	11	1	11	11	1	11	11	1	11	11
Applications													
CICS			X		X	X		X	X			X	X
DB				X				X	X	X		X	X
ETSS							X				X		
APL										X			X
CPU	X	X	X	X									
Batch (1)		X			X			X				X	
Batch (2)		X			X			X					X

Figure 5-19. Sample disk volume requirements grid.

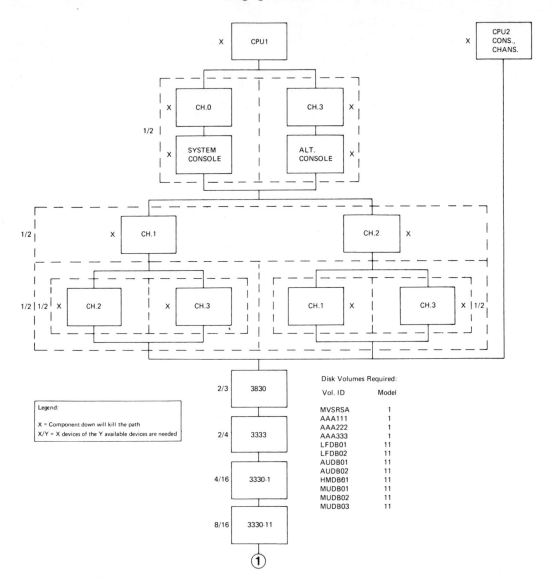

Figure 5-20. Critical path chart. (Source: IBM Corporation, © 1978.)

Analyzing Your Data

Armed with these kinds of information, a more formal analysis of how to maintain availability, at what cost, and with which components, is possible. In this phase of the effort, the applications to be examined are selected and verified as to their importance with user management, a grid is drawn up, and output is generated for a disaster recovery plan. Ultimately, a report on specific recommendations is made to management. In one IBM study, for

Failing device	CPU	CH. 1	CH. 2	CH. 3	3350	3350	3880	3705	3205
Required resource									
CPU	X								
Ch. 1		X					X		
Ch. 2			X				X		
Ch. 3				X			X		
3350	X			X			X		
3350	X			X		X	X		
3880	X	X					X		
3705	X		X					X	
3205	X			X					X
Minis	X	X						X	
RJE station	X	X						X	
CRT network	X			X					X

Figure 5-21. Failing device requirement chart.

example, it was calculated that the amount of effort over time required to perform this activity was quite short (summarized in Figure 5-22). Note that it does not take a great deal of effort with three individuals assigned to the task, regardless of the size of the installation.

As a general rule, the more critical applications are the commercial on-line ones that affect such bread-and-butter activities as selling (order entry) and cash collection (accounts receivable). Batch applications, because they can be run at varying times during a 24-hour period, as a rule provide more flexibility and therefore are less critical from the point of view of timeliness.

Once the applications have been listed in importance and the list agreed to by management, the grid can be drawn up—the key output of this whole exercise. Major system components (software) are listed in columns in

	Single Processor	Duplex Processor $\leqslant$ 158/3031	Duplex Processor $\geqslant$ 168/3032
Construct grid	$\frac{1}{2}$–1	1	1
Conduct analysis	2–3	3–4	4–6
Modify and/or develop bypass/recov. proc.	3–4	5–6	8–10
Prepare report	$\frac{1}{2}$–1	1	1–1$\frac{1}{2}$

Figure 5-22. One estimate of time (hours) needed to do the outage analysis. (Source: IBM Corporation, © 1978.)

descending order of significance to the organization, while applications are cut across the top with intersections to show that one affects the other, and where. Bypass or recovery options for major applications are also shown on such a chart. Figure 5-23 shows a matrix filled out. By using numbers to identify specific items, additional textual commentary on how one integrates with another, or can be backed up, may be described on other pages. The matrix, although it should, in its final form fit into a typed report, is easiest to work with if drawn up on large flip charts and taped to a wall so that a number of individuals can quickly see the details clearly. This is particularly necessary while the outage analysis is being performed and the actual chart created. Notice that in the column there is a mixture of applications and software, based on the significance of the code to this organization.

	SOFTWARE				CPU 1					CPU 2				SWITCHABLE CPU 2		
ITEM:	1	2	3	4	5	6	7	8	9	10	11	12	13	22	23	24
LISTED BY NUMBER	VS1	NASP	DL1	CICS	CONSOLE	CH. 1	CH. 2	CH. 3	BLOCK	CONSOLE	CH. 1	CH. 2	CH. 3	TP CONTR.	3880	3880
Bypass																
Must fix none.	X		X	X	X					X						
RE IPL	X		X		X	X										
Switch		X			X	X	X	X	X	X	X	X		X		
Restart	X	X			X					X				X		
Reconfig.			X	X												

Figure 5-23. Bypass matrix sample.

If a program is used by itself, consider it an application; if used with other applications, treat it as part of a system.

This system of grids works well with hardware, software, applications, and even people's skills (see Chapter 8 for the latter). When using hardware, list the applications in the columns and the equipment needed to support them in rows. This way, if x amount of hardware is lost (e.g., destroyed in a fire) you know what can be run right away on remaining hardware and how much of what specific equipment you need to operate the most critical applications. Specialists will usually argue that not more than 40 or so variables should be listed; more makes it too complicated to track everything properly. Thus consider tape and disk as one item, all your systems printers as another, and so on, grouping items as needed to keep the list to a manageable size.

Armed with such a grid, one can ask: What happens when a problem occurs? Specifically, what is the impact of a department's ability to run a particular application? Is there another alternative way to run an application and thus restore availability quickly (such as running another computer, using a second string of disk, etc.)? Invariably the answers to these kinds of questions generate another document, which reflects the department's collective wisdom and thinking about the impact on various systems. Figure 5-24 suggests this for some of the applications cited in Figure 5-23. Figure 5-24 illustrates the kind of document that forces DP to address rationally the issue of recovery procedures, allowing specific plans to be developed for each major component of the grid. As we argue in Chapter 8, a great deal can be done to minimize the negative impact of most serious problems, provided that certain kinds of planning and information gathering have taken place in advance. The grid is part of that effort. Without going through such an exercise, the DP department is left to survive the hazards of probable downtime on any given device or software component. We know that all departments are guaranteed to experience hardware downtime, but they do not have to endure avoidable disasters.

The last comment on outage analysis concerns the preparation of a final report detailing the work of the task force preparing the grids. The report

	Item	Problem	Bypass	Effect	Issues
1.	VS1	Waits	Hardware failure? Problem determination IPL	Lose current jobs	Review operations procedures
4.	CICS	Abend	Fix, restore, restart new copy	Lost jobs	Review procedures Check log tape
		Faulty use	Same	Lost jobs	Check procedures and recovery systems

Figure 5-24. Sample backup detail for a bypass matrix chart.

should be presented both orally and in written form to DP management and if necessary (if requiring additional money for hardware) to general executives. The written document becomes a working paper for providing continual updating of plans and thinking about the relationship of hardware to software. As hardware and application configurations change, so should this document. It should also become an integral part of the disaster recovery documentation, and thus a copy must always be in the hands of the disaster plan coordinator. One final note: an oral presentation allows the task force to answer questions about the outage analysis's methodology and perhaps suggest its applicability in other non-DP departments.

CONCLUDING SUGGESTIONS

Several considerations have traditionally provided the necessary focus for ensuring that the correct steps are taken to maintain high levels of availability. The first involves viewing uptime as availability. Running a machine most of the time never did constitute availability except perhaps in a department running monoprogramming in a batch environment. Since almost no DP department has that kind of an environment today and instead has one characterized by multiprogramming on an extensive scale, a predominance of multiple on-line systems operating concurrently is the norm. Such environments also have complicated configurations with dozens of peripherals, various CPUs linked together, and an assortment of large and sophisticated software. Thus hardware uptime itself is no longer a realistic benchmark for performance. Productivity must be measured in terms of how the overall system performs—how much that total configuration really is up and available, rather than simply any one of its components. The task before any operations manager today, therefore, is complex.

The second recommendation made in this chapter is that availability be viewed from the perspective of the user community rather than from the other end of the telescope—DP operations. As long as data processing remains a service, whether centralized or decentralized, its ultimate quality must be judged by how it can be used outside the MIS group. All the machines in the organization can run all day long, but if the user community finds their use inconvenient, too complicated, or inaccessible, availability does not exist. Service remains the bottom line, and its accessibility by users on a timely basis represents the most effective way of evaluating its usefulness. In short, that is availability.

For an organization to deliver reasonable levels of availability, a number of general steps must be taken. To recall the most important of these, data processing must manage in an integrated fashion several elements of a configuration:

- Hardware
- Systems software
- Applications

Anything less just does not work today. On the hardware side, while the main computer or intelligent controller remains the center piece of an equipment configuration, its importance can be overshadowed by the introduction of new peripherals and in greater quantity. Management must therefore recognize that (1) configurations are dynamic because they change so quickly, and (2) machines that might have broken down or been poorly used in the past may in fact today work better than other components in the system.

Fine tuning of software, scheduling, and raw cycle utilizations, among other issues, are not objectives in themselves but simply means to an end: better availability. Working in concert with the user community to establish what work has to be done, when, and at what prices, fine tuning of software and hardware can be a means of supporting those objectives. Fine tuning for the sake of squeezing more out of a machine because it is a challenge, fun, or whatever makes no sense; the cost in people is too great given the declining price of hardware today.

Availability cannot really be expected to improve in a quantum fashion without good management techniques to support a good configuration of hardware and software. The managerial structure for housing the proper control over availability that works the best are the precepts of problem management. This is not a substitute but an addition to the more traditional operational steps taken by all computer room managers in running their jobs, scheduling work, and keeping records. Problem management takes the most widely used cliché of the data processing industry—"the only constant is change"—and manages that reality. The cliché is true; many departments recognize that fact and manage better as a result, using problem management techniques.

One of the most interesting and sensible changes evident in the past five years in data processing has been the fusion of hardware and software skills within management. At one time, computer room managers knew only hardware and nothing about software. As they became operations managers, they learned a little about operating systems but not much more. As the recognition spread that availability had to be a marriage and balance of resources across software and hardware, operations managers began to acquire more technical backgrounds, incorporating systems control programs, teleprocessing monitors, data base managers, and capacity planning skills. That is why today we see such titles on DP department organization charts as Technical Support Manager, Technical Services, and Technical Support and Operations Management, all a clear indication that the two major areas must be balanced.

Since maintenance of hardware and software has always been critical in any organization, with the working relations between primary vendors and the department always important and therefore usually close, understanding the changing role of computer manufacturers in this arena is obvious and imperative. Unfortunately, few DP managers recognize how to work more effectively in this changing arena. On the one hand, they love the decline in the cost of hardware, but on the other, complain that they are not receiving service like in the "good old days." As the adage goes, you cannot have your cake and eat it too. Or can you? The choice remains in the hands of MIS management to complain or take advantage of the new ways of maintaining equipment, thereby enjoying full quality services while benefiting from the declining cost of technology.

The last activity that can contribute to a rational view of availability is the preparation of component failure impact analyses, which any department can easily carry out. With such a simple way to drive availability considerations, capacity planning, and preparations for disasters, it is a widely used method for controlling and understanding critical issues in DP. Yet many departments still do not even know what it is, particularly in intermediate-size companies with annual sales of less than $500 million. Yet it is these smaller companies whose data processing has grown the most in the past several years and thus have increased their dependence on DP the fastest. Large corporations and governments long ago recognized the advantage of such a tool and use it, while shops in smaller organizations do not, although they run a sufficient risk to require more formal managerial practices. (See Figure 5-25.)

As a final consideration, intermediate-size companies frequently operate their departments in the same way that they have for the past decade or more. Yet as their users have become more dependent on data processing, both DP managers and their executives above them invariably failed to recognize that more formal, different, and not necessarily imaginative or time-consuming techniques for controlling this technology had to be put in place.

Figure 5-25. Building blocks of availability.

Too often a disaster had to hit, hardware break down, or a critical application come on stream too late before someone recognized that things had to change. The typical scenario then was to replace the data processing manager because very rarely would the previous one initiate such steps and thus save his or her job. This is an all too familiar pattern, which teaches us the lesson that availability will be obtained by non-DP management even at the expense of traditional MIS managers. As long as executives come out of the ranks of user departments, availability will remain the bench mark by which to measure the performance of data processing.

Reform that you may preserve.

Lord Macaulay

No topic has become so critical to so many organizations as quickly as the cost of energy. Since data processing is one of industry's largest users of this resource, this chapter describes how it uses this expensive energy—specifically, how to reduce or control costs in this area. We show you how to determine what is presently being consumed and at what cost, then how to cut energy use. Finally, the chapter describes how to use data processing to control the costs of all types of energy throughout the entire organization.

CHAPTER SIX

Energy Conservation and
Data Processing

Data processing departments are some of the greatest users of electrical energy today, and consequently any conservation measures taken by the DP department have the potential of large savings to any organization. Computer equipment requires substantial amounts of electricity to operate, additional amounts go to supporting extensive air-conditioning systems, and yet more is used to light large computer centers with their growing staffs and floor space. Despite the declining amount of energy required by newer devices, more pieces of equipment are being installed at a faster rate than ever before. Therefore, the demand for additional power continues a sharp and upward trend. So does its cost. In the United States alone, for example, during the 1970s and particularly since 1976, the average cost for energy

251

has risen at over 12% each year and in some areas by more than 20% annually. At the same time, it was not an unusual situation to find growth in installed data processing equipment in the range of 25% per year, bringing the average increase expenditure in electrical energy up in the range of 37% compounded each year. When one remembers that even a medium-size data center could consume several thousands of dollars' worth of electricity each month in 1976, the significance of this growing cost can be appreciated.

At the same time that electrical costs were rising, the expense of fuels such as oil and gas were also rising for all organizations. Therefore, controlling the cost of energy consumed by data processing and using this technology to hold down the expense of all forms of energy throughout an organization has become an urgent requirement. It no longer is simply a hot topic but is a part of the normal management of a growing expense item in most organizations. Central to any strategy for the containment of energy costs is data processing. There already exists within the DP industry a number of methods used in managing energy that have proven cost effective.

Replacing older devices with cooler, less energy consuming units represents a growing strategy in many organizations. So is the application of data processing in controlling overall costs of fuels and electricity in buildings. Better management in the use of computerized devices has also proven very beneficial. In this chapter the role of energy in the data processing environment is explained as well as proven methods for restraining costs. Since an increasing number of organizations today are trying to use computers to manage buildings, the basic applications involved, together with their costs and benefits, are discussed in detail.

HOW MUCH ELECTRICITY DOES DATA PROCESSING USE?

The very first step in tackling the problem of energy consumption in data processing is to establish how and where electricity is used. Next, management has to improve the efficiency of the power used by such energy hogs as data processing. Within any data center, energy is essentially used for three purposes: to operate hardware, to air condition computer machine rooms, and to light and heat the entire department. Usage in each of these areas can conveniently be measured in terms of kilowatthours—the basic unit of measurement used by electrical companies for billing purposes. Each kilowatthour represents a certain quantity of electricity used in one hour. Thus, arriving at a value (the number of kilowatts a device uses per hour) provides a convenient common denominator for measurement. Three ways are commonly used to gauge the use of electrical power:

(1) Measuring voltage and current to develop a kilowatt unit per hour (kWh)

(2) Simply reading a watthour meter provided by the electrical company

(3) Relying on the computer manufacturer's estimates of power consumption (in kilowatts) for each device multiplied by the number of hours used

Since electrical companies bill on a monthly basis, all costs should be multiplied out to a total for a month.

Measuring voltage and current essentially involves taking a piece of readily available test equipment to measure electricity from a circuit panel to a particular piece of hardware. Any electrical engineer would then be able to translate this information into kilovolt-amperes (kVA) and from that figure, multiplied by the hours the device(s) is used, establish the amount of energy consumed. A standard watthour meter connected to the main power source leading into a computer room would also provide an accurate count of power consumed. Almost all vendors of data processing equipment can easily provide information on the power requirements for their devices by the hour and the number of generated British thermal units (Btu) per hour. Physical planning manuals issued by manufacturers of computerized equipment often carry this kind of information. Thus if you have two dozen devices in a room, look up the kVA for each, add up the total, multiply by the number of hours per month used, then by the cost per hour charged for electricity by the local power company, and you have the total cost. Do the same for the air conditioning used to support computerized equipment. For an illustration of this process, see Chapter 3. As a brief reminder, take the kVA value per device times 0.9 to obtain the kW value. Multiply this number by the hours used to yield the kWh, which is then multiplied by the cost per kWh to arrive at the expense involved.

Equipment represents a portion of the electrical usage in any room and therefore other power usage must be added to obtain a more realistic appreciation of the costs involved. Lighting consumes electricity as well. Assuming that fluorescent bulbs are used, figure usage with the following equation:

$$0.001xyz = \text{kWh}$$

where x represents the number of bulbs being lit, y the number of hours they are on, and z the input of watts per fixture. Bulb vendors can provide the data for z. As a general rule of thumb this ranges from 40 to 85, although a more common range is between 74 and 92 W. For instance, if $x = 10$ bulbs, $y = 200$ hours in a month, and $z = 40$, then $10 \times 200 \times 40 = 80,000$ kWh per month just for lighting. To carry the logic further, if your power company charges 6 cents per kWh, the cost would be 80,000 kWh $\times$ 6 cents, or \$48 per month. Other devices that would drive this number up would include card I/O and typewriters (their kVA $\times$ 0.08 $\times$ hours used to yield kWh).

A large user of power is, of course, air conditioning. One way of establishing the amount used to drive air-conditioning units is to put a meter on the line feeding power to these devices. Another, illustrated in Chapter 3, involves measuring the number of tons of air conditioning needed and going to a vendor's physical description manual to establish the kVA for the device. If you are trying to determine how much is needed, add up all Btu generated by all the data processing equipment. Figuring that you need 1 ton of air conditioning for every 12,000 Btu, with an additional 25% tonnage to account for people and lights, will lead to an accurate count of air-conditioning requirements. For more precise calculations, do the following:

(1)   For an accurate count on lighting, the Btu/hour value is arrived at by taking a light's Btu value and multiplying it by 3413; this converts the amount to kWh.

(2)   For a more precise number and cost of human-generated heat, take the average number of people in a particular area and multiply by 650 Btu per hour. The average individual generates 650 Btu/hour. Thus, if you have 10 people on average in a data center, multiply 10 by 650 to arrive at 6500 Btu/hour. This tells you how much additional air conditioning would be required and ultimately the amount of electricity and its cost to cool off. In our case, half a ton of air conditioning is needed in addition to lights and computers.

Sample Electrical Costs in a Data Center

The example below is a case study of an existing data center to suggest the number of Btu generated, the cost in electrical power, and ultimately translated into money spent for one month to run everything.

The installed equipment, with their electrical and Btu statistics, are as follows:

Device	Quantity	Power Requirements kVA (watts)		Btu
Computers	2	6.91	(6.22)	372,992
TP controller	2	10.59	(9.53)	22,457
CRT controller	2	0.26	(0.23)	815
Disk drives	52	107.80	(97.0)	332,302
Tape drives	30	50.33	(45.30)	157,652
Printers	7	28.10	(25.29)	86,341
Other I/O	7	19.71	(17.74)	63,940
Subtotal		223.70	(201.31)	1,409,491
600 bulbs		200		240,000
75 people				48,750
50 CRTs/printers		0.78	(0.70)	29,750
20 typewriters		0.20	(0.18)	3,500
Subtotal		0.98	(200.88)	322,000

To determine the air-conditioning requirements, take the total Btu involved (1,409,491 + 322,000 = 1,731,491) divided by 12,000 to arrive at the number of tons of cooling required. In our case this equals 144 tons. If each ton of air conditioning requires 2 kw, the total electricity for these devices comes to 2 × 144, or 288. Take the total wattages for the computer room, other areas of this large DP installation, and air conditioning to come to a total of 690.19 kWh. If the local power company charges 6 cents/hour, the math is 690.19 × 0.06 = $41.41 of electricity per hour. If this data center and other areas operate 600 hours per month, the electrical bill (not adjusted for inflation or price increases) would be $24,846 per month, or a total of $298,152 for one year. To make it more realistic, in this case the final bill for one year was $357,782, including local taxes and price increases along the way for energy.

The moral of this story is that electrical costs are significant. The case above involves a large data center with two fully configured major computer systems used in a major bank. A midsize installation with 25% of this hardware capacity would still spend over $100,000 each year on power. Thus in any installation, someone should look very closely at the consumption of energy.

DATA PROCESSING OPERATING ENVIRONMENT

Armed with some appreciation of how much electricity data processing can use is not enough to attack the problem of reducing the costs of energy. There are some general considerations that one must take into account involving the kind of environment data processing hardware must operate in, which cannot be overlooked or sacrificed for the sake of energy management. The consequences can be broken equipment and expensive operations —two extremely expensive conditions that result when sacrifices are made (such as computer rooms that are too cold or too hot). There are certain physical requirements for equipment which should be respected, regardless of any energy conservation program, to ensure the proper operation of these devices. Although these requirements vary from device to device and are in fact changed for the better with each succeeding generation of equipment, some generalizations can be made useful in guiding management in controlling energy usage by data processing.

Most data processing equipment should operate in a room with temperatures between 65 and 75°F and at levels of relative humidity ranging between 45 and 50%. Hardware as a rule can operate at a few degrees above 75°F, but at some risk, and with humidity levels closer to 60% and even below 45%, but again with some risk of malfunction. Some industrially hardened terminals designed for use in manufacturing or process plants can operate at much higher temperatures and at even lower humidity levels, but these devices represent the exception rather than the norm.

Using IBM equipment to illustrate more normal operating conditions suggests the environment in which DP hardware is working in today's world. The widely used 4300 series of computers can operate at temperatures of between 50°F (10°C) and 90°F (32°C) and with relative humidity levels ranging from 8 to 80%. Wet-bulb temperatures should not rise above 78°F (26°C) without asking for trouble. On the other hand, computers available in the 1970s had operating ranges of 60 to 80° and humidity variances from 20 to 80%. Chilled-water-cooled machines normally have to operate with the water system in use and without it for no more than several minutes. The temperatures cited above are for air-cooled systems only. Even with such systems and water-cooled machines, when they are turned off, the manufacturers of these devices recommend that room temperatures and humidity levels remain the same as for operating hardware. This prevents deterioration of delicate components such as logic boards, which tend to crack when stressed. Thus for storage consider temperatures between 50 and 110°F (10 and 43°C) as outer limits and humidity between 8 and 80%.

Major pieces of peripheral equipment also have general environmental specifications. For widely used data storage media, consider Figure 6-1 as a guide. Like computers, these units are also sensitive to changes in temperature and humidity. Printers, terminals, and card I/O can be considered as functional within the same guidelines established for computers and such media as disk and tape drives. Once a data center is conditioned for disk and computers, it automatically is for the less sensitive peripherals. Terminals, printers, and control units designed for use in office environments obviously have higher levels of tolerance to variations in temperature and relative humidity. Yet these devices should operate above 20% relative humidity and below 80% and at temperatures above 50°F and below 100°F. As a safety feature, most computers and complex control units have thermocheck devices which will either signal that environmental conditions are deteriorating dangerously or will actually cause the machine to shut down (power down) to prevent damage. Unfortunately, for some computers built in the 1960s, by the time a thermocheck mechanism goes into action, some damage has usually taken place and possibly some data have been lost.

Conditioning of tape and paper used in a computer room is another consideration that must never be ignored. Bringing a tape or box of cards which has been stored in a room at 100°F into the data center operating at 68°F will probably result in some failure to perform. Extremely cold tape

Device	Temperature, °F (°C)	Humidity, Relative (%)
Tape (normal)	40–90 (40–32)	20–80
Tape (long-term storage)	50–90 (10–32)	20–80
Disk packs, cartridges, modules (short-term storage)	60–90 (16–32)	10–80
Disk media (long-term storage)	40–150 (4–66)	10–80
Diskettes	50–125 (10–51)	8–80
Mag cards	50–125 (10–51)	8–80

Figure 6-1. Environmental requirements for storage media.

may break or not record data, and humid cards stick to each other. As a general rule of thumb, consumables should be at the same temperature and humidity levels as the computer room. Tape and paper items usually need several hours in the data center for conditioning, although if previously stored in widely different temperature and humidity levels, a maximum of 24 hours may be required. Disk packs, data modules, mag cards, cartridges, and so on, also need conditioning, and this can usually be done in about two hours just by being in the same room as the computer. Most data centers store data and products in rooms very similar in temperature to the machine room or keep at least one day's supply in a conditioned state, that is, at the same temperature and humidity as the equipment that will use them.

CONSERVING ENERGY WITHIN THE DP DEPARTMENT

Armed with an appreciation of the amount of energy consumed by data processing installations, it now becomes possible to determine ways to conserve its use and thereby save money. Typically, when a company goes through the exercise of establishing the costs of energy for data processing per month or year, managers are shocked at the amount. And when the numbers are adjusted upward for inflation over the following several years, together with the additions caused by more devices, the amount grows geometrically. Thus the potential for saving money really exists in the area of energy conservation. Fortunately, a number of proven methods are available to control costs.

The first technique that can be used is to install more modern equipment. Often, devices are replaced only because of the need for more or larger or faster units or because maintenance costs on older devices are rising too quickly. Equipment is hardly ever replaced because it uses too much electricity or throws out too many Btu. Yet when the need to change equipment arises, the opportunity to look at the cost of running hardware presents itself. Average electrical consumption has dropped between 65 and 80% between hardware sold today and that sold in the mid-1960s. Thus a medium-sized computer room filled with older devices might cost $5000 per month in electricity, whereas the same hardware capacity using the newest devices could possibly cut $4000 per month in costs: multiply this by twelve months and you have a savings of $48,000—not a small amount. Savings in a large data center could easily be four times as great. Furthermore, since the number of Btu would decline with the installation of more modern technology, additional savings in the cost of purchasing or maintaining massive quantities of air conditioning would drop, together with the requirements for additional expensive floor space, and hence more lighting, and also a possible decline in the number of operators (each with his or her 650 Btu). The point to remember is that electrical consumption has become a growing factor of significance in the selection of new equipment. More-over, quantifying the costs of DP power can be used exactly the same for all manner of equipment in any organization, from manufacturing equipment to copiers to ovens to all kinds of electrically driven devices. In fact, much of the new industrial hardware (non-DP) has become more efficient, smaller, less expensive, and a declining user of energy by being partially comput-erized through the use of chip technology and miniaturization, all reducing the cost of operation.

A second way to reduce data processing's use of electricity is through equipment shutdowns. Since this procedure requires careful planning in order not to disrupt an organization, careful attention must be paid to the details of this method, particularly since it is becoming increasingly fashion-able. Whether or not shutdowns are a normal practice within a company or agency, policies for implementing such an action are essential if for no other reason than that power companies are increasingly forcing organizations to reduce energy consumption. It is now quite common on hot days in the United States for individual power companies to reduce the amount of electricity being fed to their customers by 3 to 10%, to avoid brownouts or blackouts. Too often such reductions are also done with little or no warning, thus placing a premium on the shop already equipped with a plan to address the problem. As your organization becomes increasingly de-pendent on computers being up in order to operate, the problem of reduced electrical supplies becomes a more serious problem. Since no computer system can operate properly with significantly reduced quantities of elec-trical power, either other devices are powered down during shortages or the mainframe is not used. The choice is yours.

The easiest way to save on electricity is to turn off CRTs and their associated printers when not in use. Turning them on again takes less than a minute. Savings are possible here because most people leave their terminals on 24 hours a day, which is totally unnecessary. Secretaries turn off their typewriters, so why should everyone else leave devices on? A second group of devices that can be shut down are computer peripherals not being used by putting them into a "not-ready" condition, which means to the computer that the equipment in question is off. If your data center has a string of eight tape drives but in the first shift only uses two, turn off the other six for eight hours. Some DP managers force operations to stop using certain devices at different times of the day anyway just to see if the units are really required and if so, how much. Such exercises do more than simply serve as an audit of the need for equipment—they save electrical costs! Printers not used extensively in odd shifts can also be powered down, together with the many lights, which in any case probably cause the glare that people complain about in most computer rooms.

Using the data from the case study of electrical costs in our large data center, it quickly appears that $20,000 to 30,000 a year (10%) is possible. Since most energy conservation programs have 5 to 15% per year as a reasonable target, substantial savings become quite possible. Furthermore, if sufficient quantities of devices can be shut down during a particular shift, so can the air conditioning. Suppose that a data center has two 10-ton air conditioners and in the third shift cuts its Btu in half through shutdowns; then one of the air conditioners could also be powered down. Reducing air conditioning and lighting can often save more money than any equivalent piece of data processing equipment since they are such heavy users of energy. The goal is always to reduce the amount of kWh consumption, which, when multiplied by x cents each per hour, times the number of hours per year not used, can yield savings usually in the tens to hundreds of thousands of dollars.

In short, some general rules of thumb apply to cost reductions which are worth summarizing before discussing specific shutdown methodologies:

- Look at all consumers of electricity and air conditioning as energy hogs.

- Set targets for reduction to be attained slowly through trial and error over time so as not to reduce vital services or to damage equipment.

- Energy conservation is not an end-all in itself; the primary mission of the DP department is still to provide information to the organization, not to save energy.

- Document usage and savings as a lesson about what is possible within your organization and as a planning tool.

An early step in identifying what can be powered down is looking at the schedule of jobs run through a computer. Often, rescheduling work with various users can make it possible to shut down equipment for a while. It is usually the easiest way to find time slots when equipment can be silenced. More partitions in a particular shift could be used (if enough I/O is available), and streaming more jobs together with less operator interference is also a popular trick. Having fewer store-and-forward jobs (common in the early 1970s when equipment went down more often) presents more opportunities. Backup of files to tape does not have to take place all at the same time once a day but can be staggered periodically when tape drives have to be on. Backup utilities in teleprocessing monitors and data bases may also eliminate unnecessary processing. However, if tapes are used for backup only, then doing all the backups at one time may allow you to shut off other units during the process (such as card equipment) while shutting off the power on many tape drives during production periods.

A look at the blocks of idle time per device that exist over a period of one month or two suggests possible areas of savings. All operations managers will argue that they cannot power down any equipment due to their heavy work loads. Yet each of those individuals has blocks of idle time on devices that they may or may not be aware of. Thus an analysis of idle time by device will always indicate better loading schedules for equipment—just as it does for plant managers in manufacturing plants worrying about capacity and efficiency loads. Opportunities abound everywhere: card I/O used only two hours daily scattered across 24 hours can be scheduled for use in two one-hour slots in two shifts, terminals can be cut off, air-conditioning units powered down at night, and unused tape drives on a long string silenced, among others.

Other techniques and tricks to balance work loads better in order to try some shutdowns include:

- Examination of all jobs to reduce the processing of unnecessary work or the number of times a particular job is run during a week or month
- Rescheduling work loads to increase total system utilization during a shorter period of time (but not at the cost of slower processing time)
- Examining a system's software, particularly its application code, to tune them better, thereby increasing throughput while reducing processing time

A small warning is in order, however. If fine tuning code takes a great number of hours to do, it may be cheaper just to let your code run fat and sloppy, since computer cycles are far less expensive (and its electricity and Btu) than programmers.

Checklist of Do's When Implementing Shutdowns. When a schedule for shutdown has been arrived at, a number of things should be done to ensure a smooth implementation that does not cut service. These include:

(1) Notify all users in advance of scheduling shutdowns which might affect them and again an hour before it is actually done for all on-line users.

(2) Implement a soft shutdown of applications, together with securing all data and closing files.

(3) Unload peripherals of data and complete jobs currently in them while unassigning these units from the system via console commands.

(4) Implement actual power-off of peripherals and computers and any other devices not in use.

(5) Reduce use of, or turn off, environmental equipment (such as air conditioners). (See Figure 6-2.)

The time it takes to power down would probably be short, especially since various tasks can be done concurrently. The number of units that can remain shut off simultaneously varies; thus a total number of shutdown hours in a row is not as important from the point of view of energy consumption as is the total number of hours of all devices shut off. Three

Time Estimate of Shutdown Planning Requirements

Required Actions	Time Needed to Complete (Hours)
Notify local and remote users of coming shutdown	———————————
Shutdown of application processing at data center	———————————
Orderly shutdown of operating system software	———————————
Deactivation of all peripheral devices	———————————
Turning off hardware	———————————
Storage of all data medium	———————————
Raising temperatures and reducing power to data center within tolerances	———————————
Locking up computer room	———————————
Total shutdown time needed	———————————

Figure 6-2. Planning requirements of an organized shutdown. The time for these should be estimated, then tried, so that accurate data on how much time and what efforts are needed can be known. The same applies to starting up a system again.

devices of equal kWh value shut down at the same time will probably mean that they are unavailable for a shorter period of time than shutting down one at a time. The more devices that can be shut down concurrently, the greater the savings, since additional air-conditioning savings also become possible.

The actual time and amount of shutdown will have to be tested. Practice and changing circumstances suggest that in reality more time is available for shutdowns than can actually be taken, and that this situation changes almost monthly. Practicing shutdowns as a normal disaster plan management technique often suggests what is possible. Any conscientious effort of this sort will lead to meaningful shutdowns regardless of the quantity perceived or actual utilization of data processing hardware. Quantification of the hours and devices shut down translated into dollars saved makes it possible for management to judge the value of such an exercise.

A rarely used yet good opportunity for shutdowns is weekends and third shifts. Often, data processing management, recalling the delicacy of equipment and the increased number of problems that occurred in the 1960s or early 1970s when equipment was turned off, simply leave all devices on during shifts when no work is being processed. This practice is foolish because it costs energy and is needless. This wasteful practice is hardly necessary given today's technologies, which permit easy power on and off. With operating systems that can be fired up quickly (IPLed), turning off unused equipment becomes a more viable option than in the past. Thus if a data center is closed after midnight, turn the equipment off and fire it back up an hour before office hours begin in the morning. If no processing is done over a weekend, again, turn off some or all of the hardware. Remember, electrical consumption by hardware continues high when left on but without productive work. Turning off the lights and removing 650 Btu worth of operators is not enough. Left on unused, the equipment will continue to hum away, spending your energy dollars.

Often, users of computer systems will request processing over a weekend which, if properly scheduled, will maximize blocks of idle time. For instance, see if the work can be processed during a weekday shift or on a Friday evening. Another thought: gather a number of such processing requests and plan on running them all at the same time during a particular shift over a weekend. Thus, if the data center is going to be open on Saturday, for example, and the accounting department wants to come in for one day over the weekend to work on year-end closings, offer to keep its terminals up on Saturday rather than on Sunday. In installations that have more than one computer, loading work on one and not on the other over a weekend makes sense. If, however, a programmer wants to work on a weekend testing a new system that is resident on only one computer, some careful planning might be necessary to make sure that the programs are available. Otherwise, management may find it easier to say no to the programmer, arguing that no time would be available over the weekend. The other business judgment that comes into play is the problem of the single user. Is it cost effective to leave the system up just for one user who might also only need the computer for a few hours? A system that costs $2000 per hour to run may be too expensive to make available to a weekend programmer, whereas one that operates at $200 per hour might make sense. Avoid any extreme in scheduling through commonsense planning and management.

On Managing Shutdowns

An additional set of summary thoughts on shutdowns should always be kept in mind and practiced:

- Periodically test major shutdown procedures and always check changes before they are implemented. Often, initial plans are faulty and need drastic changes.

- Document all procedures and problems through logs and the minutes of regularly scheduled review meetings (once monthly seems to work for most shops).

- Impose energy conservation targets on all operations managers. These often can be set in the form of percentages of reduced electrical usage over last year's consumption (e.g., reduce usage by 5 or 10% over last year and measure a manager's performance against the target).

- Provide incentives for such reductions through recognition, money bonuses, higher job appraisals, and improved working conditions.

Managers who have implemented proper shutdowns frequently have other tips to suggest for implementing individual plans. Most suggest that you anticipate some operational, hardware, and systems problems in the early stages which, although not usually serious, are frustrating and unpredictable. Most often these can be cleared up quickly after testing and debugging. Often, a trial run will flush out almost all the problems. Other managers warn that if a shutdown of all the equipment is carried out and lasts for more than two days, the temperature in the computer room may drop too much. This condition causes severe hardware failures later; therefore, either plan on reducing air conditioning or leaving some devices on to push the temperature above 50°F (but to keep it below 80°F). A third experience is that you should anticipate being able to shut down peripherals more than computers (the one unit all peripherals, even one, needs). Operations managers often feel that if any device remains idle for more than two hours at a time, it is an excellent candidate for shutdown. This might include card I/O and often tape drives on a long string or in a shop that has dozens. Many computer rooms have multiple system printers, some of which may have large periods of idle time. People who have implemented energy conservation programs feel that a target for reduction in the range of 5% is a reasonable one to set. That target could reasonably be expected to be exceeded over a number of years. Thus for a manager to say that he or she wishes to reduce energy consumption by 5% each year over the next four years should be greeted with a high degree of confidence.

So far two general methods for reducing electrical consumption have been reviewed:—using more modern energy efficient devices and shutdowns. A third approach involves implementing conservation in the data processing environment, involving air conditioning, heating, ventilation, and humidity controls.

Humidity controls represent one opportunity for DP management. Typically, a vendor of data processing equipment will state that its hardware is designed to operate in an environment of about 50% humidity. Yet in reality, most equipment will operate effectively with no damage at a relative humidity range between 35 and 60%. By allowing an air-conditioning system to operate within that range, as opposed to a strict 50% at all times, the amount of electricity used can be reduced. Because there are so many models and sizes of air conditioners being used at widely varying levels of efficiency, it becomes impossible to offer possible ranges of savings. In very humid environments, the need may be to reduce humidity down to 60% rather than to raise it from, say, 30% to 50 or 60%. Most equipment will operate above 60% and possibly below 35%, but only for short periods of time (ranging from a few minutes to an hour) and always at the risk of damage. Therefore, one should leave a buffer of 10 to 15% humidity at either end of the scale in case the air conditioner breaks down. This way at least the room will be properly conditioned environmentally for a while longer and possibly until the air conditioner is fixed.

Most data centers have a barometer which is checked frequently. Invariably, these are devices that record humidity levels in the room around the clock so that any fluctuations in humidity can be noted. Air-conditioning maintenance personnel use such data to fine tune their machines. As a good policy, most operations managers personally review the barometer log daily or weekly. These logs also provide them with information necessary to determine if the current air-conditioning system is adequate to service a room when new and additional equipment is installed, thus serving as an early warning system that the environment is deteriorating.

Always use air-conditioning systems independently of those employed for the building as a whole. If dependent on a building-wide system, a data center could lose air conditioning when the rest of the building's machine is shut off. Also, since environmental requirements for offices are less severe than for computer rooms, data centers connected to central systems may either receive insufficient quantities of cold air or may have humidity levels that are consistently too high. The latter condition can be only partially resolved with a dehumidifier, most of which are too small to do the job properly. By giving a computer room its own air-conditioning units, management of these devices can be independent of company-wide working conditions.

On the other hand, there should be a connection between the computer room and the central air conditioner in case the DP department's breaks down. The ducts leading into the data center should be adequate enough with all the necessary blowers to ensure the same amount of air conditioning as the stand-alone system usually provides. The main system can then serve as a temporary backup, protecting expensive DP hardware while allowing processing to continue at a relatively minimal cost.

Increasingly today, large buildings are being heated and cooled simultaneously through an organized effort on the part of management to become more energy efficient. Interior rooms often have to be cooled down as a result of heat coming from people, lights, and equipment (such as typewriters and copiers), and rooms along the exterior have to be heated in the winter. Intelligent management of energy simply calls for the distribution of colder air to the center and hotter air to the periphery of a building. Data processing is increasingly playing a major role in this ecology. Taking heat from data processing equipment and funneling it out to appropriate parts of the building where needed makes sense. As we saw earlier in this chapter, a data center produces tens of thousands of Btu per hour, which can be used elsewhere rather than simply being cooled off. The easiest way to take advantage of this heat is by using a heat pump, which, in effect, absorbs heat from a computer room, transfers it to a cold-water distribution system, and then moves it to the heater in the building. Excess heat is then vented to the outside (e.g., in the summer months). Needed heat can be stored in water, later providing energy to drive the heat pump or to be used to operate a heater warming other parts of the building. (See Figure 6-3.)

A less sophisticated use of heat in the winter, which everyone uses every time the central heating system breaks down, is to open the doors of the computer room, allowing the excess heat to blow out into the rest of the data processing department. Although this is a common stratagem, it is not

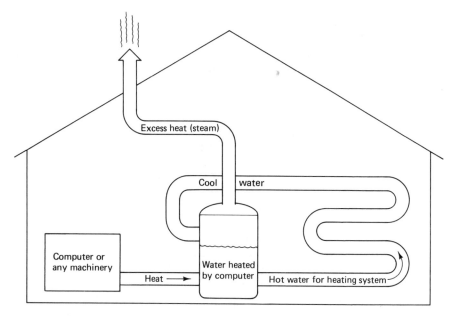

Figure 6-3. Heat transfer system.

really a wise one, since (1) the humidity in the computer room usually rises quickly to the level of the office environment, which is then too high, and (2) security becomes a problem because now anyone can wander into the area housing the computer. About the only time that opening the doors makes sense is in the middle of the summer if the air-conditioning system breaks down and processing must continue. Then open doors and fans might keep the temperature below 80%, but even then the practice is not recommended because of the humidity problem.

Getting back to the heat pump system, this method can be extremely useful. Recovered heat from the computer room, although lower than that generated by a heater (115°F from hardware), can provide a substantial amount of hot air in concert with normal heat-generating devices. In short, this method, if not currently employed, should be studied seriously, particularly if there is a large data center with several computer systems within a particular building.

Just as heat can be extracted from data processing, cooling can be brought in without simply depending on air conditioning. The most widely used method involves mixing a portion of cold air drawn from outside the building in winter and mixing it with artificially cooled air from an air-conditioning system to ensure the correct humidity levels. In the northern portions of North America, for example, air-conditioning costs are being cut sharply this way during the winter months. Remember, however, that as

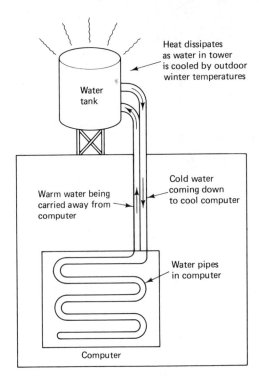

Heat dissipates
as water in tower
is cooled by outdoor
winter temperatures

Water
tank

Cold water
coming down
to cool computer

Warm water being
carried away from
computer

Water pipes
in computer

Computer

Figure 6-4. Chilled-water-cooling system using outdoor cold air and a water system to dissipate computer heat with little or no reliance on air-conditioning systems for the CPU.

a general rule, outside air is not as humid as air-conditioned air, and therefore additional humidification equipment or capability in an air-conditioning system may be required. Clearly, the costs of drawing on nature are offset by the benefits in lowered air-conditioning costs, however.

Another technique commonly employed uses a cooling tower of water, exchanging heat. Essentially, the way it works is that when temperatures outside hit 40°F or lower, water in an outside tower (usually on the roof) can be cooled sufficiently to reduce heat in a computer room without using air conditioners. Obviously, such a system would be of little benefit in such hot climates as Florida, Mexico, or southern Spain. But the point is that in combination with a normal air-conditioning system, nature once again can be made to pick up some of the responsibility for cooling a computer room. (See Figure 6-4.)

Later in this chapter yet another method for controlling environments through the use of computerized energy management systems is discussed. Suffice it to say at this point that the determination of how much and when nature or variations in hot and cold air and water can be utilized effectively can be controlled by a little mini- or microcomputer in a building separate from the computers in the DP department. But before such systems can be reviewed, it is important to understand how to ensure at least minimal levels of energy for data processing.

ENERGY SHORTAGES AND PLANNING
IN DATA PROCESSING

Brownouts, blackouts, forced cutbacks, rising costs of energy, conservation programs, and normal security considerations all dictate that attention must be paid to provide sufficient amounts of cost-effective energy with which to operate data processing equipment. Despite all the attacks on the use of energy, data processing will continue to need minimal, yet substantial quantities of electricity. A DP director does not have to resort to the use of cannons and armies to ensure minimal supplies of energy since there are specific, proven methods available which can help ensure constant access to the electricity that he or she may need.

Basically two types of problems may occur that result in power reductions or losses. In the first situation, power companies can and have often reduced the amount of electricity being fed to a particular area when demand exceeded supply. These reductions typically range from 2% to an extreme of 8% in normal supplies. What makes the situation worse is that these shortages usually come during the summer months when homeowners and business offices use more electricity, to run air conditioners. That is the time when data processing also needs the greatest amount of air conditioning. Because cutbacks have become almost a way of life, any data processing department without an energy conservation program that can adapt to a reduction in power in the range of 2 to 8% probably has a serious problem. The second common scenario involves momentary blips in which a power surge in excess of normal supply is fed into the computer room or there is a sharp decline for a few seconds in the normal flow of electricity. The situation of an uneven flow of power is a continuous problem that can occur many times each day in all departments. Most data processing equipment can stand a power fluctuation of between +6 and +10% down to −10 and −16% without damage to the device or the loss of productive services. Obviously, if someone drives a truck into an electric light pole outside your building, taking out all the power, the hard crash that data processing will experience in its systems can hardly be avoided without having expensive auxiliary backup electricity producing units tied in automatically to the hardware. As a general rule, most blips in electrical supplies are within the tolerances just described and thus pose few problems. More normally, the DP department has to worry about brownouts (usually coming in the summer months) and less often about fluctuations in voltage.

With the increase in brownouts the need for orderly shutdown procedures has become an essential element of managing a DP installation today. We have already discussed shutdown procedures which are clearly related to the problem of brownouts; suffice it to add that all installations should have a list of applications in priority of importance (need) which must be executed so that if resources are limited, the most important jobs to the organization are done first. Thus if payroll is run every Thursday, brownouts on that day should cause other applications to be suspended if need be but not the salary check run. If a plant scheduling application must be run each night to ensure the operation of a manufacturing plant, alternative backup locations to run this batch application must be arranged for as part of a normal disaster plan. Critical work should be run at odd shifts when power constraints are not as severe (the third shift is a good time). As part of a normal disaster plan, unanticipated electrical outages should be accounted for by such things as duplicate copies of files and operating systems, backup locations for processing, and a priority list of critical applications.

Normal fluctuations in power are often not fully understood by DP personnel. Local power companies, building maintenance personnel, or an engineer can easily provide data on what the pattern of electrical flow is in the building housing data processing. If statistics are not kept on the building as a whole, a sample study could be performed so that management can have an idea of how often fluctuations in voltage threaten to disrupt data processing, with possible damage to equipment as well as the loss of information in machine-readable form. Devices exist to trap this kind of information, which can be attached to transformers feeding an entire building, to the fuse box servicing the computer room, on specific machines, or even to attach to specific power lines. A study of this sort typically shows that fluctuations occur constantly each day, in many instances coming very close to causing problems. Figure 6-5 shows a sample form that can be used to track such data for a period of time. In some departments such records are kept for every day of the year, and if voltage levels remain too low, the local power company is contacted to provide better service. Occasionally such data have been used to sue local power companies for faulty service and breach of contract.

A number of approaches can be taken in attacking the problem of voltage fluctuations. One common action is simply to see if the local power company can provide a better flow of electricity. Second, if power stability is critical enough to you, install an Uninterruptible Power Supply (UPS) system, which will smooth voltage supplies just before going into the computer room. Upgrading equipment to devices that can tolerate greater fluctuations of power represents a third option. A fourth action can be to run critical jobs at those times during the day when electrical supplies are historically most reliable in your area (a practice commonly used in developing countries).

Although it is not the purpose of this book to discuss software backup considerations, some obvious points can be noted that can augment the strategies mentioned above.

- Use data base management software with checkpoint and backup utilities that allow data to be protected against unexpected interruptions of work and which record and track transactions so that at restart time, one simply continues from the point where the problem developed.

Duration of Disturbance	Number of Disturbances per ~~year~~ 1978 - Shift 1					
	Undervoltage (dips below normal rated voltage)			Overvoltage (rises above normal rated voltage)		
	to −8%	below −8% to −18%	below −18%	to +10%	to +15%	over +15%
1 cycle (17 ms) or less		1				
1+ to 6 cycles (17+ to 100 ms)	2	7				
6+ to 30 cycles (100+ ms to ½ second)			3			
30+ to 60 cycles (½+ to 1 second)						
1+ to 30 seconds						
30+ seconds to 5 minutes						
5+ to 10 minutes						
10+ minutes to 1 hour						
over 1 hour	14					

Figure 6-5. Completed sample of a power disturbance form. (Source: IBM Corporation, © 1979.)

- Usc software backup utilities built into terminal management packages. If a particular teleprocessing package fails to have such backup capability, do not buy it; install someone else's. This collection of programs can be resident in the main computer or in some front-end processor or teleprocessing controller. Built-in backup and recovery procedures and code are absolutely essential.

- Keep duplicate copies of files and programs on tape or other medium that can be loaded into the computer after a disaster should the originals be wiped out or altered as a result of an unscheduled shutdown. A common procedure is to set up restart and checkpoint procedures both in all programs and with the operators in the computer room so as to minimize the duplication of work after a problem has developed.

Reruns of work partially completed at the time a power failure occurs is a time-consuming effort and therefore a costly event. By tracking how often this occurs during a period of time (two to three months minimum seems to work well), management can gain an appreciation for the expense of people, additional processing, lost productivity, and the cost of electricity for reruns. The higher the cost, the greater the motivation will be to minimize this problem through the use of hardware and software safeguards. It would not be unreasonable, as an example, for a computer to experience several blips a month of 1 or 2 seconds but which cause three or four hours of reprocessing each time because jobs in midstream had to be started over. If it costs a department $500 per hour to run a system and in the course of one month it has 10 hours of reruns, the cost approximates $5000, which in one year could reach $60,000—pure waste. That money represents hard cash laid out in overtime salaries, increased rental on the machines, and more electricity used. The installation of a UPS device at $100,000 would have a payback of less than two years in this case and thus would represent a good option functionally and financially. The key point to remember is that the issue of electrical usage and the management of downtime is a worthwhile business activity.

Mention has been made of the UPS strategem, yet more needs to be said. Data centers that absolutely must be operational (e.g., those with large on-line systems) frequently use such devices. By shielding a data center from fluctuations in power while maintaining a reserve of electricity (anywhere from a few seconds to a half-hour, with most systems closer to 5 minutes), the damage caused by blips in power is reduced. By warning operators of a problem, an organized shutdown is made possible without losing data and with sufficient warning for users.

Although UPS devices are constantly changing, with new ones appearing all the time, they all essentially fall into three categories. The first type provides battery power from five minutes to an hour (depending on the brand) and is usually equipped with the necessary features and switches so that if

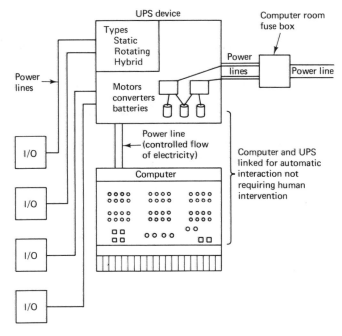

Figure 6-6. Overview of a UPS in a data center. UPS receives power from utility company line, smooths its flow into the computer (and peripherals if so desired), and can provide electricity in a blackout.

there is a power failure, the DP devices are immediately run off the batteries. Redundancy of parts in such units allows for component failure and repairs while not interrupting its support to a DP system. A second type of UPS drives a dc motor and flywheel with an induction motor, batteries, and appropriate switching devices to provide temporary electrical power. A third variant is simply a combination of the first two approaches, static and rotating. They all vary in size and power and features. A deluxe system with all the bells and whistles would have rectified chargers, inverters, batteries, motor generators, cause ac output—possibly drawn from dc sources—and be very expensive. It may also be very necessary. (See Figure 6-6.)

UPS devices are turned on and off with the computer systems they support and thus are often physically part of the collection of computer equipment in a data center. Electrical usage to operate a UPS device will be about an additional 10% over what the computer room uses without it. Actual kVA and other values can be determined for this kind of a device in the same manner as for a computer. In selecting such devices there are some general rules of thumb. First, a device that has between 15 and 30 minutes' worth of electricity will probably take care of more than 90% of all power failures. Second, if a power failure takes place with a computer that is water cooled, a UPS may also be required for the cooling system (apart from that servicing the computer), so the choice of a unit might involve being able to drive air-conditioning or water-cooling equipment along with a computer. So electrical capacity has to be an issue. Engine generators do not usually have to be purchased in a UPS configuration unless 100% availability of the computer system is essential.

CONSERVING ENERGY USING DATA PROCESSING

Besides being an energy hog, data processing, as was shown earlier in this chapter, has available to it various proven methods to hold down the cost of energy. The data processing industry as a whole has devoted considerable attention to the development of techniques that can be applied across an entire organization and not be limited simply to itself.

Essentially five different areas and techniques in conjunction with computer technology are helping. Although some of these have been discussed briefly within the context of how DP departments can initiate energy conservation programs, they merit further review. The significant approaches include:

- Heat pump systems taking computer-generated Btu and passing this heat to needed areas in a building
- Varying humidity levels
- Separate air-conditioning systems for computers and buildings
- Employing computers to manage the use of all forms of energy

Although many of these areas have been profitably exploited in the past, optimization of each is improving dramatically today as increasing numbers of organizations pay more attention to the problem of energy.

Heat Transfer Systems

As mentioned earlier, buildings are air conditioned in some form all 12 months of the year and heated for nearly half as many, presenting the unique problem of having the right amount of cold or heat at the right points in a building at a reasonable cost. Fortunately, most major air-conditioning and heating companies are selling systems that provide coordination between heat and cold movement throughout a building. No longer are they simply selling air conditioners or heaters at the expense of efficiency. Increasingly, such vendors are taking a total systems approach to the problem of heat transfer in a building, configuring systems that provide heaters and air conditioners working in coordinated fashion. The most useful of these involve the use of some sort of heat pump.

Essentially, a heat pump can take the hot air generated, say by a computer, by way of a cold-water network of pipes or a blower, and send it to the building's heating system, which can either pass that on through normal

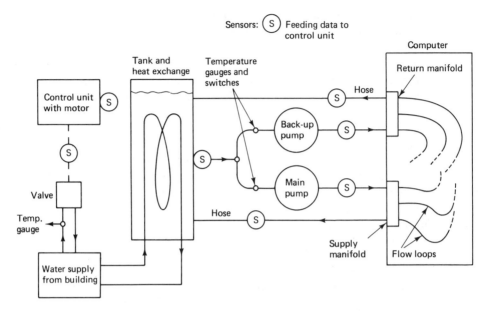

Figure 6-7. Chilled-water system for a computer.

water or air ductworks to where it is needed (in the winter) or expel the excess heat to the outside when it is not (as in the summer). Expulsion to the outdoors is simply done through the use of water towers or an evaporation unit. Other organizations are trying to capture the energy of this heat (even in the summer) for use in operating hot-water heaters more effectively to provide water for kitchens, bathrooms, and manufacturing facilities that require steam and other forms of heat. Considerable experimentation in heat systems also involving solar energy, and heat from computer and other equipment, is evident in such high-energy users as glassmaking factories and paper mills. (See Figure 6-7).

Almost all the major manufacturers of air-conditioning and heating units today feel a tremendous incentive to develop more efficient heat transfer devices. One of the leading manufacturers, Fedders Corporation, led the way in 1980 with the establishment of a solar energy division to add the resources of the sun to well-known technologies. Many practical units are available and fairly inexpensive today. Working with a traditional heating system, they provide warmth where needed and cause the normal conventional heater to work when heat transfer components fail to provide sufficient temperature to a building. The most attractive feature of a heat transfer system today is that it can take very low levels of heat—either in water or air—and transfer it efficiently, making it possible for water or air to be heated up to desired levels instead of heating from much lower temperatures, which would cost more. Thus heating 115°F, taken from a heating system, up to 140°F becomes less expensive than, for example, taking winter tap water at 40°F and raising its temperature by 100°F.

The real improvement in the past several years has come in the ability of a heat transfer system to work efficiently in gathering up even lower levels of heat into concentrated masses which need even less heating energy to come up to required temperature. There is an electrical cost associated with a heat transfer system which must be netted against potential savings. With the devices coming on the market today, the savings in fuel costs continually rise over older systems, especially when compared to heating units that did not take advantage of heat transfer principles. Just in the past five years alone, from pricing actions of OPEC, inflation, and normal price increases caused by demand increases for all forms of energy, these systems have become so price competitive that many heating units that are over five years old could be replaced today with enough energy savings to justify the reexpenditure in the new system. In short, heaters that were designed and built six or seven year ago, even if fully paid for, are often more expensive than replacing them with newer systems today.

Any engineer or building maintenance personnel trying to evaluate the amount of heat that can be recaptured from a computer or other heat-generating industrial device should consider the following factors:

- How much heat is totally required by a building (or campus of buildings)?
- How much heat dissipation over how many hours comes from each of the machines in question?
- How much heat can a heat transfer device capture and contribute to the conventional heating system in a building?
- What are the costs for energy (in kWh) to drive a combination heat transfer/boiler system?
- What additional expenses are there to amortize (such as water tanks for thermal storage, supplemental heat sources, discount for the recovery system's reliability, minicomputer to manage a total energy system, etc.)?

A comparison of today's costs extrapolated into the next two to five years, with appropriate increases for fuel costs, when netted against the expense of using a heat transfer system will show clearly that there is a substantial savings involved in any good-size building, even in a structure that is only two or three stories high. The cost of a heat transfer system becomes a fixed one-time installation expense with maintenance and ongoing energy costs being the only growing expenses to face—something you would have with any heating system. More conventional (older) heating systems have higher maintenance costs and require more energy to run. Like the newer computers, heating systems have finally become more energy conservative.

Cold Transfer Systems

Since computers still require anywhere from ¼ to 5 tons of air conditioning, using cold outdoor air in the winter is an attractive alternative to expensive air conditioning. While the need for air-conditioning machines (and therefore their operating costs) will not go away, usage and expenses are being slashed in many creative ways today. Increasingly, air-conditioning machines are being adapted so that a combination of return chilled air can be mixed with cold air drawn from the outside to provide the required amount of cooling for a computer room. Controls are available today to ensure proper levels of humidity as well. In the northwestern part of the United States or throughout Canada, for example, such an approach can profoundly reduce the costs of running air-conditioning systems for computer rooms. Figures citing savings of 20% to over 50% after expenses are not uncommon. The overhead involved in such a combination includes additional humidifying capability in the air-conditioning system, since typically outside air is not as humid as is required for a computer or office environment. Outside humidity levels in winter may be commonly between 30 and 50% while most operations managers try to maintain their computer rooms closer to 60%. Combination units can either be just for a computer machine room or be tied into the central air-conditioning system serving an entire building or complex. The key fact to remember is that some sort of a system involving the use of outdoor air invariably makes good business sense as long as your area enjoys some winter and almost regardless of the requirements of computer rooms and offices.

A second method by which outside air can be equally cost justified involves the use of chilled water and cooling towers. Simply put, if the temperature outside the building is less than 40°F (at wet-bulb temperatures), water going through a cooling tower on the roof can be cooled enough to draw heat out of a computer room using conventional industrial or computerized equipment designed to be water cooled. This method can and usually does eliminate all need for air-conditioning equipment of the traditional type for a computer room. Operating like a radiator of a car, the principle thus remains a simple one. An easy system to install, its benefit is a function of how much cold weather you have. This system would not be cost effective in Mexico, but it would be in New York, Oslo, and Vienna.

Humidity Variation Systems

Already mentioned briefly were the savings caused by having the data center live with fluctuating levels of humidity within predefined limits. Since most equipment requires levels of between 35 and 60%, a tremendous amount of latitude exists and therefore an opportunity. Since in most installation the need is to raise humidity levels (rather than lower them as in the tropics), adding water to the air is less expensive than trying to dry it out (which requires heat). It is also a well-known fact that operation of air-conditioning equipment is far less expensive if it is required to maintain humidity levels within a range rather than at a precise target (such as 50%).

When the suggestion is made to an operations manager that he or she live with a range of humidity levels, the person invariably will ask what happens if humidity exceeds 60% or drops below 35%. No—fungus does not grow on machines or, at the other extreme, computer operators do not die of thirst. Leaving aside the obvious problem of equipment malfunctions that might occur during long periods of excessively humid or dry conditions, other concerns also exist. Static electricity in dry environments (often the result of low humidity levels but not always) obviously will irritate individuals as they touch each other and everything in the room. Worse, these little shocks are often sufficient to cause malfunctions in equipment and momentary blips that can result in lost data. With too much moisture in the air, cards and paper may stick to each other and therefore not work properly in data processing equipment. The most obvious problem of all remains the malfunctioning of equipment caused by conditions not taken into account in the design of hardware. Downtime can lead to the expense of reruns, lost time, and actual damage to logic boards, all of which far exceed the benefits of maintaining erratic levels of humidity outside recommended ranges. Thus the answer is, keep within reasonable levels.

Multiple Air-Conditioning Systems

A fourth way in which data processing can optimize the cost/benefit of air conditioning is to have its own system apart from that used by the rest of the building. If a data center shares the central system, however, and the DP department operates three shifts daily (a normal situation), the central air-conditioning unit must also operate around the clock cooling the entire building. For a small building of about 300,000 square feet, for instance, the cost in energy can run into thousands of dollars per month. Even cooling a portion of the building in a zoned system can be expensive just to satisfy DP's requirements. What a waste of money. It is far less expensive just to cool the one department that must operate all the time rather than the whole building. This is not to say that the two should not be connected so that the central system can operate as a backup to the DP department's air conditioning—simply that here is an opportunity for real savings. (See Figure 6-8.)

An example illustrates how to cost-justify the possible expenses and benefits involved in a multiple air-conditioning network. Using an intermediate-size data center might require one or two 10-ton units at a purchase cost in 1980 of under $70,000 to cover acquisition, initial installation, and initial maintenance expenses. Such a system might operate for several hundred dollars per month. The central system, operating an additional two shifts, for example, in a building with 500,000 square feet would (in 1980's prices)

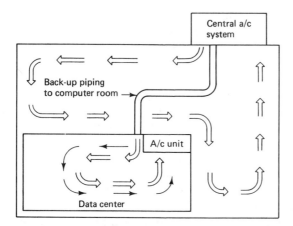

Figure 6-8. Principle of a two-way air-conditioning system using a central air-conditioning unit as backup to the data center's own system.

approximate several thousand dollars per month. If having a separate system for the DP department cut the monthly costs of air conditioning by $3000, that figure divided into $70,000 suggests that the second system begins to pay for itself in two years. That assumes there has been no price increase in the cost of energy in that time. If that is taken into account, the break-even point would be closer to 18 months. Thus the payback in operating expenses by having two separate systems can be quite short. During a brownout or severe reduction of electricity, electrical usage throughout the building can be cut back drastically while diverting available energy to the data center, which would probably have to continue operating anyway. If an organization is heavily dependent on data processing, electrical shortages thus do not have to threaten the functioning of other departments. In fact, separate air-conditioning and electrical circuits feeding a computer data center is the norm today. Rarely does a company still supply air conditioning and power from the main systems in a building.

Power Management Systems

The latest innovation in data processing's involvement in energy management involves using computers to hold down the costs of electricity, fuel, air conditioning, heating, and so on, outside the DP department—throughout an entire building. Such an application of data processing is rapidly appearing in office buildings, warehouses, manufacturing plants, schools, and other installations. Managing a building through the use of DP to control the costs of an ecological environment has proven to be a fairly simple process with high paybacks. Essentially, the objective is to make sure that energy is being used most efficiently where it is needed at all times, while reducing or eliminating waste. For example, holding down the amount of electricity used in a building can be achieved by monitoring such devices as compressors, elevators, ovens, air-conditioning units, lights, heaters, fans, escalators, furnaces, and other devices. Another general area where computers are used has been briefly mentioned already—using outdoor air to heat and cool. Called *enthalpy control,* this process of using outdoor air involves controlling temperatures throughout a building, making sure that no space is overheated or cooled and that the right resource is used optimally. This process may involve automatic on/off temperature switches (such as one might have at home), the use of fans on a timed basis, and intake and exhaust devices—all controlled by computer technology. Fortunately today, systems can be installed in which the programs to manage a building have already been written and which merely require tailoring to a particular building. Combinations of programs and computers are now being sold by a number of computer manufacturers, such as IBM and Honeywell, not solely by small energy consultants or solar energy companies. These systems allow you to set targets for consumption, track and modify usage, and probably generate more different reports on what is happening in a building than you may care to read! More seriously, this kind of information allows management for the first time to forecast costs of operation accurately while making it possible to identify problems quickly and to fix them almost immediately.

A few essential facts about electricity should be understood to make such a system attractive. Remember, such an energy management project will be concerned primarily with controlling the costs of electricity, which remains the most expensive and widely used form of energy in buildings today. Thus in controlling the costs of energy in most organizations, the real potential savings lie first with electricity and only afterward with oil and gas. Therefore, focus on electrical problems first and other forms of energy later.

As in your home, electrical companies charge for the number of kilowatt hours of power consumed in a month. The amount of usage is determined by reading a meter. Another way in which power companies measure electrical usage in commercial establishments is by taking a snapshot of usage during a particular period of time called a *demand interval.* Thus usage in a period of, say, 15 to 30 minutes is measured to establish usage. If in a 30-minute period, 20 kWh is consumed (within 0.50 hour), the power demand in our case would be 20 kWh X 0.50 hour, which yields a usage of 40 kWh/hour. Since kWh is the basic unit of measurement used by power companies to establish costs, the demand for power can now be determined for billing. Because demand is the basis for a power company's establishment of costs, it is important to keep down the *rate of use* of power per hour as much as possible. In the course of a normal day, usage by the hour varies, and therefore an opportunity to even out usage as a means of lowering the rate (amount) consumed per hour exists. In short, the goal is to slow down usage when the power company determines your rate. This can only be done from a practical point of view by trying to use the same amount of power each hour during the day rather than a lot at one time. (See Figure 6-9.)

Complicating the problem of cost control is the fact that billing is usually a combination of the number of kWh used and the rate or time when they

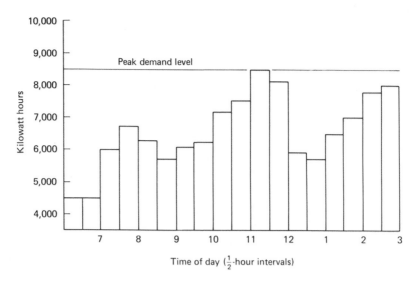

Figure 6-9. Sample chart for tracking electrical demand in one building. In this case, the peak is at 8500 kw between 11:00 and 11:30. The objective is not to lower peak demand below 8500 kw.

were consumed. Billing on a demand basis is invariably set at whatever your peak period is. Thus if utilization is highest at 8:30 to 9:00 in the morning, consumption during that period becomes the basis for billing all hours during the month—hence the motivation to keep utilization peaks down in any effort at cost control. Fairly constant rates of consumption always yield lower electrical *rates* of billing. Remember, to save on electrical costs you have to reduce *both* total consumption and the rate of usage.

Computerized energy management systems essentially monitor both consumption and demand rates through various timing methods and meters. Depending on how you are billed by the local electrical company, one or both elements can be measured and controlled. Usage either way is recorded at preset intervals or constantly. The resulting reports generated by such a system can indicate potential areas of waste to building engineers. Armed with such information, they can reduce power peaks over time. (See Figure 6-10.)

For example, suppose that at 8:00 A.M. most of the lights in the building go on together with a computer, heating system, and other commercial equipment. Since this is the time of day when people begin arriving for work, use of elevators and escalators also increases sharply and typewriters, copiers, and coffee machines are also put into use. If the local electrical company takes its snapshot at this time, when a power surge in demand is taking place, the electrical bill will be quite high. By understanding the costs involved, the building engineer would obviously conclude that the peak load had to be lowered by spreading demand increases over a longer period of time. Thus

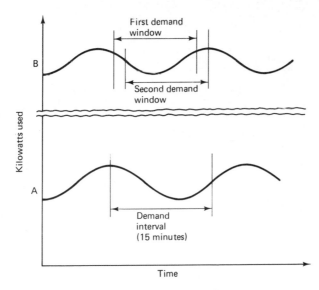

Figure 6-10. Two views of demand intervals. A shows a fixed demand level; B shows a sliding-window demand level where multiple peaks are measured. Both are typical ways of analyzing energy use by an energy management system.

the computer could be turned on at 7, the heating system fired up at 7:30, all lights automatically turned on one floor at a time starting at 7:35, and other equipment even later. There is little that can be done to stop the use of elevators and escalators at 8 unless (1) the work force reports to work at staggered intervals or (2) the number of people using an elevator each time it moves is increased. Flextime and staggered work loads are becoming increasingly popular, and limiting the use of elevators to certain floors reduces their cost of operation (e.g., elevator 1 going only to the first 10 floors, elevator 2 going only to floors 11 through 30, etc.). With these various practices, it is possible to lower peak loads together with the rate at which power is billed.

Armed with information on your sliding window of demand (also called *lagged demand*), additional fine tuning of usage can take place as building engineers work with computerized reports on usage. (See Figure 6-11.) Besides indicating what areas need to be worked on to reduce demand peaks and power loads, a computerized system can also allow management to preset certain actions for the computer to take. For instance, if usage exceeds predefined levels, the computer can be preset to turn off certain devices or warn maintenance management. Another obvious use is to turn off lights automatically at night (say at 10:00 P.M.) since most people forget to turn them off on their way home anyway. Certain elevators and escalators can be turned off automatically after normal working hours to reduce electrical usage still further. Although many of these actions could be done by a person not using a computer, people cost money and manual efforts become quite expensive and complicated in large buildings. Thus computerized controls of these obvious users of energy become cost-justified and convenient.

Such systems always produce savings without either reducing productive work in a building or making the environment uncomfortable for employees

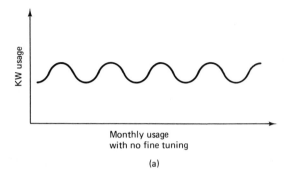

Monthly usage
with no fine tuning

(a)

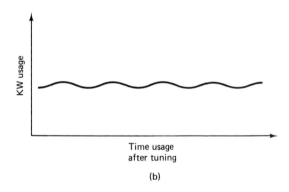

Time usage
after tuning

(b)

Figure 6-11. Monthly view of kilowatt utilization: (a) Usage before an energy management system was used; (b) effect of smoothing demand.

simply because without such a system there would be a tremendous amount of wasted energy going unchecked or unappreciated and whose elimination would have no effect on normal working conditions. Although savings vary widely, realistic potentials exist to cut costs from 10% to well over 50%. A small three-story office building with a data center today might realistically be spending $15,000 per month on electricity alone. A 25% cut would represent a savings of about $3700 × 12 months = $44,400 per year, which, when adjusted for a 15% increase in the cost of energy during one year, yields a true annual savings of $51,000. If a computerized electrical control system costs $75,000, the payback begins in 18 months. And it would work for years, saving money on ever-more-expensive electricity.

As already mentioned, computerized controls are also being applied to air-conditioning systems. Wiring a building with thermometers on all sides inside and out allows for a number of possible actions. For example, if the south side of the building at 10:00 has the sun shining on it, less hot air would be required there than in the center or northern end of the building. A computer could detect this and be programmed to turn off the air blowers on the south side, saving electricity, while concentrating more hot air where it was needed. If the majority of the people in a particular department eat lunch at noon in the cafeteria, less heat may be needed in the eating area because of the increased number of Btu everyone brought into the room. Also, less heat would be required in the empty department for 30 to 60 minutes at lunchtime. Both of these examples are common ones today, and variations are endless, limited only by common sense and imagination. The point is that these changes and controls can be effected smoothly by a computer in almost any organization.

The general benefits of an energy management system can therefore be summarized briefly:

- The cost of electricity can be reduced by reducing demand and peak loads.

- Complete coverage of energy consumption becomes possible since a computer can control a building 24 hours a day and usually up to approximately 100 different points of measurement (thermometers, devices, lights, etc.).

- Centralized total and rapid control from one point allows maintenance personnel to manage a building better as a whole.

- Disaster control becomes possible with rapid warning of problems, deviations from preset conditions, malfunctions, fires, flooding, and increases or decreases in available electricity, oil, gas, and so on.

- Analysis of the costs and benefits of one form of energy versus another for different tasks becomes possible.

Similarly, a more sophisticated system that does more than control electrical usage can be installed to monitor the use of natural gas, hot water, and heating oil to maximize the efficiency of their use. Today, modern industrial heating systems are increasingly being outfitted with microprocessors to improve the efficiency of oil and gas consumption. This can also be done by the computer managing the entire building. Detailed record keeping can generate reports that suggest to management whether or not and when it would be cheaper to use gas instead of oil or coal. Other data can suggest optimal periods of use, as with electricity, and in general suggest the kinds of benefits clearly available when controlling the costs of electricity. In short, the possibility of many variations and benefits are extensive.

Despite the variety of functions that an energy management system can have, the basic components of such an application are relatively few. A typical system that takes care of electrical management, and controls air conditioning and heating, would consist of a small computer dedicated to this one application. The system would have its own data storage devices, a printer, and a terminal console (probably located in the building maintenance office) and have attached to it whatever devices and input-measuring units are relevant for that building. These might include thermostats, thermometers from outside the building, and power lines controlling lights, elevators, and escalators. The programs in the computer would probably be purchased from a vendor and simply modified by the data processing department (usually in conjunction with the vendor) and the building's maintenance personnel—not a terribly complicated or time-consuming task. Probably, no additional DP personnel would be needed except on rare occasions when a software problem developed or a major change was anticipated as a result of someone's clever idea of a new application for the system. In short, such a system is fairly small and can be treated like any other industrial control equipment—there but quiet and unobtrusive. (See Figure 6-12.)

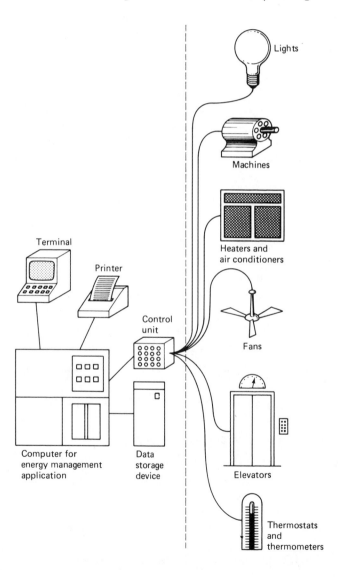

Figure 6-12. Sample energy management system.

Installing an Energy Management System

Although the technical engineering details for installing such a system could easily be expanded to fill a chapter, suffice it to point out here that some managerial issues should be kept in mind when installing such a system. Begin by trying to identify the kinds of things you want to control and in which buildings. It is best and simplest to have one system per building. After you have made a rough list of the kinds of energy consumption you wish to control (e.g., which data centers, elevators, air conditioners, etc.), you can begin the process of finding a system. Start out with the idea that electrical consumption will be the first thing to manage. You want to monitor peak loads and usage in your building by drawing data from the local utility company's meters. Go after the biggest energy users first, such as computers, lights, air conditioning, elevators, and other heavy industrial equipment. Leave the typewriters and coffee machines for last. After gathering literature from various vendors (all of whom advertise energy systems in just about every major business and industrial publication), you can make some decisions about how you want to control the use of energy.

During this investigation, there are a number of questions that must be answered in order to make the final selection of a system relevant to your operations.

- Which devices and users of energy must be controlled?
- Where are they located?
- Can they be turned off, for how long, when, and how?
- What is the energy consumption of the major users in the building (amount used and cost in money)?
- Which devices must stay on regardless of peak demands or brownouts?
- What does it cost the organization in money and lost quantifiable productivity if certain energy users are denied power or are not managed effectively through the energy system?
- What are the potential savings by investing in an energy management system?
- What will it take to gain the necessary approval for such an installation?
- What will it take to get it installed and operational?

Armed with answers to such questions, it becomes possible for management to define the important uses of energy, how and when they can be controlled, and at what cost. Emerging from this kind of analysis would be a strategy for lowering the costs of energy (both with and without the use of data processing) while making the organization keenly aware of the great expenditures going toward all forms of energy. Invariably after such an examination of the issues involved, management is shocked at the large amounts

284

of money being spent and wasted on energy. To be sure, once a system is installed, the plan as initially conceived would have to change as data on actual activity became more precise and as people learned more about the true interrelationship of energy consumption to costs in a particular environment. In short, management of a building's energy consumption over time would be done more efficiently and at a better cost. As time passes, additional monitoring devices should be installed (e.g., thermometers in places never thought of in the beginning, feeding data to the computer) which would allow for continued fine tuning of costs downward. Hardware and software to drive such a plan is relatively easy to obtain quickly. Once installed, additional modifications and additions can usually be made without stopping the computer's work and is a logical outgrowth of the normal process of good management.

CONCLUDING OBSERVATIONS

The whole issue of energy conservation has become an issue of great concern to management in general as a result of the sharp increases in the cost of fuels evident since the mid-1970s. The concern is a real one which has also become fashionable for its own sake. Although a great deal of experimentation is currently going on with conventional energy sources and even more with newer areas such as solar and thermal, common sense must prevail when dealing with this year's energy costs and next year's anticipated needs. Availability and cost over the short term will remain high—and therein lies the problem. How do we get the most for energy expenses now? Although redesigning new buildings and replacing antiquated equipment are obvious long-term solutions when coupled with alternative sources and uses of energy, we remain trapped by contractual obligations on existing hardware, buildings that we cannot move out of overnight, and accounting and managerial practices which some believe are medieval. Clearly, a proven attack on the problem of energy expenses can be made either in data processing or by using computerized technology. With nearly a decade of actual experience, one can clearly state that data processing can quickly control the rising costs of energy and frequently actually reduce its expense not only within data centers but throughout any organization. What is beautiful about this fact is that the actual process of controlling costs is not as complicated as other data processing applications which have proven useful in the past. In short, it is easier to manage the costs of energy in and around data processing than it would be to install some standard computerized applications such as plant scheduling, order-entry systems, or integrated financial applications. This means that the benefits of such an investment compete very well against other possible projects within most organizations. The ultimate fact to keep in mind is that energy conservation via data processing is a proven success story.

Things that go without saying go
even better if they are said.

Prince de Talleyrand

Too often non-DP management does not understand what hardware issues there are and even less how to measure the demands of MIS managers asking for more equipment. This chapter is devoted to showing how DP management can present hardware and technical issues in nontechnical, business terms for general management: how to present topics for decision together with specific examples that suggest clearly proven methods for improving communications and thereby relations between the DP department and the rest of the organization. Finally, we review the typical issues that non-DP management should be informed about and the benefits of such a dialogue.

CHAPTER SEVEN

Presenting DP Issues to Management and Users

Increasingly today, DP management is being called upon to explain and justify their activities to executives at the top of their organizations. Many of these executives have little or no understanding of data processing or of its vocabulary. As the costs of data processing as a whole continue to rise, together with an organization's total dependency on computerized technology in order to be competitive and profitable, executives will follow an already existing trend of paying more attention to data processing. And yet a gulf of serious misunderstanding and lack of communications separate the two groups. Because data processing management reports to the key decision makers in an organization, these high priests of computerized technology are more frequently being called upon to explain their activities in terms that executives can understand. The conversations between the two groups involve such bread-and-butter issues as application justification and development, requests for more computers, people, and money, and perhaps the most challenging, discussions about problems and concerns within data processing as they affect the entire community of users. Further pressure for meaningful dialogue comes from the fact that many DP applications by their nature force reorganizations within a company, changes that can only be sold to top management in carefully thought out presentations and reports couched in terms relevant to the decision makers.

It has been only in the past five years that DP management as a whole has felt a sharply increasing pressure to explain to executives in relevant detail what their activities are in such areas as applications and hardware acquisitions, and ultimately, their contribution to the "bottom line." This situation parallels a period of sharply growing dependence on data processing as well. Top executives today are still being asked to make major commitments to data processing without always fully appreciating what is being asked of them. Far too often DP management still discusses problems with executives in terms that are not fully understood, let alone appreciated sympathetically. It is still common to have vice-presidents and presidents of small and large companies complain about the lack of adequate communications between them and DP personnel. All too often you can hear such comments from them as: "I don't understand how data processing operates," "I am being asked to authorize the purchase of a new computer and I don't know if that is the right thing to do," "My DP manager uses too many technical terms such as 'data base,' 'CRT,' and 'on-line'; I don't understand these and really do not believe I should have to." And why should they? There is a language of business that transcends the peculiarities of marketing, distribution, manufacturing, advertising, personnel, and data processing which can serve as the workhorse of communications. This is the language you were taught to speak at home and in school, coupled with the discipline of normal practices and methods of accounting. Only rarely do technical terms have to enter a conversation and then only after being fully defined for the uninitiated.

Some executives will try to learn some of DP's "buzz" words, and another, rapidly growing number will actually have technical backgrounds in data processing. But most still do not have a genuine appreciation of data processing technology and its issues and, moreover, are firmly convinced that they do not have to. Therefore, data processing management, if they are to have the necessary dialogues with non-DP executives in order to continue carrying out their functions, must speak clearly and communicate in nontechnical terms. Many DP managers who have spent most of their adult lives in the technical womb of computers and have thus acquired a unique vocabulary associated with that technology, find it difficult to understand that there is a serious communications gap between them and the executives who ultimately make the key DP decisions. How this problem manifests itself and the ways in which some managers are effectively dealing with it are the subjects of this chapter. Its purpose, in other words, will be to explain how typical DP concerns can be expressed in nontechnical language, how decisions can be framed in sound, businesslike fashion, and how normal day-to-day communications of ongoing events can be defined without the aura of magical technical jargon surrounding them.

DECIDING WHAT NEEDS TO BE TOLD
TO MANAGEMENT

Assume that a typical manager in data processing will worry about day-to-day problems and responsibilities without having to run to upper management for decisions regarding them—because good managers do not need a great amount of handholding. Still, there are a number of issues which increasingly have to be laid at the feet of non-DP executives either for decision or action. Although these issues vary in number, substance, and degree of importance from one organization to another, normally they would include such common topics as:

- Justification of applications
- Application development plans
- Requests for money with which to acquire hardware, software, and people
- Establishment of DP policies regarding priority of application development, chargeout principles for services, and directional statements
- Approval of DP budgets
- Commitments to distributed processing, data base, and on-line applications
- Linking DP plans to corporate or divisional business plans
- For-your-information types of presentations on data processing aplications
- Status reporting on DP activities
- Defenses against criticisms regarding uptime on the computer, system availability for users, controlling costs, and speed with which applications are developed

Although the list could be expanded even further, the items cited represent the issues most commonly discussed with upper-level management. They fall into several categories: (1) directional meetings, which set policies and establish priorities; (2) status discussions, which review ongoing projects and the solutions being applied to existing problems; and (3) requests for hardware, software, people, money, and applications. Each of these strikes at the core of any organization and therefore cannot be left solely in the hands of a cadre of middle managers in data processing.

Directional meetings are perhaps the most important and require the greatest amount of delicacy on the part of DP management. For instance, increasingly, managers are finding it necessary to understand the organization's business objectives in detail so that applications development can support these objectives. This might include the establishment of warehouses in another part of the country which would then have to be serviced by terminals from a data center. This simple situation could raise the complex issue of centralized versus decentralized data processing and the effects it would have on the DP department and the company as a whole. This discussion alone represents one of the most classical issues requiring good communications between the DP department and general management. Most often it is the DP manager or director who first reaches the conclusion that information of all types in a company is a corporate asset that should be managed as if it were money or inventory. A logical outgrowth of that would be such actions as moving machine-readable data to a data base system, placing it where it is physically needed in many departments, and then giving the DP department more responsibility for the management of information. Eventually, this authority must extend from machine-readable data to all forms of information, whether in a disk drive or in a file cabinet.

Thus the common possibilities that fall out of a directional commitment require software, hardware, people to manage them, and new applications (such as office systems, word processing, text management), all of which cost a great deal of money and invariably cause reorganization of departments to the point where within a few short years the organization is fundamentally different in composition than it was before. Since these decisions cross departmental lines, a department-level manager cannot make decisions that have such profound directional implications; only general management above has that authority. Consequently, it is imperative that non-DP executives understand clearly what the data processing ramifications are of directional decisions that DP managers are asking them to make.

Discussions about the status of various DP issues are typically more susceptible to overtechnicalization in conversations and written reports than in directional meetings. Specific discussions of applications, how they will or are being developed and managed, together with the problems and decisions involved can lead to the use of a large number of data processing acronyms or, even worse, the assumption that executive management understands technical nuances of existing problems. Thus the wrong decisions are brought before such managers. Instead of deciding whether to change access methods for files, executives would rather decide whether or not to authorize the development of a specific application. The real challenge for data processing management in situations involving detailed issues is to articulate their concerns in nontechnical terms and to leave out of the discussions issues that upper management should not have to act upon, such as a decision as to which access method to use.

A simple illustration of a typical confrontation can suggest the problem in communications. If an executive asks why an on-line order-entry system is taking longer to finish than the DP department originally forecast, data processing management cannot begin to discuss unanticipated difficulties in using access methods to the data base or about the complexity of integrating modules of application code into a bisynchronous network via a back release of a teleprocessing monitor running on a current release of a system control program on the host CPU. You might as well be discussing the intricacies of nuclear fission or molecular structures. Rather, data processing would have to explain that the delay was being caused by unanticipated difficulties encountered in integrating several major programs which jointly feed the application to terminals outside the data center. An executive with no DP background can understand that.

Explaining how problems will be fixed also presents a pitfall for data processing. Technical personnel are tempted to explain too specifically how problems will be fixed. Thus poor response time for terminals should not be explained away by saying that the 2400-baud TP lines will be upgraded to 4800 conditioned lines along with implementation of a change from sequential access methods to VSAM under CICS Release 1.5. Rather, management should be told in this example that the response-time problem will be fixed by using faster telephone lines to the terminals, together with some fine tuning of the programs resident in the main computer. The message is the same in either explanation, but the second one is understandable to non-DP executives. It is the lack of such explanations that lead many to criticize the DP department for a lack of sensitivity to the problem of communications. Users do not understand the complexities of data processing but they do know when service from the DP department deteriorates. Dealing with the problem of explanations becomes in itself either a weapon that the DP department can use for its protection through explanation or the sword upon which it falls. In fairness to data processing managers, it has only been in the past few years that they have been called upon to work closely with other departments on an extensive basis. It has been just recently that they have begun to realize that their manner of communication has had to change. For that matter, even the politics of dealing with other parts of the organization have changed now that data processing often finds itself in the middle of these internal skirmishes. The brighter DP managers are realizing that their technology and proper communication of it are powerful weapons for political infighting and useful tools in helping their respective organizations. For many, this is the first time that they have ventured outside their data processing departments to do battle with peers within their companies.

Requests for executive commitments involving money, people, hardware, and software have the same pitfalls as other types of meetings. Yet it is this kind of discussion that should be easiest for data processing management to handle. The DP department has one major advantage over most other departments in just about every head-to-head rivalry for investment money: in most projects, when compared to each other in strict financial and accounting terms, money spent on data processing frequently yields faster and greater returns. Data processing is truly one area of an organization that can deliver substantial amounts of increased productivity. Yet often DP management, because it fails to request additional resources in purely businesslike terms, does not win. Thus manufacturing, distribution, sales, or some other part of the business frequently can win against competitive DP proposals and get financial commitments that might not be as attractive to the organization as a whole as an investment in data processing would be. Or, a non-DP department will gain additional resources for some data processing solution which is then implemented within its own confines or through a service bureau without utilizing the knowledge of the data processing department. Both of these situations exist in every organization and invariably are repeated several times each year. Yet executive management increasingly is resisting investments in data processing out of an ignorant but intuitive faith that computers are good for the organization. Those days are gone. If executives do not understand the benefits of a particular data processing proposal (such as the reasons for acquiring a new computer), the person who brings a business proposal to them from another part of the organization will get what they want instead.

A number of reasons are frequently cited by executives as to why they resist data processing proposals which are not properly explained to them in clear business terms. First, some executives know better; they have a working knowledge of data processing and therefore recognize a poor proposal when it is brought to them. Second, others just simply refuse to allocate substantial amounts of resources for things they do not understand and at a time when either business is doing poorly, the economy or their industry is not strong, or because the cost of capital is too high at a time when debts are probably great. Third, there are those who have been promised the moon by previous DP managers only to receive pie in the sky and performance far less than anticipated. Thus a growing concern for business discipline in all areas of an organization, a negative economic environment, and an increasing amount of both good and bad experiences with data processing are leading many executives to demand better articulation of needs by data processing. The irony of this situation is that they are willing to spend vast amounts of money on data processing. The growth rates of data processing by any measure of performance indicate this with each passing year.

Of all the requests, probably the easiest to document in strict common-sense business terms without recourse to technical language is the acquisition of a computer and its peripherals. And as will be illustrated below, the issues do not have to be couched in terms of the new technical enhancements of a new generation of equipment but can be boiled down to cost, how the money will be used, why the change should be made now, and what the implementation schedule will be like. The issues are essentially the same as for the acquisition of a new warehouse, additional office space, manufacturing equipment, or more sales people. Chapter 3 suggested the detailed staff work that had to be done in order to come up with a business case for a DP request. Although later in this chapter presenting such cases to management will be illustrated, it is important to realize that executives outside of data processing want the situations kept in simple English, without DP acronyms and technology.

More specifically, executive management wants to know several things when meeting with DP personnel on any of the three types of concerns. What is the business problem or situation involved? How does it affect the business and the performance of the DP department within the organization? What are the costs? What are the benefits? How long will it take to do? What are the low, medium, and high risks to a proposed plan of action in terms of cost in money, time, and other resources? With that kind of information in nontechnical language, an executive can begin making sensible decisions arrived at intelligently for all concerned, and probably with the kind of enthusiasm that will ensure the DP department continued monetary and political support. Moreover, such an approach will make data processing appear very competitive in comparison with other portions of the company when applying for money and other resources. Invariably, any survey of general management on the role of the DP department turns up complaints about the lack of organized, clear presentations of issues to executives. Yet they are asking for commonsense approaches to what data processing wants. Thus what management needs is English, organization of thoughts, costs and benefits, and little technical jargon.

Case Study of an Acquisition Proposal

A quick illustration of how major data processing decisions can be presented to management in simple terms proves that issues do not have to be complex. Our case involves a European manufacturing company with a small subsidiary in the United States. Taking advantage of the value of Swiss francs against the dollar, this company decided to acquire four divisions from an American competitor and now must decide whether or not to have the competitor's main data center continue processing the work of the four divisions or to do the work elsewhere. The Swiss chairman of the board decided on his own that the data processing activities of the new acquisition could no longer be done as in the past and that DP work had to be out of the competitor's data center as soon as possible for security reasons.

The DP director for the little American subsidiary was asked to put together some options and costs on how data processing might be handled.

After two months of studying the situation, he boiled the options down to four scenarios.

Option 1

- Use the competitor's data center until the end of 1982 (18 months) at a cost of $1.1 million per year.
- Select a centralized or decentralized DP solution for the new acquisition by the end of 1981.
- Hire a DP manager and others, find a computer room and offices, order and install equipment, and educate new staff, all in 1982. If not completed by then, use of the competitor's data center must be extended.
- This solution is a temporary one only, as the decision has already been made to leave the existing data center.

Option 2

- Transfer the data center work load to a service bureau as soon as possible.
- Negotiate costs and conditions (roughly $2.5 million per year) and evaluate risks.
- Select this solution, find people, hardware, space, and so on, and define when to implement (sometime in 1982 or later), adding the costs of installation to option 2.

Option 3

- Decide in favor of a central system near planned headquarters for the new acquisition.
- Hire a DP manager by August 1981.
- Hire people by the end of 1981.
- Educate them by mid-1982.
- Order hardware and get space by September 1982.
- Cut over, including teleprocessing, by November 1982.
- Estimated costs:

Hardware and software	$ 600,000/year
Personnel	290,000–320,000
Operating expenses (building, taxes, etc.)	600,000
Total	$1,500,000/year

Option 4

- Decide in favor of expanding the existing data center at the small subsidiary to take on the additional work load.
- Hire people by August 1981.
- Educate them by the end of 1981.
- Order hardware by the end of 1981.
- Cut over, including teleprocessing, by February 1982.
- Estimated costs:

Hardware and software	$ 600,000/year
Personnel	240–270,000
Operating expenses	300,000
Total	$1,200,000/year

- Transfer the workload from this data center to the corporate head-quarters of the new acquisition (with some DP staff) from 1983 on.

He then estimated what risks existed for each version and boiled it down to the following risk analysis (in terms of controlling the variables):

- Low risk in options 1 and 4
- High risk in options 2 and 3

He argued that staying in the competitor's data center (i.e., doing nothing) represented little risk since the work is being done there now and would continue until pulled away. Option 4 also represented a low risk since (1) he was there to manage it (a known factor since his management skills were understood), (2) he had room to house the computer center and people, and (3) he had some staff members who could be trained to handle the additional work. In short, options 1 and 4 had the least number of uncontrollable variables. Option 2 represented a significant risk since all work and the quality of that work would be controlled by another company (a service bureau), over which there would be little or no control over personnel, schedules, or costs. Option 3 also had significant risks because the company would have to hire a DP director (an unknown factor at that point), staff, find housing, and get the center set up. Costs were roughly comparable across all options, and speed of installation favored the risky options.

To back up the data presented to management in Europe, the American DP director included recommended hardware and software configurations, estimates of space needed, costs of supplies, and a list of the types of people needed (such as systems programmers, operators, etc.) with salary ranges. Corporate management in Europe based their final decision simply on the data presented on five flip charts (one for the situation, and four describing each option), hardly glancing at the thin binder with the backup material.

Now examine what happened in this typical scenario of events. Non-DP management performed a business act (acquisition of the four divisions in the United States) and data processing was asked to support the new additions. Corporate management knew that no part of its business should be formally controlled by a competitor and thus ordered that data processing be separated from the selling company. Operational-level management, in our case the American DP director, put together the various options for carrying out the business mission of data processing: crunching all the numbers and handling the technical details on hardware, software, staffing, and space. This mass of data was boiled down to several sheets of paper, defining briefly the options, their costs, when decisions would have to be made to meet certain self-imposed deadlines, and the risks of accomplishment. Corporate was interested in costs, the time it would take to do, and the risks of failure. In our case, the American DP director favored option 4, recommended it, and was ordered to expand his operations. He placed the least attractive option (in his mind) first, the next least attractive one next, then his second choice for a solution, and finally the one he favored, forcing the decision makers to arrive at the same logical conclusion that he had by focusing attention longest on the favored solution.

Although internal politics in both the United States and in Europe complicated the decision-making process, which the various people involved had to take into account, the final solution had some attractive features. First, all options were treated as interim solutions, so that no individual felt that decisions were cast in concrete; all could be changed with reasonable advance notice. That made decision making easier. Second, politics was taken into account in that option 4, the new acquisition, would have the possibility of gaining control over its own data center at sometime in the future. Third, the final presentation and report consisted of both oral recitations before corporate management and supporting detail in written documents. The actual decision to go ahead with an option grew out of an oral presentation.

What has just been described is a typical flow of events witnessed every day in many organizations making significant hardware decisions. It is clear that skills in presentation and in writing are critical to the success of any proposed solution.

COMMUNICATING WITH MANAGEMENT: THE ORAL PRESENTATION

Any request for a major decision invariably should be part of an oral presentation or meeting face to face with decision makers. Put another way, it is easier to reach a decision in a meeting which has reaching a conclusion as its objective than it is to work solely with written documents. And as any sales-person will tell you, written proposals are pretty but are not approved as often as are requests made orally. Therefore, decisions that require expenditures of money in sizable amounts—the acquisition of a new computer, establishment of a data center, implementation of a distributed processing plan, or the decision to computerize a significant application—are usually the subjects of meetings and presentations. A normal cycle of events which DP managers typically go through (just like vendors) would include the following:

- Exploring the initial idea
- Researching the costs and benefits by talking to vendors and people who have to implement the decision, and working with financial specialists to cost out the proposal
- Preselling the solution orally to various line managers through meetings and presentations before going to the final decision maker for a judgment
- Making a formal presentation to the person(s) authorized to make a go/no go decision

Once a data processing manager has made up his or her mind as to which solution to ask for, the first possibility of moving toward a "go" decision would be in meeting with the managers affected by the decision. The best way to describe the process is to illustrate it with an example drawn from an actual, yet typical situation, so that the nature of the cycle of events can be shown. In our case, a DP director has decided to acquire a new computer to replace the existing one. She has already chosen one and the various line managers within the DP department are in agreement. The detailed costs have been obtained from the vendor and preliminary plans for a possible installation have been worked out. Since the new machine would rent for over $100,000 per year, or could be purchased for yet a greater sum, approval must be obtained from the president of the company. As in most organizations, the president does not want to approve the acquisition unless the machine is cost-justified and the financial vice-president blesses the cost/benefit analysis.

Because a major portion of the justification for this computer comes from the installation of an on-line manufacturing system, the director has concluded that the first executive to be "sold" on the new computer must be the manufacturing vice-president. Assigning a person from her staff and working with a small task force from manufacturing, a detailed study was done to determine what applications should be installed, at what expense/benefit, and on what timetable. Manufacturing line managers have been asked to give their assessment of impact and benefits. Along the way, the manufacturing vice-president has attended some meetings to see how things were developing. In each instance, a clever DP director would make sure that:

- Bickering among the task force members was kept to a minimum for the occasion.
- No data processing terminology was used by anyone.
- The focus of each meeting was on how the DP and manufacturing departments would interact.
- Each meeting was held in a conference room that was neat, clean, and managed by one individual to ensure that necessary slide projectors, foil viewers, screens, needed extension cords, and the inevitable coffee pot were hooked up and ready to go before anyone came into the room.
- An interim status report was always presented by a manufacturing person, casting the project in a positive light and in terms relevant to senior managers present.

Finally, after the manufacturing group had finished its work, a similar exercise would take place with the financial people to cost out the impact of the project in accounting and financial terms, reflecting all its costs, not just those for the computer. Financial options would be defined and cast in terms reflecting the accounting practices of the organization. Ultimately, a similar, formal presentation would be made to the vice-president of finance to gain his concurrence and again a substantial portion of the oral presentation would probably be done by a financial manager. Any objections or concerns that would come up in such a meeting with either vice-president could either be overcome by people involved in the project or could be worked out afterward with a follow-up meeting of a less formal type to ensure that all objections had been worked out. One cannot emphasize too strongly the need to gain the approval of those people who most frequently influence a decision maker. In our case, these individuals were vice-presidents, who in turn were persuaded by managers reporting to them.

Armed with the approval of the two key influencing executives, our director of data processing would now be ready to take her proposal to the president for action. If the meetings with the two previous vice-presidents had gone very well, she would encourage them to tell the president about the status of the proposal and how impressed they were with the details presented so far. Ultimately, one of the three executives involved would go to the president and ask for time in which to present the results and to ask for a go/no go decision on the project. For the DP director, this means obtaining approval for the application and the new computer.

The meeting with the president is an important one that should be properly prepared for in advance. Typically, well-run sessions are scheduled from one to three weeks in advance and one manager becomes the host, responsible for all the details. In our case, this would be the junior executive, the DP director. The director would plan for a meeting to last from one to three hours, with a third of the time scheduled for a formal presentation of the particulars. A conference room would be reserved and it would be furnished for the number of people attending and with the tools needed (foil and slide projectors, etc.).

Who should attend such a meeting is a critical issue. Although each situation varies, it is a good rule of thumb to keep attendance to a bare minimum. It is important that the host make sure that all attendees are in basic agreement with the purpose of the meeting. If there is a problem, delay the meeting to another day so as to work out objections in advance. In our case, the meeting would be attended by the president, the two vice-presidents, the DP director, and possibly one manufacturing and or/financial manager who can make a good stand-up presentation. With a major acquisition such as a computer, the vendor would probably be there also, because he or she has considerably more experience in navigating such meetings than most DP directors and can answer any questions regarding the costs, functions, and use of the computer and make statements regarding maintenance and other forms of support.

Control over the details goes far toward ensuring that the results of the meeting will go as expected. There are some tried and tested rules that should be applied in our case. First, let the president know that he will be asked to make a decision so that as he hears the presentation and discussion, he can move toward the ultimate goal of saying yes or no. Second, confirm with all attendees, several times and right up to the last day, that they will attend and that no other obstacles to meeting exist. Third, make sure that a room is reserved for the meeting well in advance and that on the day it is to be used it is properly laid out to accommodate the attendees. There is nothing less professional than to come into a meeting and waste 15 minutes while projectors are hooked up, extra extension cords found, or chairs moved about. Do that hours before the meeting so that everyone can sit down and crisply get to work doing what they have on their mind at that moment: deciding the fate of your project.

The actual presentation should be done standing up. The reason for this is quite simple. By using flip charts, foils, or slides, one is forced to lay out the logic of a request in advance in a thoughtful manner, preparing beforehand for obvious questions and objections, which can often be overcome quickly. Also, a documented presentation serves as an outline of the discussion that follows and helps to keep the flow the way you want it. A formal presentation forces people to be led along the path of each chart and, by implication, down the logical path you have set to the decision you want. Seeing something while hearing it reinforces attention and later retention of the facts. Finally, a well-organized presentation has a better chance of acceptance than a disorganized conversation because it shows that proper homework has been done and raises a decision maker's confidence in the individual making a request and ultimately in the proposal itself.

The agenda for such a meeting flows logically from the nature of the meeting. As a general rule, all agenda essentially follow a similar outline:

- A review of the circumstances generating the study, proposal, or purpose of the meeting (such as a business problem or need)
- A review of how the problem was studied and the conclusions reached (such as the use of a joint DP–manufacturing task force)
- The various options, considered with their pros and cons (such as alternative ways of financing the acquisition of a computer)
- The solution finally agreed upon by the task force and now being recommended for approval

In our case, the presentation agenda might look like this:

- The Mission of Manufacturing in XYZ Company
- DP's Role in Supporting Manufacturing
- Problems and Needs of Manufacturing and Data Processing
- Possible DP Solutions and Recommendations

The question of manufacturing's mission might be five minutes in which the vice-president of manufacturing describes the current business problems for which he requires help from data processing. The DP director could spend five minutes on how data processing is supporting manufacturing today, followed by a review of the task force findings by the DP manager or a manufacturing person for another 15 to 30 minutes. Options would then be reviewed by the data processing executive in nontechnical terms, finally taking the president through the logic of the recommended solution.

In our case, the data processing director opened the meeting by thanking everyone for attending and for their time away from their busy schedules, and acknowledging the help and cooperation of people from various departments in making the study and recommendations possible. This is more than polite nonsense; it is a clear signal to the decision maker that what is to be presented has been sold up and down the line before coming to him. User managers then presented their portions of the review on foils showing the flow of events in manufacturing, the need for certain applications, and how the DP department could help in general. The DP manager then changed the pace of the meeting by switching to flip charts to describe the various options. In our case, the manager and manufacturing had agreed to use commercially available software packages, settling on one set which is then briefly reviewed using a half dozen or so slides loaned by the vendor for the meeting. Typically, questions and answers would fly about the room, making the presentations longer than originally planned. If all is going well, people will nod their heads in approval as each segment of the presentation is made. The president might look the vice-president of manufacturing square in the eye and ask if he wants all of this and would pay for the software. The vice-president assures the president of his need for this software and willingness to pay for it. The second half of the request involves the DP department's new computer with which to run this and other groups of applications. Since this book discusses hardware, the portion of the meeting discussing hardware is shown below as it appeared on foils.

Foil 1. Why a New Computer

- Manufacturing wants new applications that cannot fit on the existing computer.
- The sales and distribution departments have gained approval for new applications, also straining existing facilities.
- The DP department is doing more programming and is using the computer to improve productivity and to speed up the development process.
- Ten plants are supported by computer, as opposed to three when the existing computer was installed.

In short, our computer is overworked.

While this first foil is being presented, the DP manager explained that the computer had been acquired originally to do a certain amount of work, which is now greater than the computer can handle properly. The number of transactions going through it in any given hour has reached the maximum technical capability of the system, yet the demand for more work exists. Because it is aging technology, the computer does not perform as well as newer devices or support the more cost effective peripherals now available on the market. The manager assures the president that no additional fine tuning of the system is feasible; that has already been done. Note that there has been no mention of capacity loads, channel or memory utilization, data loading, transaction rate measurements, MIPs, and so on, and they should not be mentioned unless the decision maker happens to know something about them.

Foil 2. Options Considered

(1) Lease computer A.
(2) Purchase computer A.
(3) Lease computer B.
(4) Purchase computer B.

With this second foil the DP manager moves quickly into a discussion of why a particular computer was selected and how it could be financed. Foils

3 through 6 discussed the pros and cons of each option: one computer was too small, the other too large, one was more expensive, the other aging technology; there were financial constraints affecting the company; and the DP department had its limits as to how long it could commit itself to a particular device. In our case, the DP director placed the favored option last so that attention would logically and finally linger on the desired option. In this case, the manager recommended the purchase of computer B for a five-year period. Although pretax and after-tax cash outflow (discussed in Chapter 3) were shown for each of the options, the decision favoring option 4 was explained with one additional foil.

Foil 7. Why Purchase Computer B

- Capacity is sufficient to support existing and planned applications for five years.
- Technology supports new and forthcoming DP peripherals relevant to XYZ Company.
- It is the most cost-effective option.

While stepping through the logic of these three points, the data processing director emphasizes that this particular computer will satisfy known needs for the period in question (in this case, five years). If the financial vice-president is doing his job properly, he assures the president that the financial option chosen is clearly the best for XYZ Company to take at this time. A final foil showing the overall costs of the manufacturing/computer project and its benefits was then presented. Finally, the big moment arrived when the DP director looked the president squarely in the eye and asked: "May we go ahead with the project?"

As any salesperson will tell you, this is more than a moment of truth, it is one filled with fear, tension, and courage. If the tension is great enough, there are people who would swear they could hear the blood coursing through their veins in a deafening roar. With all eyes on the decision maker, he begins to feel tension and discomfort which only an answer of some sort will relieve. The best thing that a DP director or any other individual awaiting such an answer can do after asking the magic question is to say NOTH-ING, NOTHING, NOTHING, letting the president break the ice. If you or anyone says anything, the decision maker has an excuse not to answer the question. If the answer is no or is less definite, questions can be asked to identify obstacles to a "yes" and possibly overcome them immediately. A yes answer relieves the tension and makes the last couple of minutes of the meeting more peaceful.

There are two schools of thought on one key point: the implementation schedule. Some managers believe that a tentative schedule should be part of the proposal during the presentation, whereas others feel that the more detailed discussion should follow a go-ahead decision, giving the decision maker only the completion date for an option before he decides. How best to handle implementation information is a function of the personalities involved. Some decision makers want a great deal of detail up front, whereas others prefer not to be bothered with such minutia. Most managers, however, would agree that following a go decision, at least one more foil should be aired explaining what will happen next, so that everyone feels that they have moved on past the decision and are in the first phase of implementation. They argue that this approach takes a decision maker's mind off the possibility of an immediate reversal since everyone can be given something to do fast as a first step toward implementation. One final note, take your yes and run; terminate the meeting very soon after receiving a go-ahead decision before anyone airs second thoughts or says something that brings on a reversal.

Since an implementation schedule essentially remains in either school of thought as a good inclusion for any presentation, one further example is presented, drawn from a manufacturing proposal that was shown to the president of a company.

Implementation Schedule

	Jan.	Mar.	June	Sept.	Dec.
Install computer	X				
Install bill of material (BOM)		X			
Develop materials requirement planning (MRP)				X	
Begin installation of shop floor data collection					X

Next Task Force Meeting: January 5, 9:00, Room 455

In the situation presented in the case study, a one-foil listing of events such as the one just illustrated would be sufficient for the president. He or she would have asked the usual questions about how many people would be needed, dollars involved, and other resources, so that this foil would simply be a summary of the anticipated discussions. If this schedule were presented to the vice-president of manufacturing, then more detail on the functions, activities, and individuals involved would have been put together.

Considerable detail through the use of a case study has been presented since this kind of a scenario is played out often in all organizations. Again, there are several characteristics of the final meeting for the commitment, because in one form or another they exist in all conversations regarding the acquisition of data processing technology. For one thing, in none of the discussions were technical data processing terms used, nor were detailed technical issues. Such concerns were hammered out long ago within the DP department or with manufacturing and vendors. Second, the two vice-presidents and the director of data processing stressed the costs and benefits of the computer's use (manufacturing applications here) as opposed to emphasizing the computer. The hardware was simply a means to an end. Third, costs were presented in a formal financial manner just as they should be in any other business project. Fourth, the various functional groups signed off on the proposal before the key decision maker had to commit. This made a positive decision relatively easy or safe to make both politically and financially. In short, potential problems were reasonably identified and overcome before they became lethal in the hands of a smart and experienced president. Ultimately, the whole process was reasonable and logical.

COMMUNICATING WITH MANAGEMENT:
THE WRITTEN REPORT

While the big commitment meeting just described will never be the only type of structured oral presentation to management, reports to various managers and executives on a variety of issues should be a continuous process. This involves keeping open lines of communication, updating people on joint projects and problems, and institutional advertising for data processing—and it just makes good political sense, not to mention good protection. Yet most data processing managers write too many of the wrong types of letters and memorandum, keep poor records of meetings, and never take full advantage of the written word to communicate important issues throughout an organization. Yet to this author's knowledge, there is no company, government or educational institution, or organization that forbids its management from writing anyone else within the enterprise. Odds are that anything written will at least be glanced at by someone in the section of the organization you are trying to reach, and quite often it will be the person to whom the document is addressed, especially if it is written by a middle manager. Therefore, with such an opportunity to communicate, it would be a waste not to use it skillfully to advance the cause of data processing. Below are listed some typical situations that could be dealt with particularly well via the written word.

Common Types of DP Reports

- Minutes of meetings with users
- Project status
- System availability
- Proposals
- Budget-related memoranda
- Policy statements
- Tactical and strategic plans

Each of these are common, everyday types of reports that data processing managers are called upon to prepare. Because of the implications of their technology, it is often best that data processing personnel initiate the composition of such documents. They have the responsibility of understanding the technical details of computerized technology; they also have the responsibility of expressing themselves in normal nontechnical language. For instance, the status of a project should be described without continuous references to technical terms. In the installation of a computer, why raise discussions about cabling channels or generating new releases of software? Non-DP management can be told that the installation will require connecting various devices together via cables and that some modifications to computer programs will be necessary.

System availability is often a pitfall for data processing writers because of the temptation to explain in technical language why a system is not always up or to indulge in recriminations laced with DP acronyms that make little sense to those who complain about service. For instance, a manager is called upon to explain why the computer was down for over seven hours each of three days in a row. A typical response might look like this:

Subject: CPU Downtime

The CPU experienced downtime on Tuesday, Wednesday, and Thursday because of a series of problems which F.E. finally determined were caused by I/O channel checks. Our problems were compounded by a faulty diskette, which was fixed only by cutting a new one. PTFs were also applied against the SCP, all of which took my staff time to do.

That paragraph was actually written by a data processing manager and addressed to his boss, a vice-president of finance! A better way to have written this explanation might be as follows:

Subject: Computer Breakdown

Our computer malfunctioned on three consecutive days for a variety of reasons. First, maintenance personnel experienced considerable difficulty in identifying the problem, which cost us over six hours of processing time. Second, the computer failed to communicate properly with some of its peripheral devices, and some malfunctions in the operating programs controlling the computer also appeared. Necessary repairs were made to both hardware and software. Our department responded as quickly to the problems as was technically possible, and it is our belief that the causes of these failures have been eliminated.

This second version is not only in understandable English, but it also tells management what the prognosis is for the proper functioning of the computer. This vice-president wanted to know why it broke and whether he could expect that to happen in the immediate future. Channel checks, PTFs, and so on, were irrelevant to him.

Budget requests invariably are masked in clouded language that makes little sense. Using a simple example of a request for more disk drives illustrates the common problem. A data processing director decides that he needs three more disk drives to be installed next year, for a total annual cost of $45,000, because of capacity constraints. This is a normal situation faced by most DP departments almost every year. In requesting permission to acquire these units, the DP director might write the following memorandum to whoever has to grant permission:

Subject: Request for Additional Disk Drives

The expansion of the CICS network, together with anticipated needs for the on-line systems, has forced me to conclude that we will require three more disk drives by January to provide an additional 1.5 billion bytes of storage. This will cost $45,000, which I would like to have added to my budget.

Another way to present the same material to a non-DP executive might be:

Subject: Request for Supplemental Budget for DP Hardware

In the past year the number of computerized files has increased 23%, primarily because of the expanded use of the order entry system and the installation of the budget modeling application. Our ability to keep required amounts of data in machine-readable form to support these applications can be continued only by installing additional devices to store such information. These will cost $45,000 next year. I am requesting authorization to add this amount to my budget.

Some managers might even add some additional statement to the effect that there is sufficient justification within the applications to support this added expense or might attach a formal financial analysis of options.

Strategic and tactical plans often lead data processing managers down the path of technical jargon, including the use of ill-defined "buzz" words such as "word processing," "distributed processing," "networking," "centralization," and "data base." An example of a statement of strategy in such language can only suggest confusion in the minds of other managers.

Subject: Strategic Plan of Data Processing

It is the intention of this department to implement a distributed processing plan which offloads the host processor of applications for the plants driven by an SNA network and 8100s at the remotes. Data will be stored at the host site under data base where we can control the master files.

This memo would mean almost nothing to most people and simply confirm that data processing generates a great deal of useless smoke. On the other hand, the following might be clearer.

Subject: Strategic Plan of Data Processing

With the demand for computing power in all our plants increasing each year at the same time that our central computer facilities are being heavily burdened, I have concluded that the best approach in providing service to these locations is to place computing power throughout the organization as needed. This will involve installing small computers or terminals in each of the plants over the next few years, making available on a cost-effective basis those applications that are needed. The benefits

I anticipate that we will experience include:

- Exporting some of the work load from our computer to the plants is less expensive in hardware, thereby reducing operating costs.

- Providing more data processing where it is needed when it is needed should yield faster services.

- Controlling our company's information centrally by establishing policies and guidelines for its use and protection.

- Improving the quality of our information by placing responsibility for its accuracy in the hands of those most familiar with it.

- Reducing bottlenecks associated with funneling all programming and data entry through my department, making it possible for our users to process applications at times of their choosing.

Perhaps an illustration of the future network might accompany this document. (See Figure 7-1.)

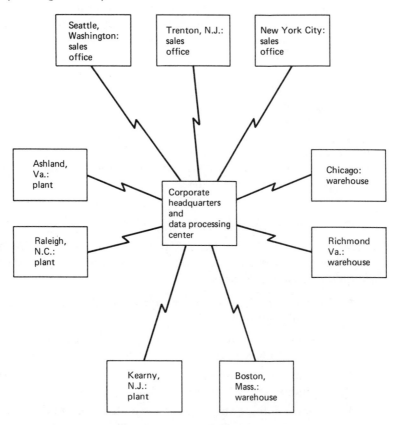

Figure 7–1. Sample chart of a distributed network.

Minutes of meetings with data processing can result in useful documentation. Regardless of whether or not it involves data processing, most minutes of meetings tend to be a running commentary of who said what to whom instead of being a summary of the topics discussed and the resolutions or issues remaining. A properly written set of minutes of a meeting should be short and conclusive. Take as an example the meeting in which the DP department asks for permission to acquire a new computer. The minutes might look like this:

Subject: Acquisition of New Computer

Attendees: J. Shell, DP Director; R.W. Brown, VP Finance; K.P. Stone, President

On October 2, 1981, Shell presented a proposal for the acquisition of a new computer to be installed in January. Three options were discussed—lease, rental, and purchase—and the financial analysis prepared by Brown's department was reviewed. It was decided for tax reasons that the computer should be acquired for installation in March, and that it be purchased. Stone requested that a final review of the financial implications be made in February to ensure that purchase remains the best form of acquisition. Shell was given responsibility for calling the meeting in February. Copies of the options are appended to these minutes.

Submitted by,

J. Shell

cc: K.P. Stone
    R.W. Brown
    J. Shell

There is no law which says that minutes have to be voluminous. In the example above, that kind of a meeting might have gone on for hours, but only important things to be remembered are its theme, what decisions were taken by whom, and what remains to be done.

Points on Style for DP Management

There are some very simple rules that every data processing manager should follow when committing anything to paper which might be read by a person unfamiliar with data processing:

- Do not use data processing language, terms, or acronyms unless they are fully defined.
- Assume that your reader knows nothing about data processing and cares even less about its intricacies.
- Assume that your reader wants to know in simple terms what your problems are, when they will be resolved, and how much it will cost.
- A good rule of thumb is to keep all correspondence to a page or less; more might not be read as thoroughly.

- For complicated reports (such as those involving financial analysis), summarize your thoughts and conclusions in a cover memo and attach the backup data as an appendix.

- When in doubt as to how a problem should be described (when it is really necessary to do so), use a non-DP analogy.

This last suggestion is one commonly underutilized when dealing with non-DP executives and managers, yet it can quickly convey your concerns. For instance, when describing why a particular computer can no longer provide sufficient capacity, "MIPS" mean nothing. On the other hand, drawing an analogy with a lawn mower designed to cut 3-inch-high grass which someone now wants to use to cut 6-inch grass might illustrate the problem of capacity. The mower might cut some or all of the taller grass, but it will not do so efficiently or as quickly as it would cut 3-inch grass. Running out of capacity can also be likened to the bucket of water that is too small: "I am being asked to carry a gallon of water in one trip with a half-gallon bucket; I need a bigger bucket; otherwise, I have to make two trips." As imprecise as an analogy might be, it is preferable and easier to work with than saying that due to overloading at peak times, processing can be accomplished only by putting the batch work load onto another shift. Analogies in tandem with more exact explanations always help and make easier the education of a non-DP executive to the problems of data processing.

The best ally of data processing is enlightened management that understands the value of computerized technology and feels comfortable with it. The use of analogies in explaining problems and situations is perhaps the most effective way in which managers can have a better understanding of why data processing is or is not performing as others might wish. After explaining that the CPU had a thermal check which caused it to power off, a DP manager could explain that it overheated and thus automatically triggered a procedure to shut it down for the same reasons that you turn off an overheating automobile engine: they cost too much to repair or replace. Analogies are limited only by one's imagination: data falls through cracks, parts wear out like socks and shirt collars, and thrashing is simply overloading circuits. Explaining how a computer works can be done most effectively with analogies. Thus the central processing unit of the computer is that portion that crunches the numbers, just as football players are the components of the game they play and memory is like the football field—that is, where the players are stored and used. Remember, analogies do not have to be brilliant, just relevant.

For effective communications to take place, it is very important to assume that your reader knows very little or nothing at all about data processing. False assumptions may lead to an inability to achieve the goals behind various reports, to misunderstandings causing faulty decisions, and to a bad press for data processing. Obviously, when working on a daily basis with a non-DP executive, most data processing managers will quickly learn how much the nontechnical person knows and is capable of learning. But there is no sympathy in ignorance; the magic is gone from data processing. It has always been and continues to be the responsibility of the author of anything to make himself or herself clear to the reader. This is just as true for data processing personnel as it is for a great novelist, poet, or playwright. It would be difficult to overemphasize the need for clarity of expression. Experienced DP managers all have stories to tell about how difficult relations were with a previous boss who they assumed knew more than he or she did. Looking at it from the nontechnical manager's point of view, technical memoranda are boring, not understandable, and therefore not relevant or worthy of consideration, let alone of positive action. In interview after interview, non-DP executives stress the same point: they cannot be sympathetic to something they do not understand.

STANDARD TOPICS FOR ROUTINE REPORTING TO MANAGEMENT

Knowing first when to communicate orally or verbally and then how makes it easier to keep non-DP management informed of developments within data processing. Leaving aside the quips from experienced veterans of the computer industry that this communication is an art, there are points to keep in mind in determining it what makes sense to discuss. Typically, in any organization a number of issues are discussed on a fairly regular and routine basis with various levels of management outside data processing. These might conveniently be listed among others as:

- Availability of the system (usually monthly, unless there is a severe problem)
- Budget performance versus planned performance (also monthly)
- Updates to the disaster plan (maybe once each year, after the auditors get after the DP department)
- Responses to audit reports on security and system audibility (once or twice annually)
- Monthly newsletters for users of data processing
- Personnel hirings, firings, promotions, and salaries (as needed)
- Updates on changing DP technologies ("gee-whiz" advertising for data processing)

Reviewing some of these reports and how they might be prepared illustrates proven methods for communicating with people outside data processing. Throughout this book, many examples of reports of these and other topics have been cited, especially on the theme of availability, with others on budget impacts and financial analysis, and minutes. However, additional types of important communication are common in well-run data processing installations.

Responses to audits should be carefully prepared. Most auditors will find some things to criticize when reviewing DP operations. If they found nothing to complain about, they probably would feel that they are not doing their job. An increasing number of data processing installations are being thoroughly audited today. This has come about because of increased governmental regulations and as a result of the growing dependence of all organizations on data processing. Therefore, the correspondence generated by audits is rising. Typically, data processing managers react negatively to criticisms raised by auditors, carping that auditors do not know what they are talking about or are simply nit picking. Yet, non-DP management will invariably require a formal written response to each item raised by an auditor. A technical resolution to each problem or a rebuttal has to be prepared, and if the criticism needs to be resolved by DP action, this must be done. To illustrate the problem, take three common audit criticisms of data processing departments: (1) lack of physical security within the department, (2) lack of sufficient audit trails through such-and-such applications, and (3) insufficient plans for a disaster should the host computer malfunction.

A positive, professional response to each of these items, regardless of the DP manager's personal view, is needed as well as a written comment on each. In our case, the DP director might respond in the following fashion:

Subject: Response to Corporate Audit of DP Operations

Three concerns were raised regarding operations within the DP department. . . . The following actions have been taken:

Regarding Physical Security: Combination locks have been installed on all doors leading to the department and the computer room. Only DP personnel with a need to know the combination will be able to use these doors, and the combination will be changed frequently. The walls of the computer room are made out of brick and block, not the sheetrock that the audit report suggested; therefore, no changes are necessary in the room. Fire prevention procedures currently in place are being reviewed to ensure that they are appropriate, and any necessary changes will be recommended within two weeks.

Regarding Audit Trails: The vendor of our teleprocessing monitor has been requested to provide additional details on how the software keeps track of all transactions. Last month a journaling system was installed to track each transaction performed on the on-line order-entry and sales systems. We are currently carrying this further by reviewing the possibility of using data base management software to protect our computerized files from possible loss or damage.

Regarding Disaster Plan: The auditors were requested to provide specific suggestions for elements of a disaster plan which they would like to scc incorporated into the existing one. As soon as these suggestions have been received, my department will adopt those relevant to our operations. In the meantime outdated portions of our plan have been updated, as they are as a matter of policy in this department on a quarterly basis.

Submitted by,
J. Shell
MIS Director
cc: Audit File
      Corporate Audit Department
      R.W. Brown
      K.P. Stone

Notice that a positive response with minimal recriminations can be communicated, together with defenses, when needed. Everyone who counts in this case was sent a copy so that key executives would not be able to complain later that DP was unresponsive to the audit. Equally important, the requirement for a response was met while leaving the details of implementation of action items up to the department head. Also, general management was not burdened with more detail than was needed to respond to the audit.

The issue of availability was discussed in an earlier chapter, but some additional comments on how to present such data to users of data processing are important. Most operational managers within a department measure uptime on the computer strictly by the number of hours in which the hardware is performing, that is, not broken or shut down. Systems managers measure uptime as the amount of time that their software is running, whereas teleprocessing managers count only the hours of teleprocessing available to users. Users of data processing only notice uptime when they can access the computer. Thus if a computer is down for an hour, the operations manager will argue that the downtime was one hour. The systems manager will next come along and say that it took his people an additional half-hour to fire up the programs once the computer came up. We now have a grand total of 90 minutes of downtime from the point of view of a user. User management will add an additional 15 minutes for the time needed by their people to be as productive as they were when the machine broke down (time needed to regain concentration and get back into the swing of things). Downtime has now grown to two hours. Since data processing provides a service, DP management in reviewing availability issues must look at the problem from both their view and that of the user, especially if it is the non-DP community whom they serve, who will complain the loudest about poor service.

If a user views the downtime as a two-hour problem, it is irrelevant to him or her that the operations manager in the computer room had problems with the hardware for one hour only. And no data processing manager will get any sympathy from a user if he or she comes in and argues that the downtime was only one hour or one and a half hours. Availability, as has been stressed before, begins with the computer and goes all the way through to the time a user is really productive with the system. Since proper management of availability calls for such a broad perspective on the part of data processing, discussing availability with users in monthly status reports or presentations should be from the perspective of the user community.

The first step for a data processing manager to take is to acknowledge that availability is more than just hardware uptime. Explain in a layperson's terms that this involves hardware, software, telephone lines, and human beings. Make sure that users have a sense of the complexity without succumbing to the temptation of giving a technical dissertation. However, when explaining malfunctions (downtime), identify where in the chain of events problems occur and what has been done to fix them. Discuss ways of jointly improving uptime (such as faster turnaround on jobs by more accurate data entry by users) while reviewing in writing procedures for the proper use of hardware (especially terminals). Lack of availability then becomes a joint problem. For example, lack of availability because a department has more work than can be handled by the number of terminals is not a DP problem. User managers should participate in forecasting the need for additional terminals and be in communication with DP so that they can be ordered in time. If a computer has to be shut down for maintenance, warn the users in writing in advance so that they can plan on getting their work done earlier or have a chance to make other arrangements (such as overtime to catch up).

Besides being good protection against unfair criticisms by users, writing a monthly availability memorandum to users is an opportunity to describe how services are being improved, what has been done to resolve known problems, and to describe forthcoming changes. This way, users can plan their own activities, better understand what the DP department is doing for them, and cooperate in improving the productivity of both groups.

DP Department Newsletters

An increasing number of data processing departments, facing an ever-growing number of users, have resorted to issuing monthly newsletters to all departments reviewing current DP activities. These are usually short, one- to four-page documents. Subjects typically discussed include:

- Resolution of common problems
- Addition of new hardware, software, and applications
- New or different services and procedures
- Changes in personnel and policies

These newsletters are proving to be more than simply good politics or institutional advertising; they are a solid line of communication with users and are considered useful by the non-DP community.

They are useful vehicles for addressing common DP problems, often heading off too much criticism by explaining why they exist and what is being done to fix them. Thus the DP department's standard pitch for more accurate data entry can be made while user success stories are highlighted. Short pieces on what constitutes system availability and how it is being improved are helpful. Just letting people know that a problem is being looked at is helpful in dispelling the image of DP as being a remote, dehumanized, necessary evil. If, for instance, response time on all terminals has deteriorated from 4 seconds to more than 10 seconds over the past several months, it is obvious that user management will be complaining. If DP feels that the only solution is to install a larger computer, stating in the newsletter that upper-level management is being asked to authorize a new machine shows progress toward resolution. If the user community knows that once on order, the new machine will be installed in four months, complaints will drop as users endure, knowing that a solution will soon be applied. Thus newsletters can increase pressure on executive management by gaining allies for data processing while lowering complaint levels.

Announcing forthcoming applications and what they will mean to the business is another typical theme of these mini-newsletters. They serve as vehicles for informing everyone what the new applications are, when they will be on stream, and what has to be done to make them easier to get up. Thus if the company is about ready to go live with an on-line accounts receivable (A/R) system using color terminals, let everyone know. If new languages or productivity packages are being installed at the data center, make this known through the newsletter. The acquisition of more disk storage capability, a new generation of terminals, or the installation of distributed processing to yet another remote location is important to make known so that everyone understands and can appreciate what is available and what they can possibly use. When new policies are established, they can be communicated via the newsletter in a more friendly fashion than through a more formal series of memoranda. For instance, if the president of the company decrees that all hardware acquisition decisions have to be made through the MIS director, publishing his or her authority to that effect lets everyone—managers and their employees—know the rules. The official memorandum on the subject will be cold and authoritarian, whereas the announcement in the newsletter can explain the benefits of the integration of hardware strategies, quantity discounts, and the assurance of technically competent advice. Moreover, such a memorandum would go out from the president to department heads only, who may or probably would not either make such decisions or would not let their employees know who did. Similar announcements about changes in personnel, acquisition of more programmers, and so on, can also be made, showing a solid commitment by the organization to support data processing with proper staffs and by the DP department to help users.

Getting started with such a newsletter is relatively easy. The first issue should go out to every supervisor, manager, and executive in the organization. Keep it short—two to six pages—and have a nice departmental name for it, as do all newspapers. Avoid DP "in" titles that might not be understood by others, such as "Bits and Bytes" or "Bit Bucket"; use a title that will be commonly understood. Some that have worked well in the past are "The Information Manager," "Data Unlimited," "Data Processing Newsletter," "Terminal Tidbits," and "Computer Bulletin," which although all are not very clever, are all easily understood by everyone. The first issue should introduce the DP organization, with a description of its strategic role within the company. There should also be a statement regarding the locations being served and an inventory of applications of major importance. In a subsequent issue a more detailed description or inventory of applications, programming languages, productivity tools, and other services can be described, together with the procedures necessary to use them.

Disaster Plan Updates

Although Chapter 8 will deal with disaster planning in data processing, since the ultimate goal of such planning is a document to help in disasters, a few things need to be reviewed here within the context of communication. Once a disaster plan has been prepared, the need to update it periodically will always exist. Invariably, when this is done, updating is not properly handled. There are a few rules that can be followed, however, to ensure that continuous updating of relevant documentation takes place. The most widely followed guidelines are:

- In each binder carrying the full disaster planning data, keep a list of people who should receive updates to their copies of the plan.
- Make sure that any changes in the plan are documented and sent out to everyone on the list.
- All changes should be typed on sheets the same size as those used in the binders, be cast in the same format as the ones they are replacing, and include instructions as to where in the binder they should go.
- All sheets going into the binder should have the date of the change typed in the same spot on the paper (such as the upper right-hand corner) so that everyone will know how old a particular page is.
- Since the disaster plan would include a list of who should take over what manager's job in the case of death or injury and thus would not be part of the disaster plan binder that everyone has, changes in an heir apparent to a job should be communicated in writing to the executive to whom the DP manager reports, to be put in that non-DP manager's copy of the binder or in a locked safe or cabinet.
- If at all possible, keep all changes in each section of a binder to one page; this makes it easier to track updates.

- Keep changes to a minimum; otherwise, people do not have the time to be constantly replacing pages in their binder.

- As a general rule, providing a series of changes on a quarterly basis seems to be rapid enough for most organizations.

POLITICS AND NEEDS

Throughout this chapter we have discussed how to communicate data processing issues, particularly as they relate to hardware, to members of an organization who probably have little or no knowledge of computers and are either afraid to learn anything or are simply not interested. Yet perception and reality are not always the same. What is true cannot be assumed to be so perceived in everyone's mind. Therefore, the purpose of oral and written reporting is to communicate forcefully, yet accurately the effective needs and concerns of data processing. What has been described in this chapter are practices employed today by other sectors of an organization—sales, distribution, manufacturing, administration—but which traditionally have not been done by all data processing departments. They have been the last department to realize that good communications is good business. Moreover, and of even greater significance, it is good politics. That ever-increasing needs for money, people, equipment, and software are forcing DP management to become more integral parts of an organization is obvious. That they need to communicate more as business managers and less as technocrats is less obvious. Yet without this kind of communication, data processing will get out of control and become the private preserves of user managers armed with their own minis, service bureaus, and even their own data centers. Experience in the 1970s showed this to be the case with engineering departments, sales and distribution organizations, and most recently, in the area of word processing and office systems.

Technical literature should remain within the confines of the DP department, while business issues as they relate to data processing must be the points of focus for MIS managers, especially when dealing with non-DP executives. Increasingly, this suggestion is becoming a working reality in many organizations. Profit and loss, paybacks, return on investment, risk analysis, applications, project leadership, smooth installations, visibility—via hardware and presentations—and clear writing style should be what users think of when judging DP on its ability to deliver systems and services and in communicating properly about them. As an industry, data processing has done an excellent job in providing applications and software, as evidenced by the increasing dependency of all organizations on this technology. But it has done a poorer job of sharing the magic and the realities of its craft with those so dependent on its success. Yet by communicating frequently and clearly, data processing personnel can contribute even more to the welfare of an organization while enhancing their own positions within it. As a final cap to this theme, a number of data processing executives and their superiors were asked for advice on DP communications. Their responses really did not vary greatly. In effect, they said:

- If something is needed, tell them what it will cost and what they will get in return for that expenditure.

- Do a formal financial analysis for all major proposals so that they can be compared against other requests for money from within the same organization.

- Requests for decisions should not be crowded with technical explanations or DP language.

- Technical "gee-whiz" discussions, although informative and entertaining, should not be part of monetary requests but rather be part of a review meeting and correspondence dealing with data processing achievements and mission.

- Relate all DP activities to the business objectives of the company rather than relying on descriptions of data processing just for its own sake.

- Until you learn otherwise, assume that managers around you know nothing of data processing.

- You cannot communicate too frequently via memorandum about the business uses of data processing; however, you can reduce the amount of technical discussions with users.

- Do not let the DP staff hide within its own department; have these people spend time in other departments dependent on computers, where they can communicate and jointly appreciate each other's activities.

- Provide nontechnical information and education on data processing in general and on potential applications not yet developed which might be relevant to the organization.

Although this list could be expanded, the message these managers carried to this author was simple: let people know more about data processing because they are interested, but keep this information in nontechnical yet business terms. With dependence on data processing continuing its rise, the need for such practical, businesslike communications will increase, and those who do not appreciate this fact will be replaced by those who do. Executives simply are not allowing DP departments to avoid conforming closely to the pattern of behavior evident in other departments. How could it be otherwise?

When the Chinese write the word "crisis," they do so in two characters, one meaning danger, the other opportunity.

Anonymous

This chapter deals with disaster planning and data processing. Since the loss of a data center can cripple or destroy an organization's ability to conduct normal business, the issue of equipment security is extremely important. In this chapter you are shown a simple and fast method of planning for a disaster so that if a catastrophe befalls your installation, fast recovery will be possible. This process is cost-justified, each step is described, and examples are taken from actual situations.

CHAPTER EIGHT

Planning for a Disaster

Disaster planning in data processing is a subject to which most MIS managers rarely pay attention, just as many people do not like to think and plan for death and therefore avoid writing wills. Both disaster planning and wills serve as useful tools in helping to ensure that assets are properly taken care of. Disaster planning is a form of good management, an insurance policy that helps to restrict the harmful effects of a catastrophe. With dependence on data processing growing sharply and reaching significant proportions in most organizations, hardly anyone today can afford to ignore the issue of disaster planning. Without it Murphy's Law applies, and everything left to itself will go from good to bad to worse. What this chapter will describe is why disaster planning should be conducted, how to cost-justify it, what is involved, and some of the elements of such an effort.

But first a definition is required. Often when discussing disaster planning, managers think that this involves putting together some sort of plan to overcome a particular catastrophe involving data processing, and usually their efforts involve just hardware. Unfortunately, this perspective is not validated by actual experience and thus makes no sense. In the first place, how can anyone predict what kinds of disaster will hit their installation—with the possible exceptions of fire and flood—and second, how can any planning for hardware recovery take place without taking into account software, people, and building facilities? Anything less comprehensive is unrealistic and reflects poor judgment. For the purpose of this chapter, disaster planning is considered as an ongoing process of gathering the kinds of information that can be used to formulate specific plans at the time of a disaster. It accepts the assumption that we cannot predict what specific kinds of disaster will afflict an installation, but that the information needed to recover from any type of a catastrophe can be pulled together in advance to support a rapid recovery. Furthermore, there are certain activities that must take place regardless of the nature of the problem, and these actions can be planned for in advance. Our definition also holds that disaster planning must encompass all aspects of data processing and must be linked heavily to a recovery program implemented with the key users of DP services. In short, disaster planning is essentially the collection and maintenance of data necessary to react to a disaster quickly when it occurs, regardless of its nature. How this can be done in a reasonable manner on a cost-effective basis is the focus of the pages that follow.

WHY DISASTER PLANNING?

Throughout this book constant reference has been made to the dependence of an organization on DP. Statistics showing that workers in all industrial societies depend overwhelmingly on data processing to perform their jobs at a time when the fastest-growing sector of the world economy are services (as opposed to agriculture or manufacturing) clearly suggests the most obvious reason for disaster planning. The loss of DP services for any significant period of time will prevent most organizations from carrying out their mission, and for a company it will mean a loss of profits, if not actual extinction. Disaster planning is directed toward avoiding the broader catastrophe by quickly controlling the effects of a data processing problem.

One might ask what the odds are of a major catastrophe hitting their DP installation. Although statistics on percentages are hard to come by, some implicit intuitive observations help to define the odds. Scarcely any DP manager has spent the past five years without working in some installation that had its CPU down for two to four days in a row at least once. That fact alone suggests the tip of a statistical iceberg of probabilities—the near miss. Next, read any data processing newspaper on a weekly basis, such as *Computerworld,* and you will find a minimum of one article per week about a catastrophe to a data center somewhere in the United States alone, and often several situations are described. Read weather reports in the newspapers and recall that every week there is a volcanic eruption, flooding, tornado, ice storm, or some other problem afflicting a whole community or region. You can add to your probabilities if you live in a high-crime area, or an area in which rioting is common. Finally, add to your exposure the possibility of sabotage by an employee within the DP installation or in another part of the organization. Sadly, any reasonable person would have to conclude that the opportunity for disaster is great. Ultimately, a manager must ask the question: "Would I want to be the MIS director caught in a disaster without some planning already done?"

Since planning requires time and attention, particularly when first starting such an effort, management is frequently reluctant to provide the necessary resources without having someone explain the need for the activity and cost-justifying it. Cost justification for disaster planning is easy to perform. Some sporadic examples illustrate how it can be done quickly.

As the first example, consider a manufacturing plant that ties in to a central data center. Each night the DP group prepares for the plant a master production schedule, together with bills of material and MRP, all of which are printed each morning at the plant. This information is then given to the employees as their marching orders for the day, telling them in effect what to make and do daily. If the data center fails to provide such information the personnel working in the plant cannot do their primary job that day. Suppose that there are 1000 workers in the plant, each receiving an average annual salary of $14,000. Divided by an average work year of 220 days, the daily payroll is as follows:

$$\frac{1000 \text{ workers} \times \$14,000}{220 \text{ days}} = \$63,637/\text{day}$$

This $63,637 does not even include the overhead costs of benefits (such as insurance and pensions), which typically is an additional 30%, in this case making a grand total of $82,728. Going back just to the hard dollar outlay daily, if the computer is down for a day, for instance, this plant still pays out $63,000 in salaries even though its workers cannot perform at the level of efficiency at which they ordinarily would. If this company had 10 plants of similar size with the same DP applications, the daily cost of a disaster just to the manufacturing side of the organization would be over $663,000 each day. Clearly, some DP planning to avoid or reduce this kind of exposure would be justified in this medium-size company.

Another example providing a commonly available form of justification is the heavy dependence on on-line applications, especially order entry and cash application. Suppose that a wholesale order house with 100 order takers using CRTs to process orders experiences a computer disaster. First, it faces the problem of the salaries involved. For our case, say that it takes two weeks to recover DP services via either new equipment or even a new data center. If each order entry clerk makes $14,000 a year, the math is obvious:

$$\frac{100 \text{ clerks} \times \$14,000}{220 \text{ days}} = \$6364/\text{day} \times 10 \text{ working days} = \$63,600$$

This is $63,000 paid out with no orders coming in. Suppose that annual sales for this company are $400,000,000. With no orders processed for two weeks, it loses 50% of the normal business it would have gained in this period (assumes that some of the lost business would be recouped later). The cost in lost sales would be determined in the following manner:

$$\frac{400,000,000}{220} = \$1,818,180 \text{ sales lost each day}$$

$$1,818,180 \times 5 \text{ days} = \$9,090,900$$

$$\frac{9,090,900}{2} = \$4,545,450 \text{ in actual sales lost}$$

If this disaster happened during the Christmas season, obviously the loss would be much greater. These two items alone—salaries and sales—suggest losses running into the millions of dollars, not taking into account the lost productivity of workers in the warehouse, shipping, or in other parts of the organization. In the pre-Christmas period, when mail-order and wholesale retail and commercial products may account for 25% of the total year's sales, the disaster might cost our sample company $22,000,000, or 5% of its annual sales, probably eliminating the entire profit for the year! Clearly, then, any executive with common sense would want to have a plan for trying to recover quickly from a DP disaster, especially if the effort does not require vast armies of technicians working on it.

Other concerns dictate the need for disaster planning involving contractual and legal commitments resulting in fines and law suits in the event of malperformance on the part of an organization. Examples abound. A programming company whose system is down for a week cannot write contracted-for programs for a project that is already late, on which there is a fine for each seven-day period that the final code is not delivered. Or, service calls are not met because the on-line field engineering dispatch application is down and therefore management does not always know where its service personnel are. There is always the military computer keeping track of when enemy rockets are being fired at a country, which cannot provide an early-warning capability because of a problem at its data center. More visible to all of us is the DP department that cannot finish cost-justified projects because its data center is destroyed; thus the organization loses the potential benefits of applications not yet completed. In short, the cost to any organization in not having a data center is quantifiable and the amount of justification for a disaster plan is increasingly easy to develop. Even in the smallest companies, the amounts involved are significant. Therefore, data processing cannot be treated as a necessary evil or an expensive part of the business to be left solely to the DP department. It is a vital component of an organization, perhaps even its heart, that must be protected.

BASIC ELEMENTS OF DISASTER PLANNING

Although disaster planning, like anything else, can be as comprehensive or as simple as you wish to make it, any practical effort has a certain number of common elements. Three different sets of considerations affect any planning effort:

- Length of time of a disaster
- Elements of a recovery plan
- Preparations for and execution of a plan

The first consideration involves asking what happens if a disaster is one or two days, a week, a month, or longer in duration. What do I do for each length of time? Are there things I should plan on for a week-long disaster that are different if my problems take longer to resolve? Some of the more common factors surrounding the element of length of duration of a disaster include:

- Long-term disasters (Do I need a new permanent data center elsewhere?)
- Short-term disaster (Do I need a temporary data center elsewhere or am I moving to a new, permanent site?)
- Component disaster (Did just one piece of equipment break down, thus requiring replacement? Do I work around a failing piece of equipment, software, and so on, with the rest of the configuration?)

Each of these issues influences the kind of actions anyone would want to take to restore a data center to the condition it was in before a disaster, providing the same level and types of services.

The second element of any recovery plan involves identifying those areas of data processing that can become involved in both a disaster and a recovery effort. Typically the issues involved are:

- Staffs
- Hardware
- Data center
- Software
- Data files

- Scheduling jobs
- Documenting jobs
- Communications
- Logistics

Staffing involves providing sufficient computer operators, programmers, systems analysts, other technical personnel, major vendors, users, and managers to reestablish services in the event of a disaster. Hardware involves recreating the configuration as it existed before or an alternative one that would support the most critical services needed most quickly by the organization. This factor alone also calls for planning for the availability of cables, the shipment of new equipment, and for installation, maintenance, and security. Having a backup computer room or somewhere to go to recreate the machine shop where equipment can be installed and operated is also important. This factor takes into account appropriate electricity, air conditioning, and office space, all properly documented for fast installation. If you cost-justified the disaster study by documenting what it would cost the organization each day for a disaster, identifying the expense of recovery and allocating funds for backup becomes possible and indeed absolutely essential as a form of internal insurance.

Software planning involves having extra copies of all programs off-site that can be loaded into a new configuration and run fast. The same applies to current and accurate copies of data files—the most important asset of both the data processing department and large sectors of the organization. Ensuring that there is an accurate, well-documented schedule of how jobs are run is found to be critical in all such situations because in the event of a disaster, with such information the same predisaster working environment can be quickly reestablished elsewhere. Together with documentation on programs, there must also exist run instructions and a schedule of those programs that should be run given various recovery conditions. Samples of how this can be done are illustrated below.

Communications planning calls for the reestablishment of telephone lines, having phones installed, and equipment, software, people, and management in place to ensure quick response. Communications management is a particularly sensitive factor here because it is in this area of DP that several vendors (e.g., computer manufacturer and telephone company) must be involved and are most numerous, requiring coordination with your own personnel. Often, it is also in the area of communications that a number of locations are involved, requiring additional coordination to ensure service to the key remote sites.

Finally, logistical considerations must not be overlooked. Making sure that copies of a well-written plan telling people where to go and when, and describing details on hotel rooms, office space, supplies, transportation, and office equipment, are located in various parts of the organization.

The third facet of any disaster planning effort calls for distinguishing between preparation for a catastrophe and the implementation of a recovery plan. Thus a certain amount of planning can always be done before a disaster hits (such as making sure that vendors know who to contact with what kind of information if a problem occurs) and gathering information on use (what files you have and which programs have to run when). But real planning to recover from a disaster takes place after the catastrophe has happened (when you know what it is), using the disaster plan as input to the process. The speed with which recovery is possible is in direct proportion to the quality of disaster planning that has taken place beforehand.

The most complicating factor in developing a disaster recovery plan is that each of the components described above is interrelated with every other one in all disasters. You need to manage people, software, hardware, and locations, regardless of the type of problem that hits the DP department. Any disaster recovery document that emerges as the output of any planning effort must reflect that interrelationship. Normal cross-referencing would indicate what should take place if the recovery effort is to be short term or longer, with a logical fallout of the staffing needed for either circumstance. The same applies to both software and hardware. Well-documented plans tend to be modular, perhaps in three-ring binders, so that portions can be updated and revised fairly easily on an ongoing basis. Before describing the effort in more detail, it is important to stress that this should not be a one-time shot but rather an ongoing program, because hardware, software, applications, people, locations, and procedures continually change in all data centers. Once established, however, updating is easy to do and takes very little time on the part of the person responsible for maintaining the document. All managers become responsible for funneling appropriate up-dates to this person, who makes sure that holders of the documented plan get copies of changes.

LONG-TERM RECOVERY PLANNING

Long-term recovery planning involves preparation and execution of plans for recovery at a site other than where the current data center is located. This is the kind of effort that would take place if the data center were burned down, flooded out, bombed, or otherwise destroyed. It might mean moving to another building in town or to another part of the country. People might have been killed or cut off from reaching the organization, or equipment and software completely lost or destroyed. Later in this chapter, we discuss the criteria needed to decide whether a long-term recovery location will have to be established. Suffice it to state now that long-term recovery means setting up shop somewhere other than where it was before and for a long period of time. When it is realized that long-term recovery has to take place, the most senior data processing manager present at the disaster takes charge. He or she does two things. First, the manager decides whether the problem requires a long-range solution, and second, he or she appoints another member of the department to be the situation manager, using the criteria established below. The situation manager has the immediate operational responsibility for carrying out the functions developed earlier in the disaster planning effort; in short, the situation manager is responsible for long-term recovery. We describe next, for each facet of the problem, the steps involved in the preparation and execution of a plan.

Staffing

The first step in putting together any recovery plan calls for identifying what the staffing requirements would be to restore the data center. For various degrees of disaster, certain kinds of skills would be needed, and these must be identified in advance. Catalog what skills each member of the department has, cross-train in those areas in which currently there is a weakness or lack of backup, and keep this list up to date as people come and go and different skills are needed. A method for communicating to people must be established regardless of the nature of the disaster, so that recovery can begin under any circumstances. There are eight steps that can be taken to prepare for proper staffing.

1.   Determine what skills are needed to support all key applications in the event of a disaster. The same applies to systems.

2.   Identify who on your staff can offer what skills and which vendors can do the same (right down to the details of having names, addresses, and home and office telephone numbers as part of the plan's documentation).

3.   Create a skills matrix that quickly outlines what talents are available by whom (see Figure 8-1 for an example).

4.   Put in place procedures to ensure that this matrix is kept up to date to account for changes in people, skills, and requirements. Both the programming and systems managers in a data center should be responsible for giving the disaster plan coordinator this information as needed. Operations should do the same.

5.   Define what tasks would have to be accomplished in the event of a disaster calling for the creation of a data center elsewhere. These should be clustered into groups or slots so that specific individuals can be assigned to groups of activities at the same time of a disaster, relying on whatever staff is left. This will indicate what gaps remain at the time that might be filled

PEOPLE (NAME)	OPERATOR	TECH. SUP.	APPLICATION SYSTEMS			APPLICATION PROGRAMS			SPECIAL SYSTEMS				REMOTE LOCATION OPERATIONS				
			MGG	FIN.	ORDERED	MFG.	FIN.	OTHER	MVS	VM	COMM.	DBASE	CHICAGO	TAMPA	DENVER	ST. LOUIS	BOSTON
A	E	E	K	K	E	E	K		E			K	K	K	K	K	K
B		E	E	E	E	K	E	E	E	E		K		K	K	K	K
C	E							K			E			E	E	E	E
D		E						E	K						K		
E	K			K	K		E	K				E		E	E	E	E
F		K						E	K		E			K	K	K	K
R		E			K	K	K	K		K								
S			E	K	E		K							K	K	K	K

K = Knowledgeable   E = Expert

Figure 8-1. Personnel skills matrix.

with either vendor personnel or with people from other locations or companies borrowed for the occasion.

6. Document the functions for each slot and review them with the people who would probably carry them out, so that they understand what would be required of them. Each staff member should have copies of this documentation both at the office and at home. Other copies should be stored at another location, probably at the predesignated backup site (such as at another data center within the organization).

7. Document the criteria that should be used for the selection of a situation manager in case a long-term recovery effort will be needed. Make sure that copies of this job description (and names of possible candidates) are put into the hands of one or more executives above the DP department so that they can provide leadership in the event that a DP director is incapacitated or killed. With such information a non-DP executive can at least select someone reasonably well qualified to lead the department in a crisis and be able to take over quickly.

8. Finally, make sure that everyone has written instructions as to how to get to a backup site, who they must report to, and how to communicate with and alert each other by telephone (e.g., who calls whom to inform them of a problem).

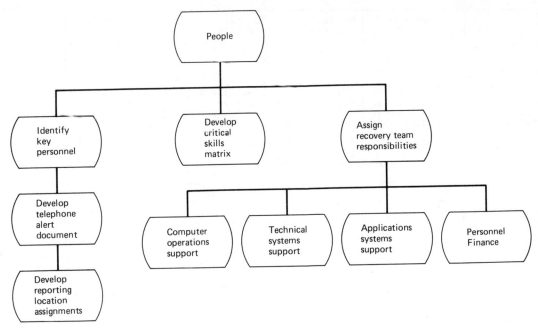

Figure 8-2. Flowchart of personnel-related tasks.

Once a disaster has taken place, four basic steps are taken regarding staffing. First, a long-term situation manager is selected immediately from the surviving managers or staff, who will have the responsibility for developing an immediate recovery plan. He or she initiates the process of alerting all staff members of the crisis via telephone. Second, once an immediate plan for recovery is settled upon, implementation begins. Third, the skills matrix is updated by someone selected by the situation manager to reflect the skills and people (some people may have been killed or cannot get to the scene) that are available, thus allowing for more precise disaster planning at this point. Fourth, the management staff now available develops a schedule of work for the operation of a data center at the recovery location. (See Figure 8-2).

Hardware

Planning for hardware problems involves the identification of how much of what kinds of equipment will be needed over what periods of time in the event of a disaster, what is cost effective for each of these degrees of severity, and what instructions must be written to make sure that vendors can conform to the requirements of a disaster plan. This information must also be kept current, because the hardware environment keeps changing. Operations managers should be responsible for keeping the disaster plan coordinator up to date on existing configurations.

Critical Applications (Decreasing Priority)

Component	A	B	C	D	E	F	G	H	I	J	K	L	M	N	O	P	Q
3033	C	C	C	C	C	C	C	C	C	C	C	C	C	C	C	C	C
3036	C	C	C	C	R	R	R	R	C	C	R	R	R	R	R	C	R
3037	C	C	C	C	C	C	C	C	C	C	C	C	C	C	C	C	C
Chiller	C	C	C	C	C	C	C	C	C	C	C	C	C	C	C	C	C
3705	C	C	R	R	C	C	C	C	C	R	R	R	R	R	R	R	R
3330		C		C			C	C									
3333	C	R	R				R		R						R	C	R
3350	R	R	R		R	C	C	C	C		R			R		R	C
3803	C	C	C	C	C		C				C			C			
3420																	
280	R	R	R	R	C		R				C		R				
281		R		R	C		R				C		R				
282	C	R		R	C		R				C		R				
283		R		R	C		R				C		R				
INP																	
Chicago	C						C	C	C	C							
Houston														C	C	C	C
Dir. opert.	C	R	R	R			C				R		R				

Figure 8-3. Component failure impact analysis. This sample form can suggest the relative value of specific machines and applications.

In the period before a disaster, when the original plan is being drawn up, seven steps should be taken to generate the planning and documentation that will be needed later.

1.   Define the equipment that will be needed to run each of the applications in a recovery situation. Often, this process of identification parallels that which takes place in identifying the software that is needed, when, and by which applications. The results of the software and hardware analysis should be presented as a component failure impact analysis matrix. Figure 8-3 illustrates what such a document might look like.

2.   It is essential that a list of major applications that must be run be developed on the basis of priority of work (most important first, second most important next, etc.) and be signed off by user and executive management so that in the event of a disaster, the most critical work is taken care

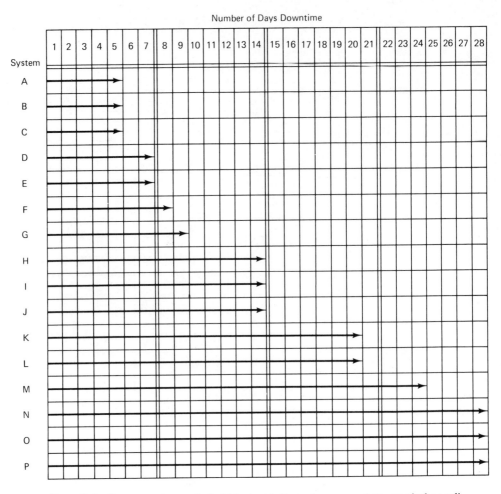

Figure 8-4. Systems outage analysis. This chart indicates how many days a particular application can be unavailable before hurting the organization.

of first and no fighting for resources takes place among users. This list should show what has to run now, those applications that should be run soon if possible, those that can wait a few days, and those that can be left for weeks or months. That kind of information must be boiled down to a matrix that can be read quickly, which would accompany the hardware chart. Figure 8-4 illustrates how this can be done.

3. First, configure a minimum system to run the most critical applications; then develop additional configurations covering different periods of time, relying on data from the two matrices. With this information everyone will know how much of what type of hardware is needed the first day, the first week, the first month, and so on, regardless of the kind of catastrophe you have on your hands.

4. Keep this documentation up to date to account for changes in hardware, applications (and their relative priorities to the company), and operating systems.

5. Obtain from the major vendors servicing the installation written statements regarding their service levels, speed, and contractual conditions for supporting an installation, and keep this documentation in the disaster planning manual.

6. Identify alternative sources of equipment in the event that your primary vendor cannot help as much as you need. These can include other vendors, leasing companies, equipment borrowed from other companies, hardware in local computer-moving-company warehouses, or configurations of other data centers within your organization that can be called on for help if needed. This step also includes making sure that vendors and backup sources have written instructions on how to help, who to contact, lists of detailed configurations (including features on a box-by-box basis), and where these items should be installed. Make sure that this kind of information is also in the hands of the primary vendors before a disaster takes place, so that at the time a simple phone call will be all that is needed to initiate the vendors' steps in a long-term recovery effort, thus allowing them to begin work immediately. People forget that cables are needed to connect equipment, so include a list of cable groups needed by machine type and required lengths.

7. A backup site should have the telephone numbers and names of the key vendors who have been designated to participate in a recovery program. Copies of required configurations should be kept with this documentation.

At the time of the disaster, a number of steps involving hardware take place next. The situation manager, or someone designated by this person, takes on the responsibility for managing the hardware phase of recovery. His or her first move is to contact the vendors so that they may begin finding and shipping equipment to a predesignated backup site. Next, the person must coordinate with the vendors the receipt and installation of new equipment, taking into account that:

- Receiving areas are informed of what is coming in.
- Electricians can quickly (if not already done) provide necessary power.
- Floor plans are reviewed and air conditioning checked and made ready.
- People, equipment, and so on, are accumulated on-site to start work quickly.
- Appropriate testing of equipment is done and maintenance and problem reporting logs are begun and maintained from the beginning

(both by the designated hardware manager and by appropriate vendor management).

Computer Site

In the event of a long-term solution to a catastrophe, you must have already selected an appropriate alternative location for the data center. Finding one and making the necessary arrangements for its use, complete with plans for flooring, electricity, air conditioning, and so on, takes time, time that no one has after the disaster occurs and thus must be locked in place long in advance. Seven planning steps cover the requirements here, and will probably take several months to complete.

1.   Articulate what the requirements would be for an alternative site for each of the relevant configurations (spaced over time—days, weeks, months) described above.

2.   Define, in writing, various alternatives for backup, which can include:

- Mutual assistance agreements with other companies
- Service bureaus
- Disaster recovery service organizations
- Duplicate hardware
- Alternative locations within your organization (including shells— empty rooms set aside and properly constructed to support a data center)

Other obvious additional candidates would be a large remote data center or space in a plant that already has minis, terminals, and so on, or a vendor's data center.

3.   Evaluation of options should account for the various costs involved, ease of access by your personnel, space, the problem of simultaneous disasters (quite possible if in the same community), transportation, lodging, and other considerations relevant to your organization.

4.   Examine the alternative locations, identifying the logistics and policies and procedures needed to take advantage of each. Obtain necessary approval from upper-level management and from executives in other organizations where the backup sites are designated.

5.   Select the appropriate locations and sign necessary contracts or letters defining terms of use and agreement prior to a disaster.

6.   As part of the disaster plan documentation, lay out an equipment plan, a plan for electricity, air conditioning, teleprocessing, and staffing, telephone numbers, and maps to use in getting to the alternative site.

7. In addition, the manager of the backup site (owner) needs written instructions on what has to be done by him or her once a decision has been made to use a location. This should define the clearing of space, notification of staff that equipment and people are coming in, providing for security, and names and telephone numbers of key people involved. He or she should also have a full copy of the disaster plan, with the exception of sensitive data about your company, which he or she would not need anyway.

At execution time, when a long-term recovery effort is needed, notify the owner of the backup site that the facility is needed. The situation manager should appoint a computer site coordinator to make sure that the owner is doing what has to be done and is taking whatever steps are necessary to receive equipment and people. This person then becomes the focal point of control, answering questions, assigning work, and coordinating among the various groups working to establish a new data center.

Software and Data

What use is hardware recovery if there is no software or data to go along with it? The effort for software and data files parallels the kinds of activities identified for hardware. You must catalog what your software is, what files you have and how big they are, applications, systems programs, documentation of all these, procedures, and updating functions; establish off-site storage of copies that are current (this must be done continuously); and arrange for their fast delivery to the new location. Six planning steps are involved.

1. Establish what data files, applications, and systems programs will be needed when for each level of disaster severity (for first day, first week, first month, etc.). This information is a logical outgrowth of the matrices developed for the system. Procedures for installing all of this on the new hardware should be established in advance as well to ensure fast setup. Do not forget to do the same for minis, micros, remote intelligent terminals, and so on. (See Figure 8-5.)

2. Establish an off-site storage facility where current and accurate copies of all data files and programs (including operating systems) can be kept safely regardless of the disaster. It must also be convenient to a recovery site (easy transportation between the two, such as good roads, nearby airport, etc.). Current procedures for backing up files and programs should be phased into those in the physical storage area. This can involve having a local storage area (say 1 mile away at another building replenished daily) and/or (but never by itself) another facility in a different town that might have its copies of materials replaced weekly or as needed.

System

Data file	A	B	C	D	E	F	G	H	I	J	K	L	M	N	O	P	Q
A	X			X						X							
B		X	X			X								X			
C		X		X			X				X						
D	X				X					X		X					X
E								X									
F			X							X	X				X	X	

Figure 8-5. Data fact impact analysis. This form suggests which data files work with which applications.

3.   Establish written procedures to ensure that backup files and programs can be shipped quickly to the new data center by a predesignated person.

4.   Take existing procedures and make necessary changes, all in writing, to provide logging, storing, and retrieving of files at the new data center. These should be at the place where backup files are stored as well.

5.   Written instructions for installing and running systems and applications' programs should exist together with the files. These can include normal operational documentation already in existence, as well as a startup control book and a set of vendor manuals for the installation and operation of all systems and application packages. Copies of these should be stored with the backup files and reflect the particular releases of the software installed today.

6.   Normal procedures for the acquisition of software and file backups should be altered enough to establish procedures for updating these when changes are made in the actual recovery plan. Another alternative backup site to the new data center must immediately be established in case there is a second disaster.

At the time of the catastrophe, the situation manager designates someone responsible for handling the files, calling on the data storage facility to ship the backup set of data and programs to the recovery data center, or have several employees actually go over and pick up these materials. Next, the person primarily responsible for the files takes charge of receiving this material at the new data center, checking to make sure that it is all there, and gets it ready for installation on the new hardware configuration as soon as the equipment is installed. At this point careful recording and filing of these data sets is essential to make sure that correct labels and records are maintained. Moreover, it is a means of making sure that the files can be found quickly (important if dealing with hundreds of disk packs or tapes). Finally, appropriate documentation necessary to install the programs and files on the hardware have to be made available at this point to the systems programmers now at the new data center.

Scheduling and Documentation

With hardware and software coming and going, the frame for hanging a logical recovery plan that results in operational applications quickly going on stream is the scheduling and documentation process. This involves establishing what jobs have to run and when, what documents and programs are needed to make this happen, and to make all of this available to those who need it at the new data center. It also means keeping a scheduling plan up to date and properly documented.

1.   The first step involves drawing up an application matrix with appropriate documentation (see Figure 8-4 for a view of the critical value of each). Documentation should include both system descriptions and operation-run books such as those used at the regular data center, which should be kept current.

2.   There should be a list of all technical documents necessary to run jobs, such as operator manuals, vendor publications, and standards documentation.

3.   Make sure that a procedure is in place to get this material over to the recovery site quickly. It could be stored with the programs and data and transported over with them, be at another location, at a key vendor's office, or whatever; but make sure that it can get to the new data center fast. Without this, no scheduling of any relevance can be done quickly enough. Vendors should also have lists of manuals that they would be able to ship immediately. All procedures involved in this step must be documented with copies at a vendor's office, at the data backup storage site, and at another location within your organization (as a minimum).

4.   At disaster time, take the matrices already developed for systems and data and develop new run schedules, incorporating them into the overall plan drawn up for the installation of new hardware, the operating system, and for firing up the most critical applications. The schedule should define which jobs have to run in what order given the degree of disaster. When this schedule is prepared, copies should be available to whoever needs them at the new site, and backup copies sent to one or more off-site locations for safety. By this point the reader should have concluded that having a copying

machine at the new data center might not be a bad idea; one can always be "liberated" from another part of the building or from a neighboring company for the occasion.

Do not forget to modify the disaster planning documentation on a normal basis as schedules and other factors change in the predisaster data center.

Once disaster has struck, four steps must be taken to ensure that scheduling and documentation aspects of the recovery are carried out. First, the situation manager must designate someone to be responsible for these functions, who in turn will ensure that documentation is now sent to the recovery location. This person is usually an operations manager, supervisor, or a senior operator put in charge. Second, the person has to meet the documents when they come in, take care of them, reorganize them if needed, and make sure that nothing is missing. Third, an actual schedule has to be drawn up by this person and a written copy handed to operators for their use as soon as hardware and software have been installed. Finally, this person sets up an operations execution log to start recording what jobs are or have been run, appropriate control totals, and problems needing resolution, so that these can be reviewed with the overall site manager in the immediate hours and days following the disaster. These will also be needed once the disaster has become history and the department reviews how it performed in the crisis with an eye to improving its recovery procedures.

Communications

Recovery from a disaster involving communications is the most complex aspect of any planning process, and some managers would argue that the effort itself can be a disaster. Essentially, however, the objective is to have plans in place, depending on the severity of the crisis, that allow the necessary software and hardware to be set up allowing communications to all the key remote sites or, if the disaster takes place at a remote location, to provide for the recovery of that installation. This would be done by relocating hardware and software or services. The effort described above for other hardware, software, data, and people apply here line by line. Thus six steps are essential during the planning phase.

1.   Accumulate from all vendors supplying communications products to your organization letters describing their support services in the event of a disaster, much as you would with the replacement of central site hardware and software. These letters should be part of the disaster manual, as they include the names, telephone numbers, and addresses of the vendors involved.

2.   Make copies of the hardware and software configurations that make up the existing network and keep these up to date, as this part of the total DP configuration changes most frequently.

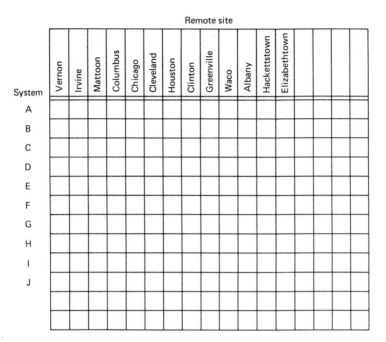

Remote site

Figure 8–6. Time transmission requirements analysis. This matrix form is used to show which systems are used by every major remote site.

Figure 8–7. Communications equipment matrix. This sample form shows what TP hardware is needed to support which remote location.

3. Do a communications component impact analysis and incorporate the documentation from this effort into the disaster manual. Figures 8-6 and 8-7 illustrate the kind of format and data needed.

4. Establish in advance different procedures for the remote sites to

deliver data to your new location and for your returns to them. Make sure that they have copies of whatever plans are created.

5.   Determine what the minimum telecommunications configuration would have to be at the disaster end of the network and tie that into the minimum application mix needed to function on day 1, in week 1, in month 1, and so on.

6.   As with other portions of the hardware configuration, draw up appropriate physical installation plans for teleprocessing (floor space, electrical requirements, etc.) as it would be at the recovery location.

When the time comes to activate these plans, step 1 calls for notifying all the vendors by telephone to pull in the necessary equipment, installation of telephone lines, and assignment of appropriate personnel at the recovery location. Because a minimum of two vendors are generally involved (the telephone company and the teleprocessing hardware manufacturer), and often three or more, careful documentation is essential; otherwise, you might wind up with everything except modems, or lots of hardware but no telephone lines. If the disaster took place at a remote site, notify the disaster-struck location where to take their data for transmittal to the host. Finally, install, test, and go live with a network to support the most critical locations and applications first, and ultimately the full network with all applications as before the disaster.

Logistics

Invariably with any major disaster, the little points that can make or break a fast recovery are often overlooked, yet as a general rule, these can always be accounted for in any planning effort. These include making plans for housing, transportation, courier services, trucking, and obtaining desks and chairs, paper and pencils, and other relevant office supplies. Most disaster planning manuals prepared by a data center omit these details, only to rue the fact when faced with an actual catastrophe. A number of simple actions avoid many of these irritating complications.

1.   Establish how many people you have to house near the new data center for the duration of the crisis. Then go to nearby hotels and gain their commitment to provide such space in the event of a disaster. Along the way, acquire the names and telephone numbers of the hotels and their managers, and directions on how to get to them. The recovery team will need this information, especially if additional people have to be brought in from other installations, from vendors, or from other data centers.

2.   Figure out what your transportation requirements would be, and make arrangements, similar to those described above, with a local car and truck rental company near the recovery data center; obtain the usual collec-

tion of names, telephone numbers, and directions. If credit cards are necessary for charging for transportation, obtain those now rather than after the disaster.

3.   Determine how to transport files, programs, and so on, and identify what courier or trucking companies would be used, obtaining names and telephone numbers, and making appropriate arrangements for service in the event of a castastrophe. This also applies to service for remote users at all locations.

4.   Duplicate everything said so far for all remote sites that have minis, micros, data collection and intelligent terminals, and CRTs (even if the assumption is made that other remote sites could be cannibalized for excess devices).

5.   Office equipment often presents a problem in a disaster situation; therefore, do with office supply vendors as with DP companies: get local addresses, telephone numbers, names, directions, and commitments to supply predetermined lists of products, keeping current as part of the disaster manual such information on basic essentials.

6.   The same applies to DP supplies. As a quick reminder, this includes tapes, paper, cards, special forms, and even little things like tape knives.

7.   You will need a petty cash fund and possibly check-writing capability; therefore, someone must be designated to have responsibility for this and should have preestablished documentation on procedures for maintaining such a function.

8.   Identify restaurants near your backup location that can supply meals (even if only coffee and sandwiches) in a time of crisis, and make appropriate arrangements, documenting addresses, names, and telephone numbers.

9.   Remember your users. In the event of a disaster, they should be able to go to a disaster manual and find instructions about what they must do to ease the burden on the new data center while also operating and feeding it data for processing in a long-term recovery situation.

10.   With all the paper flying around and the added documentation that must be prepared during a crisis, make arrangements to have one or more secretaries available to the data center who can provide services to all the managers and personnel involved. To speed things along each should have at least a typewriter, or best of all, a word-processing machine with mag card or text-processing capability to increase productivity.

11.   Test portions of the plan, as cost effectively as possible, on a periodic basis as a means of ensuring that the plan is realistic and complete. This is also an excellent but simple way to verify that the documentation is specific enough, particularly for systems programmers and operations per-

sonnel, who need to understand fully how to install and operate a system that has been thrown together quickly. Finally, it is good combat training for the troops.

Once the calamity has struck, a number of specific things must take place. Contact the hotels and others to tell them how many people have to be put up and when, with their names; assign specific personnel to hotels; reserve and obtain rental cars and airplane tickets and distribute these out to the recovery team at the time of the disaster. Preferably, have these items brought to you by the vendors involved. Notify the courier services to transport data, programs, communications to remote users, and so on, immediately. The office supply firms being used have to be contacted so that appropriate materials can be brought on-site quickly; the same applies to local computer supply firms.

A great deal of space has been allocated to the discussion of a long-term disaster situation and what has to be done because in a true disaster it may be months before a normal situation is again reached. The flooded-out data center, fire-gutted building, or sabotaged machine room takes weeks or even months to replace, and if personnel die in the process, it may take many more months to hire or train replacements. If you are going to have a catastrophe, it will last more than a few weeks and the effects will haunt your organization for months. Without planning for such a situation, the effects could be lethal to the organization or remain chronic for too long.

SHORT-TERM RECOVERY PLANNING

Short-term recovery planning assumes that you cannot operate with the current data center. Anything less disastrous is not a catastrophe but obviously hardware malfunction, a software bug, or a lack of adequate personnel. Any of these conditions is a normal operational problem and thus not the subject of disaster planning. But if there is a temporary problem that requires a move to another location in order to continue operating the data processing department for a short period, then the comments below apply. Typical situations might include the loss of electrical power for a few days, a fire destroying a portion of the data center or the building in which it is housed, evacuation of an area because of a fire at a gas station, chemical toxification of the air due to an accident at a nearby chemical plant, or natural gas leaking from a railroad accident. If the problem is perceived to be of limited duration, the recommendations below apply. As with a long-term disaster, the senior MIS manager locally first determines that the department is faced with a short-term recovery problem. Then this person appoints someone to be the situation manager. He or she, in turn, takes a modified, shortened version of the tasks already defined and implements those that are relevant (such as the movement of equipment, documentation, files, and programs, but probably not arranging for hotels and airplane tickets, assuming that the change is to somewhere nearby).

Yet there are some deviations from the previous remarks that need to be made. In regard to a computer site, since an alteration in location is only required for a short period, long-term rental contracts and the like might not be necessary. Procedures and guidelines in the eventuality of needing another location only for a short period must be worked out and documented in advance. Other than that, staffing, hardware, software, data files, scheduling, documentation, communications, and logistics remain a concern with considerations similar to those of a disaster that you would have to live with for many weeks or months and which therefore must be treated more formally and with serious intent. (See Figure 8-8.)

ADDITIONAL DISASTER DETAILS

So far the discussion has centered on identifying the key issues involved and what has to be planned for and what can be done once you are cursed with a disaster, any disaster. Obviously, specific planning can only take place once the catastrophe hits, but equally so, with good planning many of the key details can be worked out long in advance. There are other specific elements that should be understood or restated to be fully usable in any disaster planning effort.

Perhaps the most important set of details involves the specifics of doing component recovery planning. This entails what has to be done in advance and later, both at a host location and at remote sites, particularly if a major piece of equipment (such as a computer) is lost. The decision as to whether or not a disaster is short or long and if just a minor or major portion of the data center is gone goes back to the criteria established in the various component impact failure analyses and systems outage analyses charts developed as part of the normal disaster recovery manual. (See Figure 8-9 and 8-10.)

If a piece of hardware is gone and cannot be fixed, that portion of the plan calling for transferring work elsewhere or having the vendor bring in new equipment is activated. The same applies to data and software, sites, scheduling, and documentation activities. Staffing normally would not be a problem unless a key individual(s) was incapacitated or killed. Similar portions of the disaster plan apply to communications and logistics in most situations where only a portion of the facilities have been damaged. Assessing the actual damage is a task done by the senior DP manager at the site at the time of the disaster and determines what happens next.

To illustrate some of the more specific elements of any disaster plan, a series of figures are presented below, suggesting the kind of documentation that should be prepared in advance. Figure 8-11 shows a specific disk configuration with the major files that are housed, Figure 8-12 suggests the first

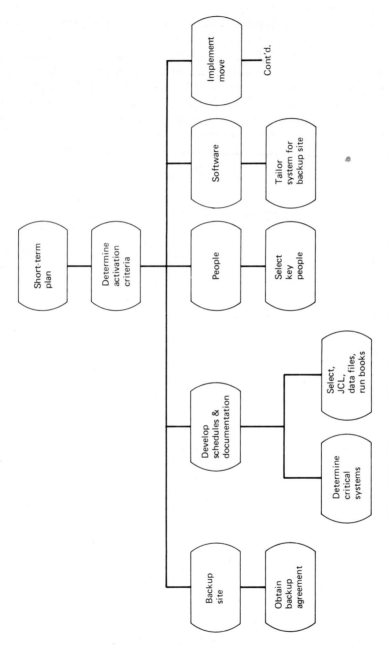

Figure 8–8. Short-term failure plan, showing short-term disaster planning efforts.

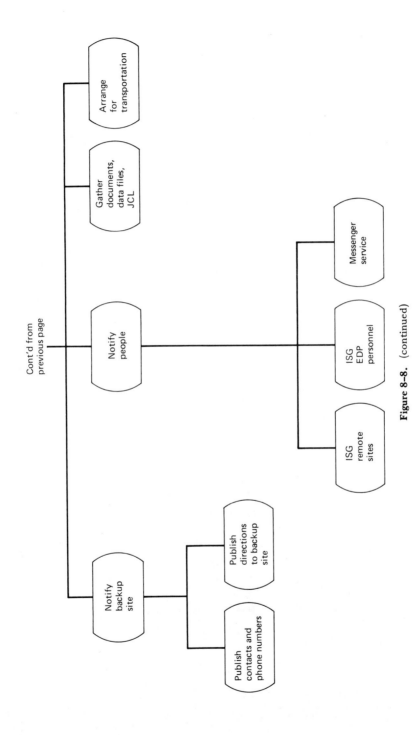

Figure 8–8. (continued)

347

Component failure plan

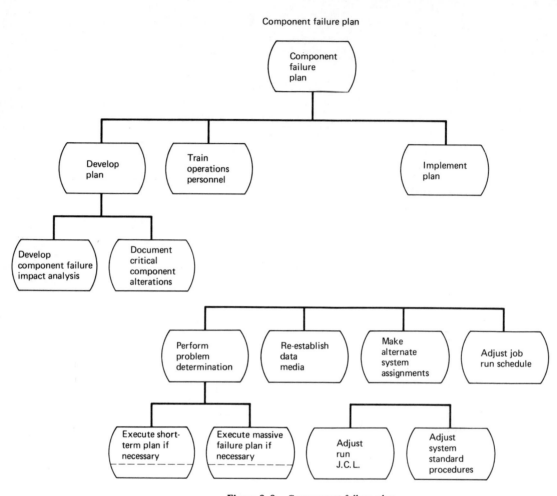

Figure 8-9. Component failure plan.

Critical
1. Operational and technical personnel cannot achieve recovery.
2. User or operations cannot access systems as defined in the systems outage matrix.

Recoverable
1. Operational and technical personnel can achieve recovery reasonably fast (such as by assigning different tape assigns).
2. The length of time of an outage does not prevent operations from meeting significant job schedules as defined by the priority of applications that must be run.

Figure 8-10. Definitions of component failure impact analysis. Defines the two sets of circumstances affecting component failure impacts. For correlation to the system as a whole, see Figure 8-3.

348

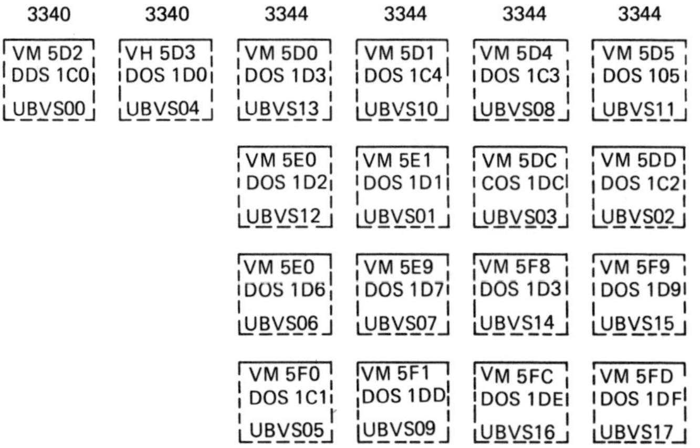

3340	3340	3344	3344	3344	3344
VM 5D2 DDS 1C0 UBVS00	VH 5D3 DOS 1D0 UBVS04	VM 5D0 DOS 1D3 UBVS13	VM 5D1 DOS 1C4 UBVS10	VM 5D4 DOS 1C3 UBVS08	VM 5D5 DOS 105 UBVS11
		VM 5E0 DOS 1D2 UBVS12	VM 5E1 DOS 1D1 UBVS01	VM 5DC COS 1DC UBVS03	VM 5DD DOS 1C2 UBVS02
		VM 5E0 DOS 1D6 UBVS06	VM 5E9 DOS 1D7 UBVS07	VM 5F8 DOS 1D3 UBVS14	VM 5F9 DOS 1D9 UBVS15
		VM 5F0 DOS 1C1 UBVS05	VM 5F1 DOS 1DD UBVS09	VM 5FC DOS 1DE UBVS16	VM 5FD DOS 1DF UBVS17

Figure 8-11. DASD file layout by disk drive.

page of a list of what files are involved, and Figure 8-13 shows the kind of form that may be used to identify what systems are used by which remote sites.

Applications always draw users' attention very quickly and therefore that of top management. It is imperative to understand what applications must be brought up first (as suggested in Figure 8-4). Additional, obvious information would include a list of applications involved, then a systems outage analysis chart suggesting which applications can be down for x number of days and no more (see Figure 8-14 for an example).

The disaster manual should also have a list and a description of the various functional responsibilities (clusters of jobs to be done) which define what the disaster team should look like for your organization. (See Figure 8-15.) This is the group charged with the responsibility for restoring services that it controls in the event of a disaster. A team designated for a major disaster should include the following functional areas described below. How many people and managers should staff each depends on how large the data center is and how many people are alive or available to do recovery work. But in one fashion or another, in all organizations, each of the functions described below has to be staffed in any disastrous circumstance.

Recovery Manager. This person has overall responsibility for the recovery and for the day-to-day operations of the backup data center. He or she may or may not be the MIS director but should at least be a manager from the data processing department. If none are available, a senior member of the department must assume this responsibility.

Personnel. One person must be responsible for arranging all lodging, transportation, and related personnel matters and would report to the recovery manager.

Systems

Data file	General Ledger	For Location	Purchasing/ Payables	Accounts Receivable	Order Processing	Distribution	Materials Control	General Financial	Planning	Operations Research	Personnel	Rough Rice	Sales Reporting	Payroll			
01												X					
02												X					
03												X					
04												X					
05												X					
06												X					
07												X					
08				X	X			X				X	X				
09	X			X	X	X	X	X	X			X	X	X			
10														X			
11														X			
12														X			
13														X			
14		X															
15		X															
16			X														
17			X														
18								X					X				

Figure 8-12. Data file layout by system suggesting impact when a system or file is not functioning.

Finance. This function would cover all disbursements of cash, working with insurance companies directly related to the recovery effort, and may possibly be handled by the individual managing personnel matters unless the cash and insurance problems are too great or numerous, in which case perhaps a member of the accounting department should become involved. Regardless of who it is, this person would report to the recovery manager.

Remote Site

System		Vernon	Irvine	Albany	Hackettstown	Elizabethtown	Special Warehouse	Master Warehouse	Uncle Ben's Warehouse	All Warehouses Combined
A	OP						40	30	10	
B	RP									25
C										
D										
E										
F										
G										
H										
I										
J										

Figure 8-13. Chart illustrating transmitting requirements in hours/months.

Short-Term Disaster Team Leader. This person, also reporting to the recovery manager, would organize and coordinate the daily operations of the disaster team at a new location.

Technical Services. This function would encompass the installation and modification of all operating software that would be dependent on available hardware at the new location. It involves its installation, effective startup for immediate processing, and eventually for the stabilization of a more permanent solution. A technical support or systems manager would usually head such a group, with one or more individuals reporting to him or her. The technical services manager would report to the short-term disaster team leader.

Data Base. Someone would be responsible for installing data base software and ensuring that files were loaded into the system in a manner that would allow the most critical applications to perform. Such a function might

Number of Days Downtime (1 Month Duration)

Systems Name	1	2	3	4	5	6	7	8	9	10	11	12	13	14	15	16	17	18	19	20	21	22	23	24	25	26	27	28
Order processing		X																										
Payroll rough price			X				X																					
A/R														X														
Purch./pay.							X							X														
G/L														X														
Dist. National control							X																					
General finance														X														
Sales analysis							X																					
Personnel																					X							

Figure 8-14. Specific systems outage analysis. This form indicates how many days a particular application can be inoperative before crippling the organization.

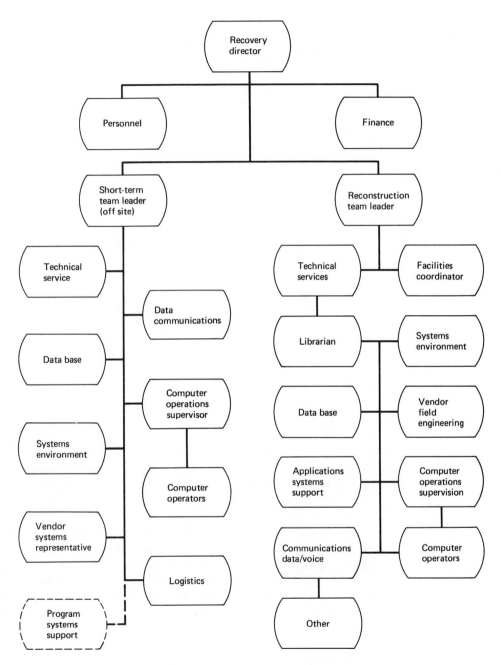

Figure 8-15. Sample disaster team.

also be under the direction of technical services except in large shops where data management is an extensive and separate function with its own manager and staff. Regardless of size, this person would report to the short-term disaster team leader.

Systems Environment. This covers modification and installation of production, application, and disk management programs, disk assignments, and job scheduling for jobs predetermined as being the most critical to operate first. The manager of this function would report either to the technical services manager or directly to the short-term disaster team leader.

Data Communications. One or more persons must have the responsibility for installing communications facilities and getting the installation "on the air" quickly. Such a person would have a telecommunications background in hardware and software and would report to the short-term disaster team leader.

Programming Support. In order to install and have operational key applications, some modifications of programs or debugging of others might require the assistance of programmers. Thus for the key applications that must go live first, programmers trained in the use of languages in which these applications are written must be on standby alert for use if needed; they would report to the technical services manager or to the short-term disaster team leader.

Hardware Operations. A manager is needed to coordinate the activities of all the operators across as many shifts as necessary to operate the equipment once it is installed. This person will make sure that the critical applications, as defined in the disaster manual, are run first. Such a manager would handle the daily operations; he or she would report to the short-term disaster team leader.

Remote Site and Logistics. Someone must have the responsibility for transmitting data to key users throughout the network who need to run the most critical applications first and would have to ensure that important reports were sent to the relevant persons quickly by mail, courier, or whatever means were determined before the disaster. This person could also handle logistical issues involving supplies and would report to the short-term disaster team leader.

Vendor Personnel. The primary vendors supplying hardware and software to the data center would have to assign either technical advisors (such as systems engineers) and/or a manager who could pull in whatever software and hardware resources were needed to install and get their company's products operational. Such persons and or staff would report to the short-term disaster team leader for the period of the crisis.

Once the initial shock of a disaster is overcome and temporary facilities established to allow normal work to continue even if in a crippled state, the next step would be to return all operations to a predisaster state in a permanent home—in short, to return to normal. Certain people and functions would be involved separate from those just described.

Reconstruction Team Leader. While the short-term disaster team leader was, in effect, putting out fires by just trying to get the immediate day-to-day work done, someone else would have to be responsible for managing the department on its way back to normal operations. This would mean planning and building new facilities, obtaining hardware and software, and coordinating the shift of work and people from the emergency and thus temporary data center to the new permanent home with all systems functioning. His or her primary objective would be to reconstruct everything back to what it was before the catastrophe and would report to the DP director. In small to intermediate-size companies, this person would be the DP manager.

Technical Services. In larger departments, this would be a separate person from the manager reporting to the short-term disaster team leader and would be responsible for the installation of a full operating system as it was before the disaster. He or she would report to the reconstruction team leader.

Library. Someone, the department's librarian if there is one, must reconstruct the entire library of manuals, publications on hardware, software, systems code, applications, operations, run books, logs, procedures and guidelines, and so on; he or she would report to the technical services manager.

Data Base. This involves the complete reconstruction of all data files to a predisaster status, incorporating new data generated after the catastrophe, including generating appropriate copies for backup. This person(s) reports to the reconstruction team leader.

Applications Systems Support. This position involves ensuring that all applications are back to their state prior to the disaster and would draw on technical services and programming staffs for help. This person reports to the reconstruction team leader.

Communications. This involves the recreation of the entire teleprocessing and voice (telephone) network at the permanent data center in the same condition as they were before the catstrophe and this person would report to the reconstruction team leader.

Facilities. One individual must be responsible for working with contractors, electricians, plumbers, and so on, to rebuild a data center with appropriate offices, conference rooms, storage facilities, supply center, library, and so on. He or she would also provide appropriate physical security to the entire DP center. Such a person would negotiate contracts, supervise the work, and ensure that the construction personnel were paid and information on the entire reconstruction gathered for insurance claims. This person should report to the reconstruction team leader and possibly also report to an administrative director or vice-president ultimately responsible for such large expenditures of money.

Systems Environment. All production, JCL, and disk assignments on a permanent basis to predisaster levels fall into this category. This person also bears the responsibility for the tricky task of integrating short-term production efforts into a permanent one that provides predisaster levels of full service. Such a person should report to the reconstruction team leader, who has ultimate responsibility for developing and implementing a specific plan to migrate all services from the temporary disaster backup facility to its permanent new home.

Computer Operations. As with the temporary installation, someone must be responsible for operations as they are reconstructed at the permanent data center to ensure that predisaster levels of service are achieved. This may be the same manager as the person off-site, if nearby; otherwise, it should probably be a different person, reporting to the reconstruction team leader. All operators would report to this supervisor at the permanent location.

Vendor Personnel. Primary vendors responsible for the installation of hardware and software, including physical planning specialists, should report to key vendor managers, who report directly to the reconstruction team leader, to ensure a rapid and smooth return to predisaster levels of service.

DISASTER PLAN EXAMPLES

To reinforce some of the principles discussed above, examples of specific types of output from one disaster planning effort are described below. In the case selected, a medium-size company with annual sales of about $250,000,000, with one major data center and a number of remote sites, is supporting a population of about 60 CRTs and a work-load mix of about 60% on-line and the rest batch, 90% of which consists of commercial and financial applications, the rest engineering for manufacturing. They used the methodology described in this chapter, and their disaster plan is contained in a fat three-ring binder. At the time that this chapter was being written (mid-1981), this company was starting to expand this skeleton plan into a second, more detailed edition using the full methodology illustrated above.

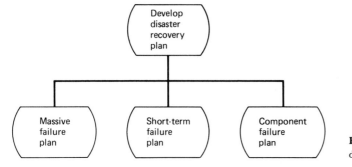

Figure 8-16. Flow of overall events in disaster planning.

The covering letter to their disaster manual stated how many copies there were in existence (six), five of which were kept at the homes of key DP managers and one within the department. A second memorandum stated that the manual was broken down into long-term and short-term disaster information. Then a series of HIPO charts were developed, accompanied by the kind of textual description presented in the preceding section of this chapter, but in more detail. Figures 8-16 through 8-23 illustrate the flow of events for long-term disasters. In the organization being discussed, a similar set of appropriate diagrams were developed for short-term crises. One final chart was drawn to illustrate quickly a component failure plan, which had an

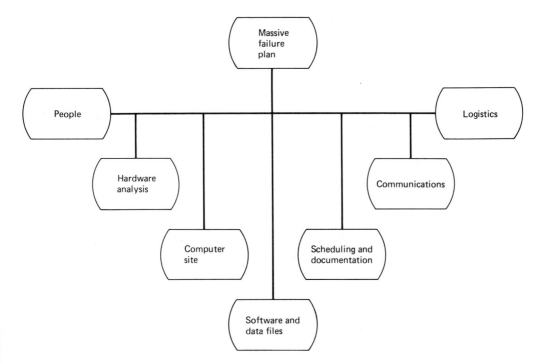

Figure 8-17. Major elements of a severe disaster plan.

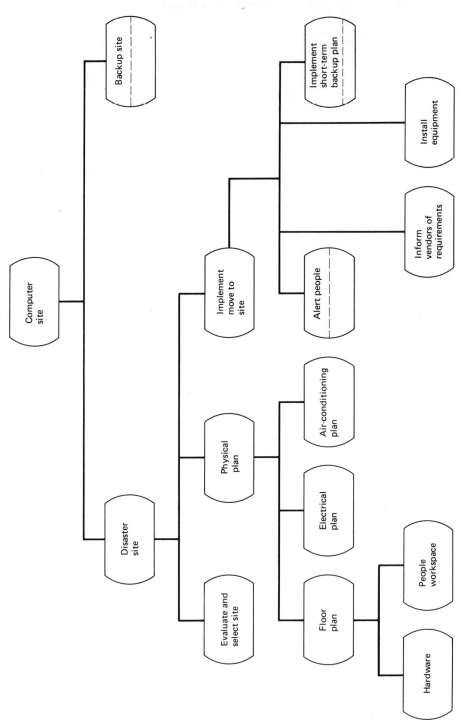

Figure 8-18. Steps preceding a move to a backup site.

358

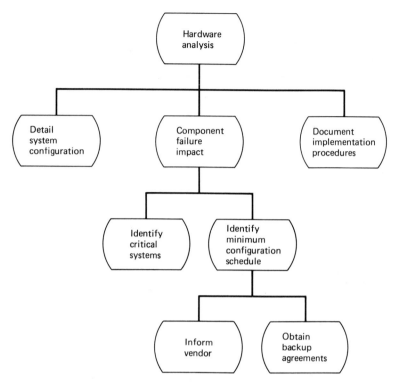

Figure 8-19. Elements of a hardware disaster planning effort.

accompanying textual description of each feature. (See Figure 8-24.) Before describing additional elements of this manual, it would be helpful to know what its organization was like:

- Introduction
- HIPO narratives
- HIPO diagrams
- Telephone-alert plan
- Personnel skills matrix
- Hardware configurations
- Component failure impact analysis
- Backup-site agreements and contracts
- Alternative-site floor plan
- Data file matrix
- Master/system file backup procedures
- Critical systems master run schedule
- Systems outage analysis

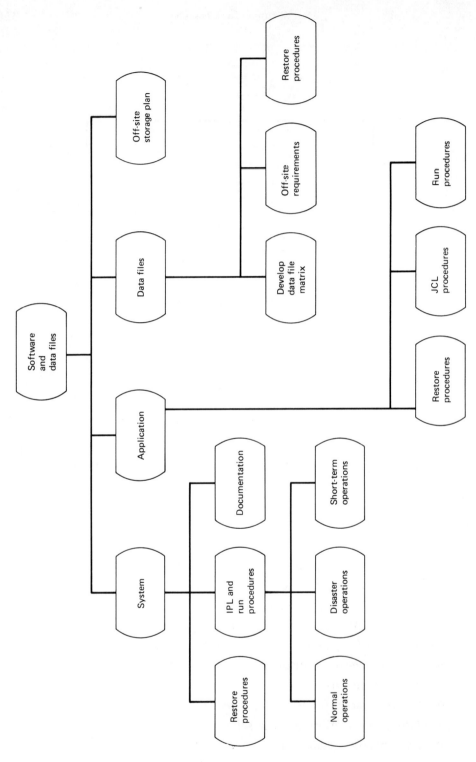

Figure 8-20. Planning software and data areas.

360

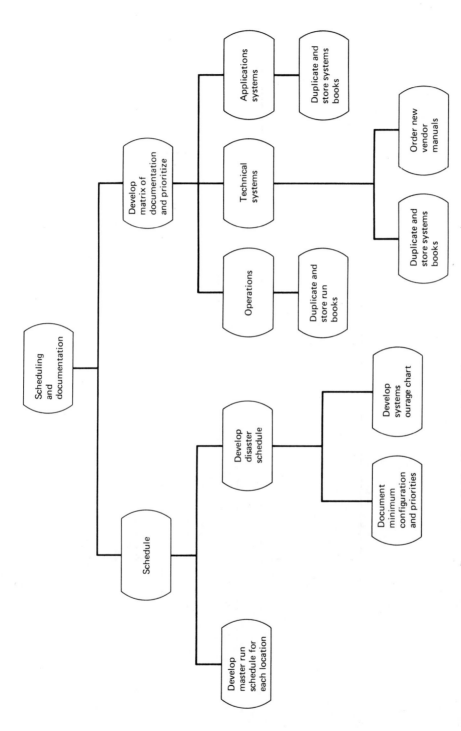

Figure 8-21. Elements of scheduling and documentation planning.

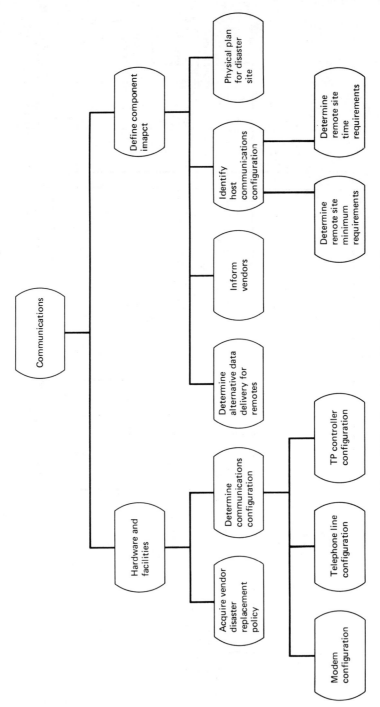

Figure 8–22. Elements considered in communications.

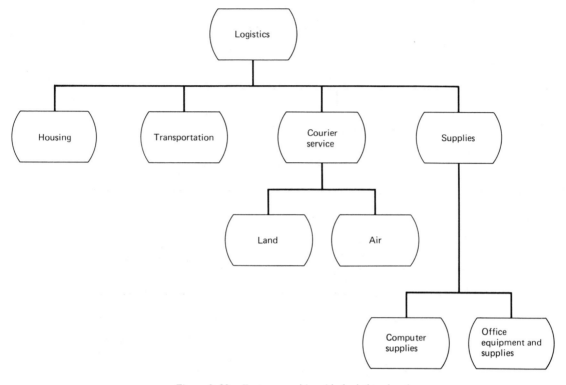

Figure 8-23. Factors considered in logistics planning.

- Critical systems documentation matrix
- Physical security considerations
- Prime vendors
- Auditor's recommendations
- Schematics of various major remote locations

Each of these major topics encompassed material relevant for either a long-term or a short-term disaster.

The telephone list had at the top the name of the DP director, who was responsible for calling each manager. They, in turn, had a list of specific people to call, with names and telephone numbers. Each manager was responsible for calling all other managers to make sure that each knew of the disaster, thus avoiding a serious breakdown in communications. Each manager also kept a copy of names and telephone numbers at home and in their cars. Additional instructions were included on how to activate a backup site, who to call, and so on. The next section had detailed descriptions of people's skills by application. They described who knew which applications, rating their skills as either expert or just familiarity, using E and K (knowledge) in

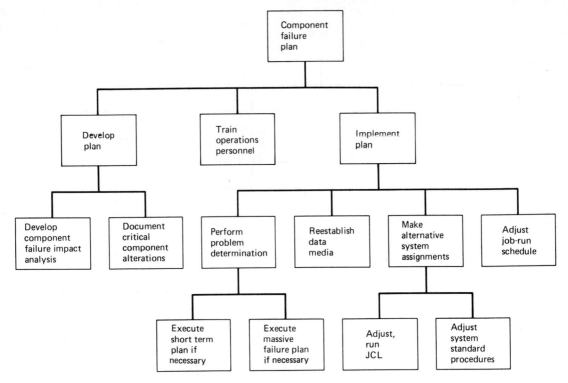

Figure 8-24. Component failure plan.

the matrix under application and name. Hardware configurations down to the feature level were provided by the computer vendor for all installed equipment. A list of manuals required from the vendor to support the software and hardware were also included. Component failure impact analysis reflected the data presented earlier in this chapter.

In the section on backup letters, letters from major vendors supporting this installation, the telephone company, and backup sites were duplicated, describing what would be done, who to contact, and their office and home telephone numbers and addresses. For the backup site in another company, the other DP director enclosed a detailed configuration of hardware and software currently installed and kept that configuration report up to date as his installation changed devices and programs. A backup site was also chosen within the company that currently housed some terminals and RJE equipment. There was a memo here describing the area, who had to do what to it in order to make it usable, and a floor plan showing what a backup system (CPU and I/O) would look like. Sufficient power and air conditioning had already been installed.

Software documentation was explicit. There was a chart illustrating what files were on which packs of disk, a narrative describing how master files were currently being backed up and how frequently, followed by a checklist of all files that could be used, to make sure none were overlooked. A copy of the master run schedule was also enclosed. This was followed by a memorandum stating that the criticalness of applications was determined by their potential impact on the company's profitability should they not be available. That is, the company could survive without certain applications longer than without others. Application flowcharts were then included for the most critical applications. Security issues were addressed by appending two publications on the subject published by the IBM Corporation.

A miniature version of the disaster manual was prepared for each of the major remote locations, showing hardware and software, space, names, telephone numbers, applications, and files in approximately one dozen pages per installation, with copies deposited at various other remote sites. These included instructions as to who was to use which as their backup. Remote-site managers were resonsible for maintaining the currency of their portion of the disaster manual.

The vendor list was one page long, citing hardware vendors, vendors for forms, tapes, ribbons, disk, and software, the names of sales and service personnel, and telephone numbers. Additional lists of hotels, restaurants, and courier services were included for an additional several pages.

This short disaster manual took two people, working part time, about three months to prepare. It currently takes one person about one hour every several months to keep it current. A revised and enlarged version will obviously take more time to prepare and to maintain. A great deal of the effort is obviously a function of the size and complexity of the installation being planned for, the personnel involved, and the personal inclinations of the MIS director involved. If a data processing department has undergone significant change and growth over the past several years (as most have), a major review of all aspects of the existing disaster plan is imperative because beyond a certain point patchwork maintenance and updating may not be sufficient.

CONCLUDING OBSERVATIONS

Common sense and disaster prevention should go hand in hand, especially when focusing on the problem of planning for a catastrophe. All the planning in the world in itself will not reduce the exposure to a problem. Anyone who spends even a short period of time within the data processing industry hears of incredible stupidity. I have two favorite and recent situations that illustrate the concern. There is the chairman of the board of a major company who became excited about the security of his company's main data center and ordered that it be housed in a bomb shelter underground. This was done, but no one made sure that the contractor building this facility put a vapor barrier between the cement and the ground around it, so the first time it rained, the computer room was blessed with 3 inches of water.

A credit card company has its main data center in San Francisco. In the event of a major earthquake there, do I have to pay the balance due this credit card company? The lesson to be learned from these two true situations is not just that stupidity exists even in well-run companies, but that risky circumstances cannot be overcome simply by good disaster planning.

Therefore, in the process of reviewing plans, take time out to see if your organization has a fundamental risk with its data center, involving crime, security, flooding, earthquakes, war, and so on, and if such problems exist, look at cost-justifying their resolution first, even if it means moving. Some of the more common examples of problems are:

- Pretty glass walls showing off the data center
- Water sprinkler systems that can leak
- Data centers on a floor immediately below bathrooms, laboratories, and machine rooms with heavy industrial equipment
- High-crime area, perhaps in an inner-city neighborhood also subject to rioting
- Facilities in a building next to a lovely river that becomes a surging torrent of disaster once every few years
- A country with considerable political instability, civil wars, or other unrest
- An old building considered a major fire hazard or in danger of collapsing

The reader can easily think of other obvious examples; the point is that these are common—they exist around us all the time. The question is: Does your installation fit any of these criteria? If so, plan on moving before planning a disaster manual. After all is said and done, all organizations want disaster plans, but more important, none ever wants to have to use them.

There are some more specific considerations regarding disaster plans that should be kept in mind. The architect of the methodology described in this chapter, Edward Allen of IBM, a leading specialist on disaster planning, constantly recommends that a number of specific actions always be taken:

- Designate in the disaster manual who is to have copies of the plan and make sure that they always receive the updates.
- One person must have overall responsibility for maintaining the plan up to date and to make sure that every copy is current at all times.
- Test portions of the disaster plan periodically to ensure that it remains relevant and usable.
- After a disaster, conduct a postdisaster audit of the manual and procedures to correct problems that developed and thus improve the overall quality of the disaster plan.

- Let top management know how important this kind of planning is and what it means to the organization if serious attention is not paid to it.

The methodologies described in this chapter have been used in various forms of disasters and thus are prudent, realistic, and cost effective. The ultimate benefit of such a process is that it is applicable to all types of data processing installations and organizations, regardless of what kind of hardware or software is installed. It is also usable in non-data-processing sectors of an organization. In a modified form it can be used to manage all types of industrial machines, manufacturing and processing plants, departments, and agencies because basically it calls for information to be gathered in a formal manner about current operations to be used quickly in the event of a disaster. At least in data processing, it is becoming an important aspect of both hardware and software management practices today.

Glossary of Data Processing Terms

This glossary of terms is not all inclusive; it includes only those phrases that are most widely used in this book.

Abend: The unanticipated end of a task in the computer.

Access Time: The time from when the computer asks for information and the time it is delivered by the system.

APAR (authorized program analysis report):   A customer's request that a vendor fix an identified problem in a program.

Availability: The degree to which a computer system or any specific component is ready to process jobs.

Batch Processing: The processing of a number of jobs gathered together in advance for completion together, usually serially, and usually hours after being submitted to the computer center. This is opposite of on-line or real-time processing, which is done on a demand basis when asked for by users.

Benchmark: In data processing the actual testing of a system in advance of installing it by running jobs on another computer to see how fast and well they perform. It is a way of measuring the performance of a computer being considered for acquisition.

Block Multiplexer Channel: A data path from peripherals to the computer in which blocks of information are brought into the system. Services a similar purpose as the byte multiplexer channel and the selector channel.

Buffer: In hardware, an area of storage set aside for data coming in or being written out to peripheral equipment (I/O).

Cathode Ray Tube (CRT): A television-type device with a keyboard used to display data from a computer or to transmit typed information into the system. It is the primary tool of users communicating with computers.

Channel: That portion of a computer, or a separate device, by which data are moved from the CPU to information storage devices and back (such as disk drives).

Code: Slang term for programs.

Communication Control Unit: A device responsible for managing the transmission and reception of information across telephone lines from remote terminals to a host computer.

Computer: A device that does mathematical and logical computations. It is the heart of a system and is driven by a system control program that governs what application programs are run and when, and manages all peripheral equipment attached to the computer configuration.

Configuration: The term used to describe all features and equipment linked together into one system made up of computer and I/O. It can also include software.

Console: That device or portion of a computer by which operators communicate with a CPU. It is usually a CRT.

Controller: A device used to manage the functions of multiple I/O performing similar functions (such as a controller for disk, another for tape, or telecommunications).

Core: Slang term for memory.

CPU (central processing unit): That portion of the computer that processes mathematical and logical calculations.

Cycles: A set amount of time that is needed to perform a specific task. It is a unit of measurement of the speed of certain devices, such as computers.

DASD: Direct-access storage device; the same as disk drives.

Data: Specific information being used by a computer system; information.

Data Base: A collection of information, at least one file long, or multiple sets of data.

Data Base Management: Either a set of programs to control information or a person (department within DP) that has the responsibility for maintaining and controlling machine-readable files.

Data Processing: The act of performing specific calculations or logical analysis on information via the computer.

Disk Drive: A piece of equipment used to store data, which can be accessed directly (to a record), as opposed to sequentially, as on tape. It is the primary data storage medium in use today.

Distributed Processing: The placement of computer power at various points within an organization or teleprocessing network where local computing can take place, as opposed to all at a centralized data center.

Downtime: Slang term that refers to a particular piece of equipment not operating; the opposite of availability.

Host Computer: Either the one computer responsible for controlling other processors or the main computer to which all users turn for processing.

Initial Program Load (IPL): The process of loading programs and operating system into a computer and beginning work; much like turning on the ignition to start a car.

Input/Output Devices (I/O): Those machines involved in sending or receiving data from a CPU, such as card readers, writers, and disk and tape drives.

Job: A complete set of data and programs making up a logical or application set; includes directions to the computer on what to do with these programs.

Line: In teleprocessing this is a slang term for the telephone link between a terminal and another computerized device, such as a host. On a CRT it is a string of characters (such as words and numbers) on the screen.

Mainframe: Another term for computer.

Megabyte: Mega is the prefix for 1 million. In data processing, memory sizes are expressed as the number of megabytes of storage positions for characters of information. Memory can, for example, be called 1 megabyte (or a meg), 2 megabytes, and so on.

Micro: A very small computer; a microcomputer.

Microprocessor: A processing unit within a computer.

Mini: A small computer; a miniprocessor.

Multiprocessing: A way of processing more than one set of jobs in the same computer at the same time.

Multiprogramming: A process whereby two or more programs may be run in an interleaved, concurrent fashion within the same computer.

Nanosecond: One thousand-millionth of a second; a measure of the speed with which computers operate.

Network: A combination of equipment located at various places all tied in to a central processor or several processors and passing data back and forth via telecommunications. Thus a series of terminals talking to a central computer would constitute a network.

Off-line: The operation of a computerized device not under the control of the computer; also a phrase suggesting that a discussion be held privately.

On-line: The operation of computerized equipment directly under the control of a processor; also refers to a user's ability to access a computer via a terminal instantaneously.

Operating System: A set of programs that manages a computer system, controlling the flow of jobs and data into the system, debugging, and device management facilities.

Pack: A device that attaches to a disk drive and is the unit in which information is stored on flat disk services through magnetic writing.

Page: A set of data which, in virtual operating systems, are brought in and out of a computer's memory.

Paging Rate: The average number of pages per second in and out of the memory portion of a computer; a way of measuring memory utilization.

Printer: A device that produces paper (hard copy) of information from a computer, such as a printed report.

Priority: The process of assigning a degree of rank so that when a computer assigns resources, the most important jobs are taken care of first.

Processor: Another word for computer.

Program: A series of machine-readable instructions to the computer on what to do with data (perform logical or arithmetic actions).

Random-Access Storage: Another way of saying direct-access storage.

Read: The process of calling into the computer data from a storage device.

Real Time: The process whereby a user can update or use files instantaneously via an on-line terminal.

Reliability: The ability of a device to perform functions for which it was designed within certain stated conditions (such as speed, volume, time up).

Reruns: Performing a set of tasks, jobs, or programs more than once because something went wrong the first time.

Response Time: The amount of time it takes for a computer to acknowledge receipt of data from an on-line terminal or for it to send data back;

always expressed in seconds and thus a measurement of the speed with which a processor works. In a batch environment, response time may even be expressed in days.

Selector Channel: A channel for I/O devices to communicate data back and forth with a computer; it services one device at a time.

Shared DASD: The ability of more than one computer system to access the same data files on disk.

Software: Another term for programs.

Storage: A storage device, such as disk, computer memory, or diskette.

System: A set of computers, peripherals, and software working together.

Tape Drive: A device that uses magnetic tape to record and store data.

Telecommunications: The process of communicating via telephone lines or satellites between a computer and remote users.

Terminal: A device used to send and receive information from a computer over a telephone or in-house cable, such as a CRT.

Throughput: A means of measuring the amount of work that can be processed in a computer in a given period of time, such as minutes, hours, or days.

Tightly Coupled: A type of configuration that allows two or more computers to share the same memory and be under the control of one copy of the system control program.

Working Storage: Temporary storage in computer memory.

Selected Bibliography

Reading the periodical literature is the easiest way to keep up with current publications and trends within the data processing industry. The leading publications include *Datapro* literature, *Infosystems, Datamation,* and *Computerworld* (a weekly newspaper). Useful also are various publications by DP vendors and consultants.

Chapter One: Hardware and the Organization

Cortada, James W. *EDP Costs and Charges: Finance, Budgets, and Cost Control in Data Processing.* Englewood Cliffs, N.J.: Prentice-Hall, Inc., 1980.

Davis, John J. "Economic Effects on DP Departments," *Data Management,* 14, No. 10 (October 1976): 41–43.

Diebold Research Program. *Trends in Systems Software: 1980, 1985, 1990.* New York: Diebold, Inc., 1975.

Dolotta, T. A., et al. *Data Processing in 1980–1985: A Study of Potential Limitations to Progress.* New York: John Wiley & Sons, Inc., 1976.

Chapter Two: Capacity Planning

Bronner, LeeRoy. *Capacity Planning Implementation.* IBM Washington Systems Center Technical Bulletin. Gaithersburg, Md.: IBM Corporation, January, 1979.

——. "Overview of the Capacity Planning Process for Production Data Processing," *IBM Systems Journal,* 19, No. 1 (1980): 4-27.

Burns, C. C. *Memory Can Increase Your Capacity.* IBM Complex Systems Technical Bulletin. Gaithersburg, Md.: IBM Corporation, July 1978.

Cooper, J. C. "A Capacity Planning Methodology," *IBM Systems Journal,* 19, No. 1 (1980): 28-45.

Dunlavey, Richard F. "Workload Management," *EDP Performance Review,* 6, No. 5 (1978): 1-6.

Jenkins, J. M. "Measuring System Capacity," *EDP Performance Review,* 5, No. 4 (1977): 1-12.

Nutt, Gary J. "Tutorial: Computer System Monitors," *Computer* (November 1975): 51-61.

Schaeffer, Howard. *Data Center Operations.* Englewood Cliffs, N.J.: Prentice-Hall, Inc., 1981.

Schiller, D. C. "System Capacity and Performance Evaluation," *IBM Systems Journal,* 19, No. 1 (1980): 46-67.

Svobodova, Liba. *Computer Performance Measurement and Evaluation Methods: Analysis and Applications.* New York: American Elsevier Publishing Co., Inc., 1976.

Chapter Three: Cost Justification

Cortada, James W. *EDP Costs and Charges: Finance, Budgets, and Cost Control in Data Processing.* Englewood Cliffs, N.J.: Prentice-Hall, Inc., 1980.

Financial Accounting Standards Board. *Statement of Financial Accounting Standards No. 13, Accounting for Leases, November 1976.* Stamford, Conn., 1976.

First Chicago Leasing Corporation. *Leveraged Leasing.* Chicago, 1973.

Gravitt, Charles A. "The Truth about Investment Tax Credit," *Computer Decisions* (July 1978): 44-48.

Joslin, Edward O. *Computer Selection: An Augmented Edition.* Fairfax Station, Va.: The Author, 1977.

Roenfeldt, Rodney L., and Robert A. Fleck, Jr. "How Much Does a Computer Really Cost?" *Computer Decisions* (November 1976): 77-78.

Seth, Ray, et al. "Information Resource Management Cost Justification Methods." *Guide International Proceedings 45,* Vol. 1, Atlanta, Ga., October 30-November 4, 1977: 183-196.

Chapter Four: Installation

Price Waterhouse & Co. *Management Controls for Data Processing.* White Plains, N.Y.: IBM Corporation, 1976.

Russell, Susan Higley, et al. *Data Processing Control Practices Report.* Prepared for the Institute of Internal Auditors, Inc. Armonk, N.Y.: IBM Corporation, 1977.

Schaeffer, Howard. *Data Center Operations.* Englewood Cliffs, N.J.: Prentice-Hall, Inc., 1981.

Chapter Five: Availability

Bird, R. A., and C. A. Hoffmann, "Systems Management," *IBM Systems Journal,* 19, No. 1 (1980): 140-159.

IBM Corporation. *Component Failure Impact Analysis—An Availability Management Technique.* White Plains, N.Y.: IBM Corporation, 1976.

——. *Problem and Change Management in Data Processing.* Lidingö, Sweden: IBM Corporation, 1976.

Schardt, R. M. "An MVS Tuning Approach," *IBM Systems Journal,* 19, No. 1 (1980): 102-119.

Chapter Six: Energy Conservation

Brill, Kenneth G. "Power Protection Equipment: A Survey," *Mini-Micro Systems* (July 1977): 41.

Budzilovich, Peter N. "Thinking of Buying a UPS?" *Computer Decisions* (May 1977): 88.

IBM Corporation. *A Guide to 50 Hertz UPS Selection.* Kingston, N.Y.: IBM Corporation, 1975.

——. *Energy Conservation and Management in Data Processing Installations.* White Plains, N.Y.: IBM Corporation, 1979.

——. *Introducing IBM Facility Control/Power Management 2, 2M, and 3.* General Information Manual. Atlanta, Ga.: IBM Corporation, 1979.

Chapter Seven: Communicating

As of this writing, there is no body of literature on ways to communicate data processing issues in nontechnical terms.

Chapter Eight: Disaster Planning

There is no body of adequate literature on the theme of disaster planning as a whole, although there are publications concerning specific backup procedures, such as those dealing with data security, for certain types of software, not specifically relevant to this chapter.

Index